Learning Conversations

In their challenging book the authors offer a radical approach to personal and organisational growth. Their new science of human learning uses reflective procedures called Learning Conversations to enable individuals of all ages, backgrounds and disciplines to become more aware of their own learning processes, to challenge the robots within, and those personal myths which often disable them as learners. By self-organising their learning they achieve insights resulting in improved attitudes and outcomes in study and work, greater personal confidence and innovativeness, and an enhanced capacity to learn.

This deeply personal yet systematic approach offers greater opportunities for self-responsibility and for the development of skills, competence and creativity.

Any organisation acting as a Self-Organised Learning entity can more constructively enhance the quality of its activities, with a pay-off for individuals and the organisation as a whole. Workforce teams, project groups, managers and top executives can create learning networks and Self-Organised Learning environments to achieve higher productivity and improved job performance, quality of service and cost-effectiveness. They can creatively overcome crises and uncertainties, and meet the challenges of our rapidly changing and competitive society by evolving flexible strategies that will help to lead to more constructive alternative futures.

Individuals, teachers, trainers and managers in public and private enterprises, consultants, planners, knowledge engineers and many more will find this an invaluable compendium of new and exciting ideas and techniques that will transform their approach and achievements.

'. . . it's a book no psychologist and no teacher should be without. It could fundamentally change the way in which we approach learning.'

David Fontana

Sheila Harri-Augstein is Senior Research Fellow and Deputy Director of the Centre for the Study of Human Learning, Brunel University of West London. Laurie Thomas is the Founder Director of the Centre for the Study of Human Learning and Carl Rogers Memorial Professor, Clayton University, USA. Together the authors have pioneered the theory and practice of Self-Organised Learning. They have presented TV and radio programmes, and run seminars and workshops in Europe, the USA, Mexico, Australia, India and the UK. Their approach has successfully been introduced into major commercial, educational and government organisations. They are the authors of *Self-Organised Learning* (Routledge & Kegan Paul, 1985).

We often mistakenly regard the identification of our learning needs as the responsibility of our teacher, trainer or manager. Self-Organised Learning not only offers each of us the opportunity of recognising and structuring such needs but enables us to adaptively construct strategies for fulfilling these effectively. The S-O-L system has enabled individuals and teams to improve their skills and competencies, and to approach the changing nature of their jobs and tasks with great confidence and motivation. It has already produced very encouraging results in the Post Office, assisting in progress towards higher productivity.

Sir Bryan Nicholson, Chairman, Post Office and
Chairman, CBI Educational Training Affairs Committee

Learning Conversations is a significant contribution to the theory and practice of Human Learning as this is being conversationally reconstructed within the new psychology which is now clearly emerging in various forms in many different parts of the world.

Professor Rom Harré

As the founder of cybernetic 'Conversation Theory', I commend Sheila Harri-Augstein and Laurie Thomas's recent book, *Learning Conversations*, as an important and significant work to be widely read. They have added to, and independently innovated along, congruent although phrased-in-their-own-metaphor directions.

Professor Gordon Pask

I regard Laurie and Sheila's work at the Centre for Human Learning as the most important endeavour of its kind in the UK. They have brought to the study of 'Human Learning' a freshness, a scholarship, and a breadth of sensitivity and understanding which bears few comparisons. Their work is actually about people. I find it practical, inventive, iconoclastic, and above all realistic. . . I believe that *Learning Conversations* is a book no psychologist or teacher should be without.

Dr David Fontana, Reader in Educational Psychology

Learning Conversations

The Self-Organised Learning Way to Personal and Organisational Growth

Sheila Harri-Augstein
and
Laurie F. Thomas

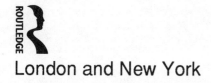

London and New York

First published 1991
by Routledge
11 New Fetter Lane, London EC4P 4EE

Simultaneously published in the USA and Canada
by Routledge
a division of Routledge, Chapman and Hall, Inc.
29 West 35th Street, New York, NY 10001

Typeset by LaserScript Limited, Mitcham, Surrey
Printed in England by Clays Ltd, St Ives plc

British Library Cataloguing in Publication Data
Harri-Augstein, Sheila
    Learning conversations
    1. Learning
    I. Title   II. Thomas, Laurie
    153.1'5

Library of Congress Cataloging in Publication Data
Harri-Augstein, E. Sheila.
    Learning conversations/Sheila Harri-Augstein
    and Laurie F. Thomas.
    p. cm.
    Includes bibliographical references.
    1. Learning, Psychology of. 2. Conversation–Psychological
    aspects.   3. Zen Buddhism–Psychology.   I. Thomas, Laurie F.
    II. Title.
    BF319.H347 1990
     153.1'5–dc20   90-31957

    ISBN 0-415-02866-3
    ISBN 0-415-02867-1 (pbk)

To Lavender Lal and our learner-centred clients, past, present and future, in recognition of all we have learned and continue to learn with them. In one sense this book belongs to them, since each has contributed to its creation.

Working with people from many walks of life across a whole range of tasks and at different levels of responsibility, involving direct line management as well as advisory, training and educational services, we have demonstrated the power and effectiveness of Learning Conversations. For ourselves and many of our clients the experience has been, and is, challenging, exciting and deeply fulfilling. This book has been written with them continuously in mind.

Contents

Illustrations

Figures

Tables

Acknowledgements

The authors are especially grateful to:

The late Don Bannister who, for seven years as Associate Professor at CSHL, offered his personal support. Don, more than most, understood that a new science of Human Learning based on the theory and practice of Learning Conversations was in the process of being constructed. In Don's words, 'the authors cast light on much of the everyday, yet somehow mysterious, experience we have of conversation, including its dual nature. We reflect to ourselves as well as exchanging with others, so that two conversations, one internal and one external, seem always to be taking place' (Foreword to *Self-Organised Learning*, Routledge & Kegan Paul, 1985).

Professor Marie Jahoda for inviting us to join her on the DES-funded project, 'Optimal Conditions for Studying Intellectually Complex Subject Matter', and for her lively support and friendship in her years at Brunel and later.

In the field of personal construct psychology, to:

Miller Mair, for his insightful metaphor of 'the person as a community of selves' which inspired us in our original development of the PAIRS, EXCHANGE and SOCIOGRID Repertory Grid computer programs as tools for amplifying the power of individual and group Learning Conversations.

Phillida Salmon, for her 'deeply personal' approach to learning, particularly in her work with children and their teachers. Her approach, together with Don's, Miller's and Fay Fransella's, has influenced us in our search for a person-centred formulation of the Learning Conversation.

In the field of cybernetics, to:

Gordon Pask, who joined Laurie over a period of ten years, in running a series of postgraduate and open seminars at Brunel on the 'Nature of Man'. Many colleagues, physicists, architects, writers, psychologists and cyberneticians, now scattered around the world, will remember the unique quality of these 'conversational encounters'. Although sharing the notion of 'the conversation' as a fundamental process, the two research groups, Systems Research and the Centre for the Study of Human Learning differed greatly in their approach. This provoked a constructive debate. A continuous exchange of ideas ensued with colleagues, in particular with Mike Elstob, David Stewart, John Race, Les Johnson, Bernard Scott, Nick Farnes, Massoud Davoudi, Dionysius Kallikourdis and Richard Jung. Later Professor Igor Aleksander and his research group and our research colleagues at the Admiralty Marine Technology Establishment led by Arthur Gardner contributed to our thinking.

In the field of education, to:

The group at CRAPEL, University of Nancy, France, and in particular to Phil Riley for his keen interest in 'Learning Conversations' as a method for adults learning a foreign language; and to the Welsh Office and the National Language Unit of Wales for sponsoring a pilot study on 'The Use of Learning-to-Learn Techniques' for adults learning Welsh.

Our friends at UAM and UNAM, Mexico, and in particular Marie Louisa Figueroa, Vida Valero and Michelle Flood (now at Toulouse) who continue to offer us a fascinating environment for developing S-O-L in the area of staff development

Our friends in Australia, especially Phil Candy who organised and hosted, with his wife Mary Anne, our whistle-stop seminars and workshops throughout the Antipodes. To Pat Diamond for his keen interest and support of our conversational repertory grid techniques for teacher training, and to Rosamund Nutting for her successful efforts in pioneering the 'Learning Conversation' approach in Continuing Education.

To Graham Crosby and Lesley Martin for pioneering some of the techniques and methods in junior schools in the South of England, thus transforming the quality of children's learning.

To colleagues at the Open University for giving us an opportunity to present Course Units, a Radio and TV programme on 'Reading as a Learning Skill' in the Post Experience Course on Reading Development.

To Mike Smith and Sally Richardson of Kingston Polytechnic for inviting us to use the Poly as one of our early test-habitats, and for later developing their own brand of learning conversations within their Learning Resources Programmes.

To colleagues and students at Loughborough and Brunel Universities for supporting our research efforts and for offering themselves as 'learning subjects' during the last two decades; and to Mel Myers at Birmingham University for supporting a series of 'S-O-L' Workshops for Educational Psychologists as part of his Post Experience Programme as well as for offering facilities for an S-O-L database.

In the fields of industry and commerce, to:

The British Post Office for inviting us to develop S-O-L within the habitat of the Royal Mail Letters Business; our thanks to the 250 Learning Coaches and their Learning Managers who are striving to practise Learning Conversations 'on the job'; and to Drew Wightman, then DHP at Edinburgh; Bill Halson, then Assistant Director, responsible for the S-O-L Cascade Project and David Smith, the S-O-L Project Manager based at

Headquarters, and Geoff Batstone, the original Learning Coach at Reading Head Post Office.

Also, to our research associates, Norman Chell, Beryl Williams and Ian Webb for their competence and dedication whilst working with us on the CSHL – Post Office project.

Again, our thanks to Pat Hedges and Andrew Taylor, both senior staff within the Royal Mail Parcel Force, who are working with us to pioneer S-O-L for their management teams.

To the British Council for supporting many visitors from overseas to attend seminars at CSHL and for sponsoring some of our educational visits abroad; and to the Institute of Training and Development who have provided support for the development of an S-O-L Diploma for managers, trainers and Learning Practitioners.

To a Yogi dramatist and Hindu philosopher at Cochin for inspiring us within seven hours of drama, mime and explanation on a roof-top in the heat of a tropical night.

On a broader canvas, to:

Homo sapiens for providing a natural laboratory for studying people as tool-makers, language producers, modellers, scientists, artists, inventors, philosophers, story-tellers and conversationalists.

Finally, a very special thank you to Catherine Kerr who courageously faced an ever-changing sea of words as she patiently and cheerfully persevered in her highly competent use of the word processor to produce all five drafts of this manuscript; and to David Stonestreet , our editor, for his patience, trust and support whilst the book was being written.

General Introduction: Personal Myths about Learning

Origins

This book attempts to represent some of the authors' practical experiences and intellectual endeavours following a discovery we made some twenty-five years ago.

As psychologists, our purpose was to develop a better theory of 'real' human learning in reaction against theories about what experimenters could teach rats, pigeons or humans in the unnatural conditions of the laboratory. We were working intensively with people in the natural habitats of home, work, sport, the community and in education to discover how they learn. We encouraged them to reflect carefully on their learning experiences and to describe these processes to us. We developed special techniques for recording their learning activities. We used these records to talk the learners back through their behaviour so that they could more precisely reconstruct their learning experiences and report them to us. Whilst we questioned their initial explanations, we treated these seriously. We conversed with them to identify descriptions which would satisfy both them and us.

Some of the subjects of these enquiries became deeply interested in their own learning processes. Indeed, they continued to investigate their learning and to reflect upon their findings long after we, the 'real' researchers, had left. Intriguingly, employers, teachers and parents went out of their way to inform us of some dramatic changes. We wondered what we had done and why it had worked for some and not for others! Then we tried to repeat and improve on these results.

Thus was the idea of a Learning Conversation originally conceived.

Since then we have conducted Learning Conversations on the shop floor and in the board room, on a frigate, on a rugby field and a skating rink, in schools, polytechnics and universities, in a bank, the post offices, and in a chain of shoe shops as well as in a number of research and development establishments. We have run short courses for officers of the Royal Navy, educational psychologists, psychotherapists and counsellors, foremen of Clarks Shoes, managers of Dunlop, Shell, ICI and Kelloggs, supervisors and managers of the Post Office, as well as teachers and other higher education staff as far afield as Madras, Mexico, Sydney and Singapore, and nearer home in Paris, Berne, Strasbourg, Cardiff, Edinburgh, Limerick and Milton Keynes. We have worked with factory managers and production teams, quality assurance and personnel staff, with sales managers and their customers. We have acted as advisers to general practitioners, architects, athletics coaches, teacher trainers, family counsellors, marriage guidance counsellors and prison governors.

The theory and practice of Self-Organised Learning (S-O-L) has thus involved action research with individuals and groups in a wide range of educational, commercial and industrial organisations. Projects have been financially supported by the Ministry of Defence, the Post Office and Manpower Services Commission, the Welsh Office, the British Council, UNESCO, the Department of Education and Science, the Social Science Research Council, the Architectural Association, the Medical Research Council, the Hotel and Catering Industry and Air Traffic and Tourist Training Boards, as well as a number of individual companies and institutions.

This massive research enterprise has pioneered the development of a conversational technology and a body of knowledge about human learning which we have called Self-Organised Learning (S-O-L). The authors' earlier book by that title used *the repertory grid* as a vehicle for introducing the philosophy upon which this book on Learning Conversations is based. This book expands on the theoretical principles of S-O-L and offers a compendium of conversational techniques well beyond those in the original volume. Within these pages a conversational paradigm for promoting human learning is fully addressed. When done well, assembling electronic circuit boards, managing a post office which can sort a million letters a day, attempting to row faster than anyone else in the world, teaching mathematics, engineering, psychology or law, being able to dress oneself without help if handicapped, studying chemistry, computer science, Russian or art, or being a 'good' and sensitive parent demands certain levels of skill, knowledge, flexibility, judgement and innovation. Each in its own way depends upon the ability to learn effectively through direct personal experience.

Learning Conversations and the process of change

Imagine a six-year-old, a sixteen-year-old, a thirty-six-year-old or a sixty-year-old anywhere in the world executing any specific task; if it is being done effectively, adaptively and with relevance to what is going on around them, they will be more than rote-skilled; they will value and be achieving *quality* in their performance, through developing their *capacity for learning*. This is particularly true in the highly competitive and rapidly changing environments of today where often the only constant appears to be the process of change itself. The home, the workplace, the school, and all the multitude of situations in which we, as human beings, experience and act out our lives are all *habitats-in-change*, demanding new levels of skill, competence and creativity. If this change is not to degenerate into chaos, breeding fear and unreasoning or even violent responses, we each need to become more self-organised and discriminatingly responsible for what we learn. By organising our learning, we can together participate in and steer the process of change. If, by default, we allow others to organise what we learn and how we learn it we abdicate our membership of the fully human race.

Our research has shown that the development of S-O-L requires an increasing awareness of the personal processes of learning. Greater insight allows more accomplished use of personal learning skills. By reflectively reviewing their direct personal experience Self-Organised Learners can better regulate the direction, quality and content of what they choose to learn. Each new event becomes an opportunity for learning, for updating skills and enhancing competence. The Learning Conversation and its reflective techniques offer tools for enriching those functional aspects of skill, competence and creativity, through which we achieve quality, personal fulfilment and, occasionally, joy. Every form of human endeavour from the billiard room to the board room, from the home to the hospital, from the sports field to the battlefield, from centres of research to the factory floor, and from weapon guidance to marriage guidance can be enhanced many times over by the ability to utilise each experience imaginatively as another learning opportunity.

The focus of attention is always the *Learning Conversation*; fundamentally, this puts learners in conversation with themselves, but it also enables them to converse more effectively with their peers, their tutor, coach, trainer, instructor, therapist, manager, spouse or occasionally even their general practitioner, osteopath, lawyer, architect, clairvoyant or stockbroker! Such a conversation is not just chit-chat about disconnected snippets of experience; rather it is a sustained activity creating an increasing awareness of the whole experiential process of learning.

Many regard this approach as radical, but our observations of pre-school children at play or the admittedly more rare fully functioning adult engaged in some equally passionate activity reveals that the seed of this self-organising ability manifests itself whenever purposive and innovative processes play themselves out in learner-friendly environments; but this seed needs nurturing. Often it falls on stony ground, withers and dies. We have only to scrutinise mankind's outstanding literature, from philosophical essays to fairy stories, from biographical accounts and scientific reports to poetry, prose and drama, to appreciate the richness of the languages available for conversing about the self-regulatory and life-enhancing processes of learning. Not enough of us use these resources for this purpose. Education and training do not guide us into such pursuits.

The process of S-O-L is itself conversational. We learn by conversing with ourselves, with others and with the world around us. The learner cannot, by definition, know what they have yet to learn, but they can reflect upon their experience, anticipate possibilities, act on the basis of these and reflect again upon each new experience. This continuing process can be encouraged and enabled through the practice of Learning Conversations.

S-O-L theory and practice

It is in the nature of this Learning Conversation that the theory which drives it and the methodology by which it is sustained are symbiotically related. They are two perspectives on the one activity, and as such are both intrinsic to it. Any 'personal theory' of the learning process must be experiential and therefore, in the final analysis, private. The theory expressed as public knowledge may only be personally appreciated through first-hand experience. The methodology is only practised effectively when informed (that is, given personal meaning) by the theory. Thus, personal understanding of, and competence in Learning Conversations is only achieved by 'having a go', reflecting on the experience, informing the experience with the 'theory' and then 'having another go', revising one's personal theory to do better each time. Once this shift towards a 'conversational paradigm' has been made, the theory becomes the practice and the practice becomes the theory. But there is always a small productive mismatch between the two. Sometimes the learner knows better than they can achieve, at other times they cannot quite understand how they produce the results they do. It is this mutual 'boot-strapping' function of the symbiosis that is so creative. Most of our more successful clients and our postgraduate students eventually comment on this. Months or even years after first believing that they have fully grasped S-O-L, they will comment that 'I am only now really beginning to understand what you mean by a Learning Conversation. It is both a philosophy and a technology which grows and expands the more you use it.'

The authors attempt to capture the excitement of this approach as they explain, demonstrate and converse through the medium of the book.

Approaches to learning

Traditional training methods, and educational practices based on curricula embodying 'expert knowledge', can and often do inadvertently reduce a person's capacity for S-O-L. The learners come to accept a non-adaptive 'expert knows best' approach which treats them as novices; empty-headed followers needing to be held on a tight leash and led in directions specified by the competent few. At best, this results in learners who know how to 'submit successfully to being taught, instructed or trained'. They develop into what we shall later describe as a series of more or less efficient robots. In new situations, they demonstrate few learning skills. Left to their own devices, they have to learn 'the hard way' ineptly and blindly from ill-digested experience. At worst, they exhibit almost pathological manifestations of rudimentary skills, disabling attitudes to personal competence, and strongly negative feelings about school, about learning or even about large sections of society. Perhaps this is not surprising, for much of the psychology and educational research on which this teaching and training is based shares the same outdated physical science paradigm of how learning may be investigated, understood and produced. We shall attempt to demonstrate why this way of studying the nature of learning will always eventually reduce to a 'teacher always knows best' approach, no matter how conscientiously its adherents seek to avoid this.

On the other hand, any too permissive approach to teaching and training based on too soft or mystical a psychology can be just as limiting for the learner. Whilst it offers, if only by default, opportunities for self-initiated learning, it does this without stimulating those insights and nurturing those skills through which such opportunities may be exploited. Such 'discovery' approaches are often based on an undeveloped, even stunted version of the personal science paradigm advocated by Carl Rogers. His writings give form to the belief that the right psychological conditions will produce a flowering of the individual. But a diffuse concern for the learner arising perhaps out of a mixed-up sentimentality does not generate these conditions; neither does the *laissez-faire* approach created when people think that they can go along with these ideas without fully understanding them.

Despite the contradictary but nevertheless strong pressures of the behaviourist and humanistic trends of the past thirty years, the better teachers have never quite fallen completely into either of these learning reduction traps. They 'intuitively' develop a conversational approach, at least for those learners with whom they feel they can be successful. Some pick the high flyers, others the lame ducks; but many a gifted teacher's understanding of their own skills remains tacit, leading to the mistaken view that 'good teachers are born, not made'. We find it more useful to believe that they make themselves, but are unable to describe how they achieve this. Their acceptance that they are 'naturally gifted' or have a 'knack' with learners has, so far prevented them from joining a scattered few in pioneering *a conversational science*, the principles of which can be formulated, tested and developed as rigorously as its better-established precursors. The experience of teachers and trainers, carefully sifted and reflected upon, could greatly enrich this endeavour.

The search for a new approach

In his Foreword to our previous book, *Self-Organised Learning*, the late Don Bannister comments that the CSHL's approach 'performs a kindly, necessary and powerful act: *it rehabilitates the concept of learning*'. The ways in which we have experimented with and defined learning cannot meaningfully be filed in the pigeon holes of 'cognition', 'motivation', 'emotion', 'behaviour', 'IQ' or 'traits'; nor into the traditional approaches of educational practice, training and therapy. These are entrenched in old psychologies and outmoded languages. Our reflective, process-based methodology begins from the boundaries of 'learning experiments' as described by George Kelly in *The Psychology of Personal Constructs* (page 77):

> the problem of learning is not merely one of determining how many or what kinds of reinforcements fix a response, but rather how does a subject personally phrase the experience and what validations of personal predictions do they reap? When a subject fails to meet the experimenter's expectations it may be inappropriate to say that 'she or he has not learned'; rather one might say that what the subject learned was not what the experimenter expected him or her to learn.

This perspective on learning has led us to question the appropriateness of various paradigms of research. In focusing on learning as a uniquely individual process, we have framed our research endeavours within a 'conversational paradigm' which is both person-centred *and* systematic. We have developed a reflective methodology and a content-free technology which preserve the integrity and humanity of individual experience, and which are demonstrably capable of enhancing people's *capacity for learning*.

In our search for a new approach we have been particularly inspired by contemporary themes introduced by a number of researchers and thinkers spanning a wide range of disciplines. These included C. Rogers (*Freedom to Learn*), A. Newell and H. Simon (*Problem Solving*), G. Kelly (*Reflexive Theory of Man as Personal Scientist*), K. Godel (*Open Systems*), G. Pask (*Mechanisms of Consciousness*), I. Illich (*Celebration of Aware-ness*), G. Jung (*Synchronicity*), M. Minsky (*Representation of Knowledge*), G. Bateson (*Ecology of Mind*), M. Warnock (*Imagination*), H. Maturana (*Forms of Knowing*), R. Pirsig (*Quality*), J. Bruner (*Strategies of Learning*), M. Polyani (*Tacit Knowing and Explicit Knowledge*), L. Zadeh (*Probablistic (fuzzy) Thinking*), R. Laing (*Incoherence within Personal Meaning*), A. Maslow (*Creative Encounter*), G. Miller, E. Galanter and K. Pribram (*Images and Plans*), K. Lorenz (*Living Matter as Mirrors of Reality*), W. McCulloch (*Embodiments of Mind*), J. Searle (*Intentionality and Understanding*), as well as the radical intuitivism of Eastern psychology and Zen practice.

Our progress has involved discarding our earlier 'physical science' stance in which our subjects' explanations were treated merely as data for our 'psychological' theory building, and also discarding the 'personal science' stance which assumes that people must explain themselves to themselves, and that the role of the experimenter is merely that of creating the conditions in which this may happen. We have contributed to the development of a 'conversational science' based on the premise that no one can explain themselves unaided, nor can they exploit their infinite (almost) potential by being facilitated by an exclusively non-directive practitioner. The unique attribute of humans is that they 'converse'. Separate nodes of meaning construction (namely, people) can pool their experiences, identify needs and purposes, critically evaluate performance strategies and develop a language for enhanced awareness of this very process. The role of the psychologist (experimenter, teacher, manager) becomes that of tool-maker and provider, observer and joint interpreter of the evolving conversational experiment in which both subject and psychologist are full but different participants. Whilst meaning is shared, each participant remains free to reconstruct new meanings and these augment the potential of the conversation. The conditions of a conversational experiment require that the content and process is controlled according to a developing recognition of the nature of what each can contribute. This cannot be totally specified before the experiment, but there are priorities. Only the sub-ject/learner can tap his or her personal *experience*, but the experimenter can observe *behaviour* and recruit methodological skills to drive the experiment forward.

Underpinning this methodology is our definition of learning as:

'the conversational construction of personally significant, relevant and viable meaning' and meaning as:

'purposeful patterns of thoughts and feelings which are the basis of our anticipations and actions'.

Thus behaviour *and* experience are seen as indicators of:

'a coherent personal process which is *itself* conversational'.

Most of education, training and psychology is built on the assumption that there are knowable best ways of learning and that these can be discovered using a scientific method which has long been discarded by contemporary philosophers (Popper), scientists (Medawar) and physicists (Heisenberg). As psychologists we know very little about the means by which personal ventures in learning are undertaken, nor why and how some individuals are more competent than others. This is the recognised gap that we have attempted to fill in developing a discipline of human learning in its own right. It has involved a new synthesis of contemporary themes from philosophy, neo-cybernetics, knowledge engineering, physiology, computer science, biology, engineering and psychology. We have carried out this work over the past twenty-five years at Brunel in pursuit of our vision that mankind can only creatively survive the challenges of this age of rapid change by evolving our *capacity for learning*. Only this can provide us with the resource to negotiate change, to prevent man-made catastrophes, to achieve success and to attain new standards of excellence and quality in our various human endeavours.

Personal beliefs, values and myths about learning

Life is a continuing opportunity for learning. *What* and *how* each of us learns depends upon what we bring to each event and what we make of each experience. For the authors or one of our clients each of the following events was a personally significant and valued learning experience.

Learning about:

- cooking 'whilst living on my own for a year in a foreign country with what was for me an unpalatable cuisine';
- divorce 'whilst living with a mum and dad hell bent on destroying each other';
- personal fulfilment 'when awarded a first-class degree after years of hard study';
- the power of the intellect 'through a succession of chats at the bar with a gifted science teacher';
- a sense of pride 'whilst stripping and re-building an old motorcycle which had been discarded as scrap';
- coping with personal crisis 'when my girlfriend fell for another bloke';
- writing 'by being forced to edit and re-write my thesis many times';

- personal care 'after surviving a nasty fall on a mountain';
- controlling one's temper 'by trying to keep cool whilst supervising difficult staff';
- maths 'by persevering to produce a short, well-formed proof';
- problem identification 'when I was forced to chair a very sticky meeting whilst the managing director was away';
- history 'by living with the Mexican Indians in the Chiappas and then reading Spanish, Mexican and North American accounts of the Conquistadores';
- scientific method 'whilst doing a fifth-form project';
- molecular biology and genetic engineering 'by getting to know a Cambridge professor rather well, reading *The Double Helix*, participating in the gossip about Crick and Watson, and becoming the mother of a test-tube baby';
- sculpture 'by spending a whole day blindfolded with a tree';
- teaching 'by working closely with my sixth formers to make sure that they developed originality of thought';
- joy and despair 'by truly sharing the experience of writing a book with Laurie';
- what is meant by a learning conversation 'by having to role play as a "learning coach" in front of my boss and my subordinates';
- man as personal scientist and psychological reflexivity 'after sharing a Chinese meal with George Kelly';
- loneliness and misery 'when I was forced to take early retirement';
- self-esteem 'when I was shunted sideways out of my job as manager of a big high street bank';
- mapping 'when I really saw how coordinate geometry mapped diagrammatic geometry on to algebra';
- ridicule 'when as a broad Cockney speaker just arrived at the posh grammar school, I was made to stand on a stool in front of the class and try to pronounce French verbs';
- limitations of the best possible training 'when I desperately tried to help deal with attacking aircraft as air intercept controller on HMS Xxxx in the Falklands';
- learning 'when I was found playing with a Dinky toy under the desk top, the Latin master reprimanding me by declining words rythmically on my head with a wooden ruler';
- training techniques 'by running four-week short courses on work study end to end for two years';
- management 'by discovering as an assistant production manager in a precision engineering firm that understanding how the equipment worked was less important than understanding how the people worked';
- conversation 'by role playing a Rogerian being taught by a Skinnerian';
- being professional 'whilst running a seminar for a group of clinical psychologists who accused me of being too self-effacing';
- teaching being different from learning 'by discovering that some of my best A-level students failed during their first year at university'.

Such experiences are neither totally subjective nor objective; their significance does not reside solely in objective reality (for instance, on the mountain or in the bar), nor are they purely subjective (for instance, 'just whatever I think and feel'). They are significantly *how* one acts, thinks, feels and reacts in a specific set of situations. People seek meaning; the conversational process of achieving personal meaning is learning.

Personally significant and valued learning through experience is not imposed by Skinnerian conditioning, nor is it achieved by inventing any reality we choose. It is achieved by exercising the *freedom to learn in 'conversational encounters' which are valued by using criteria which arise from within the experience itself.* Thus, we do not necessarily learn from life's experiences, only through awareness, reflection and review of such encounters from within a conscious system of personal beliefs, values, needs and purposes. This is a highly skilled activity. Each of our clients, including ourselves, came to value these learning experiences more fully after being 'talked-back' through the experience and then systematically helped to reflect upon it.

It may require many Learning Conversations involving an increasingly wide range of experiences before individuals gain such insights as:

- learning is a skill which can itself be learned;
- learning by experience is more effective when treated as a conscious, reflective, evaluative and developing process;
- apprenticeship or studentship, being a trainee or a probationer are all skilled activities in which what might have taken years of repeated activity can be achieved in weeks or months;
- self-organisation in learning is an insightful and purposive activity demanding greater responsibility, flexibility, skill and judgement than is required in 'submitting to being taught or instructed'; and
- developing one's capacity for learning can be challenging, creative and fun.

Learning by experience involves the complete person. How a person's learning is organised and where the locus of control resides need to be carefully considered. *Self-Organised Learners* are better able to control their individual destinies; other-organised learners are victims of their fate. We are all both.

The Self-Organised Learner continues to learn the skills of learning, thus being able to live fully in events, trusting his or her fully functioning self as a test-bed for validating his or her constructions of experience. Analogous to George Kelly's 'personal scientist', Self-Organised Learners are free to use behaviour to validate their understanding. Behaviour is not merely a series of experiments each designed to test separate hypotheses; it is a continuing conversation with reality, in which personal meaning can be further developed and more comprehensively validated. *All the artefacts of human endeavour, which together form the mind-pool of a culture, can be construed as learning resources by the Self-Organised Learner. We attain our freedom to learn by exercising judgement and achieving a selectivity that matches our requirements. It is in this exercise and the skills it develops that the capacity for self-organisation emerges and matures.*

The notion of S-O-L enables us to conceive of all knowing as relative. Any particular segment of personal meaning related to a task, topic, person or physical event can only be temporary. It will evolve with experience and as the content or purpose changes. In constructing and validating their views, people develop their own 'personal myths'. We introduce this term to designate the 'personal knowing' that results from enduring long-term conversational encounters. The term 'myth' is meant to carry all its positive, negative, allegorical and transcendental implications. There is a vast range of viable personal myths that can be developed around any topic. These myths 'work' with different qualities of effectiveness for the range of situations, purposes, people and events within which their originators develop them. Some myths are disabling, others can be very enabling. Effective personal myths arise when learners are freed to exercise whatever capacity for conversational science they currently possess. Once this process is active they develop an increasingly healthy and robust capability to create and validate effective 'theories', beliefs and values. On being exposed to public knowledge, their idiosyncratic associations, analogies, selections, reorganisations, rejections and reconstructions subtly transform it and make it personal. Even when the resulting myth appears to others as identical to a public version, the active process of S-O-L will have built it into the individual's unique experience and personal patterns of meaning, so that it ceases to be 'academic knowledge' and becomes integral to their understanding of events.

Ineffective learners are unable to revise their personal myths and so remain victims of their own inadequate constructions. At any age, personal myths can become ultra-stable, apparently unchangeable, and the person's functioning takes on a robot-like complexion. Most of us live within a system of rather rigidly held myths about ourselves, about events and others in our world, and about physical reality. We cannot change our personal myths overnight, nor should we; but accepting the relativity of personal meaning, we can purposefully and self-critically bring these myths into greater awareness. When we begin to see our myths as productive, as the best understanding we can achieve at the moment, we can create opportunities for challenging and further exploring their value and we can experience the excitement of refining, elaborating, deconstructing and re-building them. The Learning Conversation is the vehicle for charting this personal voyage.

Almost always, as we embark on this voyage with students, apprentices, teachers, managers and many other professionals, we discover a welter of tightly held, ultra-stable myths about personal learning. Most people have arrived at convictions about their own learning; their myths of themselves as learners. These have almost always been achieved on less than adequate evidence. People have either been brainwashed by someone else's assessment of them – for example, parents, teachers and peers – or, having found themselves in less than optimal conditions to learn, they have generalised the results of their experiences as a commentary on their own capabilities. Such assumptions very easily become self-validating. If you believe you are dumb, unmusical or a bit of a joker it is very easy to confirm your belief. It is more difficult to transcend it.

Tutors and instructors also develop assumptions, prejudices and understanding about the nature of learning. Sometimes they have one set of myths for understanding their students and another set for understanding themselves. Their beliefs about learning in others are created whilst teaching or instructing, which is seen as a different process from learning for oneself. Together the instructor's myth of the learner and the learner's myths of themselves create a conversational frame which largely defines the quality of what gets learned. The interaction of these myths forms the basis of the teaching–learning relationship; but whilst it remains unrecognised, this conversational frame is not negotiable. Those researchers who fail to appreciate this have refined these myths into psychological and educational theories. Their academic authority tightens the knot of learners' and teachers' mutually disabling beliefs. Conversations with learners, teachers, trainers and researchers have enabled us to explore their personal myths. The following sections examine some of these. We end this General Introduction by outlining our own myths which are the foundation of the methodology for negotiating learning conversations so that people may enhance their skill, competence and creativity.

Learners' myths

In this section we intend to concentrate on the learner's own beliefs, values and prejudices, or what we have come to term the deeply held *robot-like personal myths about one's own learning*. Our finding is that most people are *disabled learners*. Their myths disable them; but being largely unaware of how they learn they do not know how slowly or badly they do it. Unless they fail miserably in an assignment or task or are warned by their instructors, teachers or managers that they are likely to be removed from the course or sacked from the job, they remain imprisoned by their tacitly held views of themselves. Believing that their capacity for learning is inborn – that is, a matter of 'intelligence', 'personality' or the more specific 'talents' – they make little attempt to improve their skills as learners.

The universality of underdeveloped learning capacity often goes unrecognised because so many of our peers are similarly handicapping themselves. Expectations are low. The occasional exception is the maverick high flyer who develops remarkable expertise and is seen as 'gifted'. This does nothing to change the general level of expectation of what can be learned, by whom, how thoroughly and how quickly. Expectations are transformed once we see the high flyer as someone who, having learned how to learn, has learned how to fly. Most of us could be up there too, if we so chose.

We have all seen people whose life trajectory has changed and who have developed skills and competences for which they did not believe they had the 'necessary talents'. In our terms, their personal myths have been challenged and their beliefs about their own learning capacity have changed.

The following remarks made within a series of Learning Conversations were all seen as disabling myths:

- You need to have green fingers to ...
- I am no good at figures/writing ...
- I'm not clever enough to ...
- I've no sense of perspective so I can't draw ...
- I'm hopeless with mechanical things ...
- Ugh! Poetry!!
- You have to be able to handle people to ...
- It's all that paperwork that ...
- I've got this stutter that comes on when ...
- I have no feel for painting/ sculpture/ Shakespeare/ classical music ...
- I'm all fingers and thumbs when it comes to ...
- I could never open my mouth at a public meeting ...

In helping learners to reflect upon and challenge some of their myths, we have gradually identified and developed a category system.

1 The scope and nature of what may be learned;
2 Opportunities for learning;
3 Conditions that influence learning;
4 Personal processes involved in learning;
5 Personal capacity for learning.

We have used these categories to work with people who wish to become more aware of their myths, and so challenge them. Learners' myths can be broadly classified into:

1 The scope and nature of what may be learned

Examples of comments which indicate myths about what may be learned include:

- I'm just not musical, artistic, good with my hands, mathematical, good with people, patient, tough enough, political and so on;
- well, with milking cows I watched my father and got the general gist of it, then it was just a matter of practice and waiting to get better;
- I think with most things it's a question of letting it come out. It may be there but you may never find yourself in a situation in which you need to use it;
- well, there are two types of learning – one is 'parrot fashion' and the other is 'really understanding it';
- you can only learn things if you want to, if they interest you;
- I suppose that was character-building.

'What may be learned' can be further refined in two ways:

  (a) to what extent is what is to be learned outside or inside you?

  (b) How 'learnable' is 'it'?

The 'learnability' of, for example, maths, English (that is, school subjects) or football, reading, cooking, cars (leisure topics) or politics, religion, charities (beliefs), can be judged along a 'common-sense' scale. For example:

  (a) Learnable

    1 If I really worked at that I could certainly learn it.

    2 I wonder whether we could do anything together. If you conduct a learning conversation with me over....

    3 I suppose a really good teacher might bang that into me but it would be really hard going.

    4 You may pick it up in your early years but it's almost impossible later.

  (b) Unlearnable

    5 You've either got it or you haven't.

Each learner has deep-rooted assumptions about 'what is learnable'. Some will talk only in terms that refer outside themselves. They will talk in terms of topics, tasks, situations and events. Topics are 'known' or 'understood'. For most learners certain topics are 'impos- sibly difficult'. Tasks are more action-orientated, associated with producing a given result, and with performances, such as: making a flower arrangement, chairing a meeting, winning an Olympic gold medal, sustaining a good relationship or auditing a set of books. All learners will have low expectations of ever being able to do certain tasks. 'Situations' and 'events' will usually yield topics, task performances and attitudes. Again the learn- ability of situation-specific 'feelings', or the production and control of attitudes will be questioned. Attitudes that are unrecognised or expressed in objective terms are difficult to reflect upon.

Moving from the outside one step inwards, tasks decompose into skills. 'Topics' decompose into 'areas of personal knowing'. Some people will already be thinking in these terms. Others will be prepared to do so once it is suggested to them. Others will begin positively but will find it increasingly difficult to separate the skill or the knowing from the specific task or topic.

However, 'knowledge', 'skills' and 'attitudes' are still orientated towards the outside: we can move further inside. Knowledge can be discussed in terms of 'memory', 'under-standing', 'thinking skills', 'problem-solving', 'creativity'. Skills can be talked about in terms of the parts of the body involved in the performance or the perceptions or sensory system involved, the pattern of activity, its intentionality or purposiveness. Attitudes can be discussed in terms of the emotions involved and understanding how the 'thinking, feeling, perceiving, doing' system works. Terms like 'senses' or 'perception' begin to lead into discussion of appreciation and observation as in watching a football match, listening to music and so on. Can one perceive differently? Can one become a more involved observer?

Eventually it becomes possible to discuss imagery, imagination, morality, confidence, logic, intelligence, sociability and even personal health in terms of the learner's myths about their 'learnability'. It cannot be emphasised too strongly that any particular category system for myths is much less important than helping the person to begin to converse with themselves about what may be learned. Once the learner is beginning to think about the scope of what may be learned and the nature of that learning, they can confront their beliefs about what cannot be learned, what they believe are givens. Finding oneself expressing a seemingly fixed belief that 'I could never learn that' or 'I don't think that kind of thing is learned' may become the first step towards change.

2 Opportunities for learning

This category reveals learners' tacit beliefs about opportunities for learning.

(a) must be constructed by an expert;
(b) may occur naturally;
(c) can be constructed by the learner to enhance his or her own learning.

The learner's ideas about the nature of what may be learned will form personal myths about the opportunities for learning. If their thinking is restricted to (a) above then what is seen as opportunities will largely be shaped by their experiences of education and training. Naturally occurring opportunities (b) such as 'holidays' or 'meeting new people' can be further analysed into situations, events and resources. As these are reflected upon, the number of alternatives multiplies. Reflecting systematically on opportunities for learning in this way suggests that one might begin to construct these for oneself (c). This liberates the learner to explore how they can design opportunities suited to their needs and purposes.

Situations

– being stranded at Qatar airport and meeting an Indian Greek Orthodox priest;
– spending Saturday mornings with my grandfather on his allotment;
– having two days to work on the skills trainer before my crucial test on 150° intercepts;
– the field trip to Tregaron bog.

Events

– having to do a finals year project;
– a three-day negotiation with the union;
– the two-week training camp in Italy;

- competing with Ron in class for who could first finish the weekly physics test correctly;
- finding out from my GP what the surgeon did to me on the operating table.

Resources

- a set of leaflets from the World Wildlife Organisation;
- a new spreadsheet program on the departmental word processor;
- my own personal views on industrial waste;
- my friends on the design course;
- the waiter who could speak Russian and Greek;
- the information I already knew from doing a project on pollution;
- the video on a family of dolphins in Cardigan Bay.

The greatest resource of learners is their own experience. Few fully tap the rich vein of gold which is constructed within.

Self-organisation emerges as the learner continues to reflect on all these possible opportunities for learning. The richest opportunity is that which emerges as the learner becomes able to converse fully with him- or herself.

3 Conditions that influence learning

Once learners are really beginning to think about their learning they will almost always begin to talk about the conditions that influence them. These divide naturally into:

(a) conditions in the outside world;
(b) conditions in the person as a learner.

(a) Conditions in the outside world

Students from all walks of education exhibit remarkably rigid myths about the outside conditions necessary for their 'effective' learning. One engineering student moved lodgings five times in one term because he could only learn in 'total silence'. Such personal myths about conditions of learning may even operate at the level of *personal magic*, imprisoning learners within self-perpetuating cycles of feelings which often inhibit any attempt to improve their capacity to learn.

- I must sit up at a table on a hard chair.
- I learn most when I can spread out all over the floor on my cushions with all my books and papers around me.
- I must have at least 3 or 4 hours at a stretch.
- I learn most when I work in short bursts, say half an hour at a time, and then have coffee or take a walk.

- Early morning is the best studying time.
- I find 10 p.m. to 2 a.m. are my most productive times.
- I like the quiet of the library.
- I can only work when I have the radio on as background.

(b) Conditions in the person as a learner

Many of a person's beliefs about 'how I like it to be "out there" whilst I am learning' are stated in terms of 'getting oneself into the right mood'. Many people believe that they have to be in a 'state of readiness for learning'.

- I must be interested in something before I can learn it.
- I have to feel inspired before I can really write anything worthwhile.
- If I really puzzle away at a maths problem late in the evening and I can't solve it, 50 per cent of the time if I sleep on it I wake up much further forward and much clearer in the morning.
- I have this ritual of having a cup of coffee and listening to 'Deep Purple' which really gets me going if I don't feel like working.
- I find that talking things over with Alan and Mitzie often gets me in the right mood. I come back and sit up and it just flows.

What models of personal dynamics lie embedded in these myths? What assumptions about cause and effect might the Learning Conversation reveal? Many of these myths express the deep assumptions of other-organised learners. They assume that learning is something that happens to them; minimally 'I must wait for it to happen' or 'if the outside conditions are right then....' One step towards self-organisation is the 'I can teach myself' assumption. This is a useful halfway stage since the person is accepting some responsibility, but it is the 'teacher within' that takes the initiative and acts on the 'learner within'. This still leaves the learner being taught.

4 Personal processes involved in learning

These aspects of personal myths relate to the 'internal conditions' of the previous category but there is a subtle difference: now it is not our teacher within but the learner who is taking the initiative.

Examples of myths about the processes of learning

- *A clock repairer*: I learn most by doing and listening, and then persisting until I have solved the problem and have got it sounding right.
- *A judo champion*: I spent two months every day just lightly holding this Japanese

master's belt and getting a feel for how he was shifting his weight, his balance; then he let me try another throw and suddenly it all fell into place.
— *A mathematician*: I see numbers in coloured shapes and patterns; I can change them but they also have a life of their own which I can trust.
— *A student*: When I learn, I throw out most of it as rubbish and decide very carefully what I commit to memory.

This last example was elicited from a mature twenty-nine-year-old student who was convinced that his memory was of a fixed capacity and that for every new item learned, he would automatically forget one already committed to memory. In real life this myth about his learning processes coloured most of his activities. It is here that the Learning Conversation can begin to get to grips with a learner's real beliefs about how he learns. Beliefs about how one learns are usually vague and fragmented and do not afford great insights into the personal learning process so one cannot recruit them into producing enhanced performance of a task.

When asked to comment on how they learn, most people in most walks of life, including teachers, are quite inarticulate. When they do begin to describe their own processes, they do so in terms that often show very little ability to observe themselves. Their descriptions are erroneous when evaluated against records of their own learning activity. Learning Conversations within each new action research project tediously verify this. The few who can provide the more lucid accounts are almost totally task-focused or content-bound. These people can discuss how they learned this, that or the other but they cannot super-ordinate these specific learning experiences to describe the ways in which they control, or fail to control, the process of learning itself. People *struggle to learn*, often vague about their aims and purposes, and *believing that learning is something which happens to them rather than a process which can be got to grips with and improved as a skill in its own right*. Very few ever reveal criteria for evaluating their success, believing that the expert or instructor knows best. Being process-blind, they either successfully submit to being instructed or become alienated from education. Those who later are lucky with some job training opportunity fail to learn more generally about their own capacity for learning.

What fails to be appreciated in conscious awareness is that learning embodies as much feeling as thought and as much action as reflection. Our representations of personal myths are multi-faceted; kinaesthetic, iconic, auditory, tactile as well as symbolic forms; all these mediate in a process language about learning. In learning to pilot a helicopter, to control a combine harvester, to use a manual, to lead a scout patrol, to operate a computer, each form of representation plays its part, albeit almost always unconsciously. This *tacit* representation underlies and conditions how we all learn. Herein dwell our deepest myths about our processes of learning.

The 'feelers', 'visualisers' or 'memorisers' do not realise that those who can recognise their learning processes 'through their muscles' or have 'auditory memory' are *equally convinced that everyone learns as they do.* The increased capacity for learning that results from achieving *multiple controlled* 'imagery' or 'memory' by recognising one's own mode as neither inevitable nor a genetic endowment, but *as one* of many alternate modes, becomes a quantum leap in personal learning. All that is needed is a personal system whereby all the bits of information can be brought together into a coherent language about the learning process, which can be used as a vehicle for recognising and reflecting upon the process as a dynamic whole. This is part of the meta language of S-O-L. In sports coaching there has been some work on the 'inner game' but this is as yet only scratching the surface of what might be done.

Attempts at the overt expression of personal learning processes depend therefore on a deep awareness of process. Unless such internal representations can be reconstructed for reflection and review, learning competence cannot be developed. Unfortunately, training and education gives too much emphasis to content and the end products of learning, preventing learners from sensitively monitoring their own internal processes. Many end up as fairly average robots, totally vulnerable, neither able to cope with crises nor to use their initiative to adapt their skills to meet the challenges of new experiences.

5 *Personal capacity for learning*

Learning Conversations reveal myths about personal aptitudes and learning skills. Such myths are often seen as innate capacities. Learners feel that they have no 'talent' for maths, writing, performing manual tasks, managing people, controlling air intercepts, chairing a meeting, preparing good lectures, or becoming a captain's secretary; for marching, making friends, asking questions, dealing with tricky situations, coping with boredom or for giving orders.

Deeper still are myths about their own 'intelligence', 'personality' and 'learning' style, with very little awareness of the implications for their own learning. The following comments on myths about learning capacities illustrate this.

- I do not have a radar eye.
- I'd like to become an instructor but I am not clever enough.
- I can only memorise it if I write it all out in longhand.
- I'm a practical woman. I don't understand all that theory.
- I've got a natural talent with animals but not with children.
- I can read in five different languages but I'll never understand graphs and tables.
- I'm a plodder and risk-taking is definitely not for me.
- I'm a member of Mensa so I know I'm right about that.
- It takes years of experience to be able to do that well.

Only through a gradual but deepening *reflection on personal learning experiences can people distance themselves from their own thoughts, feelings, beliefs and values to observe their own myths.* Those myths that limit their horizons can then be seen as open to change. They can also come to appreciate myths for what they really are – segments of personal meaning which can themselves be brought under review and reconstructed. Although this classification of personal myths provides a useful descriptive frame, its full power lies in its use as a reflective tool in the Learning Conversation. The first step towards S-O-L lies in recognising the relativity of personal knowing as personal myths open to change.

Activity One Becoming aware of one's own personal myths about learning This activity allows you to build a taxonomy of your personal myths, so that you may reflect upon them.

Stage 1 The scope and nature of what may be learned

Start by talking your way through a typical day at home, work, college or any social event in the community. Note down separately the events or activities in which you are involved, each on 4" x 3" pieces of paper or 'cards'. Be specific: for example, making a telephone call, driving the car, reporting to my boss, writing a letter, diagnosing the fault in my washing machine, reading Chomsky's *Syntactic Structures*. Extend the day to include all possible activities. Now think about the weekend, holidays, unusual days of one kind or another. Sort your cards into two more or less equal sized piles:

I could improve   versus   That would be
at that   difficult to do
                                          anything about

Now sort each of these piles into two, and so on until you have five piles, that is, a five-point scale.

Look through '1' and think about what it is you would be learning if you were to improve. Now look through '5' – what is it that you feel is unlearnable? Look through and identify the 'types of thing' which you feel you could learn (1, 2 and 3) and the 'types of thing' which you feel unable to do much about (3, 4 and 5). Think about your 'learnability' profile and the 'outside' versus 'inside' differentiation made in category 3 earlier (page 15).

Stage 2 Opportunities for learning

Now pick some item (or class of items) in 2 or 3 of the scale. Identify the 'types' of opportunities for learning associated with this. Note this on the back of the card(s). Use the situation, people, events, cues to help you.

Work your way through all the items in 1, 2 and 3. Now sort your cards into 'types' of learning opportunity required. Be fairly discriminating. Now use the 'must be designed by an expert', 'naturally occurring' and 'could be made by me' classification to reveal the areas where you are 'other-organised', those that are 'happenstance' and those where you feel you could be self-organised.

Stage 3   Conditions that influence learning

Use your cards to record the 'conditions for learning' (external and internal) you feel are required for each item.

Stage 4   Personal processes involved

How do these relate to the opportunities?

Now add the processes of learning which you feel each item would call into play. Could these be developed as learning skills? Relate these to the 'conditions' and 'opportunities'. Now, as your personal myths about yourself as a learner emerge, what do they tell you?

Stage 5   Personal capacity for learning

Think about what is revealed about your implicit assumptions about your capacity for learning. Take one learnability item from, say, 3, 4 or 5 on the scale and challenge your own assumption. Work your way through all the items. Learn to 'wiggle your toes indepen- dently', 'get fitter', or whatever. Have fun!

The professional myths of teachers, trainers, education researchers, psychologists and other social scientists

No matter how peculiar or bizarre myths about personal learning may appear to be, there is almost certainly some professional group who has already thought about learning and studied it systematically from that point of view. Sweets and the rod (crime and punish-ment), randomness (one-shot learning), unconscious intuition (sleep learning) and mnem-onics (systematic memorising) are just a few examples. The professional literature of the past fifty years takes on a very different appearance once one begins to look at it as systematic refinement of the personal myths of teachers, trainers, psychologists and sociologists. The generators of these myths can be divided into three groups: those who wish to produce or control the learning of others, those that are interested in their own learning, and those that are interested in actively understanding the learning of others and in helping them become 'better' learners.

The first group would talk in terms of improving the quality of instruction. They largely operate from within the 'physical science paradigm'. Much of this reduces to 'behaviour-ism' which assumes that the process of instruction produces the learning and that the learner 'receives' it. The second 'humanistic' group recognises that learners produce their own learning and that 'resources for learning' will be helpful only to the extent that learners make use of them. The third group, to which the authors now belong, recognises that learners and teachers or trainers each have a part to play. They concentrate not only on the learners' processes but also on the nature and quality of the conversational frame within which they operate.

Having once identified the perspective of our professional we can begin to appreciate more clearly just what it is that they are trying to do. We can begin to see how their methods relate to their purposes. If we temporarily accept their purpose, we can make a systematic analysis of their methods and their findings. This leads us to confront a major philosophical issue: whether their whole enterprise reduces to a self-perpetuating myth. Can we see it revealed as an interlocking set of self-validating hypotheses? Did Skinner's assumptions about rats and pigeons so condition how he went about training them that the nature of his findings were already contained within his explanation? The work of Konrad Lorenz would suggest that other assumptions lead to other findings. Can we see the whole pattern of educational theory as a series of personal myths which have been more or less well researched, often elaborated and seemingly validated from within their own perspective? Each position creates methods that are remarkably well suited to obtaining the types of evidence that are required, which work from within their own framework but which do not challenge, much less escape from, the assumptions out of which they arose. Can educational research ever be any more than a vast array of well-researched and elaborated self-perpetuating myths?

The authors do not believe that the three paradigms – the physical science, the humanistic or 'personal science' and the conversational – are merely alternatives from which we take our pick. They differ in their implicit models of the nature of human beings. The first assumes that one human (an expert) should control another (the novice); the second assumes that in being free we are each on our own. The third assumes that freedom carries responsibilities for constructing our own meaning and that we can converse to cooperate in achievements which none could reach unaided.

Activity Two Becoming aware of professional myths about learning   There is much to be learned from attempting to share a discussion which the authors have generated in various forms with many different groups of professionals, teachers, trainers and social scientists. The first stage of this discussion takes the form of asking each of the participants to identify the 'theory of learning'; that is, those schools, theories or positions in the literature with which they feel most sympathetic. The members of the group each acknowledge their position and sub-groups are then formed from people of like mind. Each sub-group is then asked to plan an experiment or a learning/teaching event which they feel would most clearly demonstrate the efficacy of their theoretical position. If this proves too difficult for any sub-group they are asked to identify any one enterprise from the literature or from their own experience which they feel illustrates the power or potential of their theory.

The second stage is to identify two positions, those of sub-group A and sub-group B.

We then set up four events:

a person from sub-group A teaching/offering learning to one from sub-group A;
a person from sub-group A teaching/offering learning to one from sub-group B;
a person from sub-group B teaching/offering learning to one from sub-group B;
a person from sub-group B teaching/offering learning to one from sub-group A.

Let us suppose that A are Skinnerians and that B are Rogerians. They could equally be Freudians or adherants to Gagne, Albert Ellis, Berne, Piaget, Bruner, Broadbent, Chomsky or Searle.

As each event plays itself out it is recorded on audio or video tape. After twenty minutes have elapsed the 'event' is interrupted. The first three minutes of the tape is replayed and each of the two participants is asked to reconstruct separately what they were experiencing during the three minutes. This is done by replaying the tape and making notes. They are then asked to listen to the next three minutes and reconstruct that experience. When they begin to feel that their descriptions of their own experience are really beginning to reflect what they were perceiving, thinking, feeling and doing, they share these experiences, first with each other and then with the whole group. Each sub-group (namely, a 'theoretical position') is then asked to explain what was going on. They are then asked to explore whether some form of conversational explanation based on the espoused myths (that is, their theoretical position) of each of the two participants might also shed some light on the nature of the event.

Finally, they are asked to identify some teaching/learning event in their own recent experience and to examine that in conversational terms.

The authors have found that discussions of this type can have a considerable impact on a group which is struggling to get to grips with what we mean by:

1 the physical science paradigm,
2 the personal science paradigm, and
3 the conversational science paradigm.

It also has a salutary effect on the stance they take towards schools, theories, positions and methods in their own discipline. They begin to see how these professional myths contribute to education and training practices and to the personal myths acquired by learners. This same 'experimental design' can be used to help learners become aware of how their personal myths influence their learning. Readers are invited to create such events so that their myths are challenged.

The authors' personal myths about learning

In order to sketch in the context of our own personal myths let us consider briefly the notion of *public knowledge* (for example, as in science, literature and the law of the land). It originates in the personal myths of specific individuals. In developing their personal myths which may embody a mix of observations, interpretations, analogy, metaphor, as well as combinations of prejudice, understanding and self-validating hypothesis, the good scientist, artist, lawyer, farmer or teacher does not differ from the rest of the human race. They create public knowledge by agreement and acceptance of certain personal knowing. This is revised, negotiated, tested and re-agreed using criteria and methods which are themselves developed using the same processes. Their success, however, partly depends on recognising public knowledge and personal meaning for what they are: representations of thoughts and feelings which are open to development in the light of experience. This *is* the process of learning and it is the method of science. Those who believe that learning is a process of unquestioningly acquiring already established public knowledge will inevitably become imprisoned in their myths and will find it difficult to develop and grow.

Some of the deep personal myths about the nature of human learning held by the authors will by now have become apparent. The theory of S-O-L and practice of Learning Conversations represents the authors' own myths about freedom to learn, the processes of learning, the necessity for content-independent procedures, and the need for a language in which to reflect upon and develop learning competence. These myths have emerged from systematic observations of the many case histories studied in our programme of action research. Let us summarise them thus:

1 *Learning is an inference from behaviour or experience, preferably from both.* Behaviour is available as evidence to the external observer of learning, but experience is directly available only to the learner. A psychological exploration of learning requires its own theory of relativity in which the perspectives of the learner and the external observer are essential ingredients in the conversationally scientific explanation. We see this view of learning being the core of all good teaching–learning, training–learning, consultancy and therapy relationships.

2 *Self-Organised Learning is the conversational construction, reconstruction and exchange of personally significant, relevant and viable meanings with awareness and controlled purposiveness.* 'Meanings' form our experience and are therefore the basis of all our anticipations and actions.

3 *'Cause and effect' or 'systems of relationships' in the sense pertaining to 'explanations' within the paradigm of physical sciences can never be an adequate means for explaining how humans learn.* The process of learning requires some different concept of relatedness. It requires some other view of how one person influences another. The idea of explanation as used in the physical sciences requires transformation into the more powerful concept of 'conversation' within a fully conversational methodology for the study of human learning.

4 *Psychological relativity applies not only to the learners but also to the supporters of learning, the Learning Practitioner, Tutor or Manager.* This blurs the distinction

between teachers and learners. To be skilled learning practitioners, teachers, trainers and managers need to be Self-Organised Learners themselves. Only by fully experiencing their own processes of learning can they achieve the insights which illuminate their role as enablers of learning in others.

5 *The myth which transcends all others is that the whole nature and intentionality of teaching and training must be developed further to create systematically a 'Self-Organised Learning environment'.* Education must invent a conversational method in which the Learning Practitioner can be 'Learning Manager', 'Learning Coach', 'Technical Assistant' and 'Task Supervisor'. The Learning Manager will provide the resources and manage the S-O-L environment. The Task Supervisor will help the learner to create more and better opportunities for learning; the Learning Coach will articulate the Learning Conversation; and the Technical Assistant will provide the specialist tools and procedures for facilitating the parts of these conversations that cannot proceed unaided. For each individual this conversational method embodies its own decease, as the developing Self-Organised Learner becomes his own 'Learning Practitioner' and internalises the whole conversation with himself.

Our meta-myth is that our insights lie as significantly in our practice as they do in our theory. So as a second pass through our myths, we would ask the reader to join us in an activity.

Activity Three Constructing a personal model of the authors' myths   In Part II, Chapter 4 we describe one core procedure for conducting a Learning Conversation. It is the Personal Learning Contract (PLC). Here, we will introduce it in skeletal form as one way of structuring your conversation with us. We end this chapter by explaining some of the assumptions and ideas behind our myths. Converse with us thus:

1 Describe *your purpose(s)* for reading.
2 Plan *your strategy* – how you intend to read.
3 What do you expect will be *the outcome(s)* of your reading?
4 How will you judge the *quality of the outcome?* That is, *what criteria* will you use to judge the degree of your success or failure to achieve your purpose?
5 How will you *review the quality* of this whole process (for example, 1–4)?

Now, converse with pages 24 to 35.

Myth no 1 Perspectives of learning

Learning is an inference which we make from evidence that there has been a valued change either in someone else's activities or in our own ways of thinking, perceiving, feeling and doing something.

We each have unique access to our own experiencing so the learner is the only judge of whether and how their perceptions, thoughts and feelings have changed. A change in our behaviour is more easily observed by someone else. Indeed, if a teacher, an interviewer or an athlete wants to know how skilled they are, nowadays they are quite likely to have a video recording made of their activities so that they can later observe themselves in 'action replay'. Learners can become their own observers.

Thus, experience and behaviour are two separate sources of evidence about whether and/or what we have learned. The learner and an observer of the learner have different access to this evidence. So one quite powerful argument for a Learning Conversation is that this evidence should be shared and participatively examined. If learners are their own observers they must converse within themselves so that experience and behaviour can be amalgamated. Our learner and our observer may have different value systems; they may bring different perspectives to the valuing of the changes. When the observers have their own vested interest in the change (for example, as trainer, teacher, HMI, employer, parent, spouse and so on) there is every likelihood that the observer and the learner will disagree (take a different view) about what 'learning' has occurred. In considering learning as an inference we have identified at least three dimensions of this personal myth (see Figure 1).

Most of institutionalised learning (schools, colleges, polytechnics, universities, industrial and commercial training departments, prisons, therapy, sports coaching and so on) is based on the assumption that the learner's view and the teacher's view of what has been learned are identical. This is the implicit and therefore hidden teaching/learning contract which predominates in education. The Learning Conversation aims to make this contract explicit and, within mutually accepted boundaries, negotiable.

Whilst in practice learner-valued 'learning' and teacher-valued 'learning' may overlap (and indeed should), it is important from the point of view of the Learning Conversation to keep the two concepts separated. The learner can by their own efforts and by the nature of their self-organised processes 'produce' the learner-valued learning. In traditional teaching/training environments the teacher evaluates them. For us, the teacher has two distinct roles: first, to exhibit institutional values and intentions about what should be learned, and to negotiate these with learners; and second, to act as Learning Conversationalists, supporing the learner's endeavours to identify his or her own values and intentions about learning.

The process of learning cannot be observed from outside the learner. Only learners know what they are thinking, feeling, deciding, perceiving and doing when they are learning; and most of them are not very good at observing their own experiences. Fewer have a working language in which to report their learning processes, discuss them and consciously reflect upon them. This is another function of the Learning Conversation. Again, the sequence of behaviour associated with the process of learning can be recorded and systematically analysed, but unless learners participate in this description of their own process any explanation of how they learn remains suspect. This is why we believe that almost all psychological theories of learning are either theories of instruction or they are the psychologists' less than well informed inferences about what goes on in the learner's mind and body.

Figure 1 Perspectives on learning

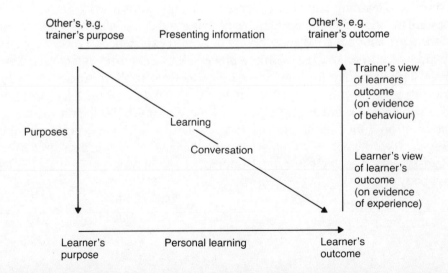

The Learning Conversation is designed to enable all learners systematically to work out their own theory about themselves as learner; and to act as their own personal scientist in systematically developing, testing, revising and elaborating this personal theory. The Learning Conversation enables the learner to challenge his or her personal myths about themselves as learner and to convert these into a viable, systematically validated set of myths that warrant the title 'personal theory'.

The inference systems directly impinging on the learning situation need not be confined to the learner and the teacher. In a fully operating S-O-L system, as the context expands, each of the three dimensions described become elaborated. With the focus remaining primarily on the inference system of the learner, all other observer positions – parent, educational authority, employer, government, manager, department, company – are legitimate. The full technology of the Personal Learning Biography can be recruited to grapple with this developing S-O-L system. This is taken up in Part III.

In addition to the learners' and the observers' perspectives on learning, there are dimensions of *time* and *quality*. The observers of learning, with their intentionalities, experiences and behaviours, operate within very different time-spans. This is what influences the psychological relativity of learning and occasionally allows quality to emerge. One can begin to imagine (or fantasise) how a 'conversational network of learning', fully engaged in the pursuit of quality, could transform personal life, education, industry, family, societies, even religion and cultures as a whole. Part V begins to play out this controlled fantasy.

Myth no. 2 Definition of S-O-L

Learning is the construction of meaning. Self-Organised Learning is the conversational construction, reconstruction and exchange of personally significant, relevant and viable meanings with awareness and controlled purposiveness. This process forms the personal experience which is the basis of all our anticipations and actions.

We arrived at this definition after deciding that 'meaning' was the nature of the relationship between conscious purposive human beings and that with which they transact. Thus meaning is prior to behaviour and experience. It does not lie completely in the human mind; nor is it a property of that to which meaning is attributed. *It is the relationship between the knower and the known.* To us, meaning does not arrive full blown; it is constructed in the transactions between the knower and the known. Further transactions may lead the knower to change their mind: that is, reconstruct their meaning.

It is a peculiar property of the relationship between two human beings – namely, between two nodes of meaning construction – that they can converse. *Conversation consists in the exchange of meaning* but this is a uniquely peculiar business. Meaning is transformed during the process of exchange. This is because meaning cannot be transmitted nor can it be received. It can only be represented. Meaning can then be constructed or reconstructed in transaction with these representations.

For the construction, reconstruction and exchange of meaning to become Self-Organised Learning

1   the meaning constructed must be *personally significant*. This means that the constructed meaning is amplified by being placed in a context of other meaning. The context is created out of past experience, current purposiveness and anticipation of the future. This living context gives the constructed meaning its personal significance.

2   the constructed meaning must have *personal relevance*. This means that the constructed meaning acquires an active place within the larger system of meaning; that it relates to this larger system in such a way as to become organised into it. On becoming incorporated it acquires relevance in relation to the *purposiveness* of the larger system.

3   it must be *personally viable*. Meaning is personally viable when it 'works for' the learner. Viable meaning leads to effective action either in relation to the outside world or in enriching the inner life of the mind, body and spirit (or the related terminology which represents analogous meanings that are significant, relevant and viable for the reader).

The sum total of all our personally significant, relevant and viable meaning is our experience as this has been constructed and reconstructed in all our past transactions and conversational exchanges. This experience, this vast pattern of meaning, is the stuff that forms our anticipations and guides all our actions into the outward world, ensuring that we are becoming more or less skilled, competent and creative, and inwards, ensuring that we are becoming more or less mentally and physically fit and healthy.

S-O-L and intentionality

Often people decide to do one thing and end up either *not* doing it or doing something else. The converse is also common. Having decided not to do something, the person ends up doing it after all. Being able to express an intention is not the same as achieving it. The process of achieving recognised intentionality involves one of two strategies. Passively one becomes reconciled with the directionalities inherent in one's construction of experience, acknowledges them, and thereby achieves intentionality by learning to anticipate the outcome of the directionalities over which one has no control. Active intentionality is achieved when awareness extends into the process out of which the constructions of experience arise. This allows a person systematically to review how he or she is constructing experience and to intervene in the construction process. They are thus able to control their own directionalities, achieving personal intentionality. Freud, Jung, Skinner, Rogers, Maslow and Laing have each had their own personal myths about this.

To the extent that a person is aware of his or her *constructions of experience* – that is, personal meanings – he or she acquires consciousness. To the extent that a person becomes aware of his or her *processes of construction* and takes control of them that person acquires self-organisation in learning. Personal Learning becomes Self-Organised to the degree to which learners become aware of their own meaning constructing processes; that is, to the extent that they become aware of how they learn and are thus able to regulate, guide and amplify their own processes of meaning construction.

Myths nos 3, 4 and 5 Relativity, the Learning Conversation and the method

Myth no. 2 invited the reader into conversation about the nature of Self-Organised Learning. The idea of exchange of meaning was spelled out in order to emphasise the conversational nature of exchange. Here we are concerned to extend the notion of the relativity of meaning and to reveal the need for a fully fledged theory of conversation.

We have suggested that the past experience of each learner provided a unique psychological perspective from within which to construct meaning. This means that even a 'shared experience' will not have the same meaning for each participant in the event. This explains the meticulous pains taken in physical science to arrive at shared meanings; that is, to agree both a language and a methodology by which different participants may generate sufficient shared past experience to become confident that *for certain purposes* they are 'modelling' well-defined areas of reality in similar ways. Modern scientists have spent 300 years learning how to do this. Even then, as the context changes or as they face new evidence or wider questions, these carefully negotiated agreements continually crumble and have to be revised and re-negotiated. This is also the nature of learning.

The physical scientist, despite all the difficulties alluded to, faces a relatively easy task compared to that facing the social scientist. Physical science has painstakingly removed any suggestions of 'mental life' from its subject matter. The gods, spirits (benevolent or evil) and the minds of the dead have all been banished from the physical scientists' view of matter. This ensures that the scientists' theories do not in themselves provoke physical matter into movement or change. This is not the case in the social sciences. In studying people, we have to take fully into account the belief that they will be perceiving the social scientists and having thoughts and feelings about them whilst the social scientist is constructing meaning about them. This makes social science difficult; or it does if you believe that by adapting the methods of the physical sciences you are going to be able to construct viable meanings about people. In fact, in its more speculative realms, the physical sciences are beginning to construct myths about matter that has a life or intelligence of its own.

Many of the frustrating anomalies of social science disappear if one acknowledges the meaning-constructing capacity of one's subject matter. To understand someone you do not treat them like uncomprehending physical matter; what you do is to *converse* with them. Once this fundamental shift is made the impossible becomes possible. If we can converse with other people we may be able to understand ourselves and them more clearly, but just as the physical scientists had to put a lot of effort into inventing and developing methods for valid investigation within their paradigm, so we shall have to spend much time and effort in converting common-sense conversation into a scientific methodology. This will be very different from the methods of the physical sciences but in its own way could become just as rigorous and effective.

In some ways, even as we start, we are 'standing on the shoulders' of the physical scientists. Conversational methods are based on the assumption of relativity. Psychological relativity can learn by analogy from the relativity of physics.

Psychological relativity has repercussions for approaches to learning and for educational policies and practice. The evolution of the conversational method is here elaborated.

Relativity and the emergence of conversations

The epistemological pedigree of the construct 'relativistic' is a long one. For Protagoras 'man is a measure of all things', a participant in the creation of all things. Excellence for this ancient Sufi is a *relationship* between humans and their experience. Sprinting on to the 'subliminal self' of Poincaré, this relationship is seen as an event within which 'awareness of both subject and object' is made possible. This relationship is prior. It is the *cause*; subject and object are the effects.

The intellectual history of our own times is also characterised by the same construct. Sapir, Whorf, Heisenberg, Einstein, Mead, Lévi-Strauss, Piaget, Kelly, Lorenz, Giorgi and Polanyi testify to the extent and importance of 'relativity'. Heisenberg showed the impossibility of measuring the complete system of an entity. Einstein constructed a universe in which even the basic dimensions of time, space and energy depend on the time, space and energy of the observer. Polanyi has explored the whole nature of the scientific enterprise in terms of the integrity of the knowing of each individual scientist. Lorenz progressively explored the realities of members of species at different levels of the phylo-genetic scale, until he saw the human as one probably unstable attempt by living matter to mirror the nature of reality. For Lévi-Strauss, the very patterns of our thoughts and feelings as competent reactions to the challenges of living in our cultural, natural, technological environment. For Mead and Shultz, reality is a social construction which receives much of its individual validation from transactions with other people who share it. Kelly expressed relativity within Personal Construct Theory.

New insights are offered into the processes of causality which influence the coincidence of events in space and time. Such insights are basic to our understanding of the nature of learning. Let us briefly sketch these out.

The struggles of Pirsig in his pursuit of 'quality' lead him into two tortuous routes of thought: the subjective considerations of the idealists and the dialectical arguments of the classical thinkers which painted the way to an objective, absolute view of truth as in scientific materialism. Neither inspired him. The 'knife of subjectivity–objectivity had cut quality in two' and killed it as a working concept. For him *quality is prior*. Quality is a third superordinate entity independent of, but related to, a dualistic subject/object metaphysical system.

Taking a different but equally long and circuitous route, Mary Warnock traces the development of the concept 'imagination'. From the romantics to Sartre, Husserl, Merleau-Ponty and Wittgenstein, she argues for the universality of *'imagination'*. It is exercised by each over all experience. We see forms in our mind's eye and we see these very forms in the world. Images themselves are not separate from our constructions of the world; they are our way of knowing. Imagination is our means of interpreting the objective world and it is also the means of forming images in the mind. These two abilities are joined in an ability to understand that forms have a certain meaning – a quality that signifies other things beyond themselves. She interprets imagination as that capacity which allows us to go beyond the barely sensory into the intellectual or thought-imbued territory of perception. For her, *imagination is prior*.

The phenomenologists were also a source for Kelly's model of 'man as a scientist' anticipating events by constructing their replicates and testing these out by action on the world and offering us the notion that *construing, making sense of our experience of the world, is prior*. Kelly was in a sense a twentieth-century sufist whose teachings were not concerned with static principles but with beliefs about man/woman and their improvements. The early humanists and Kelly resolve the classical debate on causality by taking a new/old direction. All principles, truths are relative.

The ancient Chinese mind contemplates the cosmos in a way comparable to that of the modern physicist, who has accepted that their model of the world is a decidedly psycho-physical structure. The micro-physical event includes the human observer just as much as the reality of I Ching. The 'subjective' observer has to be taken into account in any quest for 'objective' truth. Jung saw this coincidence of the physical objective and psychic subjective event as 'synchronicity', a peculiar interdependence of the observer. *A causal explanation must include the subject*. I.A. Richards makes a similar point in relation to world literature.

In many senses, synchronicity, excellence, quality, the subliminal self, imagination, uncertainty and construing are analagous descriptions of *'process'* – a process whereby the evaluation of events in a given pattern is influenced by the subject/object in a special interdependency. For the study of human learning this *interdependency is prior; it is the process of constructing meaning, through which we make sense of and act within our world*. It cannot be construed in terms of causes and effects. The process that concerns us here is better described as conversational.

From the perspective of the paradigm of conversational science, events in the outside world do not produce predictable consequences; *it is the meaning attributed to the events which become the 'conversational cause'*. Periods of psycho-physical coherence are the essence of such a conversational exchange. For us, the *conversational individual*, the conversational constructor of personal meaning, the conversational learner, is the irreducible element for investigating human learning. The conversational learner extends into the human being and entails some physical/external event. *The conversational learner is prior*. Through awareness conversational learners learn to enhance their capacity to learn and to become Self-Organised Learners. The technology of Learning Conversations is the means for achieving this. Pirsig in conversation with his motorcycle, a Zen archer, a theoretical physicist, Gerard Manley Hopkins, Yehudi Menuhin and Picasso are examples of fairly fully functioning conversational learners. All of us possess this faculty but often, as yet, only in embryonic form. Learning conversations offer a technology for enabling all those six-, sixteen-, thirty-six- and sixty-year-olds who so choose to become more fully functioning conversational learners.

The technology for creative Learning Conversations requires that an exchange is modulated through a shared understanding of how the conversation is conducted and that this model of the conversation itself remains negotiable. Such conversations are rare. People value it when it does occur, but they can rarely reconstruct it or make it happen. Such conversational encounters have been described by Maslow as those in which the criteria for appreciating them can only arise from the experience itself. They are both self-referent and self-assessed. People can achieve creative encounters within themselves, and between themselves. We call this S-O-L. Often they cannot achieve this unaided. We call the support process a Learning Conversation.

Learning Conversations may be conducted by individual learners with themselves or with their learning coach. It is the ultimate aim of every Learning Conversation that the skills in conducting it become internalised. Once this is achieved, individuals, pairs and groups can effectively conduct Learning Conversations with themselves. Sustained change often requires that a whole organisation be engaged in a Learning Conversation. Thus, a conversational learner, the conversational entity which is the locus of learning, can be represented by more than one person. A shared understanding of the nature of the conversational learner is a necessary prerequisite for creative Learning Conversations within it. Thus, a conversational learner may be an individual person, a pair, a group or team or a whole organisation. Such 'conversational entities' are each capable of Self-Organised Learning.

The miracle of the conversation

Exceptions to the traditional Aristotelian bind can be found in certain aspects of Jung's self-actualisation, Adler's creative self, Fromm's concept of man as both part of nature and separate from it, Allport's proprium which rejects the self as a discrete entity, Rogers' continuing process of becoming and in Maslow's creative encounter. For Mair a person can be construed as a community of selves; for Pask the psychological individual is an entity arising out of the properties of a communication network and for Kissinger nation might speak unto nation. For Pirsig and in Zen there are periods when man and nature merge.

These periods of *psychological coherence* are the essence of conversational exchange. But they leave us with a dilemma. The whole frame of our culture's manner of thinking about conversation is challenged. Physical science suggests that communication consists in an exchange of messages. At the behavioural level we can be observer and record what is happening. Communication networks remind us of a telephone system; there is a sender, message and receiver. Two-way communication is more complicated. The participants alternate the functions of sending and receiving. The two-person system (people) as a whole takes on characteristics which were not inherent in its separate entities. The properties arise out of how the parts exchange meaning together. How do they link? Two entities can temporarily synchronise becoming one. Both, if they are actively engaged, are developing a system of personal meaning. One is not empty of meaning while the other is talking nor is he or she necessarily receiving the message that is being sent. The exchange influences both entities and occasionally in the creative encounter the two coalesce to form one. This is the *conversational entity*.

It is this experience that suggests that Descartes did not have the whole story. I can occasionally know nature, myself, or another, therefore I have value. This suggests that it is the miracle of the conversation which might better be accepted as the basis of our becoming. This assumption clears many psychological and philosophical obstacles out of our path. The conversational entity proposition makes the way look clear.

1 I can *converse* therefore I am becoming.

2 I can *converse* with nature, with myself and with another, therefore I have value and I experience quality.

3 *Conversing is not pre-emptive*, it does not imply identity of meaning, only the sharing of experience.

4 Therefore all personal knowing is prior but is positioned in *conversational space*. That is where the meaning lies.

5 *Each position* in conversational space *has its own perspective* with reference to other positions and with reference to time and to quality.

6 Thus it is only by *appreciating a full relativity of meaning that conversation can be enhanced* and we can, as Self-Organised Learners, be free.

7 *Through the miracle of the conversation we might learn to fly.* By construing our nature we may create our own destiny. By construing our environment we may learn to converse and live in harmony with it. By construing the meaning of our own universe we have the freedom to explore, reconstruct and change.

The requirements of the conversational methodology

What are the conditions for the creation of conversational space within which personal meaning is constructed and learning can flourish? Under certain conditions the space will shrink, reducing the meaning. In other conditions the space will expand, allowing the growth of meaning. Conversational space is experienced as the context of personal meaning. It has no fixed dimensions, being always created to contain two entities in a unique interdependency. It is defined by the modes in which meaning is exchanged. Non-verbal imagery in all senses forms the language of much internal conversation. It is the manner in which this interdependency is played out that determines the dimensionality and the capacity for decay or development. Language in the most general sense is the mode in which this relationship is negotiated. Meta-language is the mode in which the process of interdependency is itself negotiable. The power of the meta-language determines the capacity for growth. The design of this conversation amplifier is represented within the technology of Learning Conversations. This book describes a well-tried form of Learning Conversations embodying a unique form of meta-language. The authors invite readers to use it and in so doing develop their own personal language for effective learning.

Activity Three (continued)   Now, to remind you of the suggested activity (page 24), reflect upon your conversation so far:

1   Has your view of your reading purpose(s) changed? Has it clarified? Is it revised?
2   Did you read in the way you planned your 'strategy'? How clearly and in what detail can you describe how you read?
3   Has your outcome(s) been achieved? Is the outcome so far in the form that you expected?
4   Are your criteria appropriate for assessing how successful you have been?
5   Does your PLC still hold or does it need revision? Can you improve on the formulation of your purpose? Have you revised your ideas about the exact nature of the strategy which will most likely achieve your purpose? Do you have a clearer idea of the nature of the outcome which you think your strategy will produce? Can you expand and/or refine the criteria by which you will judge the quality of your success? Either way, are you ready to go on or do you need to read through 1–5 again?

OK: continue to converse.

The book can be seen as an attempt to invite you to converse with our myths about S-O-L.

The main activity: converse with this book – an invitation

The words and how they are read form, as it were, the living soul of the book. 'Converse' with the words on these pages. Never let them dictate to you. Try to enter our world and understand what we mean, but argue with the ideas and test them against your own experience. Take time to formulate personally satisfying alternatives. Try out any of our techniques that interest you, then adapt and modify them to suit your own purposes. Invent further techniques of your own. Accept nothing without pulling it apart and reconstructing it in your own image. May your image change. Learn with us. Enjoy yourself.

Our invitation can be equally interpreted within contemporary Western science or within the Chinese tradition of the Tao. Either way, the power of the conversation grows within you.

You, the reader, are asked to reflect on *your way*. Here we offer you two alternatives, the Way of the Tao and the Way of Learning Conversations. Some readers may discover that these two approaches are not mutually exclusive. You might discover a third approach based on a creative synthesis between the two. Experience and behaviour, personal knowing and public knowledge, inner and outer forms of conversation, two FOCUSed repertory grids over time on one topic (CHANGE grids), two successive Personal Learning Contracts on the same topic, the task-focused and learning-focused conversation, the life and tutorial Learning Conversation, provisionality and certainty, higher-order purposes (goals) and specific sub-purposes, feedback for learning and appraisal, learner perspective and another perspective, can be interpreted as opposites which, through their opposition, represent the two universal forces of yin and yang within the personal science of Self-Organised Learning. Many more instances of such analogies can be constructed. These give rise to the forces which span cycles of Learning Events. They represent the rise and fall of change.

The Way of the Tao: the I Ching

'Why not venture a dialogue with an ancient book. There can be no harm in it, and the reader may watch a psychological procedure that has been carried out time and again throughout the millennia of Chinese civilisation representing to a Confucius or a Lao-Tse, both a supreme expression of authority and a philosophical enigma. Consider Hexagram 50.

> *(C.G. Jung in his Foreword to I Ching, Zurich, 1949)*

Ting, the Cauldron

Nine in the third place means:
The handle of the ting is altered.
One is impeded in his way of life.
The fat of the pheasant is not eaten.
Once rain falls, remorse is spent.
Good fortune comes in the end.

The I Ching is complaining, as it were, that its excellent qualities go unrecognised and hence lie fallow. It comforts itself with the hope that it is about to regain recognition.

> *(As interpreted by C. G. Jung ibid.)*

You can use the I Ching as a resource for discovering ways of conversing with our book. The yin and yang of this conversational process takes the reader outside the boundaries of Western values. This voyage of discovery may offer a new perspective on the personal interpretation of learning and of its significance in today's world.

The method

Refer to the sixty-four hexagrams, derived from eight classic trigrams, and according to one of the procedures described, prepare yourself for conversing with our book. Ask the I Ching how best to approach this book on Learning Conversations. Learn how to discover the answers it proposes. Any reader who expects the I Ching to *instruct* them how to converse had best seek one of the many more conventional educational 'How to Study' books, but readers are advised not to take on such a prescriptive approach. Let us suggest what the I Ching will do for you:

1 Explore the notion of conversation as a system of two opposing forces, yin and yang.
2 Determine your yin/yang position; that is, your own creative tension.
3 Plan whether to go with the flow of ideas, techniques and methods described in our book, or go against the flow and risk diminishing the possibilities of conversation.
4 Try to construct your own harmonious flow.
5 Discover its *resonance* – how our book relates to you.
6 Seek out suggestions as to what steps may enable you to discover the deeper patterns of meaning on offer.
7 Discover how to discover your own approach.

The Way of Learning Conversations

Consider the algorithm shown in Figure 2 and prepare yourself for conversing with the book.

The method

Make a first stab at your Personal Learning Contract (PLC). Use Figure 3 to guide you. Try to keep your PLC continuously in mind *as you read*. Use it to help you monitor your progress. Approach this actively in an open, exploratory way. Allow your intuition to play its part. The value of your PLC depends on you completing it. You may well find that you need to engage in a *series of PLCs* as you continue to converse with the book. *Use these to review your learning*. Watch the quality of your conversation develop. We invite you to use the book as a laboratory for experimenting with your own learning skills. Through this personal experience you will gain insights about Learning Conversations. You might well derive considerable enjoyment and fulfillment from this experience.

Figure 2 Algorithm: the Way of Learning Conversations

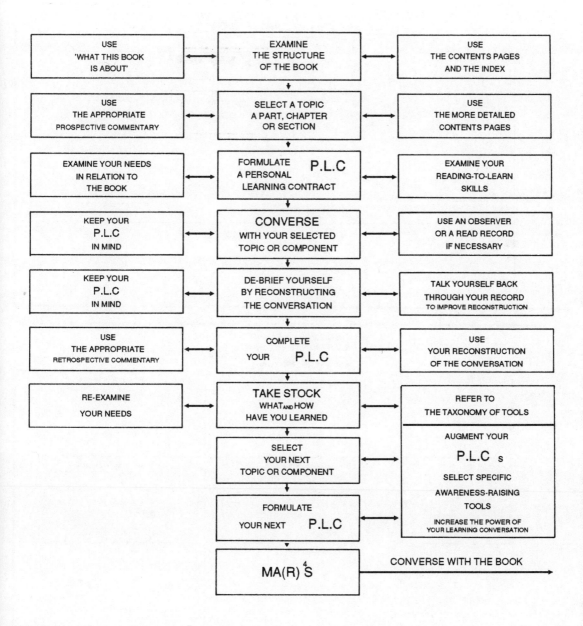

Figure 3 Your Personal Learning Contract form

	THE PERSONAL LEARNING CONTRACT FORM PLAN - NEGOTIATING THE CONTRACT
	BEFORE
P U R P O S E	WHAT IS MY PURPOSE?
S T R A T E G Y	WHAT ACTIONS?
O U T C O M E	HOW SHALL I JUDGE MY SUCESS?

THE PERSONAL LEARNING CONTRACT FORM REVIEWING THE CONRACT		
AFTER	BEFORE - AFTER DIFFERENCES	
WHAT ACTUALLY WAS MY PURPOSE?	COMPARE PURPOSE	WHAT ARE YOUR STRENGTHS?
WHAT DID I DO?	COMPARE STRATEGY	WHAT ARE YOUR WEAKNESSES?
HOW WELL DID I DO?	COMPARE OUTCOMES	WHAT SHALL I DO NEXT?

How the book is organised

The 'General Introduction' explains how the theory of S-O-L and the practice of Learning Conversations originated and how each of us are supported and constrained by our own 'personal myths' about ourselves as learners, teachers, trainers and researchers. The authors offer their own professional myths which form the basis for this book and invite readers to converse truly by offering some reflective heuristics.

To conduct effective Learning Conversations we must have reflected in depth on the nature of personal learning and how to organise one's activities and experiences to achieve it. Part I discusses this. Part II develops the idea of the Learning Conversation and elaborates on its forms and functions. The skills of learning are also addressed. Part III shows how a network of Learning Conversations can be systematised to create a Self-Organised Learning environment.

Each Part consists of two chapters and two commentaries. The *Prospective Commentary* is intended to invite the reader to engage in a Learning Conversation and provides a context, and signposts the main theme, the *Retrospective Commentary* which is intended to support the reader's reflection by indicating the value system within which the authors feel that Part might well be appreciated. For the learner to self-organise their own learning, and true to our belief that the learner must value any learning in his own terms, these Commentaries are meant to provoke reflection and review.

Chapters 1 and 2 (Part I) discuss the nature of learning. It is suggested that learning is a search for meaning, that meaning is constructed conversationally and that it is usefully viewed as modelling. This enables us to examine the nature of different types of model and to see what each will or will not enable us to know and to do. Finally, the capacity to learn is seen as a capacity to construct meaning as modelling. An explanatory model of this process shows how this capacity to learn can be gradually bootstrapped into higher and higher levels of activity.

Chapters 3 and 4 (Part II) discuss the nature of the core Learning Conversation. These chapters are primarily intended for the Learning Practitioner. To the extent that a learner or a group of learners can begin to conduct such conversations with themselves, they will begin to learn more effectively. The learner becomes their own Learning Practitioner. The idea of the three dialogues is introduced: one about personally researching the process of learning; one designed to support the learner through a period of change; and the third exploring the nature of quality in learning and discussing the referents through which the learner judges their own success and progress. *Chapter 4* introduces the idea of levels in the Learning Conversation. The central level is seen to be concerned with specific topic or task learning activities and with the Personal Learning Contract. Here the notion of self-organisation begins to grow: how is the learning to be organised, what resources are to be used, what learning skills will be required, can one plan a strategy for the learning, and can one define criteria by which the quality of the outcomes of learning may be judged? If learners cannot carry through their contract with themselves then the conversation moves to the learning-to-learn level. Here we are concerned with the improvement in learning skill so that contracts can be implemented. If the contract is successfully concluded but the results do not seem to achieve what was expected, then we move to the life or relevance level. Here the specific learning activities are reviewed within a wider context, longer time spans and larger goals.

The full power of many Learning Conversations is not realised until we reach *Chapters 5 and 6* (Part III). Here the educational institution and the private or public enterprise is seen as a potential network of Learning Conversations. The notion of Systems 7 is used to explain how defining the role of the learning coach, the tasks supervisor and the learning manager can firstly increase the potential of each individual Learning Conversation, but it can also enable groups to collaborate in ways that make it useful to view the group as learner. Further networking sees groups combining until the enterprise as a whole can be seen as a 'learner'. The MA(R)4S process is used to monitor and maintain the quality of each conversation and of the Systems 7 network as a whole. In Chapter 6 the Feedback for Learning, S-O-L Spreadsheet and Personal Learning Biography are introduced as vehicles for maintaining an S-O-L environment within a community of learners. This creates the conditions within which people can organise the evolution of constructive change.

Having established the general theory and practice of Learning Conversations in Chapters 1 to 6, the specialist tools and techniques which can be recruited to add precision, power and quality are described in the 'Functional Taxonomy of Reflective Tools'. These are categorised and ordered both for the ways in which they can be used to articulate the Learning Conversation and for the nature of the evidence of learning (experiential or behavioural) on which they rely.

Finally, some of the authors' ideas about what might possibly be achieved if Learning Conversations were taken up and applied in different institutions or sections of society are speculated upon in *General Implications: Towards the Self-Organised Learning Society*. Individual learners, teachers, entrepreneurs, athletes, scientists, managers, politicians, police, medics, journalists, therapists and priests collaborate to transform society by creating a joyful cascade of truly effective and personally relevant learning which can inform each step in the evolution of constructive change. The flow diagram illustrated in Figure 4 outlines the structure and organisation of the book. It can be used as an access device, and we suggest that readers refer to it as you work through the 'Main activity' (p. 35).

Except in the General Introduction, our policy has been not to refer to the work of others. Sources of influence are acknowledged. Readers are invited to construct their own synthesis of how our work relates to others in the field of psychology, education, training, management, expert systems, science and philosophy.

Readership: who may learn what from this book?

Each reader is invited to converse with this book from within his or her unique position. Learners are offered opportunities to observe, reflect, search, analyse, formulate, plan and act on the basis of creative encounters with themselves. Teachers, trainers, tutors, therap-ists, coaches, custodians, counsellors and consultants, as potential Learning Practitioners, are offered ways for enabling others to learn more effectively. *Managers and adminis-trators* operating in an ever-changing environment are offered ideas and techniques for developing their own learning and for rebuilding staff appraisal and career development linked to a system for managing Feedback-for-Learning. Those responsible for *teacher training* and the *training of trainers* are offered ideas and tools for rethinking what it is they are attempting to achieve and for developing learning policies in line with the New Curriculum and Open Learning Schemes. The *designers of educational technology and expert systems* may find the conversational paradigm and the learner-centred technology a useful resource. Educational researchers, social scientists and psychologists may find new insights towards a systematic, person-sensitive, conversational investigation of people, beyond the traditional experimental, anecdotal, speculatively introspective or isolated case-history and participant-observer approach.

The Learning Conversation approach allows each reader to search, construct and reconstruct their own understandings, so that they may transform their own capacity for learning and enable others to achieve greater skill, competence and creativity.

OK! Converse!

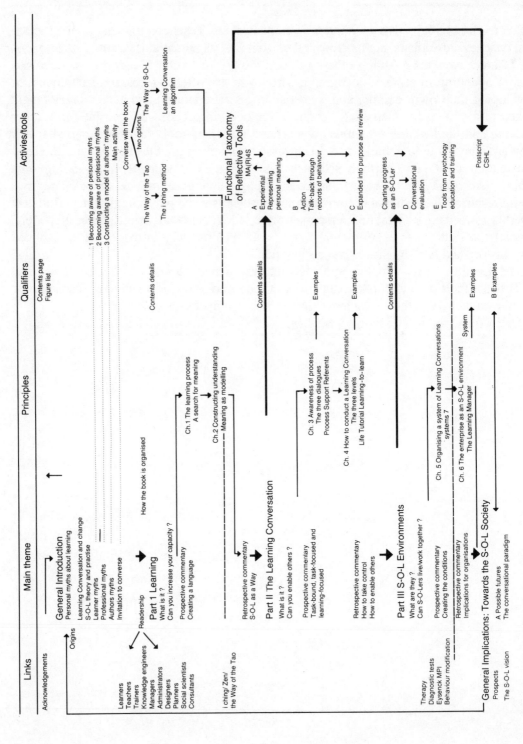

Figure 4 A flow diagram of the book

Part one

Learning

What is it?
Can you increase your capacity for it?

Contents

Prospective commentary: Creating a language for discovering what learning might become

The need for a language to talk about learning

A few years ago, in a rather high-powered industrial meeting, the production director rebuked the authors for unnecessarily complicating the negotiations by differentiating between 'learning' and 'training'. 'Forget the jargon.' 'Keep it simple.' 'In our practical world, "training" can be used to cover everything.' We insisted that since the Centre for the Study of Human Learning were being asked to introduce a system of learning conversations into his organisation, trouble might be avoided in the long run if we and he did not confuse this system with a more traditional training programme. At another meeting, some twelve months later, he was unselfconsciously using terms like 'learning strategy', 'learning contract', 'S-O-L', 'experiential evidence', 'Learning Biography', 'self-defined purpose hierarchy', 'personal meaning network' and 'Learning Conversation', and out of the blue he spontaneously turned to us and acknowledged with a grin that 'it does seem to be more practical to have some terms in which to talk about learning – particularly that aspect of it which derives from "on the job" experience'. This is not an isolated case.

In one way or another, less or more politely, most of our clients start by asking 'why do you need all that jargon?' After getting to grips with Learning Conversations, they either find themselves using our S-O-L terminology or they are creating a specialist vocabulary of their own. Usually it is some mix of the two. We take this to mean that, if we are going to increase our capacity for learning and if we are going to learn how to enable others to increase theirs, then we need tools for the job. The most powerful of these tools is a language for talking easily, sensibly and precisely with others, and with oneself, about learning. But the terminology which is created is merely the surface representation of a tacit body of knowledge forged out of shared experiences and then tested and evaluated for its power to achieve desirable outcomes. Jargon is not productive language. It does not represent such a body of knowledge, either because the complainant does not (yet) have access to it or because the presumed body of knowledge is (or appears to be) sterile. So what for some is unnecessary jargon may be practical language for others, and vice versa.

To avoid becoming jargon, the terms in which personal learning may be discussed have to be appreciated within a system of *self-generated meanings*.

So how shall we come to talk about learning in a more relevant and viable way? We have to learn to recognise events in our personal world as potential learning experiences. We have to learn to restructure our learning experiences into more useful patterns of meaning. We have to develop a language which naturally expresses these new patterns and in which we can negotiate their change and development. We can start by differentiating between 'items of experience' which we have previously, less competently, treated as being similar and we have to learn to recognise crucial similarities among 'items of experience' which we have previously, ineffectively, not related one to another. As we do this we converse with ourselves to test out our increasingly valid insights and our greater effectiveness in formulating and achieving more significant, relevant and viable learning experiences.

We have found it useful to start by assuming that 'human learning' is best treated as a *content-independent* body of knowledge. This helps us see similarities, for example, between the learning of physics, tennis, accountancy, quality control in the sorting of letters, motor-car assembly, air-traffic control, man-management skills, voice control and the fluency of speech, hotel and catering skills and viniology. Specialist practitioners and teachers often experience tremendous reluctance or difficulty in making such connections. They cannot believe that learning their subject or acquiring their expertise has anything in common with the learning of other topics, skills or attitudes. This is partly because they isolate their specialist learning from other experiences. They seldom offer themselves the opportunity to reflect upon and thus learn from the personal wealth of their own multi-disciplinary experience. We have found that it is more useful not to gloss over the obvious superficial differences between learning in different subject areas. It is more effective to work with the learner to help them discover the useful analogies and connections that can be made. The optimistic assumption that there are insights to be gained may have to precede the personal evidence to support it. Indeed, such a change in the patterns of thoughts, feelings and perceptions may be necessary before the evidence can be appreciated. We call this the process of *challenging personal robots*. If this leads to a significant change in the person's patterns of perceiving, thinking, feeling and doing it may be described as a change in personal paradigm.

By opening ourselves to explore the whole range of our experience we can each discover the rich resource within us. By learning how systematically to exchange, share and explore our experiences with others we open ourselves to infinitely rich and as yet creatively disparate resources for learning. The Learning Conversation is a method for enabling each of us to access these resources.

If we are then to treat 'human learning' as a content-independent body of knowledge, what organising principles can we use? We have found it useful to start by differentiating meanings (or usages) of the term 'learning'.

First, 'I'll learn you' may be ungrammatical, but it uncovers a pattern of meaning which is quite widespread. The difficulty arises from an inability to see real differences between 'learning' and 'being taught'. Being taught (a lesson) often carries connotations of imposed discipline and retribution for not responding correctly to 'instruction'. Learning from instruction usually implies getting it right in teachers' terms. It is interesting that some languages – for example, French, Spanish and Welsh – lack a specific vocabulary for differentiating between these terms. For us, learning entails a change that the person values, irrespective of whether somebody else is trying to teach it.

So useful difference No. 1 is:

Evaluating one's own learning   v.   Depending upon others for evaluation of 'learning'

This can be applied to the learning of any knowledge, skill or attitude and to any area of subject matter. It is subject-independent.

Second, another difference which often goes unrecognised is between the 'external evidence' that something has been learned, and the 'internal mental and/or bodily form' of that learning. Riding a bicycle, getting the right answers in a maths test, jumping higher or running faster than ever before, reciting a poem, making a letter rack in the woodwork class, playing the guitar; all these achievements may, when compared to earlier per-formance, yield evidence that something has been learned; but it is more useful to treat them merely as evidence of learning rather than as the learning itself. Learning is better thought of as a change within the person. It appears as a new or improved way of thinking or feeling about something or of perceiving it or doing it. In extreme this difference is easy to recognise. For example, an essay may be evidence of learning, but it is not the essay that has been learned, it is the knowledge, skills and understanding which were acquired in producing the essay that are learned. It is more difficult but equally valid to identify this difference when the person's performance is the evidence of learning. For example, riding the bike is evidence of learning but the 'learning' is in the person; even when she is not riding the bike, since her learning will enable her to ride the bike tomorrow.

If you have never heard of behavioural objectives, value your luck and ignore the rest of this section. If you are familiar with behavioural objectives think about the previous paragraph carefully. The behaviour may be evidence of learning but it is not the learning.

Asking learners what they have learned may help us and them to identify some aspects of their learning, but their reply does not define their learning, since most of us are not very good at observing our internal processes and reporting on the changes. The behaviourists avoided this issue by denying it (that is, by developing a language that did not deal in experience); but 'experience', 'awareness' and 'knowing' are examples of a terminology which is too useful to be dismissed. The learning conversation helps the learner to become a better observer and recorder of his or her own internal processes and thus become more aware of his or her own learning.

So useful difference No. 2 is:

External (observable) evidence of learning   v.   Learning as changes in thinking, feeling, perceiving and doing

A thorough appreciation of the significance of this difference will contribute to the development of an effective language in which to reflect upon learning.

Third, thinking about learning as 'results' or 'products' is very different from considering learning as a 'process'. Personal knowledge is a product of learning. Knowing how you came to acquire such knowledge is awareness of learning as process. The question 'How do you learn?' demands quite different answers from the question 'What have you learned?'. An in-depth appreciation of this difference is essential to understanding how you might improve your capacity for learning.

What you learn from this book will depend upon how you read it. The product of your learning may be simply that you have read it, and may be able to regurgitate parts of it. Changing the process of your learning may enable you to learn more from yourself whilst reading it than you get from the book itself.

So useful difference No. 3 is:

Learning as product, outcome or result   v.   Learning as a process

The idea of the process of learning introduces a time dimension into our considerations. With a learner who intends to become more self-organised we begin to discuss the strategies and tactics which might best achieve the learning outcomes they desire. Thus, the process of learning involves critical reflection on the organisation and timing of one's activities and how this relates to what one learns.

Fourth, another set of meanings associated with the word learning have to do with 'worth', 'quality', and 'capacity'. There is a widespread belief that a man of learning or a learned woman is to be revered and that learning to play 'philosophy' is more learned than learning to play 'billiards', but this is not necessarily so. It will depend upon what is being valued and for what reasons. An inability to describe the process of learning sensitively may blind us to the difference between a rote-learned proficiency in philosophy and a personally meaningful and creatively acquired skill in potting the black from an impossible position. The capacity for learning arises out of the range and flexibility of strategies and tactics which we can bring to the process of learning.

The capacity for learning is different from the process of learning and both are different from what is learned. The capacity for learning is often believed to be inborn. It is related to terms like 'intelligence', 'creativity' and 'genius'. Such ideas usually carry the message (reinforced by psychometrics) that there is nothing we can do about them. Much of society, and the education system it has spawned, reinforce and consolidate these ideas of inborn, pre-ordained talent or potential.

We would claim that the most powerful determinant of a person's capacity for learning is the learner's own assumptions or 'personal myths' about himself or herself as learner (see General Introduction). These 'myths' are learned in the 'hard school of life'; but this does not make them 'true'. This school may well have had a vested interest in not recognising too much potential (such as the 'Eleven Plus'). It may have had a vested interest in furthering one person's development before and beyond others (for example, the belief that boys learn science more easily than girls, or that IQ determines academic performance); or the hard school itself may be better described in terms of opportunities missed or recognised and taken at first by chance. More often this school lacks the skills needed to construct and develop such opportunities. Unfortunately it is easier to suppose that potential can be objectively evaluated and that talents are genetically endowed than it is to help people learn how to create learning opportunities and use them effectively. These personal myths have all the lethal self-limiting potency of other self-validating hypotheses. If you think you are unmusical you will not seriously attempt to learn music. If your teacher and your exam results show that you are not academically inclined you very easily accept this and every small setback validates it, whilst any 'chance' success is all too easily discounted. But self-validating hypotheses can be challenged, put to the test and opened up for further growth. The Learning Conversation challenges the myths of self-limited learning capacity.

Thus useful difference No. 4 is:

Genetically endowed capacity for learning v.   A capacity that can be infinitely expanded by increasing one's learning skills, competence and creativity

This is one of the most helpful shifts in assumptions (that is, in personal paradigm) for anyone who wishes to make full use of the ideas in this book.

Fifth and finally, in discussing learning it is useful to differentiate between 'intended learning' and 'unintended learning'. By 'unintended learning' we mean the results of those events which happen all day and every day but for which nobody prepared, nor designed them to produce learning, nobody anticipated that they would be an opportunity for learning, and yet, in the event, the learner retrospectively recognises and values a change that has taken place. This is often called learning on the job, or learning from experience, and at a conservative estimate currently comprises 90 per cent of all useful learning in our society. In contrast, intended learning involves anticipation, design and preparation and it will be evaluated with the intention clearly in mind. An event can often – indeed, always within some time-span – produce a mix of intended and unintended learning. S-O-L centres on learning that was intended and therefore organised by the learner. Other organised learning or dependent learning is learning in which the intention is that of someone other than the learner (such as teacher, trainer, examiner, employer, parent or someone else). In our learner-centred terms, unintended learning happens without the learner intending it.

The Learning Conversation is designed to enable the development of S-O-L but it recognises, accepts and recruits in all instances of unintended learning as opportunities for growth which may be reflected upon, enhanced and developed. Just as a lucky manager is said to be one who knows how to evaluate the risks of an enterprise and by careful preparation and planning minimises those risks he chooses to take, so the effective Self-Organised Learner is a lucky learner who knows how and when to put himself or herself in the path of unintended learning and how to make the most of these learning opportunities which unexpectedly come his or her way. Both the lucky manager and the skilled Self-Organised Learner also know how to execute each enterprise with prudent but fearless and decisive skill. This is another way of saying that conversational events can generate intentionalities or directionalities of their own. These are unknown to any one participant before the event, but the relationships between them and the resultant feedback processes unpredictably but logically drive the event in certain directions. The lucky manager and the sophisticated Self-Organised Learner learn to ride such unforeseen but directed events. The unlucky person and the other-organised learner tend to be overtaken or even run over by such events. They therefore avoid them or let them get away.

So useful difference No. 5 is:

Unintended learning   v.   Intended learning

The first two chapters offer an introduction to a body of knowledge which the authors conceive of as 'human learning'. Hopefully, these will enable the reader to transform our jargon into their personal language for learning.

Chapter one

The learning process: a search for meaning

People seek meaning. The creation of meaning, the process of achieving personal knowing *is* learning. A greater awareness of this process enables the Self-Organised Learner to act in ways which facilitate the growth of competence in enduring transactions with their world. Self-Organised Learners are in control of the development of their own personal learning. Ideally, social learning is a creative network of conversations between indepen-dent nodes of such personal knowing (that is, S-O-Learners), and between each node of personal knowing and the artefacts of public knowledge which are our inheritance from all such conversations in the past. Personal knowing and public knowledge are the weft and the warp of the rich fabric of civilisation. By improving the quality of personal knowing we strengthen the texture of society and enrich its patterns. In degrading personal knowing into pale imitations of limited segments of public knowledge we risk the unravelling of our social systems. Yet much of our training, education and even some therapy seems deter-mined to measure its success in these limited and self-defeating terms.

Personal knowing and public knowledge

The culture of any given society (its arts, sciences, technologies, religions and social systems) is characterised by a vast array of artefacts; products which represent the ways in which individuals and groups have sought to express and record their hard-earned meanings. A Tibetan 'Thangka' (illustrating the Peaceful Buddhas, the Buddhas of Know-ledge and the Wrathful Buddhas) which summarises Tantric-Buddhist iconography offers one beautiful example. Equally relevantly, one could have chosen a precision engineer's tool-kit, a Welsh love spoon, a personal computer, Wells Cathedral, a chemistry textbook, Bob Dylan's folk poems, the Bible, a central heating system, *Hamlet*, the Great Pyramid of Cheops, the sound and lighting system for a pop concert, a tarmac-laying machine or the three-dimensional model of DNA. Such artefacts furnish the storehouses of public know-ledge. They distil into the mind-pool of the culture (to draw an analogy with the neo-Darwinist concept of the 'gene pool').

S-O-L concerns itself with how each individual interacts with this mind-pool through its artefacts to construct personally satisfying, significant and viable meanings. Personal meanings are informed in systematic conversation with this resource, not de-formed by regimented instruction or mis-formed by an over-protective and so selectively restricted access to it. Such conversationally acquired 'meanings' will enable the individual to transact effectively with the events, people, situations and objects which make up the realities of their world. They also enable the individual to achieve better insights into their own processes.

In autocratic societies the equilibrium between processes of socialisation and those of self-actualisation is such that the structures of public knowledge dominate the processes of personal knowing. When this happens the mechanisms of self-regulated change seize up. When the purpose of the autocratic system is to impose change benevolently the result will be an unselfregulated lurch 'forward' followed by a dangerous period of stagnation. The 'mind-pool' stabilises into systems of meaning which are iteratively preserved, all too easily becoming ritual and dogma. Within such societies the individual – for instance, an architect, a plumber, a doctor, a comedian, a scientist, a ballet dancer, a farmer, a trade unionist or a mother – is instructed in some selected content of the mind-pool and practises in ways specified by that segment of the culture. It is only the inevitable inconsistencies in the mind-pool that provoke the search for personal meaning that offer a dangerous path to individual liberty and social progress.

In contemporary Western society, partly because of the pressures created by the fast-changing social and technological conditions and partly because of the person-centred philosophical creeds of the times, this tendency to preserve the status quo is unbalanced by moves towards the renaissance of the individual. The eccentric individualism of the former fortunate privileged few has become the aspiration of the new, as yet only partly emancipated, many. The pace of change is such that, for example, many of today's engineers learned their electrical theory before the microchip was developed. The personal, social and environmental problems created by our technological and commercial society will only be solved *as we search for new meanings* for such terms as 'progress', 'quality of life', 'success', 'scientific knowledge', 'craft', 'cost effectiveness', 'art', 'productivity' and 'technological knowhow'. We are on the brink of a shift in our cultural paradigm in which we could escape the dangers of the public knowledge of today becoming the chains of tomorrow's minds.

Whilst there exists an increasing emphasis on innovation, on a questioning of existing realities and on a celebration of awareness such as Illich ardently expounds, there are also pressures in other directions; towards triviality, conformity, intolerance, personal greed and the imposition of 'the correct moral values' and 'the one best' knowledge. In this structural tension lie the seeds of the paradigm shift. Which way will it go? In neither direction! We must create a new vista.

If each individual is equipped to question and search for meaning in order to establish personal viability within an environment in which the only constant is change itself, the whole mind-pool becomes a resource to inform our progress. This is in contrast to a society which 'educates' and 'trains' by pre-packaging a restricted, highly selective and eccentrically value-laden source of public knowledge to be mimicked and perpetuated. Should the valuing of this individual search after meaning become established, it will fundamentally change the nature of the mind-pool. This carries with it implications for a gradual restructuring of society itself. A creative and flexible search for personal knowing gives emphasis to the *processes of learning, the methods whereby personal meaning is achieved* rather than to the content and structure of public knowledge. Awareness and self-regulation of the processes by which meaning is attributed to experience enables the individual to engage in and influence change creatively. It is this which it is hoped will become the selective factor in the struggle for personal growth and social survival. This contrasts with the over-valuing of any specific pieces of knowledge and expertise in the content of the mind-pool itself.

As the mind-pool rapidly expands and develops we must each learn how to move around within it and transact effectively with its riches, without becoming overwhelmed. If we do not learn to do this there is a great danger that fear, confusion and submission to 'the experts' will produce the intellectual vandalism which destroys much of the mind-pool in the name of a variety of moralistic positions, including those of mass communication, simplification and togetherness.

S-O-L has a central function to play in contemporary society. Education, training and management policy could be directed towards enabling learners to:

1 identify, revive and creatively develop personally and socially validated knowledge, and

2 overcome the unreasoned pressures for the maintenance of existing structures of invalidated knowledge and the practice of robot-like mechanisms of thought and behaviour

so that alternative and more flexible ways of acting on, and experiencing the world can be sought and valued. The robot-in-man/woman then becomes servant rather than master, and the learner is freed to explore and develop personal competence. An individual can then stroll through the system of public knowledge of a given society informed by it, but remaining free to interact with it in personally meaningful ways. Despite this fairly obvious argument, current practices of education and training place too much emphasis on the perpetuation of dogma, and on the content of currently valued items of public knowledge in formulating national standards and core skills. This is achieved at the expense of the unique processes involved in achieving personal knowing. Unfortunately, knowing has its equivalents of the quick buck. Shoddy goods may be produced.

The representation of meaning

Individuals experience and represent their thoughts and feelings in many forms. Primarily they do this in the imagery of the senses. Meaning is expressed in the kinaesthetic sense of the voluntary muscle system, in the visual, auditory, tactile and olfactory sensory systems as well as in the various symbolic patterns of relationships which are continually being constructed as a person interacts with the world through mediation of language, art or technology. In riding a motorcycle, chairing a meeting, or reading a book, the emphasis given to each of these forms of representation within the total system of meaning will differ, but each plays its part, within each person's unique systems of meaning.

Our use of language plays a key role since the symbolisation of things, events, people and ideas relates richly and complexly to our sensory and behavioural experiences. Often we are only partially aware of the vast and complex system of personal meaning out of which we operate. It can become very difficult to communicate about this meaning with oneself or with others. To attempt to teach another to ride a motorcycle reveals this. Although an understanding of this skill may be represented in our personal knowing, very little of it is in an immediately negotiable symbolic form. Rather, the meaning is in the organisation of the muscles and their senses, in visual experience linked to balance and motion, in the feel of the hand on the throttle and the foot on the brake, and in a highly selective visual appreciation of events on the road.

Such mainly tacit understanding underlies the ways in which we anticipate, act out, and revise our views of our personal world. Attempts to represent this multi-faceted, tacit system of meaning externally may facilitate the reconstruction of more personally significant and viable meanings, but the forms of this external representation and our ability to map it back on to the stuff of our experience will largely determine its usefulness. Such representations can be used to *mirror* the person-in-process. Conversational reflection on these representations enables learners to review and develop their competences. To be effective these representations should reflect meaning in terms which link the original experiences with our current purposes.

With the possible exception of 'early learning' in nursery schools, education all too often over-emphasises symbolic forms of meaning at the expense of the other forms in which experience is represented inside us. Patterns of symbols cease to be means for negotiating personal meaning, becoming ends in themselves, a pattern of abstract relations divorced from the other forms in which experience is stored. A monolithic concern with symbolic understanding may well result in impoverished personal meaning: the term 'academic knowledge' often conveys this. Unfortunately, many members of the academic community have come to believe that this is what learning is all about. In some areas of public knowledge they have constructed assessment and appraisal systems which tend to perpetuate this self-destructive heresy. Too little emphasis is given to developing insights into personal processes, so that too high a percentage of 'the educational product', society's youth, are in danger of ending up as perhaps well-programmed but insightless robots, very vulnerable and therefore dangerous because they are unable to cope creatively in a rapidly changing and increasingly challenging environment. In some walks of life this state of affairs may already be upon us.

Public knowledge as a resource

During our socio-psychological evolution, humans have developed means of expression which have become very powerful instruments for embodying different classes of meaning.

- A Christian view of the act of creation as interpreted by Hieronymus Bosch depicts Adam and Eve in the original garden. On the other hand the shri-yantra in Tantric-Buddhist philosophy interprets creation as a reversal of Genesis, depicting time as a projection of human experience and knowledge. Hawkins holds a very different view of creation as represented in his mathematical formulations.
- The idea of 'womanhood' has been represented in an infinite number of ways within various cultures. Kirchner, within the movement of German expressionism, and Corot, within French impressionism, depict woman in her daily life smoking a cigarette in a café, and reading at home. In Tantric art Radah awaits Krishna, adorned for her daily life, and the woman as Goddess is depicted in the Tantric Kali. Germaine Greer and Erica Jong offer other perspectives. The relationships between men and women have been expressed in sculpture, painting and in symbolic prose. Maillol illustrates the pair as a loving couple; Henry Moore as a family unit; and Tantric art as joint seekers of self-actualisation within a sexual relationship. The Tantric view of psychological process depicts man and woman (Shiva and Shaki) in complete union joining in the totality of experience and separating into an acceptance of a subjective–objective view of the world. Henry Miller expresses this relationship differently.
- Another, rather different class of meaning is represented in the findings of science. The double-helix model of DNA, the multi-layered network models of the structure of the retina and the black holes of astronomy are fairly typical examples from Western science. A talisman for tapping the vitality of the brain represents an Eastern example. Within biochemistry, flow diagrams describe the complicated pathways of chemical processes, and computer simulation is used to design new molecular structures. Different ways of charting the human body are epitomised within the physio-anatomical systems in the tradition of analytical Western medicine and as a system of energy forces or chakras in the tradition of Eastern thought.
- In verbal language there exists a vast range of different forms of symbolism from Joycean prose, bardic stances, haiku poems, to Sufi tales. Chinese calligraphy represents 'happiness' in 100 different symbols. Kurt Vonnegut and Tom White use 'American' to represent their meaning. Noh or Pinter drama, ballet, mime, mathematical proofs, chemical formulae, maps, plans, temples, Zen drawings and Islamic carpets are all equally rich forms in which man and woman have sought to express meaning. The hot-rod, graffiti and fashion each have their own languages.

Each example as a form of representation is highly selective, enhancing some aspects of meaning at the expense of others. Each represents the end point in a specialised search for expression. *The problem is that certain artefacts or products have become the revered objects of public knowledge. They are seldom seen in context as examples of how personal meaning is sought and represented.* Even when such examples show the processes of achieving viable expression quite clearly, as in some art sequences, mathematical proofs or in music, the instructional emphasis has usually been towards reinforcing existing public languages, rather than in establishing an evolving and wide-ranging resource from which personal means of expression can continually be created.

Often in educational programmes the exploration of public knowledge has been packaged away *into separate historical studies.* Education fails to emphasise the importance of early grappling attempts to achieve new understandings, whereas it could consist of such battles. The physical science paradigm lends itself to the description of knowledge in terms of product. Particular solutions (for instance, Niels Bohr's planetary depiction of the atom) are valued as products and over-emphasised at the expense of understanding the process through which anyone could possibly have arrived at the representation of physical matter in this or any other form, and why that form is so useful. A new 'discovery method' could be formulated within a pedagogical framework describing the *conversational interaction of the learner* exploring the chosen resource. This is quite a different view of discovery learning from that embodied in the Nuffield syllabus, the GCSE syllabus and the National Syllabus or from that held by those literary and artistic exponents who believe that the process itself needs to remain forever semi-mystical.

In education, what is needed, in our view, is a curriculum which enables each individual to contemplate more clearly their own processes of knowing. This involves a continually expanding awareness of one's own meanings and how these are constructed and developed. It demands recognition of the insights to be gained from representing one's meanings and reflecting upon these representations, then reiterating this process until one values the product as an insight. Such a series of evolving representations allows for the development of a specialised personal mini-language, which can then be related to other existing forms of similar expression. This allows the learner to explore the power and sensitivity of other existing forms of representation, be they verbal languages, mathematics, choreography, chemical formulae, engineering drawings, computer languages, pop music, cordon bleu cookery, Cockney rhyming slang or the Karma Sutra.

However, even these languages are not ends in themselves; they are merely sections through continuing strands in the mind-pool, each driving ever further in our attempts to represent our meanings more adequately so that we may reflect upon them. The purpose of all education and training curricula could be to enable each one of us to join more fully in this enterprise.

The search for meaning as a consciously self-organised process

Learning Conversations enable individuals to experience the processes whereby meaning is created, and hence learn how to learn by systematically reflecting upon, and thus expanding, the terms in which they perceive, think, feel and act. Once this is fully appreciated, many of the artefacts in society can be recruited as tools in the Learning Conversation. By attributing personal meaning to the artefacts created by others, individuals can become more aware of their own processes. The contemplation of a Gerald Manley Hopkins poem, looking at a lovingly designed garden, reflecting upon a Surrealist still life by Griz or Dali, listening to the Beatles' 'Sergeant Pepper', elucidating the chemical processes and scientific significance of the surface chemistry of corrosion, can be equally powerful ways into process. Again, searching to understand the *strivings* of others – for example, Einstein's mathematical formulation of time as a fourth dimension of space, Hawking's Unified Theory of the Universe, or the notebooks of Leonardo da Vinci displaying experimentation with the visual representation of beauty through perspective, light and shade – can lead to personal insights. The problem with using such artefacts – that is, the records of others' knowledge – is that they usually represent highly developed modes for thinking and feeling about reality. *Unless the individual learner is capable of transcending these products as external representations of others' meanings to arrive at a description of the processes which enabled them to express their personal meaning in these forms, they will remain imprisoned and continue to view their world more as a series of products than as processes of learning.*

A conversational learning technology can elevate the learner to an awareness of the processes involved in constructing understanding. For instance, Kelly developed the two-dimensional repertory grid; Thomas, one of the authors, has developed this further into the FOCUSed Grid, PEGASUS and SOCIOGRID; on different lines Pask has developed Entailment Structures and THOUGHT STICKER. In Eastern science Lama Govinda has developed 'pyramid planes of existence' to depict structures of consciousness. Hierarchies, Tree-structures, Networks, Chomsky's Syntactic Structures, Minsky's Frames, Zadeh's Fuzzy sets, and computer languages from Basic to Prolog are all attempts to formulate structures for representing certain systems of meaning. All these can be recruited into a conversational learning technology.

We have already argued that many psychologists have fallen into the trap of producing an inappropriate technology for researching human learning. This is because the results of learning are presumed to be known to the experimenter already, and cannot therefore be appreciated as open-ended, as yet unknown constructions of another's system of personal knowing. Statistically based descriptions such as personality categories, IQ and creativity measures and semantic differential scales often cause individuals to feel uneasy when used as descriptions of 'the self'. Rogers' gigantic step inwards towards the process of 'becoming' laid the foundation for exploring the 'conditions of personal change' but he pays little attention to the meaning-building process itself, the unique inner processes which initiate, sustain and re-style the 'cognitive maps' of a person. Husserl opened up a new vista of phenomenological investigation, but psychology had to wait for Kelly's metaphorical conception of 'man as personal scientist' and for the development of the repertory grid as a tool for representing personal meaning. Kelly's craft initiated a breakthrough into a more humanistic technology that allows meaning to emerge in individual terms and yet retain a systematic form.

Within psychology a number of mini technologies have emerged for facilitating awareness and change. These have often been taken up, sometimes over-enthusiastically, by the training community, becoming the latest craze which has its day and seemingly sinks without trace. The Encounter Group methods, Transactional Analysis, Psycho-drama, Role Playing, and Bayles' Observation Categories for recording discussion are some examples. Within Personal Construct Psychology, the Personal Biography allows a personal self-image to emerge. As a free form of self-observation, the biography presents a useful tool once the person has experienced more systematic procedures for awareness-raising and control. The Repertory Grid allows personal constructs to emerge as a representational model of an individual's world. These constructs are hierarchically organised into a system within which meaning is attributed, stored and applied. But the use of the grid as a mirror of the process of meaning attribution depends on the skill and sensitivity of the elicitor. *As an interpretive image of personal meaning the grid only very partially captures the model building and 'acting out' process of construing.* It is the power of the conversation with the grid that comes closest to capturing this process.

In developing a technology for implementing S-O-L the repertory grid was recruited as a *conversational tool*. The compendium of examples in our book *Self-Organised Learning* show that although the grid can be a very powerful device for a Learning Conversation, it has serious limitations as a tool for representing a 'person in process'. Towards the end of that book we laid foundations for conversational tools that go beyond the grid. Simulation by computer systems tied to a graphic display may be the best yet for attempting to represent the process of constructing personal meaning. This has the advantage of being able to display process in faster than real time. But other cultures have arrived at effective conversational systems in other ways. The realisation of a Tantric model of all thought and time represents one such way. What needs to be developed is a whole library of tools, each with its own characteristics, to be recruited into the Learning Conversation. Later in this book we offer the foundations of such a taxonomy.

However sophisticated the method or procedure, only within a conversational science can we pull it out of its more static, descriptive, product-based state into becoming a tool for exploring the personal processes of learning. This cannot, by its very nature, be totally knowable. Here we edge towards Eastern thought – Zen and the Tao – but the conversational paradigm saves it from mysticism by allowing the learner to be a personal scientist, albeit a relativistic scientist, who uses the tools of conversational science to chart their own progress systematically. Here lies the power of the conversational technology.

Even within this person-sensitive technology, much of the psychological process of meaning construction remains seemingly unrevealed because it is only partially expressed in words and symbols. Polanyi comes closest to explaining this in his formulation of tacit knowing. We conceive of two separable aspects of conversational learning which appear to go on in parallel. One is the external exchange between the learner and their resource; the other is the learner's inner exchange with themselves. This is the hidden resource which feeds the outer conversation. Even when 'fully' reconstructed, one's verbal understanding of it necessarily remains incomplete. Its language is largely non-verbal and the deeper contributor to it usually takes little part in the conscious reconstruction. But it is at this deeper level that some of the more significant encounters take place and enable the learner to transmute meanings and evolve as a conversational scientist into a new phase of personal growth.

Such a conversation is as fragile as it is powerful. The conversational technology of S-O-L has to be recruited with delicacy and insight. If the conversation is approached within a 'physical science' paradigm it will fail. The Learning Practitioner is not there to explain the learner. He or she is there to help learners explain themselves to themselves. This requires that the Learning Practitioner think, feel and perceive the process from within a truly conversational paradigm. For those that have not experienced this shift in paradigm but wish to do so there is an interesting and challenging time ahead. There is a whole new system of skills and understanding to be mastered. 'Teaching', 'managing' and 'instruction' will never appear the same again. Within the physical science paradigm we would never leave liquid nitrogen exposed to the atmosphere for very long. If we did it would disappear. This might baffle those not in the know. Similarly there are many non-conversational conditions within which the search for personal meaning disappears without trace. Within the conversational paradigm this is not mysterious. It is the emphasis on learning that preserves it.

Although the fully developed Self-Organised Learner can take off within the artefacts offered by a culture, so that these become tools for arriving at a description of personal process, most of us fail to achieve this. In this chapter we have argued that education and training are partly to blame. The conversational paradigm offers a mode for articulating experience which can be applied to all forms of meaning representation. The individual becomes free to question all existing artefacts and the content these embody. Such artefacts can then become tools for the exploration of personal knowing. These tools exist in every walk of life, at every age and at every level of sophistication. So everyone can be encouraged to converse in ways which achieve this level of freedom. It depends on the recruitment of the appropriate tools and the power of the Learning Conversation.

The process of education and even therapy often fail to elevate people to a level of awareness of process, whereby they can free themselves from the shackles of dogma, self-perpetuating cycles of activity and absolutist knowledge. The construction of personal meaning needs to be brought under review during certain phases in a person's life; otherwise habitual mechanisms of construction may permanently take one over. One becomes the domain of a set of more or less competent personal robots. Not only does the conversational paradigm need to be internalised, but it must also be extended outwards into a person's life space. The mid-life crisis, the Open College, in-service training, entering school, college or university, marriage, writing a book, re-training, redundancy, retirement and even one's first job are all likely points at which the Learning Conversation can support the vulnerable individual through potential disaster to new levels of achievement.

Learning Conversation as a personal science

In the General Introduction we set the scene for Learning Conversations. We argued the need for a conversational technology for achieving S-O-L. The Conversational Learner emerged as one of the authors' 'core myths'. Here we lay the foundation of the learner as a Conversational Scientist *personally involved in researching their own meaning construction process.*

In recognising the Conversational Learner as the primary element in learning we have found it necessary to revise our view of what constitutes research, what defines a conversation and what learning may be. Learning requires that learners construct or reconstruct aspects of their reality so that meaning is attributed to new areas of experience or new meanings are attributed to old areas of experience. It also requires that the learner, sooner or later, acts on the basis of this new reality, trying out and exhibiting new or changed behaviours. Self-organisation in learning requires that the consequences of new ways of seeing reality and acting upon it should be reviewed and fed back into more personally meaningful and viable constructions of it. It also requires that the Self-Organised Learner should value his new reality or/and the consequences that accrue from new behaviours. Non-valued learning often has less acceptable names attributed to it.

Given different values and different perspectives, as described in the General Introduction, learning becomes a relativistic concept. It is a change in the relationship between the learner and his situation, personal, social and/or physical. Learning is appreciated differently depending upon the psychological position of the observer. Teacher, trainer, parent, employer, manager and many others can be observers of somebody else's learning. Only the learner has a privileged vantage point.

If educational research concerns itself with learning and the researcher/teacher defines learning in this way, then the priority of narrowly defining things in a scientifically objective way becomes suspect. The pursuit of objectivity normally involves the educational researcher in a detailed control of the experimental situation. This is how we, the authors, began (see Origins, p. 1). But studies aimed at increasing self-organisation require that the researcher/ teacher recognise that the learner has her own point of view and needs the freedom to explore each learning situation. As the learner begins to exercise greater and more sensitive choice, so the researcher/teacher loses the capacity to insist on a rigid, pre-planned, experimental design. They have the choice of becoming one among a number of pre-packaged resources, or of becoming a full participant and welcoming the student as an equal but different participant into the learning/teaching conversation. In education, staff may opt for one of three roles; they may become the other-organiser of the learning, a learning resource or a full participant in the learning/teaching conversation. They may take one role in one situation and the other in another. What happens, disastrously on occasions, is that these roles are confused and the interaction becomes neither instruction nor Learning Conversation. It founders in a mess of mutual mis-conceptions, annoyance and frustration within which personal learning mysteriously evaporates. For most of this century the educational researcher and the teacher have seemed more at home and therefore more successful at understanding pre-planned instruction. They have seemed less at ease in seeing how open-ended creative learning under the control of the learner might be investigated as rigorously and systematically by changing the paradigm of scientific investigation.

In studying the dynamics of Learning Conversations, a traditional view of objectivity is incompatible with the pursuit of self-organisation. The positions of researcher/teacher and learner are no longer entirely dissimilar. If it is acknowledged that each is an autonomous contributor to the joint enterprise, then many of the assumptions implicit in objective research, formal instruction and instructional tutoring have to be examined and negotiated afresh before the enterprise can get under way. The learner recognises that S-O-L involves him in a unique action research enterprise centred upon himself, his learning projects and his learning skills. The teacher sees him- or herself as participant adviser or consultant to the learner in this enterprise. The teacher now concerns him- or herself with understanding and making explicit the dynamics of this joint enterprise and in negotiating multiple criteria for exhibiting the degree and nature of the learning which is (or could be) inferred from various points of view. The educational researcher becomes a third participant in this enterprise. Their function is to use this privileged access to the processes of learning and teaching continually to represent and interpret these processes back to the primary participants. This re-search activity or action research method is represented later (Part II) by the authors in the form of the MA(R)4S heuristic for amplifying the conversational process.

The development of a language for learning depends upon an ability to observe, interpret and review how one learns. The process of learning acquires reality in the context of what is being learned. Thus whilst the science of human learning is independent of the particular content being learned, the practice of human learning must always have some specific focus out of which to generate the experience of learning. Self-Organised Learners recognise that learning involves them in a personally unique enterprise focused on understanding the nature of their own learning. The technology of Learning Conversations supports this process. People can learn to distance themselves from the content of their learning experiences and in achieving this, they are freed to explore and develop their learning competence. Conversational tools are designed to achieve the conscious reconstruction of the learning events, which often cannot be fully experienced during the event itself. The personal research process oscillates between structure and freedom, certainty and doubt. It depends on

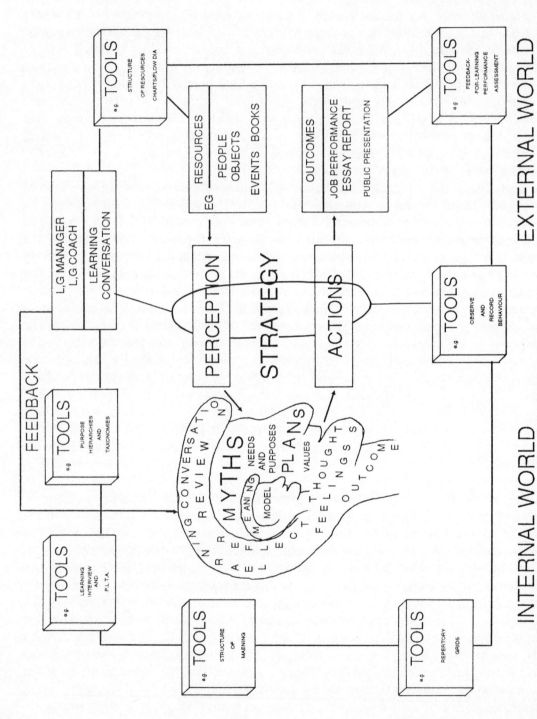

Figure 5 The Self-Organised Learner as a conversational scientist

overcomingauniversaltendencytowardsultra-stabilityandhabitualcontent-boundmodes of thought, feeling and behaviour.

Figure 5 outlines this personal research process of the conversational scientist and the role of the Learning Conversation in facilitating S-O-L.

Kelly's metaphor, 'man as personal scientist', suggests that individuals develop 'theories' about everything in their experience. These are the basis of all action and are tested, improved, revised and validated in the light of perceived consequences. This validation process can be more or less adequate both in terms of short- or long-term anticipation and in terms of the range of experience to which it is applied. The process of reviewing experience as a more or less viable system of meanings enables the person to anticipate events, act, generate feedback from what they perceive as the consequences of their actions and revise their theories in the light of ongoing experience. Inadequate constructions of meaning lead to inappropriate anticipations. Where these become locked in with an inability to appreciate the full consequences of one's actions they can be viewed as the source of what Rogers calls disruptions of natural growth. More adequate meanings enable people to achieve competence and to live creatively. This process establishes relationships between the inner world of the person and what they can appreciate or achieve in the outside world. Competences from talking to juggling, from mathematical thought to painting, from social skill to yoga, from the maintenance of motorcycles to the maintenance of personal relationships, all derive from this capacity to construct meanings which viably model ourselves in our environments.

We find it useful to conceive of the context within which this process grows as a Learning Conversation. For us, the personal scientist becomes a conversational scientist. This involves a degree of creative encounter, either with another being, with an 'intelligent' machine, or with oneself. The essence of the Learning Conversation is that there is more than one autonomous node of control within it and these nodes synchronise so that the passing of control back and forth between them achieves an encounter that neither can create separately. What is contributed by each is not predictable by the other. Indeed, what they will contribute is not predictable by the contributors themselves, since it is dependent upon what will be contributed by the other. Thus, without a totally preconceived notion of the form which the conversation will take, nor of the content, the conversants, within a conversational paradigm, enter upon a collaborative enterprise for which they can only have significant expectations. The outcome depends upon their (conversational) skill and knowhow.

Whereas practitioner and client are both clearly separate nodes of control within a conversation, the nature of the control which each exerts is different. Hence one can identify asymmetrical conversations. In the early stages of an encounter, the practitioner may control the process or shape of the conversation whilst the client determines its content, but an essential characteristic of the conversation is that it must allow for growth and for a changing, negotiable agreement about who controls what and when. When the capacity for process and content control becomes shared, the conversation takes on a symmetrical form. The very essence of becoming a Self-Organised Learner is the development of an ability to conduct symmetric Learning Conversations with oneself and to manage asymmetric and symmetric Learning Conversations with others.

The qualities of personal meaning that may be constructed

In our book *Self-Organised Learning* we have described five distinct forms taken by the personal meaning which is being constructed (see Figure 6). Let us consider the particular example of attending a lecture. The learner could be concerned to operate as a tape recorder, to try to generate the auditory equivalent of a photographic memory. If this is what the listener to the lecture is attempting we would describe the personal meaning being constructed as *rote, factual or ritualistic*. No judgement is being exercised other than to check whether it is being memorised in exactly the form in which it is being delivered. This form of meaning merely allows the learner to recall the lecture as is or anticipate a replay of the same lecture. Transferred to events other than lectures, it would allow us to recognise familiar places, things, people and events and anticipate any of these that have fixed sequences or forms.

Another way in which the learner might listen to the lecture is to construct an internally consistent and coherent but complete pattern of personal meaning. This would depend upon the listener's ability to make sense of the lecture by dividing it up into parts and seeing how these parts relate one to another. Each chunk would have a similar structure, being broken up into smaller chunks which relate one to another to produce the larger chunk. This *informational, instructional, logical, coherent, internally consistent* form of personal meaning would therefore have a *hierarchical* structure. A variation on this quality of personal meaning is one in which the 'contents' of the lecture are personally related to other informational personal meaning and, using relevance, internal consistency and coherence, are built into existing structures of this type. Such listening to a lecture would generate the feeling that one was understanding what was being said. The general form of this quality of personal meaning is that it generates 'schemata' – that is, patterns – within which the content coheres and is organised. This form of personal meaning would allow learners to recognise, anticipate and appreciate their experiences when exposed to similar events in the future. It allows multiple-entry points and paths through the experience, but it is not explanatory.

Personally *explanatory* meaning is constructed when learners relate the meaning they are constructing to things, people, events and situations in their world in ways that potentially encourage them to act in the expectation of achieving certain results. In the most simple terms the meaning is felt in terms of cause and effect: 'If I do that, then that will happen'. These meanings are *operational*. They are the basis on which the person acts.

Thus so far we have three types of personal meaning:

1 rote,
2 coherent,
3 operational/explanatory.

Let us examine these a little more closely.

Our lecturer may be talking out of a system of personally operational meaning. Our learner may be generating rote-type personal meaning. If he were very good at it, he could generate exactly the same sequence of words as were used by the lecturer, but his meaning would be in a different form. Vice versa, the lecturer may have learned his lecture parrot-fashion and yet learners may be constructing coherent or even explanatory meaning as they listen to him.

The next type of personal meaning is what we would call *constructive personal meaning*. This type of meaning grows and develops as the learner actively constructs *additional* meaning. This may take the form of additions or elaborations to existing explanatory schemata. Thus *constructive personal meaning is adding to the operational effectiveness of the learner by increasing the scope and precision – that is, the quality – of their existing competences*. Some of the sources of personally constructive meaning will be the person's ongoing experience in their world. Further sources are other people's experience, which can be reflected upon and incorporated to improve the scope or quality of one's operational understanding. Other people's experience may be expressed in their artefacts. Whatever the source, personally constructive meaning is striving to increase the learner's operational effectiveness.

The final type of personal meaning which we have found useful to identify is what we call *creative personal meaning construction*. This happens when there is a significant change in the pattern of personal meaning; when the structure of the meaning is seriously revised. This is often referred to as having a new insight or seeing things in a new light. The whole nature of the operational schemata is changed. The nature of one's skills or competences changes. We have also used the term 'personal paradigm shift' to refer to this type of learning.

The nature of each of these five types of personal meaning –

1 rote,
2 coherent,
3 explanatory,
4 constructive,
5 creative

– is different; each implies a different intent on the part of the learner. Each implies a different relationship between the learner and his or her personal meaning.

Each type of personal meaning can vary in quality. We can have 'better' or 'worse' rote-type personal meaning and we can have 'better' or 'worse' qualities of meaning within each of the other types. The important thing to note is that the learner would use quite different tests, different criteria for determining 'better' or 'worse' within each type.

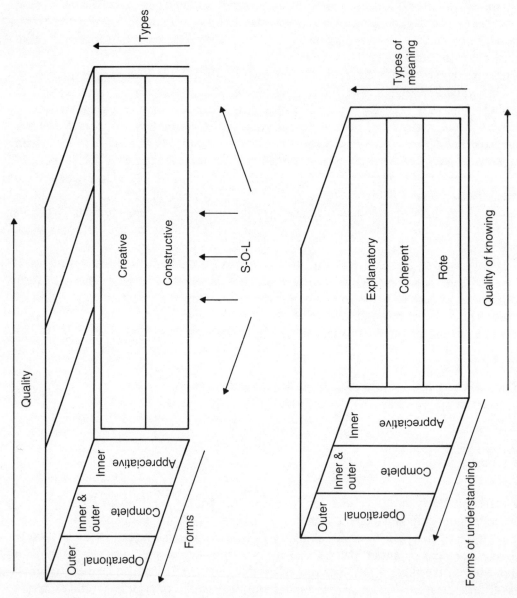

Figure 6 Five types of personal meaning

Figure 7 The capacity to learn

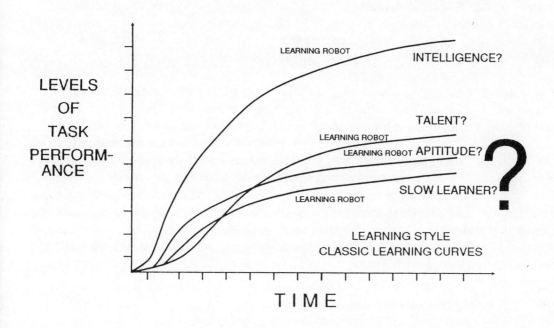

FIXED CAPACITY FOR LEARNING

LEVELS
OF
TASK
PERFORM-
ANCE

LEARNING ROBOT

INTELLIGENCE?

TALENT?

LEARNING ROBOT

LEARNING ROBOT   APITITUDE?

SLOW LEARNER?

LEARNING ROBOT

LEARNING STYLE
CLASSIC LEARNING CURVES

?

TIME

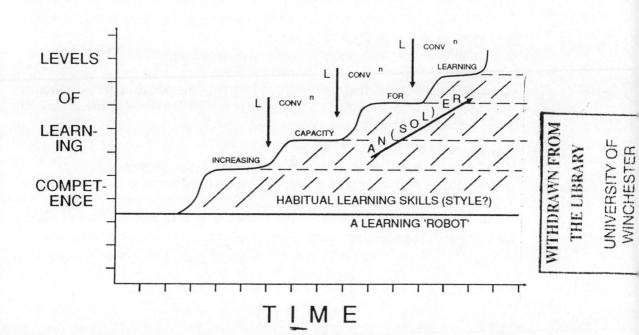

LEVELS

OF

LEARN-
ING

COMPET-
ENCE

$L \mid CONV^n$

$L \mid CONV^n$

LEARNING

$L \mid CONV^n$

FOR

E R

CAPACITY

A N (S O L)

INCREASING

HABITUAL LEARNING SKILLS (STYLE?)

A LEARNING 'ROBOT'

TIME

However, we are here considering not only the type of personal meaning which is being generated, but also the nature of the conversational learning processes which generate these meanings. The nature of the process which generates each of these types of personal meaning is different; it is monitored differently, using different criteria to regulate the conversational meaning constructing process and to 'measure' its effectiveness.

Here we begin to see how a person's capacity for learning might be changed. We might help them improve the quality of personal meaning which they generate within a given type; that is, they may learn how to generate better 'rote-type' personal meaning. Also they may learn to generate different types of personal meaning in relation to a given topic or task and thus transform their acquisition of competency and their operational efficiency. *Rote-Factual meaning* leads to exactly identical cycles of anticipation. *Coherent Instructional-Informational meaning* leads to more variable anticipations, but these are nevertheless repetitive as a logical or categorical consequence of known positions in a static structure. *Explanatory meaning* leads to anticipations which are the consequence of causal chains, system characteristics or multi-causal networks. *Constructive and creative meaning* introduces new components and structures from outside the system and anticipations will involve new parameters and patterns of consequences. The Learning Conversationalist, the Self-Organised Learner, has the capacity to converse and generate meanings at all levels and can so construct and create freedom to direct their own personal destinies. Figure 7 summarises the difference between conventional learning and the development of a capacity to learn.

Questions facing the conversational learner

1 Three meta-questions
   How, and with what special techniques, can one support a learner
   (a) to identify and question their own image of themselves as learners – that is, to investigate their own operational beliefs, myths, understandings and superstitions about their own capacity for learning,
   (b) to clarify and come to effective terms with their own brand of 'conversational science',
   (c) to re-negotiate and define their long-term learning contract operationally – either directly between the learners and the providers of the learning opportunity and/or by the learners with themselves?

2 Five questions about personal learning
   How, and with what special techniques, can a learner be supported
   (a) to negotiate their more general needs into specific and well-formulated learning purposes,
   (b) to explore and define the range of relevant learning resources available to them,
   (c) to negotiate purposes and opportunities into personally relevant learning tasks,

(d) to diagnose their particular learning expertise and weaknesses as these relate to achieving their purposes with the resources available to them,

(e) to clarify the nature of the criteria which they will use best to evaluate their own learning performance in their own terms?

3 Two general questions

How, and with what special techniques, can one support a learner

(a) to bootstrap themselves up out of the non-consciousness of over-familiar, over-learned and too habitual modes of learning into a more acute and accurate awareness of their own processes,

(b) to reflect on their constructions of experience without necessarily being forced into any one exclusive form of meaning representation?

Chapter 2 traces our pursuit to answer these questions, and Part II explains the methodology of Learning Conversations which enables the conversational scientist to become a Self-Organised Learner.

Chapter two

Constructing understanding: meaning as modelling

In Chapter 1 a view of learning as 'the search for meaning' was advanced. It is learning that makes us fully human. But what gives meaning to everyday experience? The claims are as varied as people: religion, old movies, philosophy, clothes, work, ideas, a loved one, ikebana, a cause, a career, a prestige car, voluntary service overseas, money, a good punch-up, hiking, a good meal or the Saturday afternoon football match would each be nominated by someone. What is it about such human activities that makes them meaningful, or not?

The construction and attribution of meaning to artefacts, people and events has been described as a conversation – a conversation involving the deep, tacit meanings which operate imagelessly in the depths of our mind and the more explicit, if ephemeral, expressions of these meanings as we consciously re-experience them in the 'here and now', in multi-sensory images and symbolic representations. This conversation is commonly described as the process of 'thinking and feeling'. These thoughts and feelings may remain completely within us, the conversation playing itself through as a system of visual or other sensory images, as sub-vocalised speech, or as an 'inner game' played out in covert muscular activity. The Learning Conversation can help a person to identify habitual modes in which this conversation takes place. It challenges these and, exercising richer and more apposite modes, can significantly increase a person's capacity for certain types of learning. The quality of our thoughts and feelings may be enhanced by talking with others or by reflecting upon our ongoing attempts to represent these thoughts and feelings in a more concrete form outside ourselves. So, for example, 'I feel that my ideas about learning are clarifying further as I try to express them in the form of written prose'. The inner and the outer aspects of the conversation can be discriminated. The quality of the conversation is mediated by the forms of representation in which it takes place and this influences what is transacted.

It is the quality of this reflective conversation that shapes the meanings which are constructed and it is the resulting reservoir of meanings deep within us that determines what we can perceive, what we remember, what we understand and what we can achieve.

It also determines how we feel about any or all of this, be it caviar, Cagney, Band Aid, Clogs or David Hume. This reservoir is what we call experience or, to be more precise, our past experience.

This process of constructing meaning by conversing with ourselves about our experience can be seen as 'modelling our world'. Others have suggested that such terms as the story, the 'as if' mode, the metaphor or the myth give a better feel for what we are addressing. For them, the term 'model' is too mechanistic, pseudo-scientific and engineering-like to be used to describe human processes. We prefer the term 'modelling' because it allows us to define precisely the processes involved. Modelling Theory enables us to explain the detailed function of every configuration. Even the functioning of a personal myth is illuminated by treating it as a model.

Meanings which enable skill, competence or creativity must for us be structured as viable (working and workable) models of the 'world out there'. If a tennis ball is to be hit with a racket we must anticipate the flight of the ball as it is served to us; that is, we must 'model' certain relevant aspects of how it is being served by our opponent and how, therefore, it will travel through the air. We may or may not be aware of how we do this. Sports coaching which uses various versions of 'the inner game' is based on the assumption that just playing out our viable meanings reflectively can help in testing out and developing the models in our head; and that changing the models in our head will influence and (it is hoped) improve our subsequent performance. The evidence is that quite often it does. We believe that a better understanding of 'meaning as modelling' would improve the frequency and quality of this learning process through the mediation of the inner game; but the inner game is for us just one form of those inner aspects of the conversation which are commonly designated as 'thinking and feeling' about things.

Learning as the achievement of skill, competence and creativity

How does this view of learning relate to the acquisition of skill and competence? It would suggest that as one learns to ride a bicycle one constructs and develops within one a 'structure of meaning' which enables us to do so. To interact with any part of the outside world, such as a bicycle, one must attribute meaning to it, to one with it, and to one and it together in whatever circumstances accrue. In order to interact effectively with it, it is necessary to construct patterns of meaning which enable one to act in ways that achieve our purposes.

The structure of skilled activity: the meaning, acting and perceiving cycle

A simple but powerful form for beginning to describe such a 'structure of meaning' is the *S-O-L feedback for learning cycle* in which the meaning not only shapes and triggers the activity but also creates a perceptual set, a state of selective readiness to receive

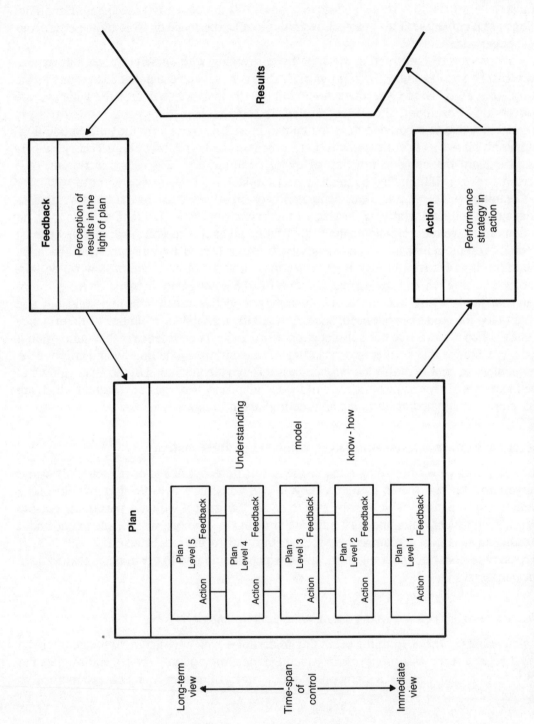

Figure 8 The meaning–acting–perceiving-feedback cycle

'knowledge of results'. Thus the meaning not only drives the activity but it anticipates the consequences of its actions and sets itself to check how well things have turned out.

The simplest form of feedback mechanism is 'error-actuated'. This is set to perceive deviations from some intended result; namely, 'errors'. This perception of 'error' is fed back negatively to change the activity in a way that will decrease (subtract from) the error next time around. The 'structure of meaning' which informs this process must be both purposeful and explanatory. It can, therefore, not only recognise 'error' as a deviation away from its purpose but it can also 'explain' to itself how the activity could produce the error and how it can therefore act to compensate for it. Such explanation to oneself is usually not expressed in words. We intuitively 'know' what to do. We have a feeling for what will work. But this form of words for acknowledging an absence of words does not mean that the explanation has not been constructed and learned, albeit in non-verbal terms.

Thus with the bicycle example the 'structure of meaning' not only shapes the bicycle riding (actions) but it also generates the purpose of riding (for example, minimally to be able to balance and propel the bike forward without putting the feet on the ground). This purpose sets the perceptual selectivity so that 'leaning over' or other early indicators of loss of balance are fed back negatively to compensate for this by turning the handlebars, shifting the weight of the body, speeding up and so on. *It is useful to think of such a structure of meaning as a model in the head; an explanatory model of bicycle riding.* When such a model drives a person's actions and sets their perceptual selectivity, and when the feedback loop is closed by the perception of what are perceived as the 'results' of the actions in the outside world, the activity becomes purposive.

Each system of 'meaning as modelling' is unique, constructed and tested through that person's unique past experience of the activity. The shape, strength and flexibility of the body influences the exact nature of the feedback information available to the rider of a bicycle. The model driving each person's bicycle riding is thus different. As they begin to gain experience, so they recognise not only what they can do but also they anticipate what they might later be able to achieve or not. Thus each develops a different pattern of purposes (such as safety, trick riding, racing, sprinting and so on). This produces their own particular pattern of performance, style and skill. This feedback model is a more cybernetic type of representation of the Self-Organised Learner as conversational scientist than advanced in Chapter 1.

In Chapter 1 we discussed the types of meaning which it is useful to think of as occurring within us. The terms 'rote', 'coherent understanding', 'explanatory meaning', 'constructive meaning' and 'creative meaning' were attached to these types. We have also suggested that at the fundamental level meanings are imageless. They are patterns of electro-chemical activity in the non-sensory, non-motor areas in the brain. At this level we are not directly conscious of the meanings that form us. As these patterns of activity play out in the specialist areas of the body and brain – that is, in muscle activity, in visual images, in words, in feelings and so forth – we may become aware of them; in other words, we are able partly to describe and represent to ourselves the meanings which we attribute to people and events and to our interactions with them. But again our 'explanations' may not be verbal. They may simply 'feel right'.

Now we can examine how these ideas about meaning allow us to use the notion of a feedback loop as a tool for helping us to organise our own learning.

Feedback for learning

What is going on as we learn to 'serve' at tennis? If our first attempt hits the net, we adjust our service to keep the ball higher. If the next serve goes out of court to the left we adjust again, and so on until we are serving as we intend. 'But!' you cry, 'there's more to it than that or we would all be aspiring Wimbledon champions.' Yes, there is, and this chapter is designed to take us some way towards understanding what is involved in becoming more highly skilled, competent and creative.

First, the feedback loops which control immediate performance are dynamic. They are in continuous action which is continuously changing. Thus what constitutes 'error' is also changing. The feedback modes also change. For example, there are feedback loops within the muscle systems. The muscles contain sensors which feed information back to the brain. To test this, we invite you to try out a brief activity. Put your hand behind your back and wiggle your finger. How do you know it wiggled? Eliminate sensations of noise (creaky joints) and touch (rubbing against other fingers) or feeling the motion in the air (perhaps temperature of the skin); this can be done by moving your finger very slowly. Now what tells you that your finger is moving? It is the 'kinaesthetic' sensors built into the muscles. They monitor the speed and acceleration of your movements. Kinaesthesis is the sense which 'tells' us how we are walking. It 'tells' the skilled games player or athlete *how* they are performing, *as* they are performing. They do not have to wait for the ball to go over the net. They know how it feels to be making a good stroke. They have learned from past experience; they have already constructed meanings. They know when they have made a bad stroke. Meanings which produce good performances are partly, but crucially, expressed in the kinaesthetic sense. Just talking about the performance, or even watching a video of yourself playing will not necessarily translate back into more effective kinaesthetic meanings. You have to get the 'feel' of it. You have to get your kinaesthetic imagery working and develop it until it is performing as a very fast and immediate monitor of the quality of your actions. The 'natural' ball player is someone who has developed this sense and can integrate it with other forms of meaning to construct mental models particularly suited to performing with bat and ball. Once we have recognised what this process is, and developed effective ways of conversing about it, many more of us could achieve significantly better performances.

Skill results from being able to attribute meaning to events in ways that enable one to recognise when to do what, to control one's actions in a precise and well-timed manner whilst one is performing a movement and allow one to recognise continually when one has successfully achieved one's immediate objectives and can move on.

Such mental models, such 'meaning as modelling', have a structure in time which is able to run ahead of events and allow anticipation from past experience about what is most likely to happen next. By past experience we mean the patterns of meaning (that is, models) that have been developed from previous attempts to act in the same or similar ways. These meanings are composed imagelessly but are expressed in a mix of sensory modes and symbolic languages when triggered into action. When the mix is right we can achieve incredible levels of skilled performance; when the mix is less appropriate the skill is less than sublime. Thus the achievement of skill arises from the composition of mental models from patterns of meaning that not only have a viable structure but are also expressed out of the optimum mix and placements in sensory and muscular controls (namely, feedback loops).

Sight and hearing are distance senses so they are best used to provide early warnings and orienting cues and to check whether the ultimate, distant outcomes are being achieved. Touch is an immediate sense that can be used to trigger the next activity, as in grasping the ball in catching it or in rotating a thumb screw. Taste and smell are largely used to monitor what we eat but smell can also serve as a distance sense, as in cooking. The kinaesthetic sense enables us to monitor and control our bodily movements immediately. Thus a dynamic perceptual set or developing state of perceptual readiness will not only be set to perceive certain events at certain times as the anticipated consequences of our ongoing activities but also it will switch from one sensory mode to another, ordering and mixing them to achieve the optimal control of one's performance. But what is optimal will depend on the structure of the meanings that drive the doing of that task (that is, those that set and keep the muscles in motion and perceptually monitor the results). The authors have used the perceptual-motor charting techniques which they helped to develop in the 1950s (the Functional Taxonomy) as a powerful tool to be used in Learning Conversations about these types of activity.

For the sake of clarity this section has used examples dealing in operational under-standing (type 3, p. 65, Chapter 1) in achieving results in the outside world, but it could equally well have used examples concerned with the inside world. For example, in reading or listening, the 'results' are located within the reader or listener and the whole activity is driven by a mental model which perceptually monitors these internal results as, say, constructive understanding (type 4, p. 65, Chapter 1) for the achievement of its purposes.

Levels of control and the hierarchical structure of skilled performance

The idea of an inner model as one coherent node of meaning operating through one feedback loop does not fully illuminate an understanding of skilled activity. For example, the ability to serve the ball does not make a complete tennis player. He or she must be able to play a whole variety of strokes each of which may be usefully conceived as a separate node of meaning within the overall mental model of playing tennis. Each node is able to drive its own particularly patterned feedback loop and feed back 'the results' to the next level in the model. The TOTE system ('TOTE' stands for 'Test, Operate, Test, Exit') has been proposed as one form of representing this idea. The levels in a system of TOTE units operate one upon another. Given the form of the operating function of each unit, they combine into a hierarchically organised model of a skill. The time span of control increases as one climbs higher in the TOTE system. Each TOTE unit is equivalent to one feedback loop. The first Test triggers the Operation of the loop, the second Test is equivalent to the 'perceptual set' which monitors the results of the Operation. If the results are not conclusive then another cycle of activity ensues. When they are conclusive an Exit signal is sent to the TOTE unit above.

For example, the best stroke-maker does not necessarily become the best tennis player. He or she has to be able to organise their strokes and move about the court to anticipate an opponent's play and string their own strokes together. So it is useful to think of skill as being achieved through nodes of meaning that are integrated at various levels of control. In tennis, serving and stroke-making are integrated into the playing of points. The winning of points is integrated into the playing of a game; and the organisation of your service game may be very different from the game you play when your opponent is serving. The games are built up into sets and the sets are won and lost to produce a match. Each of these levels of control in a game of tennis can be seen as an opportunity for the tennis player to organise his or her skill. Different players, for example Pat Cash or Steffi Graf, may exhibit different degrees or types of skill at the different levels.

The structure of meaning which can be thought to drive such a pattern of skill would be a hierarchy or tree network in which each node in the hierarchy is seen as a separate control loop triggered by the loop above and selectively driving in its turn the loops below. Such a hierarchical analysis of skilled performance can be a very powerful aid to learning. Reflecting upon the structure of the model which drives their skills and conversing with this structure enables people to achieve higher levels of performance. The hierarchical form for describing a model is much more descriptive of what is going on than merely seeing the performance as a linear sequence of activities. All forms of skill, such as cooking, tool-making, running a race, managing a factory or climbing a mountain can be illuminated by reflecting upon a hierarchical representation of the model. Later, in Parts II and the Functional Taxonomy, among the tools to be recruited into the Learning Conversation, we will elaborate on the Personal Learning Contract (PLC) and the Personal Learning Task Analysis (PLTA) which are based on these ideas of hierarchy.

Those among our readers who are familiar with computer programming will be drawing comparisons between the hierarchical structure here proposed and the idea of a nesting set of sub-routines or procedures. Those familiar with Smalltalk may think in terms of objects or those using PROLOG or LISP have the shapes and dynamics of logical structures from which to draw their inspiration to understand their own processes. But all of these forms of representation are merely that: learning aids to conversations with ourselves. Conversations which improve and enhance our understanding. They are not and should not pretend to be an objective description of what meaning 'really' is.

Learning to become more skilled by conversing with the meanings in our head

We are now a few steps nearer to having a set of conceptual tools which allow us to construct a language in which to converse with ourselves about what learning might become. The next step in our exploration is to ask how our mental models are developed, tested and brought under review. In what we will later be discussing as the task-focused Learning Conversation (Part II, Prospective Commentary) this issue is examined in depth; here it will be useful to recognise understanding and skill as separate forms of 'meaning as modelling'.

We cannot begin to construct full understanding from mere verbal (or even multi-media), one-way instruction. Nor is it possible with two-way instruction if all the 'results' are provided from within the evaluative system of the instructor without having their counterparts in the learner's model. Even when efficient, such two-way instruction only offers verbal models which may allow the learner to pass examinations and/or sound as if he may know what he is talking about. The Self-Organised Learner treats the content of the instruction as a resource which may illuminate and conversationally transform the experiential understanding which comes from reflective practice on the job. It cannot replace or substitute for the experiential model built up through real activity on the job. This is true at all levels of work and leisure activities and for all subject matters in any educational institution. The nature of the inner forms of conversation will determine the form and quality of learning being achieved. When this is robot-like the learning is robot-organised. It feels as if it were happening to us out of our control.

The Learning Conversation is the vehicle by way of which the experiential explanatory model is reviewed and through which a whole range of resources can contribute to its developing quality. To the extent that the learners are able to conduct such a conversation with themselves, or the educational process deliberately or inadvertently conducts one with them, they will develop skills, competence and creativity that are productive, on the job. Successful teachers often understand this need to get the learner to enrich the forms in which meaning is construed. To the extent that the learners cannot conduct such a conversation and get little or no aid in doing so, they will remain incompetent, learning nothing of use and at odds with themselves.

Types of feedback and learning competence

Earlier, we introduced the idea of the feedback mechanism. We described its error-actuated mode in which the difference between the result and the expectation is used to take action which will reduce this difference, thus bringing the result nearer to what was expected. This implies sufficient 'feel for' or 'understanding of' what one is doing and the results it produces in order to be able to vary what one is doing to produce the desired change. This introduces an 'unexpected' implication for learning. It may be useful whilst learning a skill deliberately to deviate from the intended (that is, make mistakes) in order to explore what produces these poorer-quality results. A greater understanding of the dynamics of the error zone around the desired result will make it easier to pick up small deviations and thus take the required action earlier so as to avoid making the error. This is part of what is meant by learning from your mistakes or by trial and error. We have applied this idea to good effect in the training of chefs. It is in itself a skilful activity and should be part of the armoury of strategies developed by every Self-Organised Learner.

However, *error-actuated functioning* is not the only form of the feedback mechanism. *Positive feedback* consists in using the deviation from expectation to push further in the same direction. It amplifies whatever results are being achieved. In, say, high jumping this would obviously be an advantage, but now we are into a more demanding form of skill. Instead of having an attainable target and learning how to get nearer and nearer to it by increasing our understanding of anything and everything that could produce deviations, we are now in the position of aiming above the top limit. What we are aiming for is some 'unexpected' result – in other words, getting above our top limit – and we need to remain sufficiently aware all the time so that when the unexpected happens we can reflect on how we achieved it and then try to use our increased understanding to repeat the effect. Even better, if we can extrapolate our understanding then we may be able to magnify the effect. By attempting to converse with themselves in this way people can move from the explanatory to the constructive levels of meaning construction. If this change endures, the learner's capacity is increased (Chapter 1). This is where imagination enters into learning. By imaginatively constructing meanings which go beyond those that are, in the learner's experience, viable, the learner can play with possibilities in his or her head. This mental testing out of the products of imaginative thought and feeling can greatly boost a learner's capacity to become skilled and competent. Some people habitually do this more than others.

The mechanism of positive feedback leads us on to a more general exploration of our perceptions of the unexpected. The unexpected most often occurs in terms which are different from those in which we are monitoring and perceiving our results. Very often this takes it outside of our perceptual 'set' (selective sensitivity) and we do not attribute meaning to it at all. This shuts us out from a tremendous amount of potential learning. It is, therefore, occasionally very useful to switch over into a more exploratory mode in which the skill may temporarily fall off but the person will be more likely to give meaning to the unexpected. A topical example of this would be the unexpected consequences of many industrial manufacturing processes for the environment. As our explanatory model grows, leaded petrol, river or sea pollution, the greenhouse effect, acid rain and the ozone layer all come within our potential control. *Freedom to anticipate events depends upon this more open type of feedback.*

Learning from the unexpected and Godel

People often feel threatened in the presence of the unexpected because they feel unable to cope, but to see the unexpected as a rich source of learning opportunities takes much of the threat out of it. To seek to explain the unexpected is the starting-point into new learning horizons. Thus to seek meaning in the unexpected is to seek to turn it into the expected and thus to expand the limits of that within which you seek explanation. Thus we can learn to thrive on the unexpected – another dimension to Self-Organised Learning.

Godel's theorem requires that the explanatory system contain at least one more dimension than the model it constructs. He demonstrates that no theory, model or understanding can be completely explained from within itself. We always need to go beyond where we are to understand where we are. By iteratively modelling its own process, this essentially open feedback mechanism necessarily converses with itself and with the world. Thus the construction of meaning is seen as a continuous conversational process which involves modelling and meta-modelling. This is the open-ended, optimistic, creative boundary of knowing. It is where the Self-Organised Learner should seek to live. The Learning Conversation is the vehicle which can take him or her to this magic place where creative construction of meaning thrives.

This is not only true for what we can learn as regards content – it is also true about what we come to know of our own capacity for learning. We can seek the unexpected within the inner aspects of our conversations and by thriving on it we can change our levels of awareness and the qualities of our consciousness. This is what we mean by saying the Self-Organised Learner constructs open-ended meaning as explanatory modelling. The modelling process can be turned on itself to change and develop its own modelling capacity. Our view of learning as skill, competence and creativity is founded on a Godel-type anticipatory mechanism, which enables us to bootstrap ourselves into a new and more powerful plane of learning. In Part II we introduce MA(R)4S (Monitor, Analyse, Record, Reflect, Review, Reconstruct, Spiral) as a conversational method specifically designed to enhance the quality of this meaning modelling conversation.

Meaning as modelling

Now that we have explored the different types of meaning which can be constructed (Chapter 1) and how feedback and TOTE systems can represent a model of skill, we are in a position to pursue our discussion of meaning as modelling.

Modelling involves anticipation, familiarity with the activity in the outside world (football, art, motorcycles, books, music) allows it to be re-presented in the sensory systems before the event. The activities in the outside world confirm and/or elaborate on the modelling.

This anticipation implies some form of modelling, and in most cases this is complex. It is not a one-to-one process in which everything is completely predicted with a probability of 1.0. It is more often a one-to-many process in which the anticipation involves an array of possibilities, and as one of these is confirmed a new anticipatory array is set up. This process of continually resolving doubt among coexistent anticipations is accompanied by the process of understanding. This drives the process of anticipatory arrays and the confirming or otherwise of a pathway through them; but all forms of modelling are not properly explanatory. Some forms of understanding run their modelling largely after the event, always having a sufficiently large array of sufficiently ill-defined possible futures to run little risk of being surprised. The details are mapped on to the events retrospectively so as to generate the feeling of understanding which is achieved. Other forms of understanding run their modelling largely in advance of events and are therefore anticipatory in a much more complete form. This type of anticipation can be recruited into the generating of skilled activity. The more retrospective understanding does not facilitate skilled behaviour although it can appear very wise. Again, the ability to converse with oneself about the nature of this activity can transform it.

Skilled behaviour depends upon the anticipatory functions of understanding described above, but it also requires effective action so the anticipatory activity divides into actions later to produce results and perceptual readiness set to monitor these results. Thus to appreciate music is not to be able to play an instrument.

Now if the skilled performer tries to express their understanding they may not be able to describe their modelling process in terms which are sufficiently complete to be helpful to someone else interested in acquiring the skill, Even if they can, the learner is often quite unable to convert their representations of their modelling back into the mus- cular and sensory forms that would produce the skill. If we take this problem into the mode of conversing with oneself then we approach one of the key mechanisms of learning. Sometimes we can perform ahead of our explicit understanding. The understanding exists in the deep, tacit meanings but we have not conversed sufficiently, or sufficiently well, within ourselves to be able to represent this understanding in forms which we can recognise and express. At other times our understanding is ahead of our ability to convert our modelling into the forms which would enable us to do things. If we can learn alternatively to leapfrog or bootstrap ourselves forward from understanding to performing and from performing to understanding we will have acquired a powerful form of learning. Meaning which is built up in this way, intricately relating theory to explaining the results of actions, and relating actions to the implicit expectations generating them, we call *constructive modelling*.

Now we can begin to see why modelling was an appropriate term to use to describe the meaning constructing activities.

Rigorous modelling theory would demand that we recognise the relationship between the model and that being modelled. The model is always less than its referent (we can never understand everything about anything) but it is not randomly less. It is deliberately constructed to replicate certain characteristics or functions at the expense of others (understanding is always selective). This introduces a dimension of quality to each of our five types of meaning. We can have good and poor rote learning but we equally have poor or good creative learning. By then running the model ahead of reality we can test out the validity of our model.

Dimensions of learning

Three dimensions of 'meaning as modelling' have now emerged. First, there are the five types or levels of meaning. Second, each of these can vary in quality. Third, there is the TOTE dimension concerned with time organisation in the 'meaning as modelling'. If learners are encouraged to explore their learning within this three-dimensional matrix they have a firm basis for developing their skills, competence and creativity (Figure 7). This involves an awareness of 'meaning as modelling' as a conversational process which informs all their activities. When this conversational process is orientated towards the outside, then the referent of the model is the outside world. Earlier we termed this 'modelling the outer world'. When the conversation is orientated towards the inside then the referent of the model is the inner self; that is, 'modelling the inner world'.

One deeply inner-orientated model is yoga-like meditation in which the whole enterprise is aimed at freeing the mind not only from action on the world outside one's skin, but also from the actions of various parts of the body. Given this starting-point, the mind or the spirit (the imageless, deep, tacit reservoir of meaning) systematically makes contact with (converses with) the imagination via meditation and the body through the yoga exercises and positions. The mind's model of the body both drives the actions and perceives the bodily results. At first, 'taking up a position' is merely a rote response to instruction, and any perception of results is crude or exploratory. If it is crude and remains so the yoga position is no more than just a rather odd exercise which stretches the body within terms which are already set by that person's previous assumption (that is, personal understanding of the nature of physical exercise). This means that a pseudo-'yoga' is instantly understood from within our existing models of health, sport and exercise. However, this level of understanding does not begin to tap the depth of experience potentially available.

If the perception of the 'bodily results' of a position is exploratory, one is ready to learn. By placing the body in an apparently peculiar position all sorts of new sensations are generated and are available as the raw material from which new non-verbal explanatory models of what we are, how our body works, how our body relates to the mind and how the mind works can be constructed. By carefully 'listening to' (taking notice of the full pattern of our sensations) the results of our actions, even when maintaining one position, we can sensitively build explanatory models which are both operational (that is, we can make our body do what we want it to) and appreciative (we begin to understand our feelings and only ask the body to do those things that at the most profound level 'feel right'). However, yoga is not the topic of this chapter; we have only used it to illustrate one form of modelling our inner world. Each form of modelling associated with the five types of meaning construction relating to our inner and our outer world can be similarly exemplified.

Throughout the book we illustrate the Learning Conversation using examples of how people model various aspects of their inner and outer world, from reading to air intercept control and from man management to the training of trainers.

What the yoga example is intended to raise for discussion is the idea that we model our own 'internal world' in the same ways that we model our 'outer world'. If our models of how we become and remain healthy are rote or internally coherent but unviable we may do ourselves much harm. If our model is explanatory but based on a physical science type of causality the model may have only very short time-spans of validity. We need to converse with our bodily selves in a constructive or even creative way. To become fully functioning, the models in our inner and outer worlds need to grow and develop together and in harmony. It is this harmonious relationship which is the basis of Self-Organised Learning. This book is offered as a contribution towards the achievement of this. Before getting to grips with the form and functioning of the Learning Conversation, we will go one step deeper to explore the underlying mechanism through which we can all amplify our *capacity for learning*.

A capacity for process that enhances learning

One way of contemplating the conversational modelling process which drives the search for meaning is to see it in analogy as a hardware/software conversation. This is the closest that we can come to acknowledge how our genetic constitution (that is, genotype) converses with our body and mind (phenotype). The *capacity for process* which allows us to run an almost infinite variety of models cannot, within conversational science, be conceived of exclusively as hardware or genotype. Self-Organised Learning is concerned with an enhancement of the *human capacity to learn*. The 'capacity for process' must itself be capable of development and change. Changes in the performance scenarios – that is, in the most obvious experiences and behaviours – is not enough for enduring growth in personal competence. To conceive of S-O-L in these terms is to set it amongst a number of mini-technologies which are beginning to abound in the education and training world. *Unless it is demonstrated that a person's capacity for learning has been transformed, S-O-L has not been achieved.*

The model which enables us to explain our universal 'capacity for process' which is itself capable of generative change takes us into the 'firmware' of conversational inter-dependency between the hardware genotype and the software phenotype (that is, thoughts, feelings and actions). This differs fundamentally from a theory such as that of Chomsky whose capacity for process model is seen essentially as an innate syntactic rule generating facility. It is closest to the Jungian notion of synchronicity, an interdependency of the psychic self and its objectification of reality, which, once appreciated, can free a person to change. The ancient Chinese mind contemplates events similarly to produce a personally meaningful picture of coincidence.

The skilled Self-Organised Learner is in a position to ask themselves not only whether and how a task can be done better, but also whether and how he or she can *learn* in a better way.

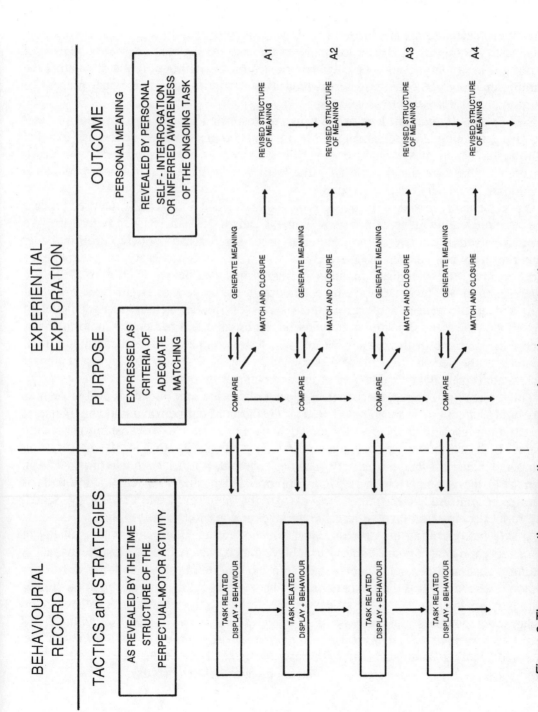

Figure 9 The conversation-generating process of meaning construction

In our Prospective Commentary for Part II we shall explain how Self-Organised Learners are able to conduct two phases of awareness-raising conversations (Figure 11). At one phase the *task* itself – namely, performance – is the primary focus of attention. The conversation acquires meaning in terms of how the learning environment (with its learning aids) assists in improving the performance of the task. At the next phase, the *process* of learning is in primary focus. The conversation acquires meaning in terms of whether the learning environment offers greater awareness and control of the personal process of learning; that is, *the capacity to learn.*

Self-Organised Learners develop their own sophisticated, Godel-type, internal mechanisms for generating feedback about their learning experiences, and relate these to external information which they recognise as results obtained as a consequence of their own behaviour. These are the flexible adaptive learners who have acquired the potential to develop into the really creative experts.

Our explanatory model of the quest for meaning as a conciously self-organised process of search must allow us to explore how humans can enhance their capacity to learn. We have conceived of a conversation-generating process which can bootstrap itself into ever higher levels of competence. A heterarchical type of model is necessary, since experience and behaviour are organised in units of increasing complexity (TOTE, p. 76). The organisation at one level achieves its coherence in the context of larger-scale organisation, and as the pattern imposed upon a series of smaller activities. Each level of organisation is essentially similar and may be represented as a perceptual motor activity, generating displays in the outside world, which are compared to expected patterns of meaning in the person's repertoire of knowledge. Figure 9 shows one representation of such a 'conversational meaning-generating and comparing model'.

This process of comparison between a person's inside and outside world is seen as generating 'structures of meaning'. These are the basis of our personal knowing (Chapter 1). Different levels in the heterarchy can be thought of as successive meaning-generating cycles. If the attribution of meaning is personally adequate – that is, if what is being compared matches – then the activity becomes coherent. If it is inadequate (mismatches), then the learner attempts to generate more appropriate meaning. It is here that the skills of learning become crucial. Mismatch is revealed in the time structure of the strategy. Search and further comparison involves a different level of conscious monitoring. This depends on a skill in controlling the process. Most learners are unskilled and as a result fail to recruit appropriate tactics and strategy to achieve match. Match leads to closure, so that the meaning generated becomes incorporated into the long-term 'store' to form part of the person's 'knowing'. It is their experience. In the short term this depends upon the immediate purpose and that part of the task being monitored. In the longer term it relates to the higher-order purposes and the task as a whole. Thus, *purpose, within a hierarchy of purposes, forms the basis against which comparisons are made and match achieved.* The Personal Learning Contract (PLC), to be described in Chapter 4 is designed specifically to aid the learner to develop greater awareness and control of this process.

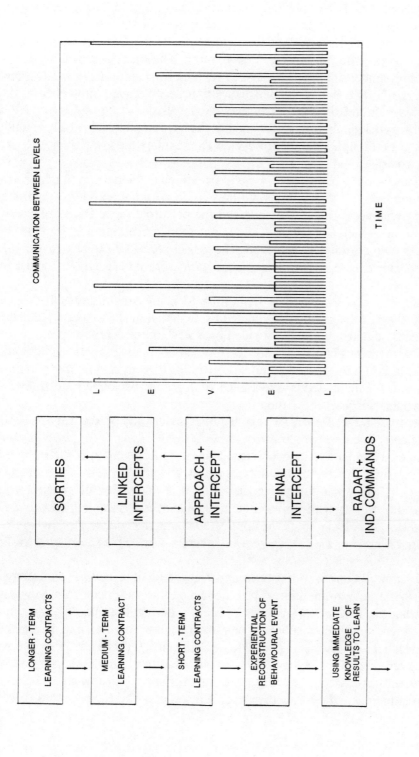

Figure 10 Time/structure of the model relating to a specific task

This model may be used to represent the patterns of behaviour and experience involved in the skills of a specific task, or it may be used to explain those involved in the skills of learning. In the former case the meanings are to do with skilled behaviour. In the latter case the meanings are to do with the activities of learning. The operation of a heterarchical meaning-generating model of skilled behaviour relating to specific tasks is illustrated in Figure 10 where the 'TOTE-like' units of organisation are integrated into coherent skilled activity. Control is exerted from the higher level downwards. Having triggered the lowest level this goes through a number of cycles and checks back to the levels above. Similarly, the second level goes through a number of cycles, triggered by the lowest-level sequence, until its cycle is complete and it refers to the level above. Such an explanatory model can represent the organisation of behaviour for *any* skill. The same model can be applied to the process of learning, where the meanings are now to do with the activity of learning, as inferred from the changes in the experience and the performance of the task. Once this transformation of the model is recognised and understood, a quantum leap into the ability to organise one's own learning is achieved. *The developing Self-Organised Learner is acquiring a repertoire of meaning associated with different levels in the learning heterarchy.*

The difference between successfully submitting to being taught and Self-Organised Learning lies in the criteria applied in the 'evaluate' component of our model. If the evaluation is entirely against referents provided by a teacher one is not in control of one's own learning. The meanings controlling the learning do not operate to change the process of doing the task. In S-O-L the learning model is operating directly and freely upon the task model whilst the task model feeds experience of learning back reciprocatingly, thus increasing the whole capacity for learning.

When the two models *synchronise*, we can begin to understand person not as a series of aptitudes and talents, but as an organism with an infinite *capacity for process*, and an infinite capacity to self-organise their process. Now the full potential of Self-Organised Learning emerges, since the task model applies to any and all skills, from commanding a ship to playing golf, writing an essay, managing the R & D division of a manufacturing company or learning to live with imprisonment. *The learning model superordinates all task models and can, with experience, be applied cost-effectively across the whole range of potential tasks. This is how the Self-Organised Learner continues to learn effectively 'on the job'.*

A dependent learner is one who has been exposed to and accepted the control system offered by a teacher, trainer or manager. They are locked into their personal myths, one of which may be that the teacher 'knows best'. Their expertise becomes the standard by which these learners judge themselves. Their own search for meaning is limited to becoming 'like teacher', otherwise it appears to be *switched off*. These are the learners who may well effectively submit to being taught but may fail to continue learning once the instructional process has ceased. They may fail to adapt creatively to change in challenging and unforeseen situations. These are the dependent robots who have ceased to search actively for personal meaning. They have little awareness of their own learning processes, lack a language to converse about learning, and are incapable of addressing the vast resources for learning 'on the job' and in life.

Retrospective commentary: S-O-L as a way of increasing your learning capacity by reflectively organising your own learning processes

Self-Organised Learning is based on a valid 'personal theory' which enables individuals to think, feel and act with skill, competence and creativity. Individuals can take control of their own learning and develop their learning skills. For the individual there are no limits; it is a negative myth to construct boundaries for one's potential skills. You can double, treble, quadruple your capacity to learn, perhaps even increase it ten- or a hundred-fold.

In the Prospective Commentary we proposed five dimensions along which it would be useful to develop a language in which to negotiate what learning might become. In Chapters 1 and 2 we elaborated some of our ideas about learning, especially the idea that learning is itself an essentially conversational process. Now it is possible to explore these five dimensions more fully.

Valued changes in meaning are changes in thoughts, feelings, perceptions and potential actions: changes in meaning as modelling. Valued changes may take the form of improved quality in the modelling from factual to creative. Disconnected factual meanings may be revised to become more coherently interrelated and internally consistent. Internally consistent meanings may be revised to produce more valid anticipations. The modelling may become more personally explanatory. Explanatory modelling may grow through the constructive incorporation of additional experience, and constructive modelling may occasionally be creatively re-modelled to produce new insights through shifts in a personal paradigm.

Learning is now seen as a conversational activity in which the quality of the process can be modelled in terms of the five types, ranging from factual to creative. Flexibility in personal control of the level of process can be seen (modelled) as an enhancement in the person's capacity for learning. To the extent that the person's myth of themselves as learner is based on the view that learning comes from teaching, training or instruction, then their view of the learning process will imply an assymmetric conversation in which the control of process lies outside. They are thus other-organised. They submit to being taught. As they begin to appreciate that the conversational process of learning need not involve a teacher, that it can become symmetrical and they can participate fully in controlling the process of learning, they become self-organised. This means that they fully accept the need and responsibility to evaluate their own learning.

The internal evidence of learning lies in the learner's experience of changes in how they think, feel and perceive. The external evidence of learning lies primarily in their behaviour or performance, and secondarily in any and all of the records or artefacts that result from this performance. The Self-Organised Learner continually pushes back the boundaries of what he or she believes to be their innate capacity for learning. The extent to which they can push back these boundaries depends on the quality of their personal explanatory model about themselves as learners. Thus their personal myths are challenged and expanded, moving from static factual meaning as modelling to a creative, open-ended, personally more explanatory modelling of the self.

These new and improved personal myths allow more learning to be better self-organised and more truly intended, but they also thrive on the unexpected as opportunities for learning that allow the myth itself to be creatively challenged and revised, thus doubly increasing the learning and the learner's capacity for it.

However, this whole bootstrapping process is not natural; it does not often occur and when it does it is man/woman/child-made. Man/woman/child constructs man/woman/child, and we do this through the mediation of the Learning Conversation. Part II, Chapters 3 and 4 offer some explanation of what a Learning Conversation might be and how it might be conducted.

So what is S-O-L and what is a Learning Conversation?

The essential characteristics of a Self-Organised Learner are:

1 To be able to accept responsibility for managing one's own learning rather than be dependent on others' initiatives and directives. This involves giving personal meaning to events in ways which work and are valued.
2 An awareness of *how* one learns: that is, to be able to reflect on the functional components of personal learning processes:
   (a) recognise needs and translate these into clearly defined purposes;
   (b) recruit appropriate resources and initiate flexible strategies for achieving these specified purposes;
   (c) recognise the quality of achieved outcomes;
   (d) critically review this cycle of activity;
   (e) plan and implement more effective cycles of learning activity to meet future needs.
3 To appreciate the dynamic nature of the personal learning process and to strive continuously for greater self-organisation so that development becomes valued and change leads to fulfilment.

4 To be able to challenge existing partially developed skills and *learn how to learn*, so that such skills are transformed to achieve higher standards of personal competency.

5 To see the value of S-O-L and to practise it as a way of life, in one's job, and in all social contexts.

6 The Self-Organised Learner digests, challenges and *re-defines S-O-L* in their own terms. This *creative aspect* of S-O-L expertise generates new dimensions of personal innovation and experimentation.

7 To strive constantly for a 'quantum-leap' improvement in one's personal *capacity for learning*. As such, S-O-L carries over into all subsequent activities. It improves an individual's ability to learn from experience 'on the job', learn from a training course, learn from experienced colleagues, and learn from their own or others' successes and mistakes.

Enabling someone to become self-organised at learning cannot be achieved through direct instruction. If this is attempted, the best that can be achieved is a successful submission to the process of being instructed. This is not S-O-L. The worst is total dependency, aliena-tion and even negatively valued learning. This is not S-O-L.

To leave each person to discover how to become a Self-Organised Learner without support takes too long. Many do not succeed and many only acquire a small part of their 'real' capacity for learning. This is not S-O-L.

The S-O-L support process must be 'conversational', offering learners as much freedom to learn as they can cope with, within a 'Learning Conversation' which is specially designed to guide and encourage them to acquire the attitude and skills of the Self-Organised Learner and progressively expand the scope and quality of their learning.

The attributes of a Learning Conversation are:

1 That it is a process of sustaining a conversation with oneself about *learning* which may be:
   (a) initiatory (as a way of approaching a new topic);
   (b) innovative (generating new ideas, suggestions, improvements);
   (c) insightful (offering an alternative understanding which breaks new ground);
   (d) reflective (tapping intuitive experience, tacit knowing, bringing processes into consciousness);
   (e) remedial (upgrading quality of thoughts, feelings and skills);
   (f) physical (development of health, posture and physiological processes);
   (g) open (exploratory, seeking alternatives, dwelling in uncertainties, exponential);
   (h) committing (ordered, linear, logical, predictable and testable);
   (i) spiralling (from linear to cyclical to spiral to chaos);
   (j) creative (from chaos to order within a regulated pattern).

2 The Learning Coach temporarily externalises this 'Learning Conversation' to improve its quality.

3   The Learning Coach makes the nature of the conversation explicit to the learner *as they learn*.

4   The Learning Coach gradually passes control of the Learning Conversation to the learner as awareness and skill is developing.

5   The Learning Conversation can now move on and upwards as individuals, pairs and groups converse, initiating 'learning networks' and a whole system of S-O-L throughout the organisation.

Increasing your capacity for learning

Towards the end of Chapter 1, we introduced the idea that an awareness of the conversational process which generates personal meaning is essential for enhancing our capacity for learning. We returned to this theme at the end of Chapter 2 where we suggested a cybernetic mechanism for amplifying our capacity for learning. The classic learning curve (Figure 7) represents a robot-like functioning, since the plateau indicates the stabilisation of a given skill at a certain level of competence. Unfortunately, this is often interpreted in terms of *ability, IQ, personality* or *learning style* and, as such, habituates into an ultrastable level of performance. The Learning Conversation challenges robot-like performance, encouraging the growth of skill, competence and creativity, so that each plateau is seen as a temporary phase, as the learner develops their capacity for learning (Figure 7).

Part two

The Learning Conversation

What is it? Can you enable others to become more self-organised?

Contents

Prospective commentary: Task-bound, task-focused and learning-focused activity – the way to Self-Organised Learning

The Self-Organised Learner can be thought to be conducting two parallel conversations. The first conversation involves the topic or task to hand. This task-focused conversation is driven by the topic or task model and comprises the doing of the task or the knowing of the topic. Left to stabilise and develop into a set of over-learned skills, these processes become increasingly robot-like. When this happens, the task-focused conversation degenerates into a series of task-bound ritual exchanges.

Two stages of awareness

The first function of the Learning Conversation is to revive the task/topic conversation into a functioning awareness, thus challenging the 'task-bound robots'. This first stage of awareness is designated the *task-focused Learning Conversation*. It mirrors the process of doing the task or knowing the topic, and thus raises the task-bound conversation back into conscious awareness.

This task-focused Learning Conversation is intermittent and extends over many cycles of task or topic activity, raising it into awareness and getting the task or topic model-building activity going again. It is concerned to lift this model-building activity up through the five layers of meaning (Chapter 1) until the model is fully 'explanatory', is being intermittently re-'constructed' in the light of developing experience and has a 'creative' component illuminating the whole enterprise. If and when this is achieved the purpose of the task-focused Learning Conversation is to expand the task or topic model and continually review and enhance its quality.

The second conversation has an extended time-span and will encompass a whole series of cycles of the task-focused Learning Conversation. This second stage of awareness *is learning-focused*. It is concerned to challenge and improve how the learning is carried out. To do this it selects and mirrors not the task or topic activity but the learning activity which is improving how the task is done or how the topic is known. Thus, it *concentrates on the learner's model of the learning process*. This may be rudimentary and itself highly robot-like. The learning-focused conversation challenges these 'learning robots' so that a more fully functioning awareness and control of learning is achieved.

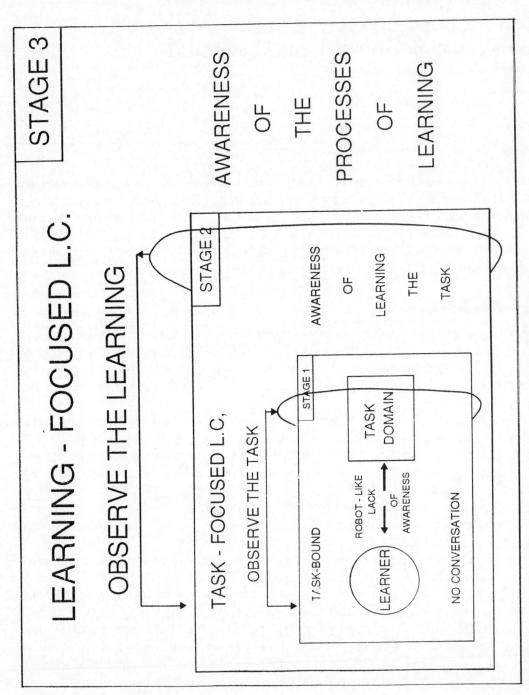

Figure 11 Task-bound, task-focused and learning-focused awareness

In many, if not most, of us the learning-focused conversation is so robot-like as to be functionally almost non-existent. Our examples of personal myths in the General Introduction illustrate this. In real life and in the natural habitats of learning, the task-focused conversation moves haphazardly in and out of a robot-like character as the strains and stresses of doing the task or knowing the topic demand. Largely knowledge- or task-bound, the conversation is seldom alive and the repetition and resulting tedium drives this into permanent resemblance to a robot. For many of us in many segments of our life, our Learning Conversations have almost ceased to grow or change at all and the whole activity is largely ritualised.

The role of the 'Learning Coach' or 'Tutor' is systematically to overhaul the learner's undernourished inner conversation by pulling this out into terms of public exchange and making this very process explicit. This externalisation of the conversation makes it available for review and development. Within our theory of Self-Organised Learning the ultimate function of the Learning Coach is to make himself or herself redundant by fully reviving and developing a system of Learning Conversations within the learner. In assuming that such inner learning conversations are potentially infinite, the success of the Learning Coach depends on how the learners can themselves become 'self-organised learning systems'. Godel's theorem (Chapter 2) leads us to understand that the task model and the learning model which drives the task-focused and learning-focused Learning Conversations can each be explained, reviewed, revised and extended by recognising the open-endedness of the meaning-constructing, model-building activity of learning. Thus, to stand outside the system (that is, model-building activity) in awareness of how one performs a task and knows a topic, and in awareness of how one learns to improve the quality of performance and the quality of coming to know the topic, is fundamental for Self-Organised Learning.

Awareness and the Learning Conversation

It is our experience as learners, teachers and as researchers of human learning that, whilst the occasional learner may hit upon some successful strategy for learning, the disabled majority of learners only become more fully functioning as they *learn to observe themselves* and to reflect upon and review their own learning activities. In the Learning Conversation they become able to recognise, represent and thus control their own constructive 'meaning as modelling' processes. They become more self-organised.

In any effective Learning Conversation, control is passed back and forth among the participants as they recognise the nature of what each has to contribute. Such conversations are usually asymmetric. In the early stages of the Learning Conversation the learner focuses almost exclusively on providing the experiential evidence on which the collaborative research into the nature of their learning is based. The Learning Coach or Tutor guides and controls it. The tutor may use one or more of the conversational tools described in detail in the Functional Taxonomy to enable the learner to explore rigorously specific aspects of their learning process. The tutor will also have an operational model of the Learning Conversation itself and will, when conditions are appropriate, share this with the learner. As the learner's awareness of his own processes increases the tutor begins to hand over control to him. The learner is encouraged to *challenge their personal myths about their own learning capacity.* As they become successful in this, they are guided to shift the emphasis of their attention and the Learning Conversation moves into the next phase. They begin to explore *how the learning can be improved.* The Learning Tutor encourages them to explore alternative models of their own processes and to develop and test in action personally acceptable models, which result in more effective performances and understandings.

Gradually, the tutor hands over control of this exploratory activity to the learner until eventually only the *quality* of the learner's personal investigation remains under the tutor's review. The total conversation is phased to enable learners to obtain insights which allow them to conduct more and more of the conversation for themselves. *The ability to conduct most of a Learning Conversation with oneself is the essence of self-organisation.*

The process of a Learning Conversation can be distinguished and described separately from its content (that is, what gets learned). The conditions for such creative conversations require that an exchange is modulated through a developing shared understanding of how the conversations will be conducted and that this model of the process itself remains negotiable. Such conversations are rare. Learners value it when it does occur, but they can rarely create the conditions to make it happen without this initial support. Each of us can identify our own special events in which we had this rare experience. It can be recognised by the experience of constructing, exchanging and negotiating personally significant relevant and viable meaning. Such creative encounters have been identified by Maslow as those in which the criteria for appreciating them can only arise out of the experience itself. They are both self-referent and self-assessed. People may achieve such creative conversation within themselves. This is the ultimate of Self-Organised Learning.

The 'science' of Learning Conversations offers an explanatory model of the conditions in which such experiences are propagated and grow. In this part of the book we attempt to sketch out this developing science. The CSHL Reflective Learning Technology attempts to amplify such conditions and thus increase the probability of creative personal learning. To be truly conversational, the technology of learning must allow relevance, validity and viability to be assessed by the learner. The criteria and referents used by the learner may be challenged and re-negotiated but they cannot be ignored, denied or arbitrarily overridden by others' perspectives without destroying the sources of self-confidence and self-sustaining effort. The Learning Conversation encourages and enables the growth of this capacity for self-organisation.

The Learning Conversation as a whole is characterised by three modes of interaction. *The central activity is the tutorial mode* and the conversation is guided towards the *learning to learn* and *life modes* only sufficiently for this central process to be enriched and progressive. In its tutorial mode the conversation leads the learner to the formulation of a series of *Personal Learning Contracts (PLCs)*. After an attempt has been made to carry out each contract, systematic review leads the learners to reflect upon their *learning competence*. Poor or inadequate learning performance and feelings of dissatisfaction about learning may come about in two very different ways.

1 Learners may have wanted to achieve their PLC and yet not have had the skills and competencies necessary to formulate and execute it effectively. The 'learning to learn' mode of the Learning Conversation leads them into a challenging of existing skills, a self-diagnosis of their strengths and of those skills which require further development. Conversational activities are then designed to help them achieve a greater capacity for learning.
2 Learners may lack motivation to achieve their PLC, although their learning performance may be adequate. The life or relevance mode of the Learning Conversation leads them to identify long-term needs and purposes and to differentiate these into shorter-term recognition of the relevance or inappropriateness of the current learning contract. It is this part of the conversation which can save days, months or even years of alienation, misery and misspent effort. The life conversation can identify the personal structure of a topic or a job situation and thus help learners chart their own paths of involvement in it.

The Learning Coach or Tutor monitors the whole process and guides the minute-by-minute interaction for the achievement of Self-Organised Learning. This is described in more detail in Chapter 4, in which specific heuristics for managing the three modes of the conversation are introduced. Choice of specific techniques – that is reflective learning tools to be recruited into the Learning Conversation – depends upon the nature of each application. Learning skills, learning situations and tasks and topics to be learned may all require specialist techniques for awareness-raising. These are described in the Functional Taxonomy of Tools.

In Chapter 3 we shall concentrate on the dialogues which form the conversation and on the nature of the conversational exchanges which guide these dialogues within all three modes referred to above.

Chapter three

On becoming aware of personal processes of learning

People are constrained by the system of thoughts and feelings (personal myths, beliefs, values, insights and prejudices) they develop about themselves as learners, and during learning they are more or less consciously building *operational* models of each situation. These models of 'personal causes and consequences' develop usually in an unregulated and unreviewed way, but nevertheless are very complex and subtle, being a system of detailed perceptual motor relationships underlying the personal ability to anticipate and control the situation. We have argued in Part I that such models are developed in every type of learning. Each of us has a wealth of tacit understandings about how what we do influences the course of events, and it is necessary to recognise this as part of the personal process of learning.

The operating models and systems of meaning we intuitively construct carry with them an implicit belief that they represent the absolute nature of the world. This is probably the cultural consequence of our Western socialisation and education processes. In practice, our models arise out of what we see others doing and what is felt to be the demand on us and our beliefs about the limits of the effects we can have on our world. Thus, the models we construct out of our experiences also constrain us and limit our skills and capacity for learning.

For those who achieve awareness of their learning processes and become self-organised, the plurality of meanings in their world is self-evident. They are the ones who are truly free to learn from experience; they can use themselves as a test-bed for validating these experiences to negotiate their needs, purposes, strategies and tactics successfully, so that satisfying outcomes are achieved and they can carry this over to subsequent Learning Events. Effective Learning Conversations have transformed their capacity for learning, not only in relation to the immediate event, but also 'for ever' afterwards. They have developed the capacity to reflect on their modelling processes, their systems of thoughts and feelings, and to bootstrap these in an ever-spiralling direction (Chapter 2).

The purpose of a Learning Conversation is to enable a person to enhance his or her capacity to learn. It is conducted as a meta-commentary around any Learning Event. The term 'meta-commentary' is used to indicate the nature of this conversation. This is concerned primarily with the process of learning; the Learning Conversation is only concerned with the content (that is, task or topic) of the Learning Event inasmuch as this can be used to illustrate, emphasise and concretise the learning processes which are being used within it. The creation of a language in which to reflect upon learning processes requires *much more than* a dictionary of terms and a syntax in which to string the terms together into phrases and sentences. The language must arise out of personally meaningful experience. Thus, there is a real sense in which each Learning Conversation creates its own 'meta-language'.

The Learning Event

A Learning Conversation can be conducted around any event. It raises the processes of learning into awareness, thus offering the learner an opportunity to experiment with new methods, strategies and tactics, and to review them in terms of how well they enable him to achieve his purpose. A child learning to read, a student learning how to take part in a seminar, an autistic child learning to play, a research engineer learning to be more creative, a high jumper learning a new technique, a head waiter learning to manage the dining room, a footballer learning to read the game, an industrial inspector learning to inspect the soles of oil-fired flat irons and a young mother learning to change a nappy are all taking part in events from which they can potentially learn. To the extent that they are unaware of their own learning processes or are uneasy about their ability to make use of the learning activity each would benefit from a Learning Conversation.

The process of learning has often become so habituated that it has dropped completely out of consciousness; worse, the learner cannot regain consciousness without completely disrupting it. For example, concentrating on how you perform any task such as driving a car, preparing an omelette or chairing a meeting, or how you listen, read, discuss or think, usually stops you from being able to do it. One major part of the Learning Conversation is concerned with helping people regain controlled awareness of their own processes. Specialist 'tools' are often useful and, on specific occasions, essential. These serve to enhance the development of a personal meta-language which enables each learner to get to grips with his or her learning and to improve its quality. Part IV elaborates on this.

A Learning Event is peculiar. The learner is purposive and yet it is in the nature of learning that you often cannot know what exactly you are going to learn until you have learned it! This means that the purpose can only be specified completely when it has been achieved! It may appear to be specified in a teaching or training situation, but that is very different from the learner coming to appreciate fully in their own terms the teacher's specified intentions.

Some preliminary description of the Learning Event in terms of its developmental phases may be useful to clarify its structure and organisation. These include:

1 negotiate needs and define purposes;
2 develop and use strategy and tactics;
3 evaluate the learning outcome;
4 review the process as a whole.

It is important to recognise that such a 'phases' description is concerned only with *one cycle* of the process at *one level of the event*. Effective learning almost always consists of a *series of such cycles* in which the purposes become progressively more clearly articulated and the outcomes become more precise and determined and well-mapped on to the purposes.

The purposes and the outcomes achieve their meaning both from their context within the larger event and from the structure of sub-events out of which they develop. Any Learning Event is itself composed of sub-events and is part of some longer-term supra-event. It is important that the Learning Conversation recognises this. The degree of self-organisation in learning which a person has already achieved indicates the 'size' of the Learning Event around which the conversation can best take place. If the event is too large it will be operationally incomprehensible to the learner; if it is too small the conversation may be experienced as trivial. Thus, reflecting on the reading of a paragraph will depend upon the purpose for reading the article as a whole and one's appreciation of the position of the paragraph within the article. It will also depend on the meaning attributed to each sentence out of which it is constructed. An effective Learning Conversation needs to take account of such levels of event. The personal meta-language requires a structure that acknowledges phases, cycles and levels.

Challenging the robot

Achieving an enhancement of learning performance usually involves serious personal change. It involves the disruption and breaking of existing, poorly organised skills and the establishment of new attitudes and personally valid ways of thinking, feeling and behaving. Many of the techniques used in the Learning Conversation have been specially devised for controlled interventions. But, however carefully the conversation is developed, the process of significant learning will always involve a 'learning trough' (see Figure 12).

To understand this, we have found it useful to think of each learner as having a set of 'personal robots'. At the task level, 'performance robots' almost unconsciously execute a sequence of non-adaptive *task-bound behaviours*. At the learning level, learning robots (the learning-by-reading robot, the learning-by-discussion robot, the learning-by-doing robot, the learning-by-listening robot) non-reflectively execute sequences of non-adaptive *learning behaviours. Each learning skill has become so automatic that it is no longer under conscious control.* Reflective techniques are required to challenge the robot, bringing each specific skill back into awareness and thus available for revision and development. But the disruption of existing skills produces a drop in effective performance. The

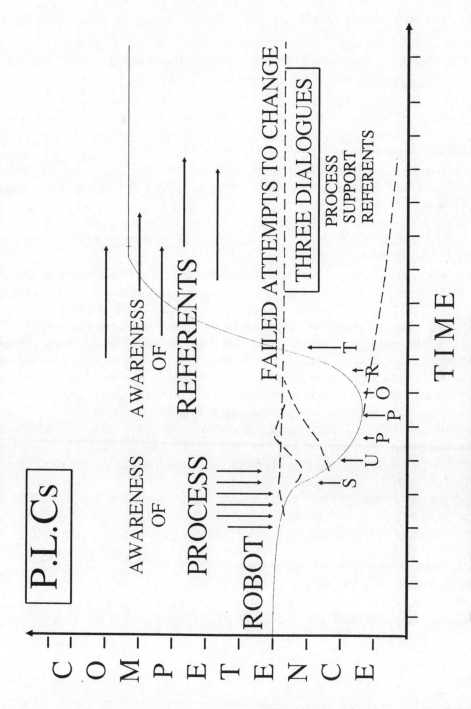

Figure 12 The learning trough: challenging the robot

learner feels that he or she is getting nowhere and becomes frustrated, hostile and anxious. Part of every Learning Conversation is concerned with offering the learner support through this learning trough. Unless this is sensitively managed, the ultra-stable robot will again take over, leaving the learner at the same level of skill as before. When effectively supported, the learner quite quickly breaks through this trough to achieve new, hitherto unconceived levels of competence, both at the task- and learning-focused levels of skill.

The need for three dialogues: process, support and referent

The Learning Conversation embodies three interwoven dialogues. One dialogue functions to raise awareness of the deeply personal processes of learning. Another dialogue offers support to the learner, particularly when he or she is experimenting with new ways of learning and often feels vulnerable when familiar habits become challenged. The third dialogue is concerned with the identification of standards: in learners themselves, in other people, and in the situation. These serve as referents for a self-assessment of the quality of learning which they are attempting to achieve. *The focus of the conversation is the reflection on process.* In managing the Learning Conversation the tutor or coach facilitates this process. This initiates a heightened awareness, and within a protected environment the learner is enabled to explore their skills and invent alternative tactics and strategies so that they achieve greater competence and creativity.

Even in the very young, the *process dialogue* taps deeply rooted unconscious habits. In most areas of activity – for example, in manual skills, social skills, reading, listening, problem-solving and in management – people have little or no understanding of their own processes. The various tools described in the Functional Taxonomy produce detailed records of learning behaviour which are used to talk learners back through their experiences. Careful reconstruction of personal experience serves to raise awareness, and gradually a personal meta-language for describing and explaining learning develops. We have found that the conversational use of the repertory grid or the Structures of Meaning and Flow Diagram techniques (the Functional Taxonomy of Tools), can serve as devices for the representation of and reflection on this developing language. It is through the effective execution of process dialogues that learners become elevated to model their own internal processes and to develop their skills adaptively. So are the skills of self-organisation of learning acquired.

The *support dialogue* enables learners to steer themselves successfully through this process of change. It involves sensitivity and an intuitive understanding on the part of the tutor or Learning Coach. Careful consideration of the methods of counsellors, therapists and even behaviourists, when separated from their pejorative and seemingly incompatible values, reveals a wealth of highly relevant techniques. For example, the work of Carl Rogers and B. F. Skinner can together offer some indicators of the ways in which this personal support should be offered. Rogers' technique is to create a very relaxed and accepting atmosphere in which there is high regard and no evaluative comment. His studies show that this frees individuals to experiment and explore their own processes in ways that are normally too threatening for them to attempt. Skinner's behavioural re-inforcement techniques enable a person to define new patterns of behaviour which they can then be carefully guided into achieving within a self-reward system. These two seemingly disparate approaches can be variously adapted and combined to produce a powerful range of methodologies by which the individual can be freed, supported and guided into new ways of thinking, feeling and behaving. But practitioners must each explore their own resources and develop those mixes of methods which are most effective for them. We have developed our own specific procedures, some of which we describe later in this chapter (p. 133).

The *referent dialogue* aims to enable the learner to appraise their own performance, but to do so must identify relevant types of referents which can be used as a basis for comparison. Part of the role of the Learning Coach or tutor is to help learners to identify such examples either in outstanding performers of the skill which they wish to acquire or as measures of quality and/or speed which they can apply to their own activities. Whatever referents learners identify in their environment, they must remain free to use them for their own purposes. In the end, the learner comes to use their own previous performances as the basis for evaluating their improvement and should be encouraged not to restrict themselves to the existing public norms nor to be discouraged by the outstanding performance of more experienced experts.

Thus, the Learning Conversation is trimorphic: one dialogue deals with *commentary on process*, another deals with *support during reflection*, and the third dialogue is concerned with *identifying referents for evaluating one's own learning competence*. The management of each dialogue depends on the dynamics of the conversation as a whole and this depends on a sensitive monitoring of the learner's efforts to change. This can only be achieved by fully understanding the nature of the Learning Conversation and how this can be adap-tively regulated.

The three dialogues in action

The authors, their students and clients have among them experienced many thousands of conversational Learning Events. These span a wide range of tasks, topics and skills and have involved 6-year-olds in nursery groups, young adults in factories, workshops, remand homes and colleges of various kinds, mature students in continuing education and re-training situations, supervisors, managers and trainers in industry and commerce, univer-sity professors, their staff and students, as well as the disabled, the dyslexic, and disadvantaged members of our society.

In this chapter we offer selected snippets of these original experiences, and our com-mentaries on these, so that the reader can appreciate the form and dynamics of the 'pro-cess', 'support' and 'referent' dialogues of the Learning Conversation. Both task-focused and learning-focused conversational events are illustrated (Prospective Commentary). The next chapter expands on this and explains how these dialogues form part of the three modes (life, tutorial and learning-to-learn levels) of the Learning Conversation, as a whole, referred to earlier.

The central aim is to support learners' strivings for achieving greater awareness of themselves so that they can review and develop the quality of their learning. Records of behaviour and devices for representing meaning serve as tools for the reconstruction of the original experience, so that this can be reflected upon from within personal criteria which guide the learner's functioning. For the learner, experience and behaviour (personal knowing and action) represents the irreducible unit for the apprehension of their learning (General Introduction). Therefore talk-back through records of behaviour function to raise awareness of personal experience, and reflections of records of personal meaning function to raise awareness of anticipations and actions. The 'Functional Taxonomy' elaborates on this. Here, we refer to these reflective tools only sufficiently to illustrate their function within the three dialogues which make up the Learning Conversation.

Records of behaviour are characterised by a display of time and structure. These can be used to elicit detailed personal explorations of the experiences involved. Records of personal meaning lack the time dimension, but can be varied in complexity and type of structure. Each therefore has specific advantages as tools for raising awareness of personal learning.

In our main example we shall concentrate on illustrating how the process, support and referent dialogues enable reflection, using both *records of behaviour* and *records of personal meaning* as starting-points. *Since reading is the immediate skill that you, our readers, are now experiencing, we shall concentrate on this skill in our main example; but throughout we have tried to comment on the generality of application.*

Competence can be developed through greater awareness and control of 'personal meaning' as this relates to specific behaviours over time. The generality of all three dialogues as essential components of the Learning Conversation is demonstrated in examples 2 and 3 in the Appendix to this chapter p. 137. These illustrate how learners can be enabled to break malfunctioning habits and to question their personal myths (thoughts and feelings) about learning in two very different areas of skill; the complex task of air-intercept control and man management. Without engagement in the three dialogues of the Learning Conversation, learners' personal myths not only become self-validating, but they also remain almost totally beyond awareness and are therefore unavailable for review. The internalisation of the three dialogues of the Learning Conversation enhances self-organisation, so that learners can continue to develop competences in specific tasks and skills and through such experiences go on to enhance their capacity to learn.

Example 1 Reading behaviour, comprehension and reading-to-learn

When people learn from text, they are seldom aware of how they are reading, nor of the cognitive and affective processes which underlie their behaviour. To the extent that they

Figure 13 A read record and the recorder

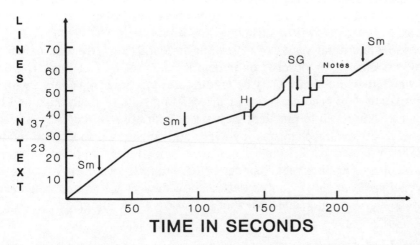

Sm - SMOOTH READ
H - HESITATION
I - ITEM READ
SG - SEARCH BACKWARDS

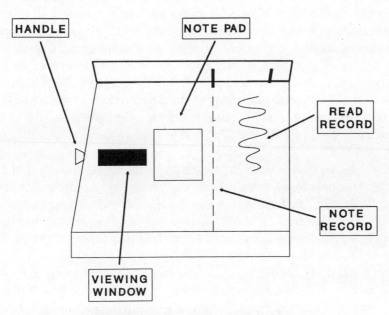

THE READING RECORDER

remain unaware, reading-to-learn remains a robot-like activity. By being supported to observe and reflect on their reading processes, learners can develop a wider and more flexible repertoire of skills which through experience becomes generalised to other learning skills such as, for example, writing, listening and discussion.

Almost always in the initial stages of a 'reading-to-learn' conversation, learners discover that they are unable to 'observe or remember themselves' reading. This is the situation from which they must start. Only by guiding learners back into contact with their direct experiences can they become aware of the existing state of their skills and bring these under review. After a little practice, they are able to observe themselves reading, analyse the deeply personal mechanisms involved, and construct a functional model of their reading-to-learn processes. Example 1 has been divided into two parts. Example 1a illustrates how records of reading behaviour can be used to raise awareness of the personal experience of reading. Example 1b concentrates on how devices for representing meaning can be used for the reconstruction and review of the process of reading.

Example 1a   Talk-back through records of reading behaviour to reconstruct experience

The Reading Recorder, Reading-to-Learn software, and various paper and pencil recording methods can be used as alternative devices for observing reading. In these various forms this tool is designed to make the behavioural processes of reading explicit as a graphical record. However, such a record needs to be sensitively recruited into the Learning Conversation to allow the learner to achieve significant states of reading awareness. The record represented in Figure 13 shows how time was spent as a learner reads a text; it shows changes in pace, hesitations, skipping, searching, back-tracking, and note-making. Uninitiated learners are unable to make accurate inferences about these reading events from the 'raw' record. The Learning Coach must be prepared to help learners acquire the perceptual skill to interpret them for themselves. The quality of learning depends on this sensitivity to the information on the record. A verbal ability to talk about a read record in descriptive terms is not the same as the perceptual ability to recognise significant events in the process of reading and to *explain* these in operationally effective ways.

Describing the behavioural events as witnessed by the time/structure of the read record does not create an operational awareness of the processes experienced in reading. It is achieved as follows. The learner is referred to the text which he or she has previously read for specifically agreed purposes and for which a record of the activity has been made, as illustrated in Figure 13. The learner is talked back through the activity by the Learning Coach (LC).

In our example, Dafydd, the learner, is an engineering student in his third year who had voluntarily enrolled on a Self-Organised Learning course because he felt that he couldn't cope with the welter of reading materials he was expected to get through. Here (as part of his third 'learning experiment') he is working on one of these texts.

Process dialogue

LC inner conversation	*LC–learner outer conversation*
I see that there are at least 3 significant changes in the time/structure of Dafydd's read record. I'm going to take him through at least 2 of these to encourage him to re-live what was going on in his head and heart at these points in the text. In the light of the difficulties he had last time I'm going to steer him away from content descriptions text into process awareness.	*LC*: Let's describe your read record together, so that you can try to explain what went on in your head as you were reading. You started at line 1 and read evenly through to line 23 where you began to slow down and read at about half your original speed until line 37. Here you stopped for about 10 seconds – was this of any significance for you?
	Learner. I am not sure. . . . Oh yes . . . (*long pause*) . . . I couldn't understand 'three-phase delta network'. *LC*: You mean *that phrase*? . . . Well, how did you deal with this then? *Learner.* I just got stuck with it . . . 'delta' really threw me.
Get him to generalise from 'delta' to notion of 'terms'.	*LC*: So what do you do when you don't understand *a term* like that? *Learner.* Terms like that make me give up reading after a bit. I stop concentrating and I get bored.
Come back to this later . . . get him to think of context cues in the text, search out meanings . . . use technical dictionary . . . reflect on lectures . . . previous work.	*LC*: Well, there are various *tactics* you could use to get behind the meanings. . . .
	Learner. This bit on lines 29–30 I found really interesting, though I disagree with the author. . . . *LC*: Why?
Content again . . . I need to make him aware of levels of meaning . . . Bloom's Taxonomy Level 5 evaluation . . . then he can explore processing a text differently for different purposes.	*Learner.* I see 'overhead lines' messing up the environment . . . on lines 34–39 I concentrated on the detailed description and then I began to wonder about other examples the author could have given.

LC inner conversation	*LC–learner outer conversation*
	LC: Now if we reflect on your *reconstructions* so far – how relevant is all this to your stated *reading purpose*? *Learner*: Well . . . (*long silence*) . . . perhaps I did get a bit bogged down with the text and I shouldn't really have spent time on arguing with the author and on *evaluating* the ideas . . . after all, I did say I was aiming to get the gist – an overview. . . . *LC*: So? *Learner*: Maybe I ought to bear in mind that I shouldn't let the author take me over if *my purpose* is to get a quick overview. . . . I suppose my *record* should be much *smoother . . . fewer hesitations* . . . no notes . . . it's quite uncanny how my *read record* traces out almost every query or thought. . . .
Good. He's becoming perceptually more sensitive to the read record. Now I can show him that this is a reflective tool that he can MA(R)4S for himself. He's let the text re-define his purpose . . . alert him to this later.	*LC*: How would you describe your *purpose* at this point?
	Learner: I wasn't thinking about *purpose* but I now see I was actually reading for *detail*.

The conversation continued back over this section of the text and read record to create a deeper awareness.

	LC: With this in mind, let's carry on then. Now, on lines 40–49 you *skipped backwards, hesitated*, read on and made some notes. What was the point of all this? *Learner*: I wanted to recall *the details* exactly and I feel that I wanted to check it later.
His notes should indicate the level of meaning he is constructing.	*LC*: Let's look at your notes. What *kind of notes* did you make?
	Learner: They are *pretty detailed*, almost a *copy of parts* of the text. *LC*: Is this your usual way of making notes or do you have *different styles for different purposes*?
He doesn't have a choice of strategies . . . like most of my learners, he's largely operating at the bottom level – literal – I suppose the tests, lecturers insist on this.	*Learner*: No, on the whole I suppose I aim for some *kind of verbatim record* of a text. I know it wasn't really necessary here to try to remember these details, but I was worried that if I didn't I might not really understand the text.

Facts are better remembered and understood when linked with higher order meanings i.e. schemata, networks. . . . Get him to do an experiment on this to coinvice him later.

When I get him to face up to this he'll need a lot of support.

I'll get him to listen to the tape of this discussion so that he identifies his own words with categories of meaning.

'disagree with author'
   – evaluation
'wonder about other examples'
   – extrapolation
'verbatim', 'details'
   – literal
I need to open this up to other possibilities next time
   – paraphrase
   – select and interpret
   – summarise
   – abstract
and the affective domain
   empathise . . .
   humour . . .
   persuasive . . .
   escape . . .
   joy . . .

LC: Do you think we can dig deeper into your worry?
Learner. I don't know what you mean.
LC: Well, what do you think might happen if you had not made notes, or made *notes of a different kind*? For instance, thinking about your purposes, some abstracts in your own words?

Learner. I've not really tested myself out on this. I suppose I'm anxious if I can't recall the text and that this will affect my marks eventually. . . . I see what you are getting at . . . *perhaps I'm scared to let go*, to really explore how I read. . . .

LC: Perhaps we should think about how 'getting the gist' relates to remembering the details . . . see that these will require different *tactics and strategies*. . . . We might get you to work on this in depth next time. In the meantime why don't you read this chapter in our book *Reading-to-Learn*, which gives a simple taxonomy of purposes and levels of meaning?

Learner. Here goes, then, into deeper waters next time. I hope all this will help me with my project and exams. . . . I'll stick to it . . . now and then I begin to see a light at the end of the tunnel. . . .

Further discussion encourages Dafydd to continue to explore the read record and to begin to appreciate why he read the text in that particular way.

Organised talk-back through the read record enables Dafydd to identify key habits and allows him to challenge these so that alternative strategies are explored in a quest for an effective understanding of the reading process as a given text is read in the context of personally relevant purposes.

Having *re-lived* the process, and *reflected* upon its meaning, the Learning Conversation becomes stringently *evaluative*. Dafydd is guided to assess his reading activity in his own terms.

So far, we have illustrated a snippet of the *process dialogue* and of how this develops over time. Supporting the learner during this talk-back is essential if feelings of anxiety and uncertainty are to be overcome and the learner is to remain in awareness long enough for the personally viable experimentation to be sustained. The following interaction illustrates this:

Support dialogue

LC inner conversation	*LC–learner outer conversation*
I've been pushing him to challenge his robot – his reading skills and competence. I sense that he's getting anxious. If I don't watch it he might switch off and we'll be back to square one or worse. . . .	*LC*: Let's take stock. *What is being achieved* so far and how *do you feel* about it?
	Learner: Usually when I learn from a book I aim to do it as fast as possible, but these sessions are really slowing me down. I'm so concentrating on trying to understand what I do as I read that I forget why I chose to read the text in the first place! It gets me down.
We do have a problem. Shift gear, support him, look for cues. . . .	*LC*: But if we look at what you have achieved in these sessions, what do you then say?
	Learner: I do seem to be getting a better idea of reading for different purposes, of processing texts differently according to my purpose, of recognising that reading for, say, appreciating the author's argument is different from reading to get the gist of a text; and again, reading for specific details is not the same as evaluating the usefulness of the text for your general understanding of a topic.

LC inner conversation	LC–learner outer conversation
Good. We have something to build on – his understanding of his reading process will help to support him through the hard bits. . . .	*LC*: Also I thought at least at times you were actually enjoying yourself!
	Learner. Well, I'm worried principally about my speed but, you are right, I have enjoyed reflecting on my reading behaviour, and the flow diagram technique you introduced me to last week certainly helps me to pick out the wood from the trees in a text. But you see I've got so much reading to do, so much work to do – all this may be a bit of a luxury.
Pressure of work is adding to the stress. . . . This will add to his understanding of his process.	*LC*: Let's take it gently for one more session and explore a wider range of reading purposes, identify further strategies and map out flow diagrams on some really difficult texts. Then we'll have a go at speeding up.
I wonder if he's doing any better on his course?	*Learner*. I'll go along with this but I need to convince myself pretty soon that this is going to be really useful to me. *LC*: We can best do this by considering how you can now begin to use some of the skills you have learned 'on the job', so to speak, to help you to process your reading more effectively in relation to your tasks. How have you been doing with your assignments?
Good. Some positive feedback here about the quality of his work. This should stop him feeling so miserable and give him confidence. I've got to make him appreciate that moving into a void in his experience leads to some uncertainty, and if he can move through this to explore the unknown positively, he will realise that real learning is an exploration which all too often frightens people off. How can I get him to enjoy this exploration?	*Learner*. Well I did get a good mark for my last lab experiment. . . . I talked to the lecturer the week before and he mentioned a journal article on a new way of bringing alternating current machinery on line. . . . I found it easy to get the main idea out of it and I was able to write it up with more insight than usual. *LC*: I want you to recognise at this stage that if you are to progress your reading skills, you have to challenge these rigid habits of yours, and that almost always involves some anxiety . . . it's like navigating in the dark . . . which way to go? . . . In fact, getting anxious (but not too anxious) and getting worse is a sign that you are getting better at learning.

LC inner conversation	LC–learner outer conversation
	Learner: I feel you are right in many ways but I'm still worried! I feel lost – it's like stumbling in the dark.
I need to be empathetic here . . . use my Carl Rogers experience . . . and I must remain congruent. . . .	LC: I know how you feel. I felt like that some time ago when I was learning to change my lecturing style. . . . Public performance of any sort was a nightmare for me until our senior counsellor talked me through my agony. . . .
	Learner: Well, when I heard your introduction to Learning Conversations for the Engineering Department I didn't think you did too badly so maybe there's hope for me.
I'll suggest a peer group support here.	LC: Don't forget you're not the only one – Sue and Bill are going through some anxiety, so why don't you three talk about this?

In giving emphasis to the *support dialogue*, the Learning Coach needs to develop sensitivity to the learner's doubts and uncertainty which may lead to a closing up of awareness. Facial expression, changes in behaviour patterns, unusual mannerisms which may develop over time and negative comments such as 'I'll never get this right', 'I'm going on with this all day, even if it kills me', 'I'm beginning to hate flow diagrams', 'I'm slowing down', 'I'm fed up today', 'shrinks meddling in learning need to examine their own skulls' provide some indications of a build-up of stress!

Part of the conversational skill is to *empathise* with the learner. Is he re-living the reading experience, or is he or she simply going through the motions of reproducing the behaviour? Talking a person back into the experience is an important component of the awareness-raising technique. Whilst there is obviously no objective check on the validity of the re-creation of the experiential process, there are numerous corroborative indicators. Spontaneous remarks which relate to the content and to the monitoring and decision-making processes, together with the learner's apparent recognition of their earlier experience, all add up. Part of the skill is to be able to talk a person back into their earlier process and through this to develop gradually an evaluative commentary, so that she or he is able to review the process of learning. This requires a specialist language. During the talk-back, the learner becomes more aware of the components of this language and of the relationships they personally construct between these. Figure 14 offers in simple form extracts of this developing language with reference to reading-to-learn. The reader is invited to compare this with the Personal Thesaurus of learning air intercept control shown in Figure 18 and the Personal Thesaurus of S-O-L shown in Figure 19 in the Appendix. Readers may also usefully refer to the Functional Taxonomy for examples of how the process language plays itself out through records of a wide variety of tasks and skills.

This 'process' language allows the learner to move towards greater self-organisation in

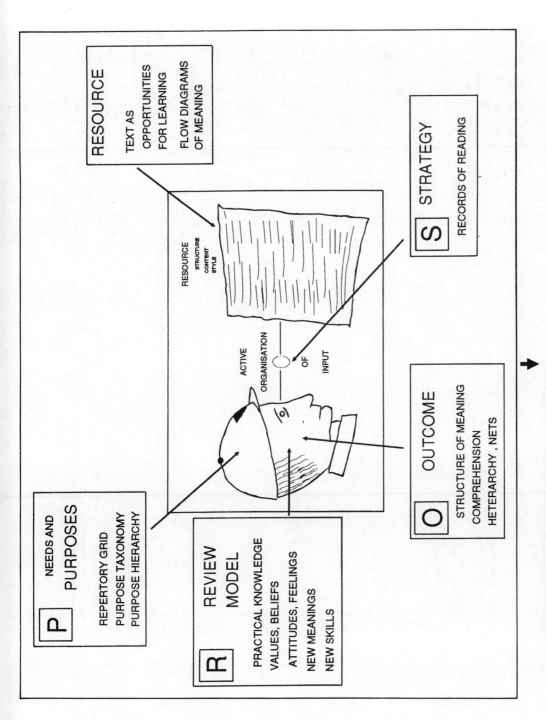

Figure 14 A developing language for reading-to-learn

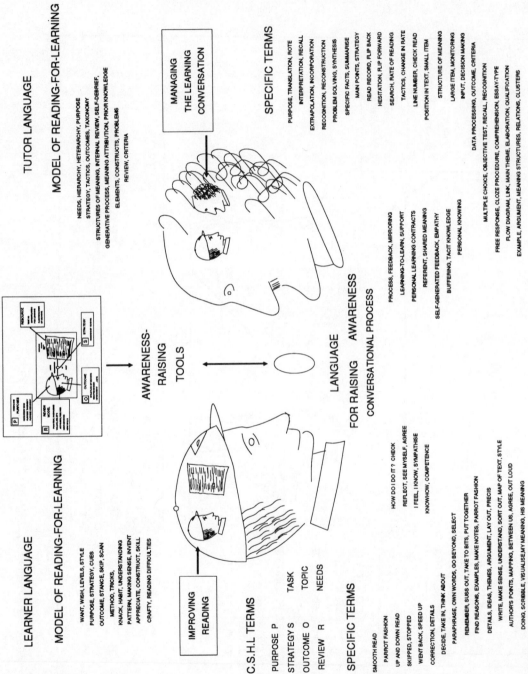

TUTOR LANGUAGE

MODEL OF READING-FOR-LEARNING

NEEDS, HIERARCHY, HIETERARHY, PURPOSE
STRATEGY, TACTICS, OUTCOMES, TAXONOMY
STRUCTURES OF MEANING, INTERNAL REVIEW, SELF-DEBRIEF,
GENERATIVE PROCESS, MEANING ATTRIBUTION, PRIOR KNOWLEDGE
ELEMENTS, CONSTRUCTS, PROBLEMS
REVIEW, CRITERIA

MANAGING
THE LEARNING
CONVERSATION

SPECIFIC TERMS

PURPOSE, TRANSLATION, ROTE
INTERPRETATION, RECALL
EXTRAPOLATION, INCORPORATION
RECOGNITION, RECONSTRUCTION
PROBLEM SOLVING, SYNTHESIS
SPECIFIC FACTS, SUMMARISE
MAIN POINTS, STRATEGY
READ RECORD, FLIP BACK
HESITATION, FLIP FORWARD
SEARCH, RATE OF READING
TACTICS, CHANGE IN RATE
LINE NUMBER, CHECK READ
POSITION IN TEXT, SMALL ITEM
STRUCTURE OF MEANING
LARGE ITEM, MONITORING
INPUT, DECISION MAKING
DATA PROCESSING, OUTCOME, CRITERIA
MULTIPLE CHOICE, OBJECTIVE TEST, RECALL, RECOGNITION
FREE RESPONSE, CLOZE PROCEDURE, COMPREHENSION, ESSAY-TYPE
FLOW DIAGRAM, LINK, MAIN THEME, ELABORATION, QUALIFICATION
EXAMPLE, ARGUMENT, MEANING STRUCTURES, RELATIONS, CLUSTERS

AWARENESS-
RAISING
TOOLS

LANGUAGE
FOR RAISING   AWARENESS
CONVERSATIONAL PROCESS

PROCESS, FEEDBACK, MIRRORING
LEARNING-TO-LEARN, SUPPORT
PERSONAL LEARNING CONTRACTS
REFERENT, SHARED MEANING
SELF-GENERATED FEEDBACK, EMPATHY
BUFFERING, TACIT KNOWLEDGE
PERSONAL KNOWING

LEARNER LANGUAGE

MODEL OF READING-FOR-LEARNING

WANT, WISH, LEVELS, STYLE
PURPOSE, STRATEGY, CUES
OUTCOME, STANCE, SKIP, SCAN
METHOD, TRICKS,
KNACK, HABIT, UNDERSTANDING
PATTERN, MAKING SENSE, INVENT
APPRECIATE, CONSTRUCT, SKILL
CRAFTY, READING DIFFICULTIES

IMPROVING
READING

C.S.H.L. TERMS

PURPOSE P   TASK
STRATEGY S   TOPIC
OUTCOME O   NEEDS
REVIEW   R

SPECIFIC TERMS

SMOOTH READ
PARROT FASHION
UP AND DOWN READ   HOW DO I DO IT? CHECK
SKIPPED, STOPPED   REFLECT, SEE MYSELF, AGREE
WENT BACK, SPEED UP   I FEEL, I KNOW, SYMPATHISE
CORRECTION, DETAILS   KNOWHOW, COMPETENCE
DECIDE, TAKE IN, THINK ABOUT
PARAPHRASE, OWN WORDS, GO BEYOND, SELECT
REMEMBER, SUSS OUT, TAKE TO BITS, PUT TOGETHER
FIND REASONS, EXAMPLES, MAKE NOTES, PARROT FASHION
DETAILS, IDEAS, THEMES, ARGUMENT, LAY OUT, PRECIS
WRITE, MAKE SENSE, UNDERSTAND, SORT OUT, MAP OF TEXT, STYLE
AUTHOR'S POINTS, MAPPING, BETWEEN US, AGREE, OUT LOUD
DOING, SCRIBBLE, VISUALISE, MY MEANING, HIS MEANING

Figure 14 continued

reading. The learner discovers that many factors contribute to influence the quality of the eyeball to print interaction and the attribution of personal meaning: for instance, personal interest, values, prior knowledge, and the articulation of specific purposes, text-processing skills, and the criteria for evaluating the quality of the meanings achieved. *The 'language of awareness' becomes the key for learning. It allows learners, often for the first time, fully to recognise their intuitive learning experiences and behaviours as an area of potential skill.* A more detailed description of the conversational use of read records involving process is to be found elsewhere (CSHL publications 'Postscript', p. 372).

To conclude this relatively simple example, let us explain how the *referent dialogue* is gradually built into the Learning Conversation as it develops in depth and quality.

Referent dialogue

LC inner conversation	LC–learner outer conversation
I must get him to take responsibility for judging how well he is doing – self-assessment – then I can get him to expand and refine his criteria. He is beginning to rely on his own primary process. I can build on this and then gradually get him to take on board others' assessments as useful but secondary.	*LC*: So far, we have deliberately not commented on the *effectiveness* of your newly developed reading skills . . . in other words, OK, you demonstrate a much better grasp of how reading *tactics and strategies* combine to achieve *specific outcomes* of reading and your repertoire of *reading purposes* is evolving from session to session, but essentially so far we have been exploring how and why you read . . . what goes on in your head in *process terms, but not how well. . . .* *Learner*: Yes, at first it was over my head, but I really do *think of reading* in an entirely new light now. Before it was, well . . . just reading, really . . . and most of the time, word for word, line by line, as I was taught at primary school. I don't seem to have thought of it since, other than as a fact-finding task, often not very well. What's more, I am beginning to see that I have a host of personal reasons for reading, beyond the academic, and that my *appreciation of reading* as a whole is changing. It's like having a *double conversation* with a text. One bit of me just reads and the other bit of me super-reads, knows what to do, how to do it, how and when I can go into a sort of overdrive. I actually talk to the author, but I don't let him take me over any more. *I select, argue, analyse, even deliberately miss out bits* without feeling guilty and I think I know what you mean by reading for content, i.e. the subject matter, and reading for process, i.e. improving my skills. *LC*: So let's concentrate on what you mean by *improving*. . . . How do you know you are more *effective*? How can you *assess the quality of your reading*? . . . In your own terms?

LC inner conversation	*LC–learner outer conversation*
I've got to get him to appreciate that there are process measures of reading skills and that these are independent of content-based assessments; also that process and content assessment must first be in his own terms.	*Learner.* I've actually *hardly ever deliberately assessed my reading*, except perhaps in terms of how slow or fast I read. How do I begin? (*long pause*)
	Anyway, in the end the final verdict is not mine, is it? (*long pause*) Well, I can see how, if I've defined a purpose, if I've borne this in mind as I read, if I've developed this and even changed the main thrust of it for reasons I can defend . . . and if the read records show how I read differently for different purposes *I must use this as evidence to measure my progress. Quality* creeps in somewhere – depth of understanding achieved in relation to the content, but also in relation to the process. Reading is becoming alive for me – *is that a measure*? How do I know I've understood the text? How do I know I've read effectively? I could easily still delude myself, I suppose! All I know is I couldn't talk about reading in this way before these sessions – but what is that a measure of?
	LC: One dimension is to consider whether you are reading flexibly, i.e. reading *speedily*, and with *quality*, recruiting the appropriate tactics to achieve outcomes which you *value in the short and long term.*
He's beginning to ask the right questions.	*Learner.* Do you mean, for instance, that if I wanted to recall a specific principle, fact or argument, or for that matter any statement in the text which I might choose, that I would know in advance how to go about this; how to plan and to adjust my reading so that I actually do recall the items I choose not just immediately, but when I need this at some later point? Or to take a very different instance, suppose I just wanted to relax and enjoy certain qualities in the writing itself, the prose, the imagery, the use of vocabulary, would I be able to pursue this in ways which would maximise my pleasure? . . . And what does one mean by quality of understanding? Can this be measured in terms of purpose and strategy and possibly other critieria . . . *quality of meanings achieved? How can we measure quality*?
	LC: What would *your criteria* be?

LC inner conversation	LC–learner outer conversation
Now we are getting deeper into acknowledging a difference between learning-focused and task-focused assessment. I'll reflect this back to him and also introduce the idea of using a peer group as referent.	*Learner:* Intuitive personal satisfaction, that's important; being able to justify the economy and, yes, even beauty of my skills and, let's face it, getting good marks in my essays and my presentations as a result!
	LC: What you're saying is that, first, you've got to work to develop criteria for self-assessment in terms of your control of the reading process and the meanings achieved . . . then perhaps exchange this experience with other learners in your group. . . . This may help to enhance your self-assessment a bit. Then, of course, any evidences you can collect of how your reading influences your own academic progress . . . these are the underpinnings of developing a self-critical approach. You need to develop a network of referent – do you see?
	Learner: I see there are several perspectives, not just one correct expert view, but in the end what you've been getting at is that I ought to criticise or praise myself, isn't it? I'll work on it, OK? Is this what you want?
I'll have to stand him back on his heels so that he recognises his dependence on me.	*LC:* Only if you do. All I want is to offer you possibilities for exploration and to help you on the way. I actually do *trust in your own judgement because you've shown me that you've earned it!* I *feel* you're on the way to self-organising your own learning.

Thus, by means of the *'referent dialogue'* Dafydd is encouraged to reflect upon and review his own developing criteria for a self-assessment of the quality of his reading. Our example so far illustrates how Dafydd, a young student engineer, is engaged in the 'process', 'support' and 'referent' dialogues of a Learning Conversation. Mature students, as well as industrial managers, have used this approach to improve the quality of their learning through reading. Equally relevantly, children can enhance their reading skills when they are encouraged to address their processes of learning directly. Let us continue example 1a by illustrating this briefly as follows:

Susie (aged 8), Nick (aged 9) and reading-to-learn

The following brief transcript illustrates how a school teacher, who had been using our various *paper and pencil methods for recording reading* to develop her own reading skills, began to use this approach with a group of her 8 to 10-year-old pupils. Once they had grasped the method, they worked in pairs independently of the teacher. She was then able to manage the whole class of thirty-two, and in a very short time these young pupils were using their personal read records and many of the other reflective tools described in the 'Functional Taxonomy of Tools' to develop their learning skills. You, our readers, are left to appreciate without further comment how Susie and Nick's Learning Conversations address the process of reading.

First read

Susie: I've made a record of how you read the story about the otter . . . do you want to see it?

Nick: How long did I take then?

Susie: How long do you think you took?

Nick: About 7 minutes.

Susie: Wrong. You took 12 . . . here is the record of when you started – see, 2.01 – and here you finished – 2.13.

Nick: My record looks all the same with little stops every few lines, except I stopped for a long time at the title and at the picture.

Susie: You said you were going to read it so that you could tell me what's in it . . . tell me the story.

Nick: Well, it's about three otters, Dilly, Dally and Bubbles. They were playing in the pool and Dilly caught a little white duck, and Dally watched carefully as Bubbles, who was the biggest, tried to take it away and took its wing off . . . and in the end, Bubbles had a broken tail, Dally had cuts on her nose, Dilly hid in a deep pool behind the big boulder, and . . .

Susie: You forgot the bit about the whistle blowing, and the tall girl called Catherine with a big broom in her hand, and the man with a gun, and . . .

Nick: Well, I can't remember everything when I read a story.

Susie: Look at your record. See the bits you forgot – you didn't stop in any of these places . . . in fact, look, you speeded up a bit.

Nick: Well, I found them boring . . . and I wanted to find out what happened at the end.

Susie: But if you want to remember all the story, you've got to read it properly, bit by bit. Now, if you only wanted to remember the important or exciting bits, that's different. . . . When Miss Martin did this with me, I had different purposes and I could remember different things each time I read.

Nick: Let's see how you can remember the important bits then – let's read that book on butterflies for our class project. I'll do you this time.

Second read

Nick: Your record isn't very different from mine, except you went back and read the first half again and so you took longer.

Susie: I wanted to stop at the important bits but I couldn't decide which they were.

Nick: You stopped in the middle for a long time and towards the end. I bet you don't know why.

Susie: I stopped there because . . . well, because . . . well, I was thinking I had forgotten most of before, and I was thinking that didn't matter if they weren't the important bits, but I got in a muddle . . . and at the end . . . where I stopped I tried to remember it all and I couldn't . . . so I went back and read a lot of it again and I can remember that, but it's not the important bits.

Nick: Let's do it again. Don't think of it as a story, you mustn't try to remember everything. Your read record should show how you were looking back and forth for clues – remember what Miss Martin did with us? Clues for the important bits.

Susie: I'll try the same chapter on butterflies again. . . .

Nick: Your record has got to be different.

Susie: OK.

Third read

Nick: You've stopped in five places and you've gone back and forth twice from line 29 to lines 14, 15, 16 and 17, you've gone back from line 37 to 24 and you made notes. . . .

Susie: I'll try to tell you the important bits:
  1 Butterflies are insects and they are cold-blooded, so they hibernate when it gets cold . . . that's there on the record.
  2 Eggs hatch into larvae – caterpillars – and then into a chrysalis that hangs from a leaf.
  3 Butterflies are found all over the world and there are thousands of varieties.

Nick: Well, the first bit you said is not exactly the same as it says but you've said the gist of lines 9 to 17, and the second bit you said is on lines 25 to 29, and . . .

Susie: See, I couldn't tell you the details, and I'm not sure I've got all the important bits, but . . .

Nick: Let's see how Bill and Mary are doing . . . we've got to report back to Miss Martin at 3 o'clock.

Susie: Remember when we started, we read the same way, long and slow, and tried to remember it all. . . . I was much better than you. . . . Afterwards when I read the last time, my record was like a rabbit's track, back and forth and I could tell you some of the important bits, but not the details about colours, and names, and countries. . . .

Nick: We'll ask Miss Martin if she thinks you've remembered the important bits.

Example 1b   Talk-back through records of personal meaning for comprehension, and review of reading strategies and outcomes

Whilst words – that is, graphemes and phonemes – run serially across a page, the reader uses these as cues to create a complex 'pattern of meaning' in his head. The full significance of reading behaviour cannot be fully appreciated by the learner until this pattern of meaning can be exhibited. *Patterns of meaning derive from the processing of the text, and awareness of this enables personal reading strategies to be identified.*

The flow diagram technique was developed by the authors to exhibit in structured form the non-linearity of the meanings which the reader attributes to a text. The technique is described in the Functional Taxonomy of Tools. By assigning categories such as 'main ideas' 'qualifiers', and 'elaborations' and by numbering the 'meaning items' in a text, it becomes possible to classify each item and show the relationships between them. It can be used to exhibit the structure of meaning in a sentence, paragraph, chapter or even a whole book. On p. 42 is a flow diagram of *this* book. Here we illustrate how the read record and flow diagram can together be used as tools for the learner to become more explicitly aware of the ways in which meaning is attributed as they hesitate, slow down and skip forward and backward in their search through the text. The learner is able to reflect on how the read record maps on to the flow diagram and to the original text and to review the quality of his understanding in relation to the purpose of reading.

Thus *the read record and the flow diagram can be combined* as a procedure for developing the process dialogue beyond the more open and provisional *reconstruction* phase into the more deeply self-evaluative phase when the quality of the reading strategies and learning outcomes are reviewed.

Having created an awareness of reading by talk-back through the reading record as in Example 1a, the flow diagram is then introduced. *Figure 15* shows how specific categories and items of text can be displayed so that the original linear sequence is preserved, but the structure of the text is unravelled.

By constructing a personally relevant flow diagram and mapping this on to the read record the learner becomes more explicitly aware of the ways in which meaning is attributed as he processes the text. Suppose, for example, that the record shows that the reader stopped on lines 'x' and 'y' and made notes; and suppose that 'x' and 'y' map on to the 'qualifications' and 'elaborations' columns of the flow diagram. What can we infer? The presumption is that the reader is looking for specific details. If that was not the purpose – if, for instance, the reader was trying to select the main idea – then the strategy will have gone sadly astray. *The record and the flow diagram provide clear evidence from the learner's own behaviour and experience.* They are tools for a deep engagement in the process dialogue, heightening awareness of the reading experience.

In the Learning Conversation the reader is guided to interpret how such evidences related to the original text and to the stated reading purpose. Gradually, the learner picks up the notion of how 'smooth', 'item', 'search', 'check' and 'inferential' read tactics can

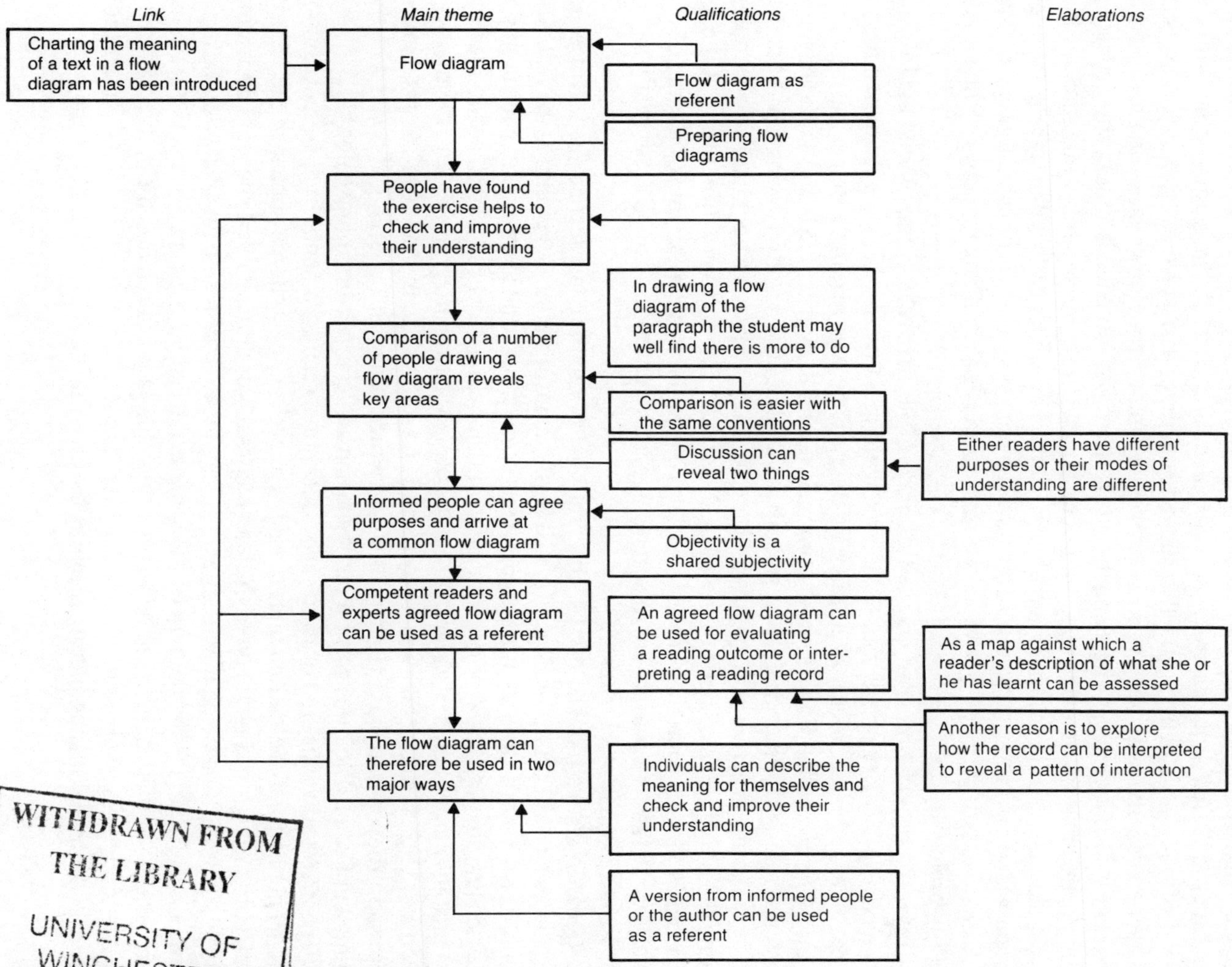

Figure 15 The structure of a flow diagram

Link

Charting the meaning of a text in a flow diagram has been introduced

Main theme

Flow diagram

People have found the exercise helps to check and improve their understanding

Comparison of a number of people drawing a flow diagram reveals key areas

Informed people can agree purposes and arrive at a common flow diagram

Competent readers and experts agreed flow diagram can be used as a referent

The flow diagram can therefore be used in two major ways

Qualifications

Flow diagram as referent

Preparing flow diagrams

In drawing a flow diagram of the paragraph the student may well find there is more to do

Comparison is easier with the same conventions

Discussion can reveal two things

Objectivity is a shared subjectivity

An agreed flow diagram can be used for evaluating a reading outcome or inter-preting a reading record

Individuals can describe the meaning for themselves and check and improve their understanding

A version from informed people or the author can be used as a referent

Elaborations

Either readers have different purposes or their modes of understanding are different

As a map against which a reader's description of what she or he has learnt can be assessed

Another reason is to explore how the record can be interpreted to reveal a pattern of interaction be differently combined to achieve different purposes. This is not easy. The tutor has to recruit the support dialogue to keep the learner motivated and to help her shift her disintegrating skill from a worsening trough (see Figure 10, p. 85) to a much higher level of competence.

Figure 16 shows an actual record of how Rhiannon read a very long sentence from a chapter 'On the Struggle for Existence' from Darwin's *Origin of Species*. She was reading it in order to *identify and abstract the main idea*. She was relatively unfamiliar with the theory of natural selection, and the subject matter of the selected sentence was both abstract and complex. In dealing with 'universals and abstractions', according to Bloom's Taxonomy (Bibliography), the semantic structure of the sentence is highly sophisticated. A linguistic analysis revealed that numerous phrase structure and transformational rules operate to generate its complex surface structure. The sentence has therefore a complex semantic and syntactic structure. The reading recorder, in this case addressed by the Reading-to-Learn software, shows how four 'read tactics' combine to identify Rhiannon's reading protocol.

Figure 16 provides a more detailed display of the first read tactic plotted against the sentence itself. The sentence was set out one word to a line so that when Rhiannon read it on the screen, the recorder logged this exactly as if she was reading a longer passage line by line. The horizontal line shows the time taken, and the vertical axis shows the position of each word in the sentence. In this 'smooth read' Rhiannon reported during talk-back that she was aiming to arrive at a synopsis of the sentence. When asked what she was doing during the hesitation at the end of the read, she said: 'I find this very difficult. . . . I'd only the vaguest idea of what the sentence was about. I couldn't begin to think in terms of my purpose. . . . I think I was trying to sort out a plan of action . . . but all I can really say is that I knew I had to read it again.'

Figure 16 shows that she used a different kind of tactic in her second read. However, the sentence is still processed linearly: that is, she reads from the beginning to the end. She groups certain words into six phrases or 'items of meaning' and at the end of each item she reported that she was 'checking the meaning of that item in my head'. We have divided the sentence into these items of meaning in illustrating the flow diagram. Extra attention was given to item 2 'because this was a key phrase and relevant to my purpose'. Items 3 and 4 were sub-grouped into word clusters or single words because 'I got bogged down with the detail, and I had difficulties sorting out the terms and complicated phraseology'.

Figure 16 shows that in her third read Rhiannon executed an entirely different kind of read tactic. She was being much more selective and search patterns appear in the record. In mapping her flow diagram on to the read record it was apparent that she was connecting items 2, 5 and 6. These she identifies as the 'key idea'. This also coincides with the main theme on the tutor's flow diagram of the sentence. It is by no means always the case that there is an immediate agreement between a flow diagram offered into the conversation by the tutor and the flow diagram generated by the learner. Part of the Learning Conversation is here concerned with negotiating meaning by firstly using the learner's flow diagram and

Figure 16 Rhiannon's reading strategy

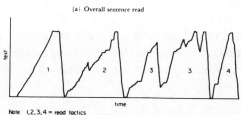

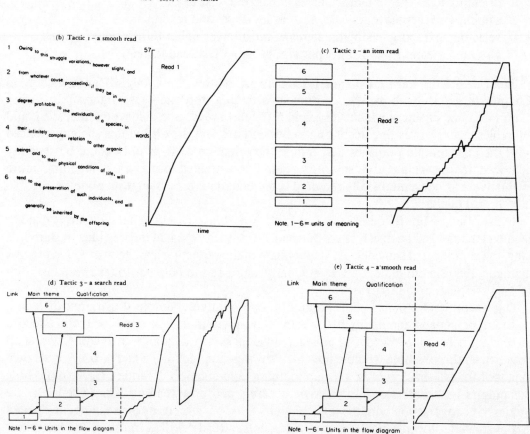

read record to achieve a detailed understanding (process dialogue), and then introducing a flow diagram produced by another learner or an expert, to extend the referents for understanding (referent dialogue).

In the fourth read tactic Rhiannon read smoothly and quickly (Figure 16). However, in contrast to the first smooth read, an entirely different cognitive process is taking place in her head. She said it was a 'check' read. Rhiannon commented that she was trying to create some meaning compatible with her specified purpose. In the hesitation at the end she said: 'I was recalling the main idea in my own words – more or less.'

During this process of reflection, reconstruction and review, Rhiannon began to discover that reading to achieve a satisfying outcome which specifically related to her self-defined purpose depended on an awareness of how she processed the text, second by second. Summarising the key idea in a complex text which was unfamiliar to her depended on:

1   orienting to the general message as in her first read tactic;
2   sampling the sentence for relevancy as in her second read tactic;
3   selecting and reorganising the items of meaning as in her third read tactic; and
4   checking meaning against her purpose as in her last read tactic.

This reading-to-learn encounter proved to be of the utmost significance to her. In Chapter 4 we show how she continued with this approach less intensively, using paragraphs and chapters which she found difficult to read. She discovered that she could adapt her tactics of reading according to her purpose and the difficulties she experienced with the text. Simple purposes demanding the selection of facts only could be speedily achieved in one relatively 'smooth' read. Sophisticated purposes demanding more evaluative and inferential skills required more elaborate processing, involving a flexible mix of read tactics.

In the example briefly described, Rhiannon was able to assess in her own terms that her reading strategy had been effective. She had successfully located the key idea in Darwin's long and complicated sentence. At a later phase of the reflective and reconstructive process dialogue, the referent dialogue was gradually addressed to help her to take responsibility for assessing her own progress.

Our example so far has concentrated on one relatively simple illustration of how a record of personal meaning, in this case the flow diagram, can be combined with a record of reading behaviour in order to enhance awareness of the quality of reading. We shall now extend this example to show how the flow diagram technique can be used on its own as a tool for talk-back within a group learning conversation. Learners can explore how meaning is best understood in relativistic terms and how reading comprehension is a process of conversation with the text, whereby personal structures of meaning are created and evaluated. For instance, a group of students, already skilled in using flow diagrams for reflecting on the quality of their reading outcomes, used this technique to review their comprehension skills in reading chapter-length texts recommended to them as part of their course work. To illustrate how process, support and referent dialogues interweave within the group Learning Conversation, we include our analysis of a sample of transcript.

Sample of a group Learning Conversation using the flow diagram to identify strategies in reading

Student	Transcript	Category of analysis
P	First thing is to agree on the size of the meaning units for analysis.	Agree conventions
R	There's no point in one taking sentences, another taking paragraphs, or groups of sentences or paras; we'll end up with different flow diagrams and we won't be able to share our experiences.	
B	Why don't we all take the paras, then we can do a rough analysis and if we get into trouble, we can do a detailed analysis of sentences in some of the difficult paras.	
P, R, B.	OK.	
F	We've got to start by trusting ourselves. Let's just experiment and do it quickly and we can go back and do bits again if we change our minds.	Support dialogue
D	If we get in a mess, we'll get Sheila in to sort us out.	Referent dialogue
F	Let's check through our purposes for reading Perry again before we start . . . mine was to try to get a bird's eye view so that I can see which paras are important. . . .	Process dialogue
B	Mine was to zoom in on the abstractions and then see where the others fit . . .	Process dialogue
P	Mine was just to summarise and generally have a go . . .	Process dialogue
B	So what do we do with the first chunk? Let's look at our notes and read records now.	Process dialogue
D	I don't understand how you (F) could spend so long on that first para with all those hesitations and notes. That's nothing to do with the central message.	
B	I agree with D.	Referent dialogue
R	. . . and so do I.	
F	I seem to see everything in the first 5 paras as important – I stopped and made notes everywhere. I'll listen to you lot for a bit. Maybe I can then see this clearer . . .	Process dialogue
D	Don't worry. If you don't agree with our analysis, yell out and we'll check what you think.	Support dialogue
P	Now para 2 has a lot of meat in it; let's stick that in the main theme for now.	Process dialogue
D	Para 3 too.	

R & B	OK.	Support dialogue
F	Para 4 is definitely *details* . . .	Process dialogue
R	OK.	Support dialogue
B	I think paras 7 and 1 are the same – they're to do with the author making asides, signposts on the way	Process dialogue
P	OK for now.	Support dialogue
R	Paras 7 to 17 need a lot of weeding out. My read record is full of stops, searches back and fore: we'll have to look at each in detail and maybe do a sentence flow analysis of para 9 and maybe 17. . . . We've each searched differently in the text – is it bad prose or is it us?	Process dialogue
F	Actually, I'm beginning to enjoy this, but I think we've got a long way to go before we can agree a flow diagram which makes sense . . .	Support dialogue
D	Well, stop flapping about and let's get on with it then.	Support dialogue
P	OK, we were all reading to describe the text in a structured flow form . . . and we've now got a rough chart that we're all reasonably happy with.	Agree conventions
B	So let's look at our read records and check out how our patterns of reading map on to our agreed chart.	Agree conventions
F	Let's check why we're doing all this.	Process dialogue
P	It's to see who's got a 'good' reading strategy, follow the method Sheila gave us, OK?	Referent dialogue
F	'Good' means where the hesitations, notes, check reads, and searches between paras actually map on to the main theme paras in our agreed flow diagram, is that right?	Referent dialogue
P, B, R	Yes!	Support dialogue
F	Well, mine's a mess, it doesn't map on at all. I seem to find most paras important. I hesitate and make notes everywhere.	Process dialogue
B	Well, learn to select, think in flow diagram terms, put 3-D specs on, and try to see the bits in relation to each other, try again on another chapter.	Process dialogue
F	But how do you do it, B. what goes on in your mind?	Process
B	Well, I skimmed the para . . . see my record? . . . then I go back and find the core . . . see, it's at the beginning of para 5 . . . in the middle of para 7 and at the end of para 9 . . . I	

stopped and made a note summarising those important bits. There's no fixed rule, even one author does it differently in the same chapter. You've got to suss it out from the sense. . . . Look, your read record goes on and on, same old pattern, like a zombie. . . .

F	But then, how do you know that para 7 is a main theme as a whole then, and para 5?	Referent
B	Well, I check it out against the paras before and after, and try to keep a helicopter view so that in my head I zoom in and out. You've got to carry the message as a whole in your head, weigh one bit against another.	Process
F	I don't do that.	Referent
B	That's it then, try . . .	Support
F	I never was any good at this in school. I was better at music and maths.	Support
P	Well, see it as maths, then . . . see it as operations in your head: compare, differentiate, check equals, reduce down, check like a proof. You'll be all right then.	Support
F	Maybe if I saw it like music, with patterns, crescendos, lyrical bits, diminuendos, I might try to like it . . .	Support
B	You might get as good at it as you are at playing the flute.	Support
D	You could even see it as dance . . . if you don't enjoy it, what's the point?	Support
F	Dance with words? Nietzsche said that too! It's all to do with recognising different patterns. See text as maths, music, dance, even mime . . . the staff will think we've gone bonkers . . . what are we learning?	Support
R	Well, let's get on with it, none of us have got a reading strategy that's really any good. According to Sheila, we've got to prove to ourselves that what goes on in our minds as we read can be traced in our read records, and we should be able to match this first on to our own flow diagram, then on to a flow diagram we've agreed together, and then on to a master diagram she prepared from a detailed analysis involving 5 staff. So it's 3 types of check.	Referent
P	But in the end, after doing that each of us decides how well we read, how our purpose relates economically and effectively to our read records and to our flow diagram . . . it's up to us. . . .	Referent
D	We've summarised prose for years, we're supposed to teach kids to do it, and look we're pretty hopeless at it ourselves. We're not really scientific. . . . That's what I am learning. I do it mostly according to whim and fancy, and look, most times I get away with it though . . .	Process

B	Well, what about when you got an E in your Ed. Psych. project, wasn't that because it was too long and your arguments didn't have any punch? Perhaps you're not scientific when you read . . . nor when you write . . . and not scientific generally when you learn?	Referent
P	Look, we'd better get to grips with all this, we're supposed to call the TV cameras in to film us doing a good Learning Conversation for the BBC OU programme. Let's get it right before we do. . . .	Support
F	I think we should let them in now anyway, and see the real thing in the raw . . . what have we got to lose?	Support

They displayed their personal meanings in a structured form and began to appreciate that, rather than search for the 'absolute meaning', the meaning in a text is essentially subjective, but that this can be shared. Students have found one of its most creative contributions to be the identification of how a structure at one level, say a paragraph, is created by a patterning of structures at a lower level, say sentences, and from the context of its position at a higher level, say a section. They have also found it personally satisfying to exchange their personal flow diagrams with each other, to try to arrive at an agreed structure. The transcript illustrates one such encounter. Each of five student teachers read the text 'The Use and Misuse of Reading' by Perry (on the Brunel Reading Recorder) and spent three hours in an intense Learning Conversation.

Not all agreed with the final form of the flow diagram, but each had learnt how to use the technique as a reflective device to review their own unique processes of meaning attribution, in terms of how well this expresses the successful outcome of their purpose. Three intensive group sessions involving different texts and purposes enabled each participant to become much more perceptually aware of their processing of a text. In the words of one of them, 'I now see text standing out like a 3-D jigsaw puzzle', and in the words of another, 'I don't have to do flow diagrams any more – they happen in my head as I read'.

The types of Learning Conversation briefly sampled in Examples 1a and 1b are not exclusive to adult learning. Susie and Nick's Learning Conversation is one of many within our junior- and middle-school projects. Children, in pairs and small groups, have demonstrated an equally powerful grasp of these techniques and have transformed their reading skills as a result.

The 'process', 'support' and 'referent' dialogues revisited

The illustrations in Examples 1a and 1b and in Examples 2 and 3 in the Appendix enable us to expand on our introductory explantion of the three dialogues.

The process dialogue elaborated: the need to model learning

The process dialogue allows the learner to develop various components of the reflective language for awareness of how they learn. We have devised a seven-step conversational heuristic called MA(R)4S which enables the learner to model his or her unique processes of learning. Underlying the examples so far illustrated, the MA(R)4S heuristic has been recruited by the tutor or Learning Coach to manage the dynamics of the process dialogue. Whilst the surface evidences of the process dialogue in any given Learning Conversation will be specific to it, the deep structure is driven by MA(R)4S, and is common to all instances.

MA(R)4S stands for:

1 *M – monitor*: Observe yourself in action (process) and keep (remember or record) a sequential record (file, protocol) of what is happening.
2 *A – analyse*: Run the record (memory) of 1 through the model (pattern of meanings) which drove the event (monitored in 1) to identify and pull out those features essential to an adequate reconstruction (thought, feeling and perception).
3 *R – record*: Make an external record (e.g. the read record or the repertory grid) which summarises sufficiently to enable an adequate reconstruction of one's intentions later.
4 *R – reconstruct*: Run the record through the model to re-recruit and revise the original experience including (in particular) that which was *not* captured in the monitoring and that which slipped out of the analysis and record stages (i.e. the inner game). (Since MA(R)4S is essentially a hierarchically organised process, the most telling level of reconstruction may be tapped minutes, hours or days later.)
5 *R – reflect*: Having reconstructed the experience as veridically as possible, now *evaluate* it in terms of the original intentionality of the event(s). Detect inadequacies, flows, mismatch, poor timing, wrong emphasis, badly distributed effort, and so on.
6 *R – re-view*: Take the model apart, amend and reconstruct it so that it will more veridically embody the structure of the domain being modelled and thus when run faster than real time will better anticipate events.
7 *S – spiral*: Try another event and go through the cycle again (e.g. fixed role therapy, play another match, sit another exam, talk again in public).

Engagement in a MA(R)4S process conversation releases powerful insights which generate the specific terms and concepts for describing learning in unique ways for each individual. *It represents the heuristic which enables a shift in awareness from task-bound to task-focused and to learning-focused conversations* (Prospective Commentary).

Monitoring, analysing and recording articulate our experience. This feeds our developing language, enabling us to bring more aspects of the process under control. Prior knowledge, values and beliefs, feelings and skills as well as the content of the event (people, things, happenings and subject matter) all influence purpose and strategy and the quality of learning outcomes. *Reconstruction, reflection and review* support the further construction of this deeply personal language, much of which is non-verbal.

The process dialogue is both iterative and hierarchical. For each specific task, one clarifies a purpose, operates a strategy, specifies an outcome and assesses the quality of the process by reviewing the whole operation. *Review* may lead to the reassessment of purpose, and the MA(R)4S process *spirals* us upwards. This is taken up further in the next chapter where the components of the process dialogue are elaborated in a particular way as part of the 'tutorial conversation'. This provides the framework for the *Personal Learning Contract (PLC)*. We have already commented that learning, modelling meaning, is organised hierarchically and that during learning one's awareness moves up and down through different TOTE levels of organisation (Chapters 1 and 2). Purposes are located in a hierarchy of purposes – likewise strategy and outcomes. *It is the MA(R)4S process in the constructive and creative levels of 'meaning modelling' which operates to drive the process dialogue in ways which initiate an enhanced capacity to learn.* Finally, the whole process dialogue will have *phases of provisionality*, experimentation, uncertainty and apparent chaos, as well as *phases of convergence*, certainty and commitment. The gradual shift from one to another forms part of the pattern through which 'personal observers' or Self-Organised Learners pursue their research.

MA(R)4S conversations allow the process language to be negotiated and further developed. The learning process is observed (monitored, analysed and recorded) using the hard evidence provided by the awareness-raising tools, and an explanation offered by the learner. The whole process is assessed (reconstructed, reflected upon and re-viewed) for effectiveness. As part of the Learning Conversation, a meta-commentary is offered about the nature of this language and about the need for generating personal feedback for developing it. Thus one major function of the Learning Coach or tutor's activities is to offer *a meta-commentary on the process dialogue, thus raising the learner's awareness of it, whilst at the same time providing the tools for the learner to comprehend it through direct experience.*

Another important function is sensitive management of a gradual evolution of *feedback* from *externally offered* (that is, in terms of the meaning system of others) to *self-generated* (in terms of the meaning system of the learner). Only when the learner is unable to generate feedback does the tutor offer this. Managing 'structure and freedom' within the process dialogue is crucial. As the learner generates his or her own process dialogue by meta-commentary on the interactions involved, there is a shift towards personal learning autonomy. The learner begins to reflect on and develop his capacity for modelling meaning, and to *internalise the process dialogue*. The tutor moves between directive, guided and discovery modes of management. Directive intervention involves the tutor in taking over most of the interpretation of the records of learning. In guidance, some components of process language are offered to enable the learner to interpret her own records. For discovery, learners are encouraged to develop their own language for interpreting the records with minimum tutor intervention. The tutor may then take on the role of mentor, offering counter-arguments or propositions, or even occasionally of madonna, shielding the learner from existing structures and the constraints of all public knowledge, whilst they generate their own personal knowing (Chapter 1).

The 'management rules' for regulating this process dialogue must be born out of each conversational experience. The aim is to *catalyse the learner's own strivings for awareness*, enabling learners to invent their own understanding of their learning process and to generate their own personally relevant feedback. This commentary on process is summarised as follows:

1 Describing and interpreting the experiential process and negotiating a meta-language for reflecting on it through implementation of the MA(R)4S heuristic;
2 Controlled movement between offered feedback and self-generated feedback;
3 Structure and freedom in regulating the dialogue.

The support dialogue elaborated: the need for support through the process of change

Some of our case studies show that learners become uncertain when exploring their learning processes. Often they become over-anxious and may exhibit extreme hostility when testing out the limits of their skill and understanding. In attempting to improve, they often get worse! As a result they retreat into the safety and security of 'stasis'; that is, personally known routines of learning. *The support dialogue is concerned with helping the learner to remain an observer of his or her own process long enough to explore it in depth*, and *to achieve new levels of competence.*

Many psycho-social factors are involved in support. Developing *mutual trust* and *'buffering'* are two outstanding requirements. Trust is important in bridging that void between the uncertainty of being in process and the security of stasis. The tutor and learner may have to work hard and long to achieve this type of relationship. Assessing the boundaries of this support dialogue is often difficult. Is it over-indulgent or is it highly relevant to explore emotional, social and intellectual issues more wide-ranging than the topic or skill being explored? As the learner gradually recognises an honest intention to help him explore and review his own competence, trust in the relationship develops.

In lowering awareness of stress the tutor 'buffers' the learner's tense and anxious state, enabling them together to transform that energy locked up in anxiety into a creative force. Thus supported, the learner can explore hitherto unknown areas of skill. Buffering depends on offering 'unconditional positive regard', 'empathy' and 'congruence'. As in Rogerian therapy, this often proves to be a demanding experience for both participants, requiring sensitivity and skill in the Learning Conversation.

Managing the support dialogue depends on developing sensitivity to the changing inner states of the learner. Cues such as changes in posture, facial expression or negative remarks about learning are used as indicators for switching into a support dialogue. We have on occasions used biofeedback monitors to detect changes in physiological states as a resource for validating the need for engagement in a support dialogue, and also for exploring with learners how they can recruit an awareness of such inner states as a resource to help them personally move through the stresses which build up as their learning robots become challenged. This area needs much more investigation and development, particularly with reference to learning complex tasks, topics and skills. Athletics coaching and monitoring pilots' performance have already shown the potential of physiological monitoring for improving competence. The support dialogue is summarised as follows:

1 breakthrough to mutual trust;
2 buffering: converting anxiety and hostility into a creative form of energy; and
3 sensitivity to stress experienced by the learner.

The referent dialogue elaborated: judging one's own performance

Having encouraged the learner to develop a language for exploring process and supported an in-depth exploration of it, the Learning Coach or tutor's function is not yet over. How will the learner be able to judge the level of competence which he has achieved?

A recurring problem experienced by many (if not all) people is that they often decide to do one thing and end up either not doing it or doing something else! The converse is also experienced: having decided not to do something, the person ends up doing it after all. Being able to express an intention is not equivalent to achieving it. The process of achieving recognised purposes involves one of two strategies: the passive or the active. Passively, one becomes reconciled with directionalities or needs inherent in one's construction of experience, acknowledges them, and thereby achieves purposefulness by learning to anticipate the outcome of the directionalities over which one has no control. This is called 'acknowledging your own limitations and learning to live with them' or 'learning to make the most of oneself'. A whisky blender on one of our repertory grid courses said he was revered for his skill, which he had acquired during forty years with the same firm. Whilst knowing that he used the 'green stick' to maintain his judgement during blending, he was totally unable and disinclined to explore how. He would not construe his own processes of construction. But only by so doing could he hope to pass on his skills rapidly and efficiently to another.

The nature of this 'passive purposefulness' is only revealed if an attempt is made to interfere with it. Active purposefulness is achieved when awareness extends into the process out of which the constructions of experience arise. This enables learners to review systematically how they are constructing their experiences and to intervene in the construction process. They are, thus, able (when they have learned to modulate their interventions) to control their own directionalities, achieving true purposefulness.

The internal process for evaluating the process of learning can recruit its 'criterion set' from three different sources:

1 the inside world (for example, Carl Rogers' fully functioning person uses his or her own organism as the ultimate test of fitness);

2 the outside world, including other people (for instance, significant others, peer groups, subordinates and so on);

3 other people as a community of meaning (such as the dimensionality of public knowledge, be it science, plumbing, art, classic literature or do-it-yourself handbooks).

Learners can compare their understanding with others *through exchanging strategies, purposes and outcomes.* In progressing through a sequence of personal, interpersonal and group review the learner can relate her own assessment to a publicly agreed system of assessment. Managing this dialogue is concerned with helping the learner to run, or jump rather than stand still within her own passivity, thus helping her to choose appropriate referents. This referent dialogue is summarised as follows:

1 Using oneself, i.e. personal process, as referent;

2 Using another as referent; and

3 Using a referent group and managing the choice of referents.

Internalising the three dialogues: Self-Organised Learning

Any one sample of a coherent Learning Conversation may contain components of all the three dialogues, 'process', 'support' and 'referent'. The process dialogue is driven by the MA(R)4S heuristic; the support dialogue is informed by a more than Rogerian model of facilitation; and the referent dialogue recruits our own understanding of self-appraisal, peer groups, feedback, continuous assessment, knowledge of results, subjective and objective measures of performance, testing, examining and accreditation and so on. These interrelate richly and in a complex way in any given exchange between the Learning Coach and the learner. As part of the developing conversation, the Learning Coach must offer the learner a *meta-commentary* on the nature and function of the three dialogues as these take place. Thus, in addition to providing the reflective learning tools, and guiding the dynamics of the flow of the conversation for the achievement of awareness of process, the *Learning Coach is enabling the learner to develop the model of the Learning Conversation itself* so that the learner may comprehend it. With experience and support, learners internalise these three dialogues and take over the management of the Learning Conversation for themselves. People differ in the ease with which they can internalise and sustain each of the dialogues. Effective internalisation of the Learning Conversation sets the learner well on the road to continue learning 'on the job' and through life. Frozen internal conversations disable learners, and it is only when the educational and training climate can offer externally supported Learning Conversations that the frozen processes are revived and the learner is set free to grow.

The structuring of Learning Conversations within short-, medium- and longer-term time-spans leads to a 'figure-of-eight' flow of the three modes or levels of the conversation; namely, *tutorial, life* and *learning to learn* (Chapter 4). *All three dialogues play themselves out within each of these modes*. Process, support and referent dialogues at the tutorial level are concerned with medium- to longer-term strategic aspects of learning, the planning of goals, and the execution of purposes over days, weeks, months or even years. This depends on the establishment of explicit *Personal Learning Contracts* (PLCs) where the content of the learning is negotiated, the needs are articulated into purposes, the resources identified and the strategies put into action and evaluated. The content may originally be task-focused (Prospective Commentary) but as personal evidences of learning accumulate, the skills of learning become the content; that is, learning-focused. Awareness and review of strategic aspects of learning become the central focus of attention. A diagnosis of the strengths and weaknesses of learning becomes possible, so that an evermore elaborating repertoire of strategies can be developed. *This approach is in complete contrast to the less adaptive task-bound approach of 'study skills' prevalent in education, training and management development.*

As the tutorial level is guided into the learning-to-learn level, the three dialogues become concerned with detailed short-term interaction of specific habits and skills so that these are challenged and rebuilt. Self-debriefs using records of behaviour in a second by second MA(R)4S process play a crucial role here. Success leads the learner back into the longer-term tutorial level of the PLC. At the life level, the three dialogues focus on learning needs and purposes in the longer term and when these begin to flow and motivation is recharged, the cycle of conversation is again channelled towards the achievement of the PLC. Thus, the three dialogues are fundamental to all three modes of the Learning Conversation and take on a different form in each; the PLC at the *tutorial level*, the negotiation cycle at the *life level*, and the self-directed debrief at the *learning to learn level*.

Self-Organised Learners are continually 'finding themselves' in each new activity. They may be dons or dustmen, moguls or mechanics, gamblers or bluebell girls, farmers or film-stars, the disabled or the devout. They may be juniors, teenagers, semi-skilled adults or professionals at all levels and walks of life. What they share is the ability to create life conversations around them. Life takes on structure and purpose; it is exciting and fully engaging. One needs only to listen out for the snippets of commentaries by 'natural' Self-Organised Learners which one picks out occasionally in biographies or in radio interviews to illustrate this.

In our view, education is only justifiable if it adds to the number of nodes for real life MA(R)4S process conversations and thus contributes to the quality of living and the competence of individuals, enterprises, and society as a whole. Thus, the Learning Conversation in its totality (learning to learn, life and tutorial conversations) is only justifiable if it contributes to greater capabilities in learning from experience, as individuals, pairs or groups 'converse' with their worlds.

Appendix

Example 2   Computer-aided learning

We have used computer logs as *records of performance* to enable Royal Navy trainees to enhance their awareness of how they learn various complex tasks, including ship command and control and air-intercept control. In the latter, aspects of the task addressed by the machine include safe fighter control in a congested air space and intercept control relating to intercept geometry. The built-in *learning aids* include the use of back-tracks that enable the learner to appreciate more readily how his sequence of decision-making produces the results he obtains; a *stop* facility for reflection and review of tactics and strategy; *replay* to enable the learner to 're-live' and therefore reflect on the process of learning so that different tactics can be invented and attempted alongside the previous attempts; *varitime* so that the *replay* can be observed in faster and slower than real time; and an *event log* of everything that has occurred during practice. These 'learning aids' create different manifestations of feedback about the learning task.

Used in an exploratory way within an otherwise intense training course (in which the pressure for success is very high, owing to the enormous expense involved in training) this proved very effective as an approach for developing learning competence. Aptitude tests offer inadequate selection procedures and the failure rate is very high. How do trainees learn the task?

Patterns in the sky: a simulator which invites the user into a Learning Conversation

Whilst learning on the simulator, each trainee plans his learning purposes for a given intercept type, his intended strategy, and considers possible criteria for assessing the quality of his outcome; that is, achieving a good intercept. Using the built-in reflective learning tools (the 'Functional Taxonomy') he then operates the simulator and tries to complete a particular intercept. As he masters the intercepts he can carry through a complete sortie on the machine.

Supported by the Learning Coach, the trainee debriefs himself as he stops, replays or inspects the log data to enable him to reflect upon and review his purposes, strategies and outcomes. Thus a process dialogue concerned with learning the skills of intercept control is gradually developed. By comparing one replay attempt with the next, progress can be reviewed as learning develops; by reflection upon 'what was I intending to do when I turned to port there?', 'why did I decide to start the final turn there?' and 'since the results showed I was too early, what must I now do to correct this error?' he learns to review his own performance. By freezing the replay using the stop facility, he can create space for reflection about 'why the decision at that point contributed to success or failure'. In using himself as a test-bed for evaluation, a referent dialogue is being developed. This gives him an opportunity to consult peers or an instructor. He can also consult 'an expert' built into the machine; namely computer solutions to particular intercepts. This extends the referent dialogue further and forces him to exercise judgement since in applying certain rules the computer can on occasions be very stupid. He goes on to use the experience of learning to compare his prospective and retrospective views of performance on the task. How well did he achieve his purposes? How effective was his strategy? How good was his outcome? What must he do next?

In using self-generated 'knowledge of results' to arrive at future learning needs, and in using the learning devices for reflection and contemplation, and in referring to other sources for guidance when he needs this, the trainee is enabled to take more control of the direction and quality of his learning. He learns to personalise the rules formally taught on the course in the context of the dynamics of his own learning process. This learning experience enables him to develop a new way of thinking about his own learning skills as he learns to perform the task.

In one debriefing session after a poor intercept, one trainee chose to reflect upon what he meant by 'coming in too early' and 'coming in too late', and so revise his next course of action. Although working on a simulator, trainees report that they feel it is the real thing, and a support dialogue with the manager of the Learning Conversation is often critical in steering the learner out of a tendency to revert to a repetitive practice mode of learning when experiencing stress. It was only by 'living with the tension' that a real breakthrough in skill and confidence was achieved. The personally generated causal explanations that emerged were very different from the logical intercept geometry concepts formally taught on the course. *Each learner has to construct his personal model of the task and a model of how he learns this for an effective operational control of the aircraft.* For instance, in assessing 'heading', 'angle of turn', 'separation of the fighter from the target' and 'relative speed of fighter and target', eyeball judgements, the crucial points of decision and control, had to be developed to a very precise degree of accuracy. All this has to be reflected upon in the context of safety rules relating to other aircraft. Using replay to reflect upon the 'pathway through the sky' as shown by the back-tracks, he learns to make better judgements about the effectiveness of his control of a single intercept and the overall sortie. A self-debrief of his event log data gives a second-by-second history of his performance. This enables the learner to grasp the commonalities between specific intercept types. An awareness of how he achieved this understanding enables him to tackle increasingly difficult intercepts more successfully with less trial and less error. He learns what is involved in working out the dynamic geometry of 'the radius of turn', 'the reciprocal' and the 'relative angle of bearing' between fighter and target.

One learner using all the learning aids addressed by the simulator progressed from eight unsuccessful attempts before achieving an intercept on the simplest intercept type (180-degree turn), to five on an intermediate (90-degree turn), to three for a very complex intercept type (150-degree turn) with the target at variable speed). Another learner who did not use the learning aids whilst practising on the simulator got increasingly worse and failed to complete the sortie. Moreover, he was unable to debrief himself adequately and had to rely on the instructor to do this for him. In our terms, he was unable to generate his own feedback and remained dependent on external direction. The former went on to explore other aspects of this complex task, such as the appropriateness of particular intercept types given the context of wind direction, position of the sun, fuel level of the aircraft, and so on. He then went on to invent his own scenarios. This longer-term and more varied exploration of the task takes him closer to the real 'on the job' training situation with real aircraft and real pilots which he is having to deal with every day of his course. This he tackled with confidence and skill, much to the surprise of the expert instructors, who usually have to be very supportive and instructive in the early days of live training.

Figure 17 The tracking of an intercept

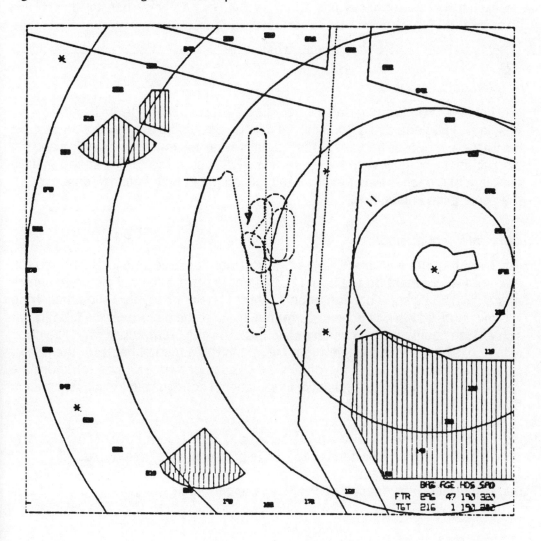

In the sample transcript which follows, the process of learning this complex skill is made partially explicit. Readers should try to identify the process, referent and support dialogues, and to work out for themselves how these interweave in the evolving Learning Conversation. Figure 17 shows the radar screen, the shaded 'no go' areas, and the tracking of the intercept.

Learning to do a 'Charlie' intercept (a 30-minute session)

Pete was totally unable to reflect consciously on his learning during the intercept attempts. Absorbed in doing the task, he was a victim of his own operating robot, unable to develop his performance adaptively. In this transcript he is attempting to model his own thoughts, feelings and actions in the process of self-debriefing during the replays, and then he goes on to explore how a conscious monitoring of his learning helps him to improve his performance.

First intercept attempt

Pete: I can't remember what happened when I approached the amber lane – ah yes, look, I neglected to go back to 'all codes'. Should be a reflex action by now; it's illegal, dangerous to cross. Then I didn't re-assess my target heading and my displacement is all wrong . . . but I was right about the target speed initially although my reaction was too slow and I failed to get him. I cut my losses rather than chase the impossible.

Second intercept attempt

Pete: I went in late with my final turn, then I got flustered and I had an aircraft mix-up. I was caught on the hop. . . . I've got to have a mental picture of which aircraft is doing what. That fighter on the screen belongs to me, I should be flying it in my mind. If I haven't got a clear mental picture, the picture on the tube (radar screen) isn't going to be of much use to me. . . . I can't remember what I've done with him, so I can't follow it through. I've got to get a mental habit . . . the fighter is me, I've got to change my identity. . . . I'm uncertain as I control; there's a conflict in my mind; I shut off a lot of information; I concentrate too closely on one thing.

LC: What have you learned, then?

Pete: To see the sortie as a whole, all the time . . . and I didn't brief myself properly on the parameters . . . I wasn't prepared in my mind for a 'weave-plus'.

LC: You must anticipate the unexpected.

Pete: I must always suspect – even if things appear to be going well – then I'll pick up the deviations much more quickly. If I'd turned head on then I'd have cut him off, a certain hit. . . . I know the answer to that situation but I failed to execute it.

LC: Can you get back to the thinking you were doing at the point of decision?

Pete: I turned him to starboard instead of to port – but now I've got the situation in my head, I'll use it in the future.

LC: In a sense, you've got a model of it running in your head, then?

Pete: Yes, but my model isn't sufficiently predictive. I've got to translate what I've been shown on the board to using it quickly in my own experience . . . it's hard . . . I don't have all the options clear. . . .

LC: You're constructing them as you go on, that's fine, that's learning . . .

Pete: It's like building bricks, isn't it? To my instructor it's common sense, but experience comes from the hassle.

LC: But in these replays and in your head on the tube you've got to watch yourself, reflect and not let yourself get caught up in it.

Pete: Yes, I got very upset at the Amber Lane incident. I wanted to get up and kick myself. I've done it several times before. . . . I've got to un-learn, teach an old dog a new trick. . . .

LC: What about learning to keep 'reality' in the head? It's faster in the air than it appears here.

Pete: I've got to work on my reaction time.

Third intercept attempt

Pete: I've got to consider the sun. I've got an option to turn port or starboard. I've got to optimise the position of my fighter and obviously it's better to be on the sun side of my target.

I said he's doing 400 and then I let this go . . . problem solved . . . unfortunately, life isn't like that. I've got to learn to deal with what is now, not what happened 2–3 minutes ago.

LC: These are all learning exercises and this was your first attempt at a complicated manoeuvre, but you must be aware that you repeated errors. Think of your learning curve as spiralling upwards. . . .

Pete: I've got my fighter turning to port and the target was in fact turning south. I've got two ports, I should have heard warning bells. . . . If the displacement is too narrow I've got to turn across the T's nose at a range which lets him see me . . . then it's a dog fight. I can't cope with it on radar. . . . I must not let myself get in this position.

LC: Looking back on your three intercepts, try to review your learning.

Pete: I've got to get feedback quickly. I've got to learn a 'radar eye', e.g. the white blobs flashing means danger. . . . I've got to split my mind – one bit controlling and doing, the other bit thinking and watching. I've got to feel I'm in the cockpit with the same view as the pilot . . . one bit of me – the thinking bit – has got to teach the other bit – the action bit . . . he's the old dog that needs to learn new tricks. The thinking bit has got to see it all, analyse it, play out the consequenses faster than it happens . . . yes, model it.

In observing their own learning on the simulator, trainees approached the task with different needs and expectations, defined their purposes differently and invented different strategies for achieving these. Opportunities to explore these differences by testing out the effectiveness of the imagined models and plans helped the trainees to diagnose their own strengths and weaknesses. This enabled more refined strategies to be evolved in order to change behaviour and produce a more effective performance on the task. Self-awareness leading to reflection and review involved as much feeling as thought. Perhaps even more than in the reading-to-learn example, the trainees had to grapple with a high-adrenalin state and over-anxiety, as well as negative feelings about their training, their own view of themselves, and occasionally of their instructors. The simulator with its built-in reflective learning aids offered clear and precise manifestations of the learning process, involving external process, referent and support dialogues with the Learning Coach, so that a personal assessment of success and self-awareness of learning could quite quickly be achieved. These were then incorporated into separate software which will enable the machine to carry on the Learning Conversation with the trainee. This software could be adapted for many other tasks.

We have tried to show in this example that by using a different type of behavioural record to reconstruct experience from that described in Example 1, we have found that the learner can develop a personal language for reflection upon how the specific task (air intercept control) is being learned. A personal thesaurus of the developing language involved in learning this complex skill is shown in Figure 18.

Example 3   Learning to reconstruct experience: the CHANGE grid

In Chapter 9 of *Self-Organised Learning*, we explained the CHANGE grid technique, and several examples were given. Without illustrating the grid, we shall briefly demonstrate how process, support and referent dialogues interact in a REFLECT grid conversation.

Jo was a manager in a very large organisation. He described himself as a sales engineer, and not doing very well in his job. The tight construct clusters in his first repertory grid highlighted that Jo saw all of his tasks in technical terms. 'Technical discipline' was a core construct which he insisted was the essence of his job. He agreed to think about the selling component of his job for a month and was then invited to complete a CHANGE grid and to continue the REFLECT conversation. The procedure involved adding new elements which extend the range of the topic and new constructs which expand his repertoire of thoughts and feelings, and rating original and added constructs on old and new elements.

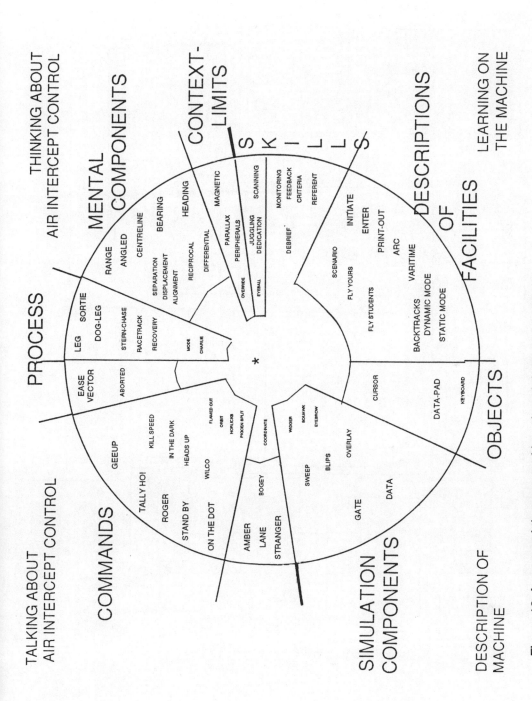

Figure 18 A personal thesaurus of learning air intercept control

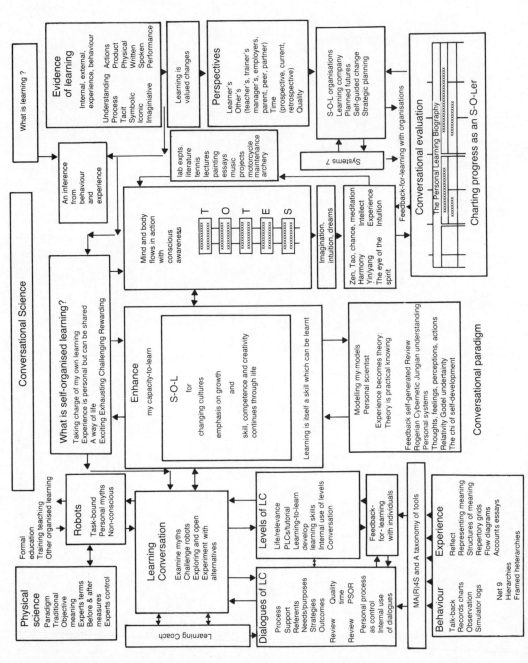

Figure 19 A personal thesaurus of S-O-L

An exploration of a job from a different perspective.

Transcript

Consultant: The overall pattern in your CHANGE grid demonstrates clearly that when you introduce man-management tasks involving 'cost' as elements . . . (which, do you remember, you completely left out of your first grid?) . . . you see all except one in a very negative mode. Again, all the technical tasks are seen most positively. Let's look at the odd one out.

Jo: This event has a high cost component, yet I see it positively, as with all my technical tasks. . . . It doesn't make sense – I really see it negatively.

Consultant: It has such a close correlation with all the positively viewed elements (95 per cent). I can't believe you; there must be some meaning, some validation in it. Try to dig deeper – but I'll go along with you if you insist there's no rational explanation for it.

Jo: I get very upset when you say that. I insist that you're wrong. I don't want to think about it any more.

Consultant: Perhaps, only if you do think about it, will you get to grips with the problem of why you're not doing well in your job. I know I'm pushing hard, but I feel this is crucial . . .

Jo: If I try to really think, I do know why I see it as positive, because it's nothing to do with me . . . yes, that's it . . . another manager does that, it's not my responsibility you see, so I can see it positively. I don't carry the can if that goes wrong, i.e. if we overspend on the budget. . . .

Consultant: Well, that's a breakthrough, it really is, but I've got a feeling that unless you can identify and view the cost part of your job positively, it will affect the quality of service you offer your customers and your management effectiveness in the Sales Division.

  Another thing – have you noticed that none of your element clusters are to do with people – how do your customers fit into your tasks, then? How do you view them?

Jo: I want to listen to you; I don't mind being pushed really. I know I asked you to keep my nose to the ground, but where do I go, what shall I do next week? I'm floundering, I'll never make a good manager in this area.

Consultant: Why did you choose this job in the first place? You said you had a choice of sections when you moved up from being a production supervisor – you must have got some deep reasons. . . .

Jo: It was the challenge, and getting out of the rut of the factory . . . I do want to do well in my job, I'll tackle every task in the next few weeks as if they are to do with people and to do with cost; I'll put the technical aspect out of my head altogether, I really will. If you don't see me again, you'll know why.

Consultant: I'll see you next week by coming to work with you at the coal face, and then we'll try to extend our CHANGE grid conversation and see how your thoughts and feelings may be changing. Try to develop an open mind about each task. It seems to me that your gut says yes, you want to get better but your performing robot says no. If need be, I'll spend a whole day with you 'on the job'.

Jo: Maybe you are right. I'll chivvy myself to keep trying to see some of these tasks I do in a more human yet cost-effective way, and I'll try to play down the technical bit, but I'll do it on my own two feet, thanks.

Consultant: OK then. You may find that as you have a go 'on the job' you might get worse at the technical aspect of your job – that's to be expected. Don't worry about it at this stage.

Jo: If I do that, I'll crack up altogether. If I see this happening can I get in touch?

Consultant: From what you said earlier . . . I may sound hard, but before you do get in touch, try to really live with it, with the pain of it, for a bit. It doesn't matter if you get worse for a little while, does it? You know you are good on the technical side; just try to see that in experimenting with a fundamentally new way of thinking about your job, skills do disintegrate – but it's only temporary, if you stay in there. Keep your mind open, trust yourself to learn, work out positive strategies – you will find a way through to a new and better view of your job as a whole. I'll be at the end of the phone, or if you really need me at the coal face, don't worry, I'll definitely come.

Jo: I promise to stick with it then.

Consultant: I'll see the Sales Director, just let him know you're working on your own self-development plan. Obviously I won't tell him what you're up to – just so that he can create a space for you, put less pressure on you, just for a bit. Is this a good idea?

Jo: I'd appreciate that, I really would.

Through successive Learning Conversations involving all three dialogues, as learners engage in awareness-raising activities on various tasks, topics and skills, a developing language for Self-Organised Learning is acquired. A Personal Thesaurus elicited from one experienced Learning Coach is summarised in Figure 19.

Chapter four

How to conduct a Learning Conversation

In its entirety, a Learning Conversation starts from the *life conversation* which provides the context within which the learner initially orientates and defines their expectations. But it rapidly moves to the *tutorial conversation* which is formulated in terms of *the Personal Learning Contract (PLC)*.

The tutorial level of the Learning Conversation

Some understanding of the context, coupled with the completion of one cycle of a PLC, is sufficient for the management of the *tutorial level* of the conversation in the short term. A given topic, task, and specific purposes for learning will have been negotiated, and intended and actual strategies, as well as expected and real outcomes, will have been compared and reviewed. Personal strengths and areas for development will have been provisionally identified and preliminary plans for the next stage will have been made.

There are several possible directions in which the Learning Conversation can then proceed but the central aim is to sustain the tutorial level exploring fully the strategic aspects of learning. Several cycles of PLCs are necessary in order to gain sufficient awareness to enable the learner to begin reviewing the quality of learning. The initial two or three PLCs need to be managed in an open and provisional way so as to support experimentation with alternate possibilities. As the personal evidences of learning accumulate, subsequent PLCs need to become more committed, highly specific and very precisely defined so that detailed aspects of the learning process can be thoroughly explored. These divergent and convergent phases, of provisionality and certainty, are a marked characteristic of the rhythmic pattern of the cycles of PLCs within any given topic and task. Indeed, such alternating phases are characteristic of the Learning Conversation as a whole. Management of PLCs in the long term depends on their growing relevance to the learner's larger goals and higher-order needs and purposes.

Almost always the first PLC attempts are *task-focused* (Prospective Commentary). For example, the learner may choose to:

'improve my ways of establishing discipline';
'learn accountancy skills';
'update my knowledge of control systems';
'create greater interest in my lectures';
'be more thought-provoking as a chairman';
'organise my study time better';
'be a better leader of a research team';
'learn about information technology so that I can become a better manager';
'become a better rugby coach';
'summarise an article so that the core meaning stands out';
'try to get higher scores in my algebra class';
'develop greater dexterity in my tennis strokes'.

Either by continuing several cycles of PLCs within the same topic in an ever-expanding mode, or by exploring other topics, the learner can continue to review the accumulating evidences about *how they go about learning*. Only then are learners in a position to begin to set themselves *learning-focused* PLCs. For instance, they may choose to:

'learn how to observe a given event more holistically';
'explore how to improve my use of discussion as a vehicle for learning about a topic';
'learn to think more evaluatively';
'learn to identify and use a wide range of "forms" in essay writing';
'learn how I can set out to learn about management skills';
'change the ways in which I think, feel and talk to myself about my family';
'learn how to go about learning a foreign language';
'learn how to be less dogmatic in seminars';
'learn about problem-solving algorithms and how to invent my own';
'learn to perform more innovatively as a half-back';
'learn how I can deal with my pain threshold differently';
'learn how to anticipate things more accurately';
'develop a more strategic approach to reading so that I can summarise reports more effectively';
'invent new ways of setting about learning'.

Thus, for the learner cumulative cycles of PLCs based on an ever-widening range of topics, tasks and skills at the *task-focused level* and an ever widening range of learning skills at the *learning-focused level* yield more powerful evidences about themselves as learners. They are now able to plan specific directions for constructive changes in their approach to learning. They can begin to enhance their capacity to learn. They become more self-organised as learners.

At any stage in this personal endeavour, any evidences which yield information about inadequacies of skill, based on the learner's own criteria of evaluation, will result in the

Learning Conversation being shifted to the *learning-to-learn level*. This requires specific conversational techniques for decisively challenging ultra-stable myths and habits, robot-like skills, or rigidly held attitudes, beliefs and prejudices. Talk-back through records of personal meaning or through records of behaviour offer precision in the control of this learning-to-learn conversation. For instance, purpose hierarchies, personal purpose tax-onomies, outcomes represented as Structures of Meaning, review charts, or behavioural records of specific activities can be introduced into the conversation. Combinations of behavioural and experiential records can be powerfully recruited for mapping actual learning outcomes onto the criteria specified in the original PLC. Later in this chapter we illustrate this. These reflective activities will identify specific learning-to-learn tasks. Success at the learning-to-learn level allows the conversation to return to the tutorial level. The main learning activity then recommences.

As an approximate guide, three to five cycles of PLCs covering at least three to five topics and tasks, with at least three sorties into the learning-to-learn level, are essential for generating sufficient personal experiences for the learner to achieve effective, long-term change in learning skills. As this experience is developing, the Learning Coach needs to explore and comment and advise on the deeply personal mechanisms underlying the learner's 'meaning as modelling' activities (Chapters 1 and 2), to enable them to achieve greater awareness of how they set about to learn. Emerging from this joint negotiation, they together decide on the next round of exploration, and the tutorial conversation continues but with greater emphasis on the *patterns in sequences of PLC cycles as a whole*. The Learning Coach pays increasing attention to the learner's developing awareness of how he or she controls his or her own learning. The final aim of the Learning Conversation is that the processes which shape it become internalised by the learner, so that they can achieve a personal metamorphosis into a Self-Organised Learner, thus taking over most functions of the Learning Coach.

As the tutorial and learning-to-learn conversations continue to develop and greater awareness of the personal principles of causality involved in these endeavours is achieved, almost always the learner begins seriously to question the relevance of the tasks and topics being explored in his life's activities as a whole. This is when engagement in the life conversation becomes important. A second visit to the life conversation at this stage may be longer and more meaningful compared with that which took place when the Learning Conversation was initially launched (see p. 147). Specific techniques such as the repertory grid or the learning interview procedure (the Functional Taxonomy) will facilitate a deeper exploration of the significance of the task, topic or skill within the pattern of 'the job', 'the marriage', or 'the studentship' as a whole. Either the learner will perceive their relevance with deeper insight and will therefore continue along the same trajectory but with revitalised motiva- tion, or he or she may see their utter inappropriateness, in which case the learner may well decide to change the direction of his or her life's activities. Failure to appreciate the significance of the relationship between short-, medium- and longer-term goals usually leads to a general withdrawal of energy and to a more superficial and stagnant approach to life.

Each of the following statements:

'Why have I spent three years in the Royal Marines, when my one cherished wish is to become a stage manager?'

'Why have I spent five years in the technical branch, when what I really want to do is work with people?'

'I can't see the sense of staying at this tech – I'd like to start my own business now';

'There's nothing more I want from this job [as R & D director of a pharmaceutical company], I could open a restaurant or create an arboretum on my farm; either of these would satisfy me more';

'Till now management for me has been to do with productivity and cost-effectiveness; I'd like to start again and see it as to do with people';

'After fifteen years as a supervisor I begin to see how I could help others to learn to do their job better';

'I only enrolled on this course [an intense sixteen-week course as an air traffic controller] because I didn't want to be sent overseas';

'Having had three kids, now grown up, I thought I should take an Open University degree, but really all I wanted was a change in my life';

'I landed here studying chemistry, which I hate, because my parents wanted me to, but I don't know what I want from life' –

emerged from actual life conversations and led to decisions which either involved a continuation of existing activities with deeper intent, or to fundamental changes in lifestyle. Either way, the pattern of the Learning Conversation will change. Some will elect to expand their PLCs within their existing tasks, topics or skills in an endeavour to enhance their capacity to learn; others may, eventually, recommence their PLC activities but within the domains of their newly chosen lives.

The dynamics of the Learning Conversation as it shifts from level to level takes on a 'figure-of-eight' configuration, starting with a sortie into the life conversation, moving into the central tutorial conversation and then flowing through the learning-to-learn, life and tutorial levels, as the learner gradually evolves into a Self-Organised Learner (Figure 20a).

The PLC as an all-purpose vehicle

As a systematic means of implementing the tutorial conversation, a well-formulated procedure for its management has been developed (Figure 20b). Specific conversational heuristics enable the learner to plan, implement and retrospectively review his or her learning activities. These have been thoroughly tested out in a number of projects and as a consequence, elaborated and modified to meet specific requirements. These heuristics are

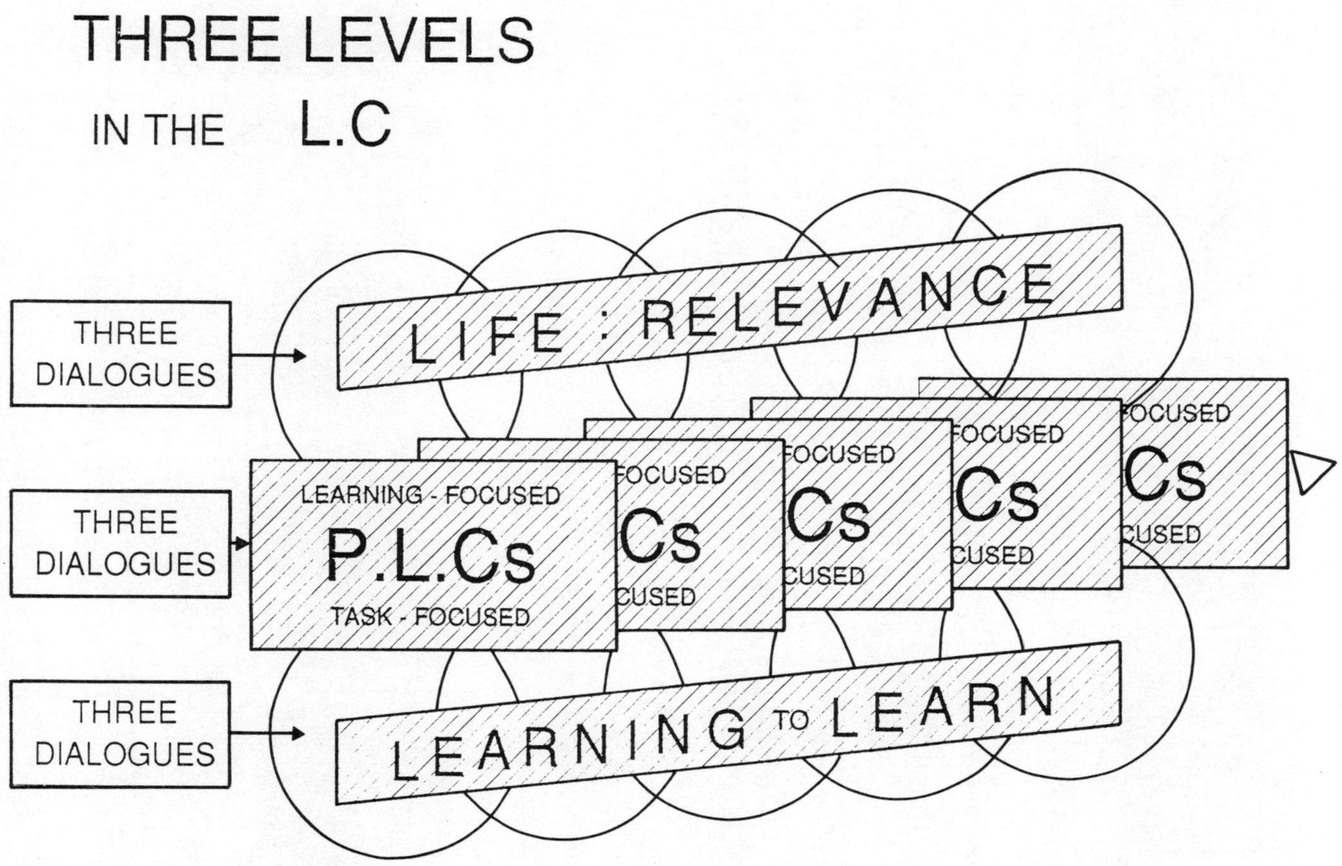

THREE LEVELS
IN THE L.C

Figure 20a The life–tutorial–learning-to-learn conversation

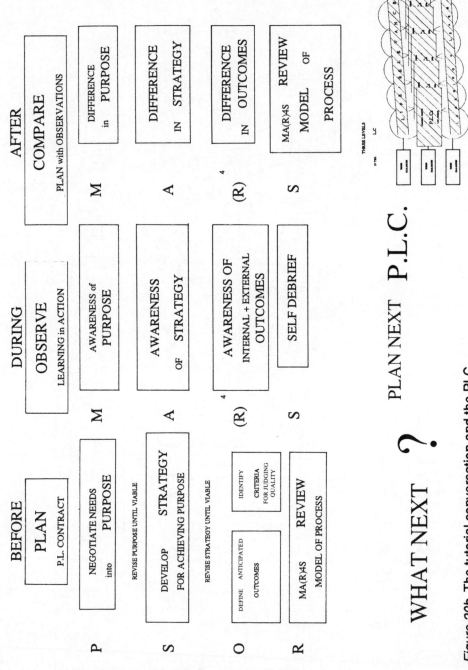

PERSONAL LEARNING CONTRACT

TASK - FOCUSED: LEARNING - FOCUSED

BEFORE	DURING	AFTER
PLAN	OBSERVE	COMPARE
P.L. CONTRACT	LEARNING in ACTION	PLAN with OBSERVATIONS

P — NEGOTIATE NEEDS into PURPOSE

M — AWARENESS of PURPOSE

M — DIFFERENCE in PURPOSE

REVISE PURPOSE UNTIL VIABLE

S — DEVELOP STRATEGY FOR ACHIEVING PURPOSE

A — AWARENESS OF STRATEGY

A — DIFFERENCE IN STRATEGY

REVISE STRATEGY UNTIL VIABLE

O — DEFINE ANTICIPATED OUTCOMES | IDENTIFY CRITERIA FOR JUDGING QUALITY

(R) — AWARENESS OF INTERNAL + EXTERNAL OUTCOMES

(R) — DIFFERENCE IN OUTCOMES

R — MA(R)4S REVIEW MODEL OF PROCESS

S — SELF DEBRIEF

S — MA(R)4S REVIEW MODEL OF PROCESS

WHAT NEXT ?   PLAN NEXT   P.L.C.

THREE LEVELS

Figure 20b The tutorial conversation and the PLC

all addressed within the PLC. This takes the form of paper and pencil procedures as well as the suite of computer programs called CHAT (Postscript).

Many potential Self-Organised Learners are unable to take on responsibility for their own learning, not because they do not wish to, but because they do not know how. The PLC is a conversational vehicle which supports them. It starts as a simple algorithm for identifying:

– *a topic*	T
– a *task* in relation to the topic	T
– specific *purposes* in relation to the task	P
– a *strategy* for achieving these purposes	S
– the anticipated and actual *outcome*	O
– criteria for *reviewing* the quality of the outcome	R
– and *reviewing* this cyclic process as a whole	R

Purposes, strategies and outcomes exist as part of a nesting set of intentions, behaviours and results. Purposes can be defined within a structure of overall purposes and related sub-purposes to give a hierarchy. As purposes become elaborated and implemented so strategies become organised hierarchically, and the outcomes – that is, personal meanings – take on the form of a hierarchy of structures of meaning. During this process of elaboration, refinement and experimentation it becomes possible to reflect upon and identify relevant resources for learning. As these are assessed, it becomes possible to plan and implement one or more alternative strategies for achieving specified purposes. This activity takes place within a given time structure. The PLC is thus a dynamic conversational vehicle for actualising this process of learning. It represents the core mechanism for driving the tutorial conversation which focuses on the operational aspects of learning.

By planning, carrying out and reviewing their learning in the framework offered by the PLC, individuals can develop their capacity to learn. There are essentially five main activities within the PLC:

1 negotiating a learning activity before the event;
2 carrying this out in an actual situation;
3 self-debrief of actions taken;
4 reviewing the PLC by retrospective comparison with (1);
5 self-diagnosis of learning strengths and weaknesses and planning a new cycle of PLC.

These represent the essential activities for enabling the learner to develop the constructive and creative levels of 'meaning as modelling' described in Chapter 1. It is this experience that enables him or her to monitor and control learning in personally relevant, significant and viable ways.

In its simplest form the PLC heuristic is illustrated in Figure 20c.

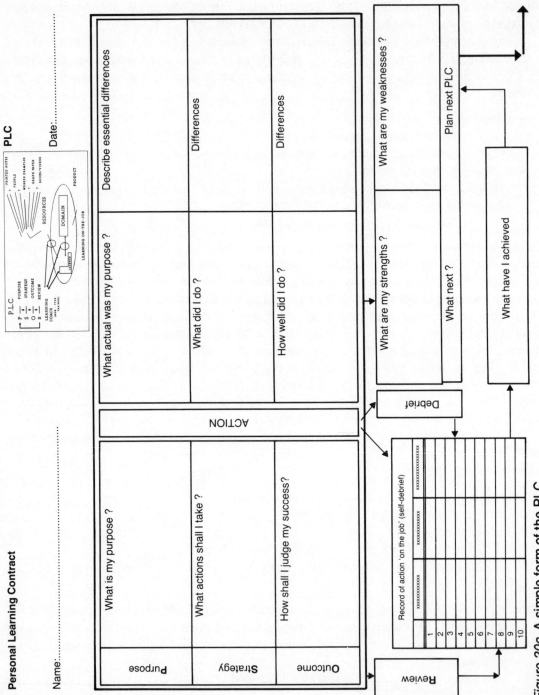

Figure 20c A simple form of the PLC

Let us briefly explain the purpose, strategy, outcome and review (PSOR) components of the PLC.

Purpose – P

People learn for different purposes. The possibilities are infinite. It is purpose which gives direction to the active intentionality which characterises us all as human beings. Strategies for the input and processing of our 'items of meaning' need to be varied according to our specific purposes. In order to be able to assess the effectiveness of our processing of the events in our world, we have to have some referent and that can only be against purpose. Thus reflection on process requires a clarification of purpose. This is the way to specificity, but it is not a once-and-for-all activity; it is in the very nature of learning that purposes can not be fully declared in advance. Reflecting on purpose therefore has elements of provisionality and will need updating during the reconstruction, reflection and reviewing process.

Strategy – S

In learning there are many potential strategies for each learner; this depends upon purpose and prior knowledge, experience, beliefs and prejudices. The person who operates with one monolithic strategy (for example, exclusively argumentative in discussion, highly critical in listening or totally receptive in reading), processes their world with 'tunnelled vision', and is unlikely to be flexible and innovative. The Self-Organised Learner varies their strategy appropriately. Learning style is a question of developing a repertoire of tactics and strategies to meet all personal needs in a flexible and creative way. The current fashion of 'profiling' learning style to select learning opportunities to suit the learner trades off short-term and limited gains against the immeasurably greater advantages of developing one's learning capacity.

Outcome – O

By 'outcome' we mean the results of learning. Broadly, learning outcomes can be defined as changes which take place in how we think, feel and act. In the end it is the outcome which provides the criteria for evaluating effectiveness. The Self-Organised Learner is self-critical and uses their own experiences of purposes and strategies as a test-bed for evaluating their effectiveness.

Review – R

Purpose affects strategy and is affected by it. Strategy produces outcome, and the outcome when related to purpose provides the criteria for measuring effectiveness. Together these components provide some key components of our language for conversing about process. Review extends more widely than against purpose; it involves an appraisal of the whole learning process.

We shall now proceed to illustrate how the PLC implements the *tutorial conversation* and, as appropriate, evolves into both *life* and *learning-to-learn conversations*, giving a 'figure-of-eight' dynamic flow to the whole process.

The PLC in action: the tutorial conversation with sorties into the life and learning-to-learn conversation

Students have used the PLC for reflecting on how they learn a practical type of activity; for instance laboratory experiments, building a model of a ship, an engine, or the genetic components of a virus, creating a sculpture, using a directions chart to familiarise themselves with a complex piece of apparatus or machine, producing a new play, or performing a new musical composition. They have also used it for reflecting on their learning of more academic tasks such as the preparation of essays or reports, making good personal notes, reading difficult texts demanding complex evaluative or summarising skills, listening effectively in lectures, using the seminar or tutorial situation as a medium for effective learning. Trainees in industry or the services have used the PLC to reflect on how they learn specific skills, either 'on the job' or on a simulator. Managers have used the PLC as a private reflective device for developing both technical and man-management skills. A group of managers have used it for developing their problem-solving skills and for brain-storming about long-term strategic planning. A group of university and polytechnic staff have used it as a means for reviewing the ways in which they have gone about restructuring their departments.

Let us illustrate a few of these activities in an attempt to convey the flavour of the PLC in action. We shall begin by developing further the reading example illustrated in the last chapter. As a complete contrast, our second example shows how the PLC has been used to enable trainee officers in the Royal Navy to learn some of the complex skills involved in ship command and control.

Example 1   Gwen, Rhiannon and reading-to-learn

Gwen

Gwen was an Open University Post Experience student pursuing the Reading Development course. She taught in a comprehensive school and had special responsibilities for the teaching of advanced reading. As her course tutor, one of the authors used the PLC to encourage her to reflect on her own repertoire of purposes for reading and to explore how she set about to read texts to achieve different purposes. After the initial life conversation in which the FOCUSed repertory grid was used to identify her 'natural' repertoire of reading purposes, it took five cycles of PLCs for Gwen to discover that basically *she only had one strategy for reading*. Reference to her FOCUSed grid confirmed this single-minded and monolithic approach to reading. Her nine constructs were remarkably un-differentiated. The majority of her responses showed that purposes for her own studies and for her work as a teacher were 'logical', to do with everyday reality, 'practical', 'factual', and 'instructive' and that on the whole she 'disliked' this type of reading. However, a small number of responses revealed that she did 'enjoy' reading for 'imagery', 'reflection', 'elucidate my own view', 'being creative' and 'to fantasise' but she did not read many texts with these purposes in mind nor did she associate any of these purposes with her work and her studies. She agreed that she should work on this.

In her later PLCs Gwen began to expand her choice of texts and to develop more creative purposes for reading. In the action stage of each PLC she used the Brunel Reading Recorder (Chapter 3) and through the 'process dialogue' she was aided to debrief herself about her reading tactics and strategies and how these related to her reading purposes. Although she thought she should try to 'read differently' for 'different purposes' every read record showed a similar pattern of reading behaviour. Figure 21 summarises her basic reading strategy.

Figure 21 Gwen's basic reading strategy

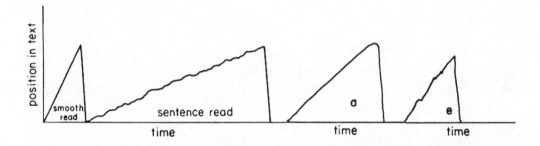

Quite simply, she used three types of reading tactics, combined in the same pattern for each reading strategy. 'Item' read meant that she processed the text in a linear sequence, and stopped at certain points 'to try and remember the bits'. According to the text, and her difficulties with it, items would sometimes be paragraphs, or even groups of paragraphs. 'Smooth' read meant that she was checking the whole text again and at the end she tried to recall it all. 'Check' read meant that she slowed down and hesitated at certain points in the text where she had experienced difficulties. She was able to explain this in the process dialogue of the Learning Conversation quite fluently. She did exhibit some awareness of tactics and strategy but this was not differentiated in relation to specific purposes.

Figure 22 Three types of reading strategy

A reading strategy found to be effective for summarising a difficult text

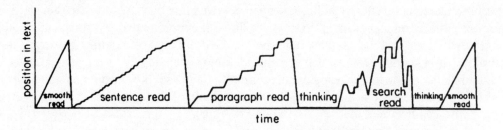

A reading strategy found to be effective for answering multiple-choice questions

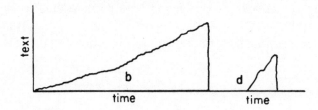

The search read strategy.

Life conversation   At the end of the fifth PLC the Learning Conversation was shifted once more into the life/relevance level, and talk-back using a record of personal meaning with the CHANGE grid procedure was used to explore how her repertoire of reading purposes was developing. This is explained in detail in our book *Self-Organised Learning*. One major discovery was that the expanding repertoire of reflective and creative purposes now involved much thought and were 'very difficult'. The read records in her PLCs showed she had no different strategy for achieving these types of purposes. This also correlated with her low grades in her own essays and tests. Yet, she was responsible for teaching advanced reading skills to young teenagers! This realisation shocked her considerably. The conversation was again shifted to the tutorial level and Gwen recommenced her PLC activities for a term and eagerly tried to complete eleven contracts quite fully. Gradually, she was able to build on her existing awareness, try out new reading tactics and explore how she could vary the pattern of these as she read a large variety of texts for different purposes, both in her own studies and in her work. This tutorial conversation became a real voyage of discovery for Gwen. Figure 22 illustrates three of her well-differentiated strategies for reading for different purposes.

Gwen introduced one new 'search' read into her repertoire of tactics and combined these differently in each of her strategies. Also, the time she took for reading the same size of text for different purposes had become much more varied and she had learned to read more flexibly and economically.

Not only did she considerably develop her capacity for using text as a resource for learning, but also subsequent evidence showed that she taught reading differently and that this had very significant effects on the quality of her pupils' reading.

Gwen was awarded a Grade 1 (top mark) in the Post Experience Reading Course. According to her the PLC tutorial conversations and the life conversation using talk-back based on the FOCUSed and CHANGE grid techniques had significantly contributed to her award. Gwen is no longer a teacher. She is running her own bookshop in a university town and on Saturday mornings is conducting her own master classes in reading. Each member of the tutorial group was offered similar opportunities for Learning Conversations. The OU examination results for this group showed a significantly higher distribution of Grades 1 and 2 than any other tutorial group in the country.

Rhiannon

Rhiannon's 'figure-of-eight' Learning Conversations took on a different form from Gwen's, although the basic discovery after the initial life-level conversation and the first round of PLCs was the same. Like Gwen, Rhiannon had very little awareness of her own repertoire of reading purposes nor of how different purposes influenced the ways she set about to read. 'Purpose' was something which was usually 'set by somebody else' and reading 'just happened' – or 'didn't happen when boredom took over'. Rhiannon had no idea at all how to evaluate her own outcomes of reading; this had always been done by somebody else. This was the tacit paradigm of reading which, as a teacher herself, she would pass on to her young pupils.

It took Rhiannon two terms and seventeen PLCs, with several sorties into the learning-to-learn conversation, before she really got to grips with the notion that purposeful reading was a complex skill requiring well-differentiated strategies.

Learning to learn   Unlike Gwen, Rhiannon's initial PLCs showed that her read records were totally undifferentiated. She read each text, for each purpose, in exactly the same way. This consisted of a long, unregulated and haphazard meandering through the text from the beginning to the end. It took her a long time. Process-based dialogues between Rhiannon and her tutor revealed that she had no concept for 'tactics' nor for what 'reading purpose' meant in operational terms. She even had difficulty in reading individual sentences if these were lengthy or grammatically complex.

Rhiannon chose some complex pieces of text from her course recommended reading list and these were copied onto the word processor so that the selected texts could be addressed by the Reading-to-Learn software. These were formatted so that her reading of individual words and phrases could be logged by the computer. She used a reading taxonomy developed by one of the authors and attempted to read different texts for different purposes. In Chapter 3, Example 1b, we illustrated some of Rhiannon's attempts.

Rhiannon's personal experiment at the learning-to-learn level, in which her basic reading skills were being challenged, reflected upon, re-explored and further developed, involved frequent engagements in the support dialogue. Often her results showed that she was getting worse: for example, she took longer to read, she couldn't remember what she had read, and she couldn't operationalise the reading purposes that she herself had chosen. Sometimes Rhiannon did not show up for her Learning Conversation sessions but she always reappeared later, offering some feeble excuse. This is one of the reasons why, in her case, it took two terms for her to build on her reading-to-learn skills. One particular supportive transaction revealed that she had been 'laughed at in school for making mistakes when she was asked to read out loud'. When her tutor, acting as her Learning Coach, confessed that the same thing had happened to her, it was a turning-point in her learning, and once more Rhiannon's energies were guided into the process dialogue towards exploring and reflecting upon her reading skills. Another supportive transaction revealed she still 'read out loud silently in her head' despite previous attempts to 'get rid of this'. She also lamented the fact that no one had ever talked to her about her reading skills, which were obviously handicapping her learning.

Learning to read had consisted of choosing a book, reading out loud, being corrected for her pronunciation and fluency and listening to others reading out loud. In a subsequent 'self-debrief' (process-based dialogue) she discovered that the only strategy she appeared to use in reading was the 'read out loud in my head' method; that is, word by word or phrase by phrase in a linear sequence. Then as part of a later support dialogue she said that 'there must be lots of teachers like me, with a reading handicap'. One supportive move introduced by her Learning Coach involved getting the whole tutorial group together to exchange these awareness-raising experiences, and Rhiannon quickly found she was not alone. Gently but firmly Rhiannon was encouraged to go on defining new purposes, inventing her own reading tactics and combining these in ways which, based on her own criteria, would lead to effective strategies. All this took place at the detailed sentence level of text organisation referred to in Example 1b in Chapter 3.

Gradually, in several sequences of referent dialogues, she was asked to justify her sentence-reading strategies in terms of the different kinds of outcomes she was achieving. She began to talk about the quality of reading and how she could begin to assess this for herself. She identified some literature on 'evaluation skills' and, together with some of her peers, began to discuss and exchange ideas on this. The group used the flow diagram technique (the Functional Taxonomy) as one method to help them explore and identify criteria for the evaluation of reading comprehension.

Eventually, after many learning-to-learn sorties involving a detailed exploration of individual sentences, with many intense self-debrief sessions, Rhiannon emerged to continue her larger-scale reading-to-learn experiments at the tutorial level. She completed several PLCs and tackled many articles and chapters in her attempt to build on her newly acquired awareness of reading as a complete skill.

For Rhiannon, this was her first experience of a 'language of learning awareness' and she became very enthusiastic about exploring how she could use the PLC method with her own pupils. She went on to comment that in offering 'language experience' and 'experience exchange' in the classroom, she would have to think further about 'what variety of language', 'what type of experience', and 'what form of exchange'. In meeting this challenge, as a teacher herself she would try different ways of using PLCs to elevate the quality of her classroom transactions so that her pupils could be enabled to get a 'metaview' of what personal learning was about.

At the end of her OU Post Experience year she no longer saw working with books as 'just reading'. She saw this as a 'search', 'developing my own view' and 'inferring relationships', 'appreciating style' and 'reading for facts'. As with Gwen, Rhiannon also decided to leave schoolteaching. She went on to do a Ph.D. in Human Learning and is now head of a university education department with special responsibility for developing short courses in S-O-L for adults in continuing education.

Example 2   Learning HUNKS

In our first example we have tried to illustrate a *learning-focused* Learning Conversation based on reading-to-learn as a complex skill. To illustrate the generality of the PLC and the Learning Conversation approach we shall now describe how a computer-driven simulator can be used, not just for routine practice, but as a vehicle for exploration of a *task-focused* Learning Conversation. The example chosen shows how 'trainee officers' develop their learning skills as they set about to learn a complex task involving command and control.

In this second example, the PLC is addressed by the CSHL-CHAT software and it was used as a 'learning shell' around a war game, guiding the learner's exploration of the simulated task (the Functional Taxonomy). The simulator addresses 'HUNKS', a war game, and the trainee Naval officers were using this to explore their tactical skills of ship command and control. Thus, the learner/machine interface consisted of the HUNKS keyboard and screen and the CHAT keyboard and screen used as a conversational aid for learning HUNKS. The Learning Coach (in this case both of the authors) guided the machine-based Learning Conversation when 'human' support was requested by the learner. The example has been grossly simplified for purposes of illustration.

Let us start by presenting one example of Dave and Tony, well into the third and fourth cycles of their PLCs (Table 1). Both are examples of a task-focused Learning Conversation.

Table 2 presents one early example of Dave's task-focused PLC and illustrates its rudimentary form in contrast to his later PLC (Table 1).

Table 3 presents one example of a *learning-focused* PLC produced by Tony.

This is also in a rudimentary form. When a new and complex task is being learnt, it takes many cycles of PLCs at the *task-focused* level before the learner can shift awareness sufficiently to begin to recognise a truly *learning-focused* conversation. In our project, trainee officers reported that this shift in insight did not take place until a long and intensive exploration had been completed. It is perhaps an axiom of any research that one must first produce the phenomenon and be able to reproduce it before one can systematically investigate how to increase the amount of it and achieve this more quickly and effectively. What is true of scientific research is equally true for the Self-Organised Learner researching his or her own learning processes. The early examples of the task-focused and the rudimentary example of the learning focused PLC illustrate this evolving process.

In this example we have shown the prospective negotiation and retrospective review stages of the PLC. The richness of the action and self-debrief stages of the PLC are illustrated in the Functional Taxonomy (p. 259). Dave's comments as he learned to play the game and both Dave and Tony's self-debriefs are also presented in the Functional Taxonomy of Tools (p. 259).

The life conversation was activated many times in between the numerous task-focused PLCs. Much of this involved recruiting past experiences into the war game and exploring the relevance of these game experiences for their on-the-job naval defence activities. Tony began to talk about the game as a simulation of 'real war'. Referring to the Falklands he began to think about the commanders responsible for the safety of the ships and the men under his command. This way of reflecting led him to rethink the balance of priorities on which his PLCs had been based. He also reflected on his young years before joining the Royal Navy when, as a hippie in India, he had become apprenticed for two years to a Zen priest. He began to rethink his PLCs within a more 'humanistic' mode.

He reported that later, when he had been an education student, he had found academic psychology very different from this more 'humanistic' life experience. In fact he described his own approach to academic learning as 'mathematical', 'formal' – in keeping with the ways 'he had been taught and instructed'. In the life conversation he reflected that he had quite intuitively classified the humanistic Zen type of experience as incompatible with learning. In the developing life conversation Tony went on to consider the idea of learning as *humanistic but also as systematic and scientific*. He began to see how he could construct a working bridge between these two separate areas of personal experience. He began to consider how he himself could learn in a more humanistic way. Tony eventually became an instructor himself and developed high-powered learning techniques of his own as his career progressed. Our management of this life conversation moved into the constructive and creative levels of reflection upon personal processes (Chapter 1). Tony's example

Table 1 Dave and Tony's task-focused PLCs

Topic before Discover enemy submarines	*Topic redefined in light of experience* Discover and locate enemy submarines.
Purpose before To detect enemy submarines	*Purpose redefined in light of experience* To detect enemy submarines in relation to my submarines' positions and estimate their speed and direction.

Strategy before
Use skills to understand how I
and the enemy move. Also use
sonar device
	Strategy defined in light of experience
	To develop skills whereby I can work out the position, speed
	and direction of the enemy submarines.
	These skills include:
	(1) Knowledge of how submarines move;
	(2) Inner skills of logically thinking things out using all the
	    information I have – both from earlier moves and current
	    moves;
	(3) Thinking things out in advance, checking the implications of
	    new information and pursuing this only as far as time allows
	    so that I do not miss inputting any necessary commands;
	(4) Understand the full implications of all the 'rules';
	(5) To formulate this strategy in terms that make it more
	    general, more precise and more easily used.

Outcome before To know the positions of the enemy submarines	*Outcome redefined in light of experience* To understand the strategy for finding and locating enemy submarines. Use the strategy to find submarines.

Criteria before
How quickly and accurately do I
locate the enemy submarines?
	Criteria redefined in light of experience
	(1) Increased confidence in using my strategy.
	(2) Check exactly how quickly and accurately I located the
	    enemy submarines by careful inspection during replay.
	(3) More relaxed but alert while playing the game.
	(4) I miss fewer submarines (hopefully I find all three)
	(5) Use all the knowledge I have acquired so far, make no
	    mistakes and go on applying it in subsequent games.
	(6) Rapidly improve my defensive strategy in subsequent
	    games.

No. resources identified before	*Resources recognised in light of experience* The games booklet, files of previous games, file of this game. My ability to carefully check these files and identify my mistakes. Use people around as resources. Reflect as I play the game thus using the game as a resource.

Table 1 continued

Topic before Test out two variations on my earlier naive attempt to intercept the enemy	*Topic redefined in light of experience* Test out three strategy variations on my earlier naive attempt to intercept the enemy.
Purpose before To see if holding a static array of my submarines increases my kill rate	*Purpose redefined in light of experience* To see if scanning across the screen slowly improves detection and possible hits.
Strategy before Move submarines in triangular array and then move appropriately when a detection happens so as to get more accurate bearings	*Strategy redefined in light of experience* As before – plus carefully calculate when to rely on sonar and when to use missiles.
Revised strategy before *(after doing hierarchy)* Move submarines into shallow triangular array.Move array (E/W) back and fore at speed 1 to increase chances of detection. On detection move one non-detecting submarine to get another bearing. Deploy third submarine to cover.Use missiles as detection device (3x3)	
Outcome before *Make fewer initial moves.* Move to pick up first detected enemy submarine with two of our own submarines at East.	*Outcome redefined in light of experience* Three phases of action: (1) Grouping into array; (2) Scanning array across screen until detection is achieved; (3) Attempt to sink enemy.
Criteria before If I get a double bearing and I manage to kill an enemy submarine.	*Criteria redefined in light of experience* Making two good passive detections (including double bearing) and making one or more near kills.

Table 2 Dave's early version of a task-focused PLC

Task
Defend my country

Topic
Strategies of defence

Purpose
To defend own land and to defend own ships as a force

Strategy
Optimally position all my ships, keeping in mind main purpose
Use 2 ships to stay back
Use 1 ship in attack mode

Outcome
Successful; destroy attacking force
All ships would be protected, but would sacrifice- if necessary

Criteria
Maximum sphere of influence
No ships lost to achieve aims
Greatest good for greatest number
Least harm

Table 3 Tony's early version of a learning-focused PLC

Task
Improve my learning skills

Topic
Play *Hunks* to become aware of how I learn it

Purpose
To reflect upon and improve my learning skills

Strategy
To improve my assessment of distances and my judgement in moving and firing: and to do this by systematically trying out different methods of learning and immediately checking the effectiveness of my learning from the replay files. One method that I know I use is blind practice, another is trial and error

Outcome
Accelerating improvement in my assessment of distance and more accurate moving and firing. Better learning of subsequent *Hunks* skills, by having identified a wider range of learning

Criteria
Ability to learn better and more quickly in the future by knowing my learning skills and when and how to use them

shows how PLCs, whilst being the vehicle for a tutorial Learning Conversation, can flow relevantly and coherently into the life conversation, with the double advantage of improving the quality of the learning and also fundamentally influencing the individual's progress in later life. It also illustrates how a man/machine system which addresses some aspects of the Learning Conversation, when supported by a Learning Coach, can be an effective tool for Self-Organised Learning.

In the Appendix at the end of this chapter, without further comment, we offer some more examples of PLCs. Table 4 illustrates how the paper and pencil form of the PLC has been used by supervisors in letter sorting offices of the Post Office. Tables 5 and 6 are presented in the form of computer print-outs from the CSHL-CHAT software. One shows a sixth-former using the PLC for learning about the topic of microbiology. The other shows a manager using the PLC for reflecting on man-management skills.

The conversational 'figure-of-eight' and the development of our capacity to learn

Learners often remark upon how revealing and rewarding the PLC (that is, tutorial Learning Conversation) can be. But the tangible evidence, the completed personal contract forms, the personal notes, or in the case of the CHAT software the printouts, seem to be only a partial record of what has taken place. Despite all the power and precision of the PLC in articulating a strategic, process-based conversation, and despite the care and sensitivity of the Learning Coach in the use of the talk-back procedures based on records of the learner's experience and action, much of what is most useful happens in the *conversational process itself*. It is not recorded in what remains. The inner psychological processes provoked by the PLC remain unrevealed in the overt exchanges. This *inner process* often illuminates the hidden power of the reflective learning technology described in the Functional Taxonomy of Tools. It is the resource from which the learner feeds the external Learning Conversation (Chapter 2).

It is within the very nature of the conversational process (as we have argued in the General Introduction and in Part I) that this conversation remains incomplete, much of its language is non-verbal, and the second deeper contributor to it usually takes very little part in the conscious reconstruction. But it is this deeper level which pulses with change: significant changes which reveal themselves later as new perceptions, insights, expectations and ways of behaving. *It is through tapping the inner resource at this deep level that the learner's capacity to learn can be significantly enhanced.*

In this chapter we have attempted to show how the PLC, augmented by the three dialogues fundamental to the Learning Conversation – process reflection, support through the troughs of learning, and referents for evaluating competence – recruiting specific behavioural and experiential records as tools for enhancing awareness, can challenge personal robots and facilitates the development of learning competence. Supported by the Learning Coach, a conversational technology functions for the achievement of the active, meaning-building, event-anticipating processes of learning.

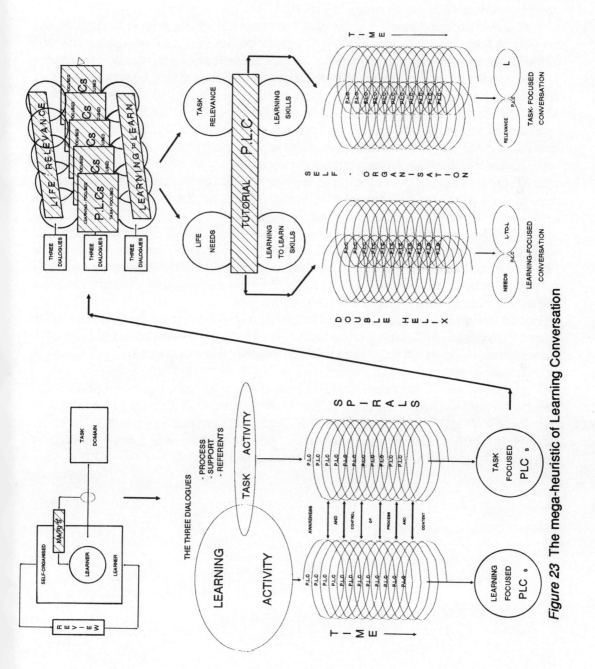

Figure 23 The mega-heuristic of Learning Conversation

We can now begin to see the power of the Learning Conversation as a whole in facilitating the development of Self-Organised Learning. The ultimate psychological encounter is the learner's conversations with him- or herself. This is what is meant by *internalising the Learning Conversation*. It facilitates a Godel-type awareness and understanding of personal processes, which can lead to an enhancement of skill, competence and creativity (Prospective Commentary to Part II).

We have also attempted to show that the movements between tutorial, life and learning-to-learn levels in the Learning Conversation are not to be treated as 'one-off' events but as an evolving, 'figure-of-eight', spiralling conversational process. Its extension in time, space and quality (General Introduction) will bootstrap the conversation into a continuous spiralling activity (Chapter 2) which can be fuelled by the process of MA(R)4S. The core *tutorial conversation* leads to reflection and self-diagnosis of processes of learning a task or topic and processes of learning about learning. This leads into the *life* and *learning-to-learn conversation*. It is the dynamic tension between the *task-focused* and *learning-focused* tutorial conversations as these develop and between the tutorial conversation and either the life or learning-to-learn conversation as these develop, that imparts a power for facilitating Self-Organised Learning. *The Learning Conversation as a whole represents the mega-heuristic through which the spiralling double helix of task-focused and learning-focused conversations are created, set into motion and maintained.* By analogy, the paired bases of the 'learning code' are constructed by the Self-Organised Learner in the form of bipolar constructs within their developing system of meanings, as they free themselves from the 'order' and status quo of educational, social and even genetic control. Figure 23 illustrates this.

Part III describes how the Learning Conversation can be systematically organised to form a Self-Organised Learning environment. It introduces 'Systems 7' as a vehicle for conversational support not only for individuals, but for groups and whole organisations to explore their learning.

The 'Functional Taxonomy' builds on the notion of learning as modelling the construction of meaning introduced in Part I, the heuristics of Learning Conversations introduced in Part II, and the Systems 7 Self-Organised Learning environment in Part III to explain further and to exemplify how the 'conversational tools' facilitate a self-sustaining growth in learning skill, competence and creativity.

Appendix
Table 4 Example 3 – PLCs of two supervisors in the Post Office

Personal Learning Contract (PLC)

Name: A.G...............................   Date:...............

	What is my purpose?	*What actual was my purpose?*	*Describe essential differences*
Purpose	To ensure that 1st & 2nd letter & pkt traffic reaches all depts as quickly as possible	To see that as well that mail is transferred quickly – all non-essential traffic, i.e. vans no longer needed are removed from yard, to reduce fumes and make the area a safer and cleaner place to work	At collection time up to 20.30,vehicles needed to be in yard/loading bay. It's essential to have a quick turn round for drivers on another collection to be unloaded with the minimum amount of delay without losing the safety element
	What actions shall I take?	*What did I do?*	*Differences*
Strategy	Start of duty making sure non-essential vehicles are removed, yard is free from rubbish & anything liable to cause accidents	Using the 2 postal drivers at my disposal I cleared the Y/LB of non-essential traffic. With the aid of cleaning staff made the Y/LB free from used skips, empty mail sacks, trolleys	The Y/LB became a safer place to work in with less fumes & more room for extra large vehicles, i.e. PCO 40 trailer & Crowcastle 40 Watford, etc.
	How shall I judge my success?	*How well did I do?*	*Differences*
Outcome	By the continual flow of mail both inward & outward and by assuring drivers of the shortest turn round time	95% of all collections were turned round within 5 minutes of arrival. 5% time lost on security I/C Group 4 having to lock main doors for up to 30 minutes at a time. No major upset, no accidents	No long-term hold up of mails. Having the right staff for the right job at the right time
		What are my strengths?	*What are my weaknesses?*
		Confidence in my ability to foresee possible jams in my system. Having staff on hand to despatch bulk mail drops, move non-essential vehicles. Ability to spot potential safety hazards	Not having an extra pair of eyes to watch yard area as well as loading bay as this caused slight problems during xmas period

Table 4 Example 3 *continued*

Personal Learning Contract (PLC)

Name ..B.W......... 　　　　　　　　　　　　　　　　　　 Date ....

	What is my purpose?	What actual was my purpose?	Describe the essential differences
Purpose	To run the station efficiently	To be able to cope with staff who are not always within your grasp or sight	A regular walk around the platforms is a good guide to how the station is running. You can spot any problem building up
	What actions shall I take?	*What did I do?*	*Differences*
Strategy	Check for correct amount of PHGs and postmen on duties	Checked duty – O/T sheets – diary and daily railway time changes	Be ready for alternative outlets when large carriers, PPTs are cancelled. Also last minute platform changes
	How shall I judge my success?	*How well did I do?*	*Differences*
Outcome	If the station was run efficiently without too many problems not having PHGs staff moved too many times from their normal duties	Apart from a change of a PPT from platform 10 to 3 which was overcome – the staff were moved to a minimum. The purpose I set out to do was achieved	You must judge when a situation is or will be arising that you will not be able to cope with your normal staff and how many extra staff you will need and for how long
		What are my strengths? To be able to handle the unexpected situation	*What are my weaknesses?* Not knowing all the staff by their surnames

Table 5 Example 4 – a sixth-former's PLC

Name....
Task....Essay – Genetic code

——————— Before ————————

These are the descriptions of your learning contract which you gave before you started the task.

Topic

```
┌──────── Topic ────────┐
│  The rules about      │
│  how the genes        │
│  control the cell     │
└───────────────────────┘
```

Purpose

```
┌──────── Purpose ──────┐
│  To understand        │
│  and  remember all    │
│  details about how    │
│  the code works       │
└───────────────────────┘
```

Strategy

```
┌──────── Strategy ─────┐
│  Go over class notes – │
│  read articles by Crick │
│  and Watson and scan   │
│  the double helix      │
└───────────────────────┘
```

Outcome

```
┌──────── Outcome ──────┐
│  Lots of notes –      │
│  a good plan          │
│  and the final essay  │
└───────────────────────┘
```

Criteria

```
┌──────────── Criteria ────────┐
│  Notes with key points        │
│  underlined well-structured   │
│  essay and being able to      │
│  remember the principles      │
│  in a week's time             │
└───────────────────────────────┘
```

Name....
Task....Essay – Genetic code

——————— Before ————————

These are the descriptions of your learning resources which you gave before you started the task.

```
┌──────── Resources ────────┐
│  Handouts; class notes;    │
│  *Scientific American;*    │
│  my memory;                │
│  and my girl               │
└────────────────────────────┘
```

```
┌──────── Resources ────────┐
│  3D model of DNA;          │
│  microfiche; BBC tapes;    │
│  Nick's essay on nucleic   │
│  acids; try to remember    │
│  school visit to science   │
│  museum                    │
└────────────────────────────┘
```

Name....
Task....Essay – Genetic code
———————— Before ————————

These are descriptions of your topic hierarchy which you gave before you started the task.

——————— Topic ———————
The rules about how the genes control the cell

——————— Context ———————
To cover microbiology part of the A level syllabus, if I can, very well

——————— Sub-section 1 ———————
Double helix

——————— Sub-section 2 ———————
DNA chemistry

——————— Sub-section 3 ———————
Order of bases

——————— Sub-section 4 ———————
Code sequence

Name....
Task....Essay – Genetic code
———————— Before ————————

These are descriptions of your purpose hierarchy which you gave before you started the task.

——————— Purpose ———————
To understand and remember all details about how the code works

——————— Context ———————
To be able to answer exam questions well

——————— Sub-section 1 ———————
To appreciate problem

——————— Sub-section 2 ———————
List my difficulties

——————— Sub-section 3 ———————
Keep record of references

Name....
Task....Essay – Genetic code

──────── Before ────────

These are the descriptions of your strategy hierarchy which you gave before you started the task.

┌──────── Strategy────────┐
│ Go over class notes – read articles by │
│ Crick and Watson and scan the double │
│ helix │
└─────────────────────────┘

┌──────── Context ────────┐
│ Plan my time schedule │
└─────────────────────────┘

┌──────── Sub-section 1 ────────┐
│ Reflect on what I know │
└───────────────────────────────┘

┌──────── Sub-section 2────────┐
│ Read selectively │
└──────────────────────────────┘

┌──────── Sub-section 3 ────────┐
│ Search for core points │
└───────────────────────────────┘

┌──────── Sub-section 4 ────────┐
│ Check with Mike if I don't │
│ understand │
└───────────────────────────────┘

┌──────── Sub-section 5 ────────┐
│ Memorise arguments til I │
│ really know them │
└───────────────────────────────┘

Name....
Task....Essay – Genetic code

──────── Before ────────

Revised Contract

These are the descriptions of your learning contract which you gave before you started the task.

Topic

┌──────── Topic ────────┐
│ The rules about how the genes │
│ control the cell │
└───────────────────────┘

Purposes

┌──────── Purposes ────────┐
│ To appreciate the problem; capture the │
│ excitement; to understand how the │
│ code works; to remember all the │
│ details; list the sources for the future; │
│ reflect on my difficulties │
└──────────────────────────┘

Strategies

┌──────── Strategies────────┐
│ Find out what I know; history – │
│ importance of, sleep on it, search for │
│ core points – note these; select some │
│ details – note logically; list rules – │
│ memorise; check with Mick │
└───────────────────────────┘

Outcome

┌──────── Outcome ────────┐
│ Good background information; know │
│ how the cell works; how protein is │
│ made; know techniques; draw model; │
│ 3-level notes on topic and produce an │
│ original essay │
└─────────────────────────┘

Criteria

┌──────── Criteria ────────┐
│ Notes with key points underlined, well-│
│ structured essay and being able to │
│ remember the principles in a week's │
│ time │
└──────────────────────────┘

Name....

Task....to review the total learning contract activity for review – essay – Genetic code

Review of your learning contract

These are the definitions which you gave for each
component before and after tackling the task.

——————— Before ——————————————————— After ———————

Topic
The rules about how the genes control
the cell

Topic
The same but add background
knowledge and implications for
bio-engineering

Purposes
To appreciate the problem; to capture the
excitement; to understand how the code
works; to remember all the details; list
the sources for the future; reflect
on my difficulties

Purposes
The same: but add who are the current
experts; what's hard fact and supported
by experiment; what's still in doubt; find
out more about how I learn

Strategies
Find out what I know; history – importance
of, sleep on it; search for core points –
note these; select some details – note;
logically list rules – memorise; check with
Mick

Strategies
The same: plus work out methods for
memorising; sort out messy notes; create
some system; pester people more;
relax and enjoy it more

Outcome
Good background information; know how
the cell works; how protein is made; know
techniques; draw model; 3-level notes on
topic and produce an original essay

Outcome
The same; plus make a real model – and
play with it – more important than notes

Criteria
How involved I am; can I explain/teach
someone else like Pam? Assess
relevance to industry; imagine significance
to health; how well I managed

Criteria
Notes with key points underlined, well-
structured essay and being able to
remember the principles in a week's time

What have you learnt about setting up contracts?

What have you learnt about yourself as a learner?

Comments:

Use this to plan what you do next.

Compare the task resources given

———————— Before ——————————————————— After ———————

┌—— Resources ——┐
│ Handouts; class notes;
│ *Scientific American*;
│ my memory
│ and my girl
└————————————————┘

————————————— Not defined ———————————

┌—— Resources ——————————┐
│ 3D model of DNA; microfiche; BBC
│ Tapes; Nick's essay on nucleic
│ acids; try to remember school visit
│ to science museum
└————————————————————————————————┘

Reflect on why you did not complete this

Comments:

Compare your before and after lists. Reflect on the nature of any differences.
How will you assess your resource needs next time?

Comments:

This is a comparison of topic hierarchies.

———————— Before ———————————————————— After ———————

┌—— Context ——┐
│ To cover microbiology part, if I can very
│ well, of the A level syllabus
└——————————————————————————┘

————————————— Not defined ———————————

┌—— Sub-section 1 ——┐
│ Double helix
└————————————————————┘

┌—— Sub-section 2 ——┐
│ DNA chemistry
└————————————————————┘

```
┌──── Sub-section 3 ────┐
│ Order of bases        │
└───────────────────────┘
```

```
┌──── Sub-section 4 ────┐
│ Code sequence         │
└───────────────────────┘
```

Reflect on why you did not complete this.

Comments:

How did constructing your hierarchy help you to refine,
elaborate and revise your topic definition?

Comments:

This is a comparison of purpose hierarchies.

──────── Before ────────   ──── After ────

```
┌──────── Context ────────┐          ──── Not defined ────
│ To be able to answer exam questions well │
└─────────────────────────┘
```

```
┌──── Sub-section 1 ────┐
│ To appreciate problem │
└───────────────────────┘
```

```
┌──── Sub-section 2 ────┐
│ List my difficulties  │
└───────────────────────┘
```

```
┌──── Sub-section 3 ────┐
│ Keep record of references │
└───────────────────────┘
```

Reflect on why you did not complete this.

Comments:

How did constructing your hierarchy help you to refine,
elaborate and revise your purpose definition?

Comments:

This is a comparison of the strategy hierarchies.

———————— Before ————————————————— After ————————

—————— Context ——————
| Plan my time schedule |

——————— Not defined ———————

—— Sub-section 1——
| Reflect on what I know |

—— Sub-section 2 ——
| Read selectively |

—— Sub-section 3——
| Order of bases |

—— Sub-section 4 ——
| Check with Mike if I don't understand |

—— Sub-section 5 ——
| Memorise arguments till I really know them |

Reflect on why you did not complete this.

Comments:

How did constructing your hierarchy help you to refine, elaborate and revise your strategy definition?

Comments:

| This helped, but I need to dig much deeper into this – particularly about how my strategy operationalises my purposes |

This is a comparison of the outcome hierarchies.

———————— Before ————————————————————— After ————————

———————— Not defined ———————————— ———————— Not defined ————————

Reflect on why you did not attempt this.

Comments:

This is a comparison of the criteria hierarchies.

———————— Before ————————————————————— After ————————

Reflect on why you did not attempt this.

Comments:

> I need more experience in tackling
> PLCs – I find it difficult to elaborate
> my outcome expectations

Name....
Task....Review – Essay – Genetic code

———————— After ————————

Revision

These are the descriptions of your learning
resources which you gave after you finished
the task.

———————— Resources ————————

> More or less as before and what I knew
> already; newspaper report on Crick's Nobel
> prize; chatting on the phone to a research
> specialist my mum knew

Revision

Name....
Task....Review – Essay – Genetic code

――――――― After ―――――――   ――――――― After ―――――――

These are the descriptions of your purpose hierarchy which you gave after you finished the task.

――――― Purposes ―――――
The same: but add who are the current experts; what's hard fact and supported by experiment; what's still in doubt; find out more about how I learn

―――Context―――
The same

――― Sub-section 1―――
Compare my understanding with Susie

――― Sub-section 2 ―――
What's very new?

――― Sub-section 3 ―――
What's still in doubt

――― Sub-section 4 ―――
The rest the same as before and carefully plan my learning

These are the descriptions of your strategy hierarchy which you gave after you finished the task.

――――― Strategies ―――――
The same: plus work out methods for memorising; sort out messy notes; create some system; pester people more; relax and enjoy it more

――― Context ―――
More or less the same

――― Sub-section 1―――
Draw a coloured model and play with it

――― Sub-section 2 ―――
Make index for notes

――― Sub-section 3 ―――
Face up to my feelings of worry and insecurity

――― Sub-section 4 ―――
Push myself to talk to the experts, if I get a chance

――― Sub-section 5 ―――
Use my initiative more

――― Sub-section 6 ―――
Laugh if things go wrong but try again

――― Sub-section 7 ―――
Fight harder against distractions; get my priorities right

Revision

Name....
Task....Review – Essay – Genetic code

_____ After_____

These are the descriptions of your criteria hierarchy which you gave after you finished the task.

┌──────── Criteria ────────┐
How involved I am; can I explain/teach someone else like Pam? Assess relevance to industry; imagine significance to health; how well I managed
└──────────────────────────┘

┌──────── Context ────────┐
OK
└─────────────────────────┘

┌──────── Sub-section 1 ────────┐
Good feeling inside
└───────────────────────────────┘

┌──────── Sub-section 2 ────────┐
Make absolutely sure I understand – not a criterion?
└───────────────────────────────┘

┌──────── Sub-section 3 ────────┐
Notes are well organised as maps and keys to underlinings
└───────────────────────────────┘

┌──────── Sub-section 4 ────────┐
Remember weeks later
└───────────────────────────────┘

┌──────── Sub-section 5 ────────┐
Can imagine model of DNA and how RNA and amino acid sequences link
└───────────────────────────────┘

┌──────── Sub-section 6 ────────┐
How well did I cope with learning problems?
└───────────────────────────────┘

┌──────── Sub-section 7 ────────┐
Distinguish between hypothesis and fact
└───────────────────────────────┘

┌──────── Sub-section 8 ────────┐
Draw a good flow plan of my essay
└───────────────────────────────┘

┌──────── Sub-section 9 ────────┐
That the mark I give my essay tallies with what I actually get
└───────────────────────────────┘

Review of purpose, strategy and outcome and your learning contract activities.

How well did the 'outcome' of your learning capture your purposes?

Comments:

How well did your 'criteria' allow you to assess
the outcomes of your learning contract?

Comments:

How effectively did your 'strategies' enable you to translate
your purposes into successful learning?

Comments:

How well did your 'purposes' describe what you wanted
your learning activity to achieve?

Comments:

How effectively did you select and use your resources?

Comments:

What have you learnt about defining a learning contract?

Comments:

Review your strengths and weaknesses as a learner!

Comments:

How would you tackle a similar learning task next time?

Comments:

> My strategies need sharpening; my criteria
> gave me a good feel on the whole; I ought to
> think more about my purposes in future; I
> have a lot to learn about how I tackle learning
> but I am trying to use my initiative more and I
> am trying to work more confidently

Table 6 Example 5 – a manager's PLC

Name....
Task....managing

─────── Before ───────

These are the descriptions of your learning contract which you gave before you started the task.

Topic

```
┌──────── Topic ────────┐
│ The skills of managing people at    │
│ work and at home                    │
└─────────────────────────────────────┘
```

Purpose

```
┌──────── Purpose ────────┐
│ To cope better with living          │
└─────────────────────────────────────┘
```

Strategy

```
┌──────── Strategy ────────┐
│ By observing myself and others      │
└─────────────────────────────────────┘
```

Outcome

```
┌──────── Outcome ────────┐
│ Less tension and more creative work │
└─────────────────────────────────────┘
```

```
┌──────── Criteria ────────┐
│ People in my life will be friendlier, │
│ more creative and happier – more open │
└───────────────────────────────────────┘
```

Name....
Task....managing

─────── Before ───────

These are the descriptions of your learning resources which you gave before you started the task.

```
┌──────── Resource ────────┐
│ Colleagues                          │
└─────────────────────────────────────┘
```

```
┌──────── Resource ────────┐
│ Members of my family                │
└─────────────────────────────────────┘
```

```
┌──────── Resource ────────┐
│ My students and my clients          │
└─────────────────────────────────────┘
```

```
┌──────── Resource ────────┐
│ Direct experience of running courses │
│ on this topic and of managing        │
│ my own staff                         │
└──────────────────────────────────────┘
```

```
┌──────── Resource ────────┐
│ Experts I know                      │
└─────────────────────────────────────┘
```

Name....
Task....Managing

─────── Before ───────

These are the descriptions of your topic hierarchy which you gave before you started the task.

```
┌──────── Topic ────────┐
│ The skills of managing people at work │
│ and at home                           │
└───────────────────────────────────────┘
```

```
┌──────── Context ────────┐
│ An exploration of what management      │
│ ought to be about, without a political bias │
└────────────────────────────────────────┘
```

Name....Demonstration
Task....Managing

─────── Before ───────

These are the descriptions of your purpose hierarchy which you gave before you started the task.

```
┌──────── Purpose ────────┐
│ To cope better with living          │
└─────────────────────────────────────┘
```

```
┌──────── Context ────────┐
│ To develop a personal model of      │
│ management                          │
└─────────────────────────────────────┘
```

———— Sub-section 1————
Social skills

———— Sub-section 2————
Psychological know-how

———— Sub-section 3————
Counselling

———— Sub-section 4————
Interpersonal control

———— Sub-section 5————
Conversation as a science

————Sub-section 1————
Practise specific skills

————Sub-section 2————
Discuss my findings

Name....
Task....Managing

———— Before ————

These are the descriptions of your strategy
hierarchy which you gave before you
started the task.

———— Strategy————
By observing myself and others

———— Context————
Adopt a conversational paradigm

———— Sub-section 1————
Use video

———— Sub-section 2————
Make notes of behaviours

———— Sub-section 3————
Elicit subjective reports and
structures of meaning

Name....
Task....Managing

———— Before ————

These are the descriptions of your outcome
hierarchy which you gave before you
started the task.

———— Outcome————
Less tension and more creative work

———— Context————
Creative conversational networks

———— Sub-section 1————
Trust and reliability

———— Sub-section 2————
Shared leadership

———— Sub-section 3————
No animosity

———— Sub-section 4————
Effective actions in the world
by everyone concerned

Name....
Task....Managing

———— Before ————

These are the descriptions of your criteria
hierarchy which you gave before you
started the task.

───── Criteria ─────
People in my life will be friendlier, more
creative and happier – more open

───── Context─────
Others would see that my management
space is worth copying

────── Sub-section 1 ──────
Observing the social
atmosphere

────── Sub-section 2──────
Asking the people concerned
how they feel

────── Sub-section 3──────
Success of those concerned

────── Sub-section 4──────
Their attitude to me

Name....
Task....Review managing

─────── After ───────

These are the descriptions of your learning
contract which you gave after you
finished the task.

Topic

─────Topic─────
Managing people at work and at home
and in all other social situations

Purpose

─────Purpose ─────
To creatively engage in living, and to
initiate this in others in my world

Name....Demonstration
Task....Review managing

─────── After ───────

These are the descriptions of your outcome
hierarchy which you gave after you
finished the task.

───── Resource ─────
A friend as adviser

───── Resource─────
Sticky situations which gave me
the opportunity to watch how I
controlled events

───── Resource─────
Stamina and determination when
things went badly

Strategy

```
 ┌──── Strategy ────┐
 │ Observation and interpretation │
 │ of the evidence │
 └──────────────────┘
```

```
                      ┌──── Resource ────┐
                      │ Trust  in myself and others │
                      └──────────────────┘
```

Outcome

```
 ┌──── Outcome ────┐
 │ To see management as the │
 │ facilitation of others learning │
 └──────────────────┘
```

```
                      ┌──── Resource ────┐
                      │ Access to people who are experts in │
                      │ training animals – sheep-dogs, lions │
                      │ and even geese – not pigeons │
                      └──────────────────┘
```

Criteria

```
 ┌──── Criteria ────┐
 │ They will not be taken over by others but │
 │ will be skilled at negotiating │
 │ understanding and agreement │
 └──────────────────┘
```

For your learning contracts notebook

Name....

Task...to review the total learning contract activity for review – managing

Review of your learning contract

These are the definitions which you gave for each
component before and after tackling the task.

──────── Before ────────   ──────── After ────────

```
 ┌────Topic ────┐                ┌────Topic────┐
 │ The skills of managing people at home │   │ And in all other social situations │
 │ and at  work │                │             │
 └──────────────┘                └─────────────┘
```

```
 ┌────Purpose ────┐              ┌────Purpose ────┐
 │ To cope better with living │  │ To creatively engage in living, and to │
 │                │              │ initiate this in others in my world │
 └────────────────┘             └────────────────┘
```

```
 ┌──── Strategy────┐             ┌──── Strategy ────┐
 │ By observing myself and others │   │ Observation and  interpretation │
 │                │              │ of the evidence │
 └────────────────┘             └──────────────────┘
```

```
 ┌──── Outcome ────┐            ┌──── Outcome ────┐
 │ Less tension and more creative work │   │ To see management as the │
 │                 │            │ facilitation of others' learning │
 └─────────────────┘           └──────────────────┘
```

```
 ┌──── Criteria ────┐           ┌──── Criteria ────┐
 │ People in my life will be friendlier, more │   │ They will not be taken over by others but │
 │ creative and happier – more open │   │ will be skilled at negotiating │
 │                  │           │ understanding and agreement │
 └──────────────────┘          └──────────────────┘
```

What have you learnt about setting up learning contracts?

What have you learnt about yourself as a learner?

Comments:

Use this to plan what you do next

Compare the task resources given

────── Before ──────   ────── After ──────

──── Resource ────	──── Resource ────
Colleagues	A friend as adviser

──── Resource ────	──── Resource ────
Members of my family	Sticky situations which gave me the opportunity to watch how I controlled events

──── Resource ────	──── Resource ────
My students and my clients	Stamina and determination when things went badly

──── Resource ────	──── Resource ────
Direct experience of running courses on this topic and of managing my own staff	Trust in myself and others

──── Resource ────	──── Resource ────
Experts I know	Access to people who are experts in training animals – sheep dogs, lions and even geese – not pigeons

Compare your before and after lists.
Reflect on the nature of any differences.

How will you assess your resource needs next time?

Comments:

This is a comparison of topic hierarchies.

────── Before ──────   ────── After ──────

——— Context ———
```
An exploration of what management ought
to be about, without a political bias
```

——————— Not defined ———————

——— Sub-section 1 ———
```
Social skills
```

——— Sub-section 2 ———
```
Psychological know-how
```

——— Sub-section 3 ———
```
Counselling
```

——— Sub-section 4 ———
```
Interpersonal control
```

——— Sub-section 5 ———
```
Conversation as a science
```

Reflect on why you did not complete this.

Comments:

How did constructing your hierarchy help you to refine,
elaborate and revise your topic definition?

Comments:

This is a comparison of the purpose hierarchies

——————— Before ——————— After ———————

——— Context ———
```
To develop a personal model
of management
```

——————— Not defined ———————

——— Sub-section 1 ———
```
Practise specific skills
```

——— Sub-section 2 ———
```
Discuss my findings
```

Reflect on why you did not complete this.

Comments:

How did constructing your hierarchy help you to refine,
elaborate and revise your purpose definition?

Comments:

_____

This is a comparison of the strategy hierarchies

———————— Before ————————————————— After ————————

———————— Context ————————   ———————— Not defined ————————
┌─────────────────────────────┐
│ Adopt a conversational paradigm │
└─────────────────────────────┘

———————— Sub-section 1————————
┌─────────────────────────────┐
│ Use video   │
└─────────────────────────────┘

———————— Sub-section 2————————
┌─────────────────────────────┐
│ Make notes of behaviours   │
└─────────────────────────────┘

———————— Sub-section 3————————
┌─────────────────────────────┐
│ Elicit subjective reports and │
│ structures of meaning   │
└─────────────────────────────┘

Reflect on why you did not complete this.

Comments:

How did constructing your hierarchy help you to refine,
elaborate and revise your strategy definition?

Comments:

_____

This is a comparison of the outcome hierarchies.

———————— Before ————————————————— After ————————

———————— Context ————————   ———————— Not defined ————————
┌─────────────────────────────┐
│ Creative conversational networks │
└─────────────────────────────┘

———————— Sub-section 1————————
┌─────────────────────────────┐
│ Trust and reliability   │
└─────────────────────────────┘

———————— Sub-section 2————————
┌─────────────────────────────┐
│ Shared leadership   │
└─────────────────────────────┘

```
┌─── Sub-section 3 ─────────┐
│ No animosity              │
└───────────────────────────┘
```

```
┌─── Sub-section 4 ─────────┐
│ Effective actions in the world │
│ by everyone concerned     │
└───────────────────────────┘
```

Reflect on why you did not complete this.

Comments:

How did constructing your hierarchy help you to refine,
elaborate and revise your outcome definition?

Comments:

This is a comparison of the criteria hierarchies.

──────── Before ─────────────────────────────── After ────────

```
┌─── Context ──────────────┐          ──────── Not defined ────────
│ Others would see that my management │
│ space is worth copying   │
└───────────────────────────┘
```

```
┌─── Sub-section 1 ─────────┐
│ Observing the social atmosphere │
└───────────────────────────┘
```

```
┌─── Sub-section 2 ─────────┐
│ Asking the people concerned │
│ how they feel             │
└───────────────────────────┘
```

```
┌─── Sub-section 3 ─────────┐
│ Success of those concerned │
└───────────────────────────┘
```

```
┌─── Sub-section 4 ─────────┐
│ Their attitude to me      │
└───────────────────────────┘
```

Reflect on why you did not complete this.

Comments:

How did constructing your hierarchy help you to refine,
elaborate and revise your criteria definition?

Comments:

Name....
Task....Review – managing

—————————— After ——————————

These are the descriptions of your learning
contract which you gave after you
finished the task.

Topic

```
——————— Topic ———————
The same
```

Purpose

```
——————— Purpose ———————
To learn appraisal, problem-solving,
technical and administrative skills
```

Strategy

```
——————— Strategy ———————
Using specific techniques, which I now
know exist, and  invent some of my own
```

Outcome

```
——————— Outcome ———————
That others would agree that
I manage well
```

Criteria

```
——————— Criteria ———————
They will be characterised by a striving
for the perfectionist human capacity
to enhance their destiny
```

Name....
Task....Review – managing

——————— After ———————

These are the descriptions of your topic hierarchy which you gave after you finished the task.

┌─────── Topic ───────┐
| The same |
└─────────────────────┘

┌─────── Context ───────┐
| The same |
└───────────────────────┘

┌─── Sub-section 1 ───┐
| Appraisal procedures |
└─────────────────────┘

┌─── Sub-section 2 ───┐
| Self-assessment forms |
└─────────────────────┘

Name....
Task....Review – managing

——————— After ———————

These are the descriptions of your purpose hierarchy which you gave after you finished the task.

┌─────── Purpose ───────┐
| To learn appraisal, counselling, problem-solving, technical and administrative skills |
└───────────────────────┘

┌─────── Context ───────┐
| To negotiate understanding |
└───────────────────────┘

┌─── Sub-section1 ───┐
| Practise problem-solving algorithms |
└────────────────────┘

┌─── Sub-section 2 ───┐
| Go on an administrative course |
└─────────────────────┘

Name....
Task....Review – managing

——————— After ———————

These are the descriptions of your strategy hierarchy which you gave after you finished the task.

┌─────── Strategy ───────┐
| Using specific techniques, which I now know exist, and invent some of my own |
└────────────────────────┘

┌─────── Context ───────┐
| Record processes and products |
└───────────────────────┘

┌─── Sub-section 1 ───┐
| In groups with assistance |
└─────────────────────┘

Name....
Task....Review – managing

——————— After ———————

These are the descriptions of your purpose hierarchy which you gave after you finished the task.

┌─────── Outcome ───────┐
| That others would agree that I manage well |
└───────────────────────┘

┌─────── Context ───────┐
| That I pass my management exams and become a director |
└───────────────────────┘

┌─── Sub-section 2 ───┐
| Survive relationships |
└─────────────────────┘

┌─────── Sub-section 2 ───────
│ On courses
└──────────────────────────┘

┌─────── Sub-section 3 ───────
│ Whilst working
└──────────────────────────┘

Name....
Task....Review – managing

─────────── After ───────────

These are the descriptions of your criteria
hierarchy which you gave after you
finished the task.

┌─────── Criteria ───────
│ They will be characterised by a striving for
│ perfectioning our human capacity to enhance
│ the *quality* of our destiny
└───────────────────────┘

┌─────── Context ───────
│ Fully functioning beings
└──────────────────────┘

┌─────── Sub-section 1 ───────
│ Surviving crisis
└──────────────────────────┘

┌─────── Sub-section 2 ───────
│ Greater perceptiveness
└──────────────────────────┘

Review of purpose, strategy and outcome and your learning contract activities.

How well did the 'outcome' of your learning capture your purposes?

Comments:

How well did your 'criteria' allow you to assess
the outcomes of your learning contract?

Comments:

How effectively did your 'strategy' allow you to translate
your purpose into successful learning?

Comments:

How well did your 'purpose' describe what you wanted
 your learning activity to achieve?

Comments:

How effectively did you select and use your resources?

Comments:

What have you learnt about defining a learning contract?

Comments:

Review your strengths and weaknesses as a learner!

Comments:

How would you tackle a similar learning task next time?

Comments:

> I'm thinking about all these questions;
> I need more time to experiment and
> reflect. I'm not ready to review my
> progress yet... .

Retrospective commentary: How to take control of learning and enable others to internalise the Learning Conversation

Chapters 3 and 4 have advanced our explanatory model of 'Learning Conversations' for promoting Self-Organised Learning and illustrated this by means of some conversational examples. This conversational activity facilitates an enhancement of our capacity to learn (Chapter 2). It represents the foundation of a conversational science for S-O-L. It operationalises our approach to learning as a personal experiment and our definition of learning as the construction of meaning (General Introduction). It embodies a series of heuristics for the development of S-O-L based on 'meaning as modelling' (Part I).

When are words not enough?

The Learning Conversation can be enhanced by recruiting specialist tools which can *Monitor, Analyse, Record, Reflect, Reconstruct and Review learning*. This is the process of MA(R)4S which adds quality and power to the conversation. The danger of such tools is that they are often more visible, concrete and enduring than the verbal part of the conversation. To the naïve observer or the aspiring Learning Practitioner who has not fully appreciated the centrality of the conversational process in achieving the changes which release the self-organising power of the learner, the tool can appear to be not just a lever that amplifies the power of the conversation but it can seem to be doing the main job. When this happens, what was a Learning Conversation can rapidly deteriorate into a series of clever gimmicks which mysteriously fail to produce the results that they did in the hands of the skilled practitioner.

Our explanatory model of the Learning Conversation manifests itself in the three dialogues, the three levels, and their figure-of-eight configuration, in the hierarchical organisation of each 'meaning as modelling' activity and in the alternating divergent and convergent phases of each Learning Event. Tools can be introduced to increase its power, quality and precision. One category of tools amplifies the awareness we can achieve by reflecting upon our *representations of experience*. Another category of tools *records our actions* and selectively represents or replays our behaviours so that we can use these to reconstruct our experience. These two sources of evidence can be systematically combined within the Learning Conversation to give us new insights and awareness.

The reflective tools and the Learning Conversation complement each other as the conversational technology services the processes of Self-Organised Learning. The Functional Taxonomy of Tools presented towards the end of the book attempts to convey the flavour of this endeavour. Throughout the book we refer to the reflective learning tools which support the Learning Conversation. The taxonomy concerns itself with an outline description of each tool and how it is used. By using these tools to research their own learning, individuals can consciously control their own processes leading to an enhancement of skill, competence and creativity. In presenting these reflective tools within a *functional taxonomy*, we transcend the specifics of each tool to show how together they provide a *conversational technology*. Readers are invited to refer to this taxonomy as they go through Parts I, II and III and to use some of the tools as they converse with the book through their own PLCs. In developing their skills as a learning practitioner, they should try out each tool as they converse with their own clients. Thus, the Functional Taxonomy of Tools can be seen as a resource for augmenting the power of the Learning Conversation.

To conclude Part II, let us briefly consider some of the wider *parameters which govern the context within which S-O-L can be implemented and developed.*

At the boundaries of S-O-L, several issues emerge for consideration. For example:

1 How do Learning Conversations play themselves out in the context of the learning –teaching–training environment?
2 How does the practice of Learning Conversations relate to teaching methods, training programmes, instruction procedures, briefings, and supervisory and management practices?
3 When does the teacher, trainer, manager or consultant operationally recruit Learning Conversations into their interactions with their learner?
4 How does the practitioner take into account the various perspectives from which learning can be observed and evaluated (General Introduction)?
5 What are the conditions for conducting Learning Conversations with groups and institutions over a long period of time?

We are not here concerned with the political, social and economic aspects of S-O-L. We touch on these in the General Implications (p. 334). Our purpose here is to sketch out the 'environmental conditions' which are prerequisites for the development of S-O-L. Failure to recognise their relevance will seriously hamper attempts to grow Learning Conversations other than in their most incidental forms.

Most teachers, trainers and even therapists, most consultants, custodians and counsellors (TCs), and many managers intend to bring about *preconceived changes* in the behaviour and/or experience of their 'clients'. They are employed to ensure that people acquire certain attitudes and knowledge, and to perform certain skills. Sometimes the nature of these changes is very well defined; often they are precisely specified; but even when apparently open, the purpose of the proposed learning will almost always have been preconceived, even if only vaguely. Indeed, most TCs and managers would feel that they are failing in their duties to their learners, clients and subordinates if they had not diagnosed needs and planned the programme of change. Often this pre-empts most of the decisions about the content and process of learning and Learning Conversations wither away.

As learners join in the enterprise, they are inevitably entering into a rather unbalanced contract. A basic requirement of an environment for S-O-L is a series of methods, procedures and techniques for making the nature of the Teaching–Learning (T–L) contract explicit and for conversing sensibly about it. Systems 7, introduced in Part III, attempts this. Learners' freedom to negotiate equally in the formulation of the T–L Contract depends not only on their appreciation of the variety of perspectives within which their learning can be observed and evaluated, but also on their awareness of the range of possible teaching–learning activities. Here, a simple classification is proposed, merely to challenge reflection and provoke you, the reader, to review some viable alternatives for yourself.

The Teacher, Trainer, Manager Learning contract (T–L contract)

In every teaching–learning situation, training course and management enterprise there is an implicit or explicit contract. Often this is operated as a mix of informal and formal events. For the educational, training or management system to be transformed into a *conversational learning system*, a detailed specification of these outer contextual qualitative dimensions becomes essential. This has presented us with an exciting challenge. In Part III, Chapters 5 and 6, we develop this theme, but let us consider some specific dimensions which directly influence the development of a capacity to learn.

Figure 24 summarises the five modes which together can operationalise a teacher–trainer–manager learning system for promoting S-O-L. These are described more fully in other CSHL publications (the Postscript).

A coordinated scheme of teaching–learning relationships

'Sitting by Nellie' or learning by 'demonstration'

First, the opportunity for the learner(s) to observe the demonstration at work is negotiated. This may involve arranging a visit, setting up an experiment, arranging that the work situation is cleared so that the observers can see, hear, smell what is going on.

Second, the 'rules of the game' should be set. Is the observer allowed to ask questions? If so, when? Is the 'demo' to be recorded, for example, by cameras, audio or video? Can the observers make notes?

Third, how real is the 'demo'? Is reality being adjusted for the sake of understanding? If so, how clearly is this exhibited to the observers? Can the nature and reasons for such adjustments be discussed before, during or after the event?

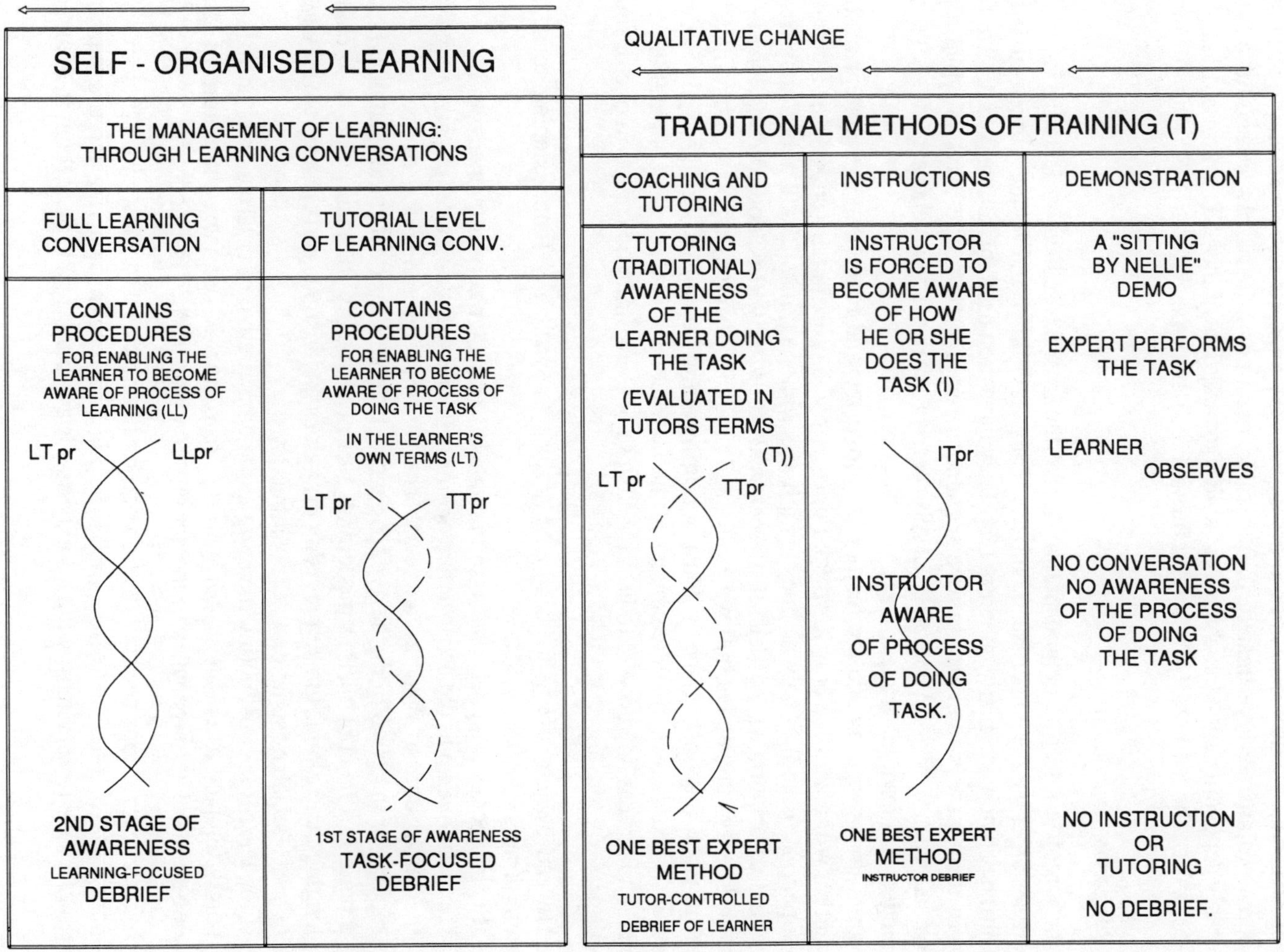

Figure 24 **The five modes of the Teaching–Learning contract**

Fourth, is the demo an isolated event or is it part of a larger learning–training contract?

Fifth, is the process of observation (that is, the skill and ingenuity of the learner in making use of the demo) to be discussed before, during and/or after the event?

It is clear that the usefulness of the demo will vary considerably depending upon how the conversations are coordinated. In particular, demos will be highly successful or fail miserably depending upon the observers' ability to make use of them. The more skilled and self-organised the learners, the more useful will the demos be.

Learning from instruction

Instruction differs from a demonstration in that the instructors have reflected upon their expertise, or upon the expertise of others. They have analysed it and looked at it to determine just how internally coherent it is. They have then used this analysis to determine what in their view is the best possible sequence of explanation. The ways in which the conversations are coordinated will largely determine the effectiveness of the use of instruction as a resource for learning.

Again, the ways in which the learner is monitoring and modelling the content of the instruction will determine how it works. For example, a probationary supervisor listening to a supervisor describe 'how he does his job and what he thinks it's all about' may treat the whole description as 'gospel'. If he sees it like this, he will be constructing meaning which is largely unrelated to his own earlier and probably different experience of how it is when he is on the floor. If he is constructing meaning at the rote or descriptive level (Chapter 2) and he feels that the content of the instruction is not exactly compatible with the real situation as he knows it to be, then his use of the instruction can go in one of four directions.

1 He can switch off in his head and 'refuse to waste my time listening to such clap-trap'.
2 He can decide to model it as is, so that later he can internally converse with it.
3 He can move up to the constructive and/or creative levels of modelling and attend to the instruction so that he can revise and improve his modelling of the job of a supervisor in light of the other's experience. He retains his own values and insight as a basis for the construction modelling. Just occasionally the instruction is so challenging that he finds himself revising his values and insights and creating a new view of what the job or some part of it is all about.
4 If the learner is constructing meaning at the constructive or creative level he will be sorely tempted to debate issues with the instructor. In our view the nature of this debate will determine whether the activity continues to be 'instruction'.

The S-O-L conversations need negotiation of the rules of the instruction game. If an expert has spent a lot of time and effort preparing his explanation, and if a large group of competent S-O-Learners know what his expertise is and they want to hear about it, then the rules of the game should allow this to happen. Any debate should happen separately. This is how instruction works best. Within this set of rules there is room for a pattern of question and answer which can be used skilfully on both sides to help the learner to understand what is being presented and allow the instructor to check understanding and adapt his presentation accordingly.

The coordinating S-O-L conversation in the wider sense is monitoring learning and learning skill. It is negotiating the nature of the learning–training horizons and distilling shared needs. It is recognising the range of expertise available and the distribution of instructional skill associated with this. It is then setting up the instructional events accordingly. Where the expert does not have the instructional skills required, it is often much more effective to have a 'translator' to collaborate with the expert so that they make the presentation together. The more 'listening skill' and 'questioning skill' the learners have, the less the need for translators, because the learners can offer their own translation service directly to the expert. This is the main threat to training that lies in facilitating S-O-L within an enterprise. It forces the teacher or trainer to become more than just a translator or middle-man between the expert and the learner.

The instructional or 'expert' tutorial

When the possibility of 'debate' between the instructor and the expert was revealed, we questioned whether the consequent activity should be called instruction. Where, in the context of instruction, the learner is constructing meaning at the constructive or creative levels, then they must restrict their conversation with the instructor to questions of fact – that is, explanation – as this is seen from within the instructor's value system or they will enter into debate. By debate we mean that the learner will exhibit an alternative (restricted, elaborated, refined, extended, extrapolated or different) meaning and will be willing to defend it or even to press for its acceptance. This process of debate is the essential feature of what we are calling tutoring, but again there are ground rules. In such a tutorial the conversation is asymmetric. The tutor is the arbiter of what in the end is 'correct'. The usual tutorial activity is for the learner to offer a representation of his or her meaning and for the tutor to evaluate it. He or she will also carry out some diagnostic work to clarify just what is wrong with the learner's understanding. This activity can be quite extensive, with the tutor spending significant periods of time helping the learner to explain exactly what his or her meaning is, but ultimately the purpose of this 'conversational' activity is to help the learner to get it right in the tutor's terms. This tutorial instruction can be very powerful. It can be developed for use in groups. It can also be incredibly useful to S-O-Learners so long as they realise that the understanding that is achieved does not have to be accepted personally by them as the 'right answer'. Given this integrity of personal knowing, the in-depth understanding of the other's position achieved by this method can be very useful indeed.

If they insist on raising their doubts with the tutor various things can happen. The tutor may recognise the validity of their criticism and undertake to go back to his or her resources to rethink the nature of their expertise and return with the 'really right' answer. This is what a good instructor (using 'instructor' to mean translator of the expertise) should do. If the instructor does find an authority for the 'really right' answer which satisfies the learner, then the position of the instructor is maintained. If the learner persists in dis-agreeing (rather than not understanding), then the debate has moved beyond the instruc-tional tutorial.

The consultative tutorial

This is in fact the limit of many trainers' and teachers' modelling of their functions and skills. Their refusal or inability to take the process of debate beyond this point is the source of much of the discontent with the current state of training and education. Beyond lies a new field of professional expertise. It lies in being able to manage a process of conver-sation which *is symmetrical at least at the content level*. Each contributor is acknowledged to have a right to his or her own personal knowing and is put under no obligation to agree either with the experts or with other learners. The rules of this balanced exchange or discussion situation are to do with an obligation to understand the other's position fully in his or her own terms, and given this process of sharing others' understanding, to be prepared to admit the possibility of negotiating a common or group understanding. To achieve such a level of shared understanding will involve much activity at the constructive and creative level of meaning construction (Chapter 2), and much monitoring and model-ling of the process of meaning construction. It will involve being able to recognise give-over, take-over, compromise and creative reconstruction as these terms are used in the Functional Taxonomy of Tools (Structures of Meaning) and it will involve being able to operate at a level of awareness not called for within the tutorial role as we have so far defined it. Some are, of course, already operating in this way. It is what is accepted within the university type of tutorial.

The tutorial learning conversation

S-O-L and Learning Conversations can help students to see more clearly what it is they are doing and that it will help them to do it more and more effectively. When this occurs we transcend the boundary of content-based conversations into *fully functioning awareness of processes of learning*, from the traditional tutorial to the *tutorial, life, and learning-to-learn conversation* (Chapter 4).

This formulation of the process of demonstrating, instructing and tutoring helps us to place it within the pattern of teaching–learning conversations. Demonstrations are speci-fically available as a resource for learning. The process of instruction and the instructional tutorial in the terms that we have described it is a way of placing a translator between the expert and the learner. The more skilled and self-organised the learner, the less of this translation service does he need.

It is part of the Task Supervisor's job in conversation with the Learning Coach (MA(R)4S, implementing the learning–training contract within Systems 7; Part III, Chapter 5) to see if, when and how instruction is made available. It is our contention that the effort put into enabling learners to improve their capacity for learning would take away the need for what teachers and trainers often find to be the most tedious and repetitive aspects of instruction. The role of the teacher–trainer becomes that of a *Learning Practitioner* whose job it is to *manage Self-Organised Learning*. This will involve modelling the teaching–learning relationships in ways which allow the practitioner to offer learners a *coordinated scheme of learning opportunities* on the lines we have described. Such a system can transform the T–L contract to give emphasis to:

1 *the process of learning* as well as its content, i.e. tasks or topics;
2 *personal needs and purposes* as well as other defined goals and objectives;
3 personal strategies as well as directed strategies;
4 *self-review* as well as expert assessment; and
5 the notion of the teacher, trainer, instructor, consultant and manager as a *Learning Practitioner or 'manager of learning'*.

Each event in the T–L contract can be construed within a system of S-O-L in which the learners and the Learning Practitioner converse about the content of the learning and about how this is best achieved. We conceive of this as Systems 7, which is explained in Part III, Chapter 5.

The 'seven faces' of conversational exchange specify some of the operating configurations. Each of these has relevance in managing an environment of S-O-L. Together, the learners (individuals, pairs, teams and the institution) and Learning Practitioner negotiate the timing and control of these contextual configurations, within which the more widely defined parameters of S-O-L are operable. *Figure 25* summarises the 'seven faces' which contribute to the management of the T–L contract.

The *four task-focused* configurations relate to the *traditional modes* illustrated in Figure 21. One of the three *learning-focused* configurations relates to counselling methods and the remaining two are exclusive to the Learning Conversation. The seven configurations together combine to operate a system for S-O-L. Thus, a T–L contract must address the whole sequence of training–learning methods represented in the *five modes* already outlined in Figure 21 from *demos* to *instruction* to *traditional tutoring* to *tutorial Learning Conversations* (PLCs) and to S-O-L as a whole. Once this proposition is recognised and implemented, there remains the question of how such a system for S-O-L can be managed within groups; that is, teams, sections, departments, and within institutions as a whole. Part III describes 'Systems 7' which creates a S-O-L environment for group learning.

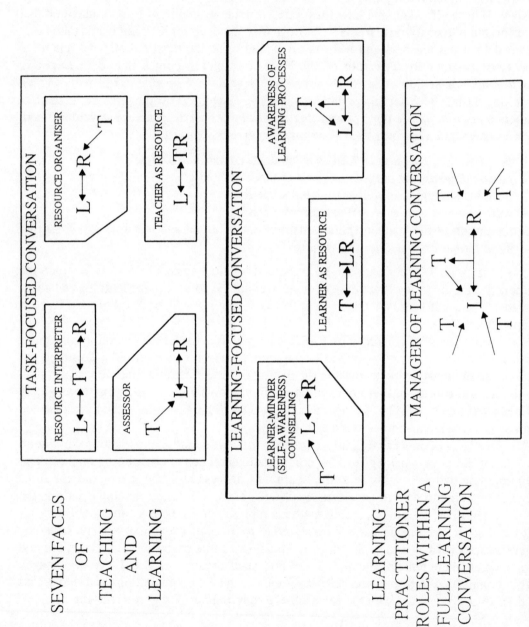

Figure 25 The seven faces of the Teaching–Learning Contract

Part three

Self-Organised Learning Environments
What are they? Can Self-Organised Learners live, work and learn together?

Contents

Prospective commentary: Creating the conditions to enable Self-Organised Learning

Part III moves the Learning Conversation into an organisational setting. This Prospective Commentary builds a bridge from one-to-one Learning Conversations through three stages to seeing the group-as-a-whole as Self-Organised Learner.

Chapters 3 and 4 have shown how a Learning Practitioner can work with an individual to enable them to increase their capacity for learning. To keep these explanations uncluttered, the Learning Conversation was described as if it was always 'one-to-one' in the sense that two people only were involved; and also in the sense that these two work on their own, without allegiance to any group or institution. In Chapters 5 and 6 this model of the Learning Conversation will be elaborated to bootstrap us out of these assumptions. However, before exploring how the theory and practice of Learning Conversations has been developed for introduction into public and private enterprises, let us examine how far we can get with the ideas already presented.

Stage 1   The 'one-to-one' situation

Thus far, the Learning Practitioner has appeared as an independent 'coach' on whom the learner can call. This activity is entirely separate from any group membership or institutional affiliations of the learner. Examples might be:

- Parents who employ a Learning Practitioner to work individually with their daughter or son to enable them to make better use of their educational opportunities, be these at school, college or university;
- A mature student employing the Learning Practitioner to enable him or her to develop their learning capacity to exploit better some of the many opportunities for open, distance, continuing or professional in-service education and training;
- A managing director or the chairman of the board privately employing a valued consultant to help them cope better with their job;
- A youth club leader who is voluntarily assisting teenagers on the dole;
- Professional tennis and golf players, who often have a personal coach who works closely with them to raise their game.

– Psychoanalysts and practitioners of other forms of psychotherapy supporting their clients in their attempts to penetrate the causes of their sufferings.

In all these examples the contractual relationship between the Learning Practitioner and their client is negotiated 'one-to-one'. Skill in conducting in-depth Learning Conversations is a valuable asset for such practitioners to possess. They might transform their effectiveness by recognising how their clients can amplify their capacity for learning. The clients can be encouraged to make their expectations progressively more clear, and the Learning Practitioners' job is to ensure that the clients' aspirations become and remain realistic, yet develop imaginatively as the relationship becomes productive.

Stage 2   The 'individual in a group' situation

Given a series of such 'one-to-one contracts' it can be more cost-effective for a Learning Practitioner to generate the Learning Conversations with individuals in a group. Many of the tools (the 'Functional Taxonomy of Tools') lend themselves to group work (for example, repertory grid, structures of meaning, work study techniques and so on). Much of the detailed conversation can take place in small sub-groups. The Learning Practitioner can monitor a number of sub-groups at the same time; but this calls for more skill and experience than working one-to-one. The breakthrough to this level of working comes when Learning Practitioners have conducted a sufficient number of one-to-one Learning Conversations to begin to see the repeating patterns of interaction. *Such group situations acquire meaning when the conversational process is modelled in ways that are free from specific content.* Practitioners learn to appreciate how the process of a Learning Conversation is progressing in a group. They can anticipate the various ways in which things can go wrong and the hazards that can arise. They also learn to sense the quality of an interaction at a more general level, recognising signals that indicate the need for closer attention. In its initial stages, group work calls for the close supervision of insightful Learning Practitioners, otherwise the outer, busy-looking behaviour will not be associated with an inner, high quality of experience; of the 'meaning as modelling' required to produce real personal change. It is more difficult to work with groups because one must learn when to trust its members to sustain productive conversation and when to intervene to help them raise the quality.

Group activity is often not only more cost-effective but more productive. Learners can exchange and share their experiences bringing more personal reality to the testing of the modelling on which their understanding is based. They can build on one another's ideas constructively, criticising and shaping them, and they can support one another through periods of change. As peers with similar vulnerabilities they find it easier to weave some of the strands of the support dialogue. The MA(R)4S modelling facility, first introduced in Chapter 2 and elaborated in Chapter 3, offers reflection, reconstruction and review to maintain and improve the quality of all the individual conversations. This conversational review activity needs to be built into group learning processes from the beginning.

The Learning Practitioner cannot monitor the individual learning processes of everyone in the group. Work in sub-groups has to be arranged so that one person observes and systematically records another's learning activity. Talk-back through this record helps the learner reconstruct the process of learning. This recording and talk-back through the process of learning can become the full conversational modelling activity implied by the term MA(R)4S (learning interface). We have found that the judicial use of audio and video recording can provide a solid back-up for this activity; but having a recording does not in itself ensure that it is used effectively. The Functional Taxonomy of Tools describes some of the tools that can be recruited into this conversational reconstruction. After a number of such process dialogues *the learner begins to seek and to acquire better skills of self-observation.* These in turn can be encouraged and reinforced with the amplification provided by various conversational tools. Some of the CSHL computer software is specifically designed to be used in this way (Post Script). In the shorter term, the use of these tools vastly improves the quality of observation at the interface. In the longer term, they offer learners the opportunity to test out and develop their own powers of self-observation until the tools are no longer required to achieve the results. Learners becomes perceptually sensitive to the interface, effectively monitoring and modelling their own processes of learning.

This sensitising of the learners to the quality of their own learning activity is one of the keys to effective group work. Learners can monitor the detailed quality of their own processes with support offered by a learning partner acting as observer. The Learning Practitioners can stand back and give more attention to longer-term aspects. They can monitor the progress of each Learning Conversation diagnosing what is wrong and intervening minimally but strategically to bring each conversation back on course.

An MA(R)4S modelling activity is also essential to monitor the quality of the Learning Practitioner's activities. Again, this MA(R)4S (Learning Coach) process is driven by a model developed from the descriptions and explanations given in Chapters 3 and 4. It is here that the skill and evaluated experience acquired in conducting a variety of 'one-to-one' Learning Conversations will emerge. It appears as 'a feel' for a good Learning Conversation which derives from the operational model built up from experience, perceptually tuning them in to what is going on; but this feel will be no better or worse than the meaning which the Learning Coach has constructed out of his or her experience. It needs to be continually tested and reviewed so that part of it develops in a form especially suited to group work. In particular, Learning Practitioners need to provide those aspects of the MA(R)4S processes, both learning interface and Learning Coach not yet being filled by the group members (that is, learners).

Working in threes is particularly sympathetic to the requirements of the group Learning Conversation. Two are needed as 'learner' and 'Learning Coach' and the other acts as 'observer' of the process offering an amplified opportunity for the MA(R)4S activities to blossom. The requirement to review fairly often draws the separate silent internal commentaries out into the open. The MA(R)4S activity should be developed as an ongoing (real time) monitoring and modelling of the quality of the Learning Conversation.

By rotation, the roles the self-observational and reflective skill is further encouraged. In particular we have found that if 'the observer' knows that they will be called on later to comment as part of the MA(R)4S modelling activity, then they develop a very sensitive eye and ear. They become benevolently, yet constructively, critical of what is missing from the conversation; where it stumbled or was less effective than it might have been, and where the process seems to have been flowing along nicely, achieving purposes in a happy, intelligent and productive manner. They will also find that they can give hints and advice about the nitty-gritty of the conversation: how a form of words, a posture, a facial expression or more generalised attitude contributed to or interfered with the flow and tenure of the conversation. This not only helps the others but it is real personal learning for the observer.

Dividing up a larger group into triads generates quality conversation with the maximum participation, but it is useful, at the beginning and end of each session, to work with the whole group. In the earlier phase, everybody hears the discussion, can participate in it and come to a shared understanding of what is required. In the final phase, full groups can be used to get the sub-groups to exchange and share their experiences. This is best done by first getting all those who have been 'the learners' in the sub-conversations to report on their experience and on how the Learning Conversation had gone for them. The 'trainee Learning Coaches'' points of view are then heard in the light of the results they appear to have obtained. Finally, 'the observers' feed their views back. This group sharing activity is very helpful in offering an opportunity for learners vicariously to increase their experience of what to expect. It allows issues to be raised and questions to be answered. It also places the Learning Practitioner back 'in the know' and in the driving seat.

Whilst threes and full group working provides a rough guide as to how to proceed, some of our best group activities have been carefully time-structured with individual work, work in twos and threes, and in larger sub-groupings dovetailing one into another as the nature of the work, of the people and of what they wish to learn dictates. As experience grows one can expand, elaborate and develop one's own properly validated set of group working strategies.

These group experiences provide a very good groundwork for people learning to conduct such conversations with others and with themselves. They also provide the right atmosphere and intensity of conversation to enable people to exchange significant experiences and thus really learn from one another. Even in a few hours people are amazed how far they can get. Such group work can also provide a salutary experience from time to time for people who believe themselves already to be skilled as Self-Organised Learners. It offers them a protected but 'up-close' opportunity to see how other skilled learners converse with themselves and one another. It also exposes them to the insightful and constructive commentaries of peers who have closely observed how they conduct themselves in the Learning Conversation both as learner, as Learning Coach and as MA(R)4S (learning interface) and MAR(4)S (Learning Coach) 'monitoring and modelling' observers.

Working in this way and ensuring that the powers of self-observation are developing sufficiently to maintain and improve the quality of the conversation, one can rapidly move to a point where members of the group are having fully fledged Learning Conversations with one another. The Learning Practitioner can then step back, monitoring this network of learning activity, making inputs from time to time. We have found that people who learn to become more self-organised using Learning Conversations within a group find it easier to move towards internalising the Learning Conversation. This is because they are familiar with the process from all three points of view – learner, Learning Coach and observer of the Learning Conversation. On the other hand, certain people at certain stages in the conversation need the security, skill, insight and trust that is best generated by an experienced Learning Coach in the one-to-one situation. As with everything, only 'understanding' based on well-tried operational modelling of what learners and learning partners can achieve at their current levels of skill can give the insight to guide the distribution of efforts between one-to-one and group Learning Conversations.

In such groups the Learning Practitioners' responsibilities are to each separate individual learner. Working in groups is merely a means to this end.

Once Learning Practitioners begin to operate within some organisational framework their allegiances are no longer so clear-cut. They still have obligations to the learners, but they and the learners also have obligations to the larger enterprise. A group or an organisation which provides its members with Learning Conversations could, in theory, employ enough full-time Learning Practitioners to make them available on a confidential, one-to-one basis to any of their members who wish to use them. Each employee could be left free to clarify their expectations and negotiate their own learning horizons. In practice, most organisations will want to put some time constraints on this activity and to limit it to work-related topics. Even without these constraints it is not quite as unlikely as it may sound for an institution to offer such a personal service to its members. If a company, government agency or college wants to increase the effectiveness of its workforce, having each member become a more efficient and Self-Organised Learner can be a very cost-effective approach. Increased job performance and savings in training and time spent learning on the job will soon more than cover the cost of the Learning Practitioners; and the S-O-Learners will continue to learn more effectively from all new experience. The initial investment in employing 'specialist Learning Practitioners' to work on a 'one-to-one' basis prevents most organisations from pursuing this policy.

As a compromise many institutions try to provide such a 'one-to-one' service more economically by getting existing staff to accept a Learning Practitioner function as part of their job. Educational institutions offer 'personal tutoring'. Some industrial and commercial organisations also offer 'personal tutoring' services in the form of what is called counselling or coaching concerned with improving job performance, career development, personal growth or self-development. Unfortunately, as is widely acknowledged, many tutors in education and elsewhere have not learned how to offer an effective personal tutoring service. Untutored physicists, geography teachers, industrial supervisors and operational managers, to mention but a few, misconstrue their personal tutoring role. They either fall into an uneasy, very informal, chatty role in which they pursue ill-defined purposes related to 'helping you with any personal problems which I hope you haven't got' or they take refuge in their subject expertise or job know-how and offer some form of performance appraisal mixed with remedial instruction. This happens because the learner does not know what to expect and the tutor does not know what else to offer. The theory and practice of Learning Conversations, even within the constraints of the 'one-to-one' relationship, can provide these tutors with a much clearer definition of their role. They are offered a firm basis for modelling what they might be doing. However, Learning Conversations need not always be conducted on a 'one-to-one' basis, In Chapters 5 and 6 the whole conception of 'Learning Conversations' is re-examined. What can be constructed on the foundation of the core conversational processes introduced in Chapters 1 to 4?

The idea of Learning Conversations in groups has now been introduced. Using the tools on offer (the Functional Taxonomy of Tools), Learning Practitioners are able to work with more than one learner at the same time. This can be achieved by having groups of learners together but having each learner converse reflectively with her- or himself. The *'process'* of conversation is guided by the Learning Practitioner and is the same for everybody; but each learner contributes her own content, represents it, reflects on it and reconstructs it within the general framework of the Learning Conversation. One can also work with more than one learner at the same time by dividing them into pairs or threes and having them carry through much of the conversational work together. This releases the Learning Practitioners to act in an overall monitoring or supervising role where they can control the quality and pattern of the conversation. It also allows them time to deal with a distilled residue of one-to-one activity which requires their experience and special skills.

In Chapter 5 *the model of the Learning Conversation is itself expanded to show how its power can be amplified many times over*. This is achieved by locating the core conversation as described in Chapters 3 and 4 within a pattern of contributory conversations which come together to form what the authors have designated 'Systems 7'. This is a modelling of the 'conversational environment' within which Self-Organised Learning can be developed and supported to extremely high levels of effectiveness. It can be treated as a guide to how a group or an organisation might create a 'network of conversations' within which each of its members is enabled to become an effective Self-Organised Learner. Finally, in Chapter 5, the Systems 7 operations are used reflexively to show how individual Self-Organised Learners can more fully model the processes by which they are able to continue to increase their capacity for learning.

In Chapter 6, Systems 7 is used to show how Self-Organised Learning can be applied to the activities of a group. *Any group* which wants to pursue a shared purpose (such as a family, a sports team, a work group or even the whole enterprise) *can be seen as one integrated Self-Organised Learning system*. This does not mean simply an aggregate of individual Self-Organised Learners. It means that the members of the group have learned to share their modelling of its activities. This *shared modelling* enables them effectively and economically to distribute and flexibly to coordinate their activities. They have also learned when and how to communicate with each other in ways that enable the group-as-a-whole to become self-organised in its learning. *The group becomes more than just the sum of its parts*. It can learn more, and more effectively, than all of its constituent members could do learning separately. These ideas are then applied to groups working with groups. Gradually *the idea of a Self-Organised Learning enterprise emerges*.

Stage 3   Real teams – 'the group as a whole' as learner

In the General Introduction we offered our personal myth that learning is a concept that we infer from selected evidence which will comprise some mix of 'records of behaviour' and 'representations of experience'. There is nothing in this myth to restrict the idea of learning to an individual person. It is usual, but it is not necessary.

Once one gets used to this idea, it is quite easy to think of the *behaviour of a group as something over and above just being the sum of the behaviours of all its members*. If we can think about the group's behaviour we can record it. Once we have a series of records of a group's behavioural activity taken over a period of time, we can begin to pose the question, 'Is there any evidence that this group is learning?' Now we are posed with a choice. We can either reply, 'No! The evidence is not a record of the behaviour of the group, it is an intermingled set of records of the behaviour of a number of separate individual people who happen to be interacting or even conversing.' If we answer in this way we might go on to say that we can see plenty of evidence that each individual has learned something and that we are sure that if we were to indulge in learning interviews with them we would quickly generate experiential evidence to support and elaborate this claim. This is one way of dealing with group situations. But, alone, we have not found it to be the most productive. It does not explain what at best we mean by team work.

If we go along with the idea that a group can learn something, which is usefully treated as something more or different from the sum of all the individual learnings of its members, we have found that various new avenues are opened to us. The first major avenue is that we can conceive of conducting a Learning Conversation (one and the same Learning Conversation) *with the group as a whole*. Without reviewing the history of Gestalt, Jung, Field Theory, General Systems Theory and neo-Cybernetics, let us agree that if we look we can find some fairly powerful supporters, not least among the theologians, for this particular personal myth. Our discussion of the idea of a 'conversational entity' which may be part of an individual or may transcend many individuals gives us the intellectual tools for beginning to think about how we might deal with the experience of a group. There is no need to push this discussion further here. Suffice it to say that we have found it very useful and productive to think in terms of a group learning.

The group's behaviour can be described in terms of what gets done rather than who does it. This is analagous to saying that if we were looking for evidence of learning in any individual we would be interested in what gets done, how effectively, at what level of quality and so on. It is only when we become interested in reflecting on strategies that we become concerned with how things get done. So with the group, as we see evidence of learning taking place we can begin to discuss strategies. As the process of learning develops we can usefully evoke a MA(R)4S (2G) (group learning interface) to describe how the group represents its own activities to itself, thus achieving increased awareness of its process of learning.

Most groups which develop or are formed within an organisation have a work purpose beyond that of helping each of their members to become more effective at learning from experience on the job. Once the group has identified its purpose conversationally (and not just had it imposed by dictat from the outside, perhaps in terms which are at variance with the experience of its members) it is possible to initiate a Learning Conversation with the group as a whole. They can together learn to achieve their group purpose more effectively. In working with a group in this way the Learning Coach drives the conversation, controlling how the process develops in very much the same way as he or she would with an individual learner. *The members of the group work together as 'learner'.* This means that they must fully understand one another and the implications of what they are doing. They must agree as to their method of work and as to any distribution of activities, but the division of labour must not entail any division of understanding unless this is fully discussed and accepted by each member of the group. It can be quite useful to have one's own resident 'expert' but this should never involve the group as a whole abdicating responsibility for some part of its learning.

Everything that has been said about individual Learning Conversations in Chapters 3 and 4 can now be applied to the group situation once these essential differences have been taken into account. For example, if the group is setting itself a task-focused learning contract then they together have to identify a learning need. They must negotiate this into a viable learning purpose. This purpose may appropriately be broken down into sub-purposes which in terms of the working situation of the group are best tackled by certain sub-groups (including individuals). The group as a whole then decides its strategy and if the purpose has been subdivided, the various sub-groups develop sub-strategies accordingly. These plans are all brought back to the group as a whole for coordinating and for checking that everything is consistent and in line with the overall purpose. This type of negotiation can be very revealing, uncovering differing assumptions and perceptions which may have remained hidden for years. It would be unusual if the purpose remained unchallenged and the group did not find out much about its own functioning during such a session. A careful record should be kept of how the group as a whole as 'learner' goes about its learning activities. Using some of the group awareness-raising techniques described in the Functional Taxonomy of Tools, audio and video taping can be useful in short initial exercises but, as group work tends to take more time and to be spread over larger physical areas than that of individual learners, so much of the awareness-raising has to be done by talk-back through direct observation. If one can get two related work groups together taking turns as 'learner' and 'observer', this not only serves the direct purposes of that Learning Conversation but also serves to bring the two groups together in a most useful, deep and work-oriented way.

Once the initial conceptual leap to seeing the 'group as a whole' as learner has been made, much else follows. The group becomes aware of how it reacts to demands for change. Does it, and if so, how does it set about learning? For a group to become a Self-Organised Learner requires that its members communicate in rather a different way. It requires that the group become much more aware of how it functions and that it, as a whole, accepts responsibility for what does or does not get done and what does or does not get learned. This is what a team aims to do.

Apart, perhaps, from some initial group mind-stretching exercises, the learning activities of the 'group as a whole' are as much learning from real live experience on the job as is individual learning. The group learning activity does therefore get built into the ongoing work activity in the same way as individual learning. The group set themselves objectives and reflect on what they need to learn to achieve these objectives. Having tried, they are debriefed and again diagnose their strengths and weaknesses as a group (not as individuals). They then negotiate their new learning objective and devise strategies for achieving these.

It is important that the group evaluate its own performance, and that this is done in terms of how the group functions, both formally and informally. Individuals may become motivated (as Self-Organised Learners) to learn to become more effective as individuals, but this is not the primary concern of the group as a whole. In the same way as it does the individual learner no good to lament those weaknesses which he does not believe he can change, so it does the group as a whole no good to blame its shortcomings on individual members. In the same way as the Learning Conversation can help the individual discover how much he can achieve with 'me as I am' and 'as I can become', so the Learning Conversation can help a group discover just how much it can achieve 'as it is' and 'as it can become' by conversing with itself through the Learning Conversation.

The reader may find the 'group as a whole' terminology and the idea of treating the group as a learner rather bizarre or contrived; but it is the result of having worked in many other ways with groups. We have found that it takes some of the mystification out of the idea of team work and team building. First, it allows the whole power of the Learning Conversation to be concentrated on the group as a learning entity. Second, it puts many of the management group methods from TA to T groups, from Lego tower building to computer-aided business games, and from team briefing to team building, back into perspective as learning aids and tools to be recruited into the ongoing Learning Conversation with the group as and when required (the Functional Taxonomy). It also reveals why what is learned by a group as a whole on a course away from the work situation disappears almost entirely when the individual group members return to their own separate work situations.

A sound test of a true group Learning Conversation is to examine whether, and how, the strategy a group develops is a truly cooperative enterprise. If it is seen not to be functioning effectively as a learning group, this observation should send warning signals to the Learning Coach about whether the group is dominated by one person or whether the apparent group purpose cannot better be seen as a mix of one or more individual purposes perhaps repeated with subtle variations in each individual. Similarly, in identifying the expected learning outcome and in negotiating the criteria by which they will recognise a successful outcome, the Learning Coach soon learns to recognise group learning activity. Part of the Learning Coach's job is to develop a MA(R)4S (2G) (group learning interface) process by which the group begin to recognise group learning as additional to and different from individual learning. They can then work at enriching the amount and quality of what they can achieve together.

It is important to acknowledge that if a group learns, it can only retain and build on what it is learning whilst it continues to operate as a group. Individual members may find that the group learning experience offers them a very good opportunity for (Self-Organised) Learning something very useful to them as an individual. This will feed back into and thus enhance the quality of the group. But it is not the group learning. This consists in what the group can do and know together, which individual members cannot do or know separately. It is a conversational property of the group. The idea of group Learning Conversations can transform the power of the system of Learning Conversations developed within the organisation.

Another way of presenting these notions is to talk in terms of 'self-controlled change through awareness'. The awareness consists in a shared modelling of the processes of change. The self-controlling function results from using this awareness to reflect upon and identify the mechanisms of change within the enterprise; and in influencing these mechanisms to produce the changes best-suited to the needs of the enterprise. Chapter 6 introduces a specific scheme for *conversational evaluation of projects within an enterprise*. This incorporates these ideas into a practical system. Being conversational, and therefore ongoing, this process of evaluation is not retrospective. *It runs in real time, producing feedback of those parameters of the performance of the enterprise which are most helpful in driving and guiding the processes of change.*

Chapters 5 and 6 outline how Self-Organised Learners can learn to increase their capacity for working and learning together.

Chapter five

The Learning Practitioner: organising a system of Learning Conversations

Conversations about learning take place in every organisation. They will probably be scattered and unrelated one to another; and there may not be very many of them. These conversations could appear in the form of a greatly experienced man nearing retirement informally taking young newcomers 'under his wing'. These 'elders' take a real interest in the youngsters far beyond merely instructing them in the job. Much of their conversation is spent reminiscing about 'the old days', since the times when the older man first joined the firm or the school. Tedious though this may appear from the outside, threaded through it is a caring attitude, a concern for how the newcomer is getting to grips with things and a willingness to listen to their problems. This ability to converse catches the interest of the novice, increases awareness and supports him or her in a search for personal meaning in the work.

Conversations about learning can also occur among a group of people concerned with some project; work study, budgeting, a new curriculum, quality assurance, a special training programme, a new examination scheme, introducing new technology, fighting a redundancy plan or coping with the new micro-computers in an automated office. These people have from necessity had to learn. They learn from one another, pooling their resources and working out their own solutions to their own problems. People who have been involved in such innovative enterprises often look back on that period nostalgically, as an exciting, stimulating and enjoyable episode in their working life. They feel that they were really alive, acquiring new skills and learning significantly about themselves, about one another and about their jobs. Such an experience is almost always associated with intense, high-quality conversations among the members of the group, and in each person's head.

More mundanely, in most organisations, people talk 'shop' over meal breaks, exchanging experience and solving many little problems; experienced people help their less experienced colleagues; and just occasionally one person becomes the centre of a small learning network; not through their technical expertise but because they seem able to encourage and facilitate Learning Conversations among the others.

Despite these examples, good-quality conversations concerned with learning are few and far between in most organisations, and those that do take place are almost always task-focused. The quality is often not good, and the conversations are not usually sustained. Very little happens which might increase people's capacity for learning. In most organisations there are departments and areas in which no such conversations take place. There is usually very little conversation about learning between departments or up and down the chains of command.

These two chapters describe how a coherent network of Learning Conversations can be developed within an organisation. They can be built into a robust system which rapidly becomes cost-effective. What the authors have come to call Systems 7 represents a way of modelling how an organisation can become a Self-Organised Learning environment for each of its members. Systems 7 amplifies the results of each conversation so that not only does each individual become self-organised, but groups, departments and the organisation as a whole achieve greater awareness, becoming more concerned with learning, with self-controlled change and with creating the type of future in which the organisation and its members wish to live, work and get their livelihood or their education.

Systems 7

Systems 7 is the term given to part of the authors' personal myth about how an organisation can become a fully fledged 'learning environment'. By the end of this chapter we will have shared this myth with you. It is hoped that you will then appreciate it and perhaps even find it contributing to your 'operational modelling' of how to help people increase the power of their learning.

Systems 7 has five nodes and seven systems:

Node 1 The Learning Domain
Node 2 The Learner
Node 3 The Learning Coach
Node 4 The Task Supervisor
Node 5 The Learning Manager

The systems are conversations which create awareness and facilitate self-organisation:

System 1 within the Learning Domain
System 2 on the Process of Learning
System 3 on the Learning Conversation
System 4 on Creating Learning Opportunities
System 5 on setting the Horizons of Learning
System 6 on the Management of Learning
System 7 on creating a Learning Policy.

The five nodes are:
Node 1 The Learning Domain – The learning domain is the whole set of resources, including any task domain, from which and in which the learner may learn.

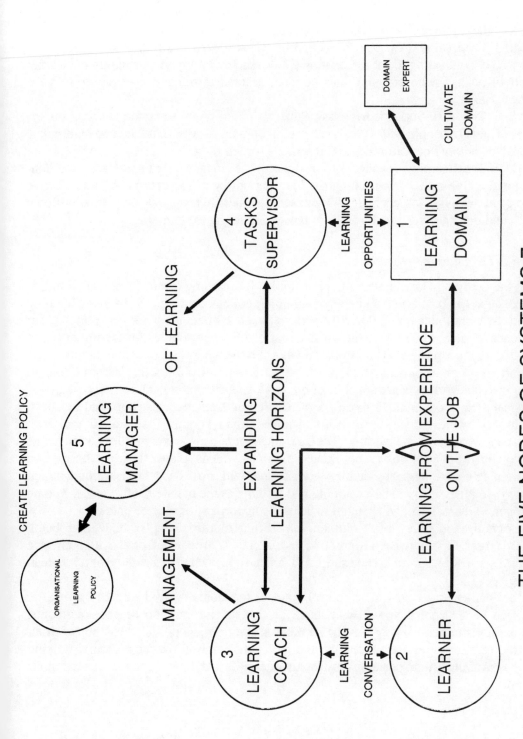

THE FIVE NODES OF SYSTEMS 7

Figure 26 The five nodes of Systems 7

Node 2 The Learner – The Learner is every learner (everybody). The learner is the worker in the work learning domain, as in 'learning on the job', or the student in an education or training domain, as in first going to primary school or university, or new recruits to the Cabinet, as in first becoming Home Secretary.

Node 3 The Learning Coach – The Learning Coach is the Learning Practitioner in his or her role of conducting the core Learning Conversation, or anyone, including the learner himself or herself, who can and does conduct a core Learning Conversation with the learner.

Node 4 The Task Supervisor – Task Supervisors are there to create learning opportunities. They are people who know the learning domain so well that they can manipulate it to provide tailored opportunities and resources for learning.

Node 5 The Learning Manager – The Learning Manager coordinates all these conversational activities, thus translating the learning policy of the enterprise into effective horizons of learning for each Self-Organised Learner. They create the organisational space, conditions and support for Self-Organised Learning to flourish.

System 1 The Learning Domain

It is in the Learning Domain that all opportunities for learning occur. In education all the resources that can be made available by a school or college contribute to form the learning domain. At work the learning domain overlaps the area where the work gets done. In our experience learners often fail to tap the richness of the opportunities for learning offered in a work area. Learning also takes place away from the workplace or school, at home, on the sports field or in pursuit of some leisure activity. Not only is the learning domain greater than the work or educational location, it is also different in kind. It is more than just a physical area, it contains all those people, including trainers, instructors and teachers, who are seen by the learner as sources or resources from whom they can learn in their own terms about what they want to know. The Learning Domain also contains ideas, knowledge and knowhow. Some of this is represented in books, videos, plans, files, databases, in a good training course, series of lectures or visits and field trips. Thus the Learning Domain is an evolving feast, growing, developing and refining as the members of Systems 7 come to recognise where, what, when and how learning opportunities may be created.

The organisation's view of the domain may differ from that held by the learner, being smaller, larger or otherwise different in kind. This is true whether the domain is a submarine, a school, a farm, a shoe shop, a machine shop, a chapel, a college or a Mexican village.

If the learner is an air-traffic-control trainee, the domain would be the air-traffic workplace in the control tower with its radar screens, information boards, intercoms, telephones, instruments, as well as the simulators and debriefs provided by their instructors. One trainee might learn more 'on the job' rather than in the more formal training situations. Another might prefer his instructor's debriefs and the less formal interrogations at the bar. Thus, each creates his or her own learning domain from within the possibilities provided by the organisation.

The MA(R)4S facility within System 1 allows the learning domain to reflect on its own activities. This enables it to grow adaptively. For instance, in the work situation, new demands on productivity, cost effectiveness and quality change the nature of the work domain and this will have repercussions for the learner's engagement with it. Again, as a result of the new GCSE, schools are in the process of radically changing the syllabuses, media and methods of teaching. This will have repercussions for the Learning Domain.

Thus the Learning Domain with its associated MA(R)4S activity becomes System 1 within our Systems 7.

System 2 *The Learners in their Learning Domain*

The conversation generated between nodes 1 and 2 is central to our concerns, being the learner in his domain of opportunity. Here we are, for example:

- talking about a rugby team involved in a training session,
- a supervisor in the Mech section of a Post Office MLO,
- an Indian faced with an Oxfam group in his village,
- the Open University student who is a full-time house-husband faced with his first package through the post,
- the baby in its Skinnerian playpen, or
- the amputee coming to terms with her new artificial limb.

In Chapters 3 and 4 we have tried to show that the learner's monitoring and modelling of this learning activity is what creates the awareness out of which self-organisation may grow. The MA(R)4S (2) (learning interface) represents the mechanism which amplifies this awareness. Where a learner has ceased to reflect upon the process of learning, or where the quality of this reflection needs to be improved, it is the function of the Learning Conversation to get this MA(R)4S (2) (learning interface) mechanism working effectively. Many of the techniques of the Learning Conversation and many of the tools described in Chapters 7 and 8 have been designed to enable us to achieve this. This is the System 2 within our Systems 7.

System 3 *The core Learning Conversation*

Nodes 1, 2 and 3, the learning domain, the learner and the Learning Coach, come together in the Learning Conversation. As we have seen earlier, the MA(R)4S (2) (learning interface) monitors how the learner interacts with the domain. It helps to make the learners' 'meaning as modelling' more effective. This is normally merely the learner's own observing of themselves in action and their remembering and reflecting upon what they have been doing. The power of the MA(R)4S (2) (learning interface) may be amplified as required using any of the techniques mentioned in Chapters 3 and 4 or described in the Functional Taxonomy of Tools.

Node 3, the Learning Coach, brings awareness and a capacity for reflection to the learning activity.

Students may be preparing for exams,
a Post Office MLO may be preparing for the Christmas rush, or
a voluntary organisation may be preparing an Indian community to help themselves.

Node 3, the Learning Coach, initiates a Learning Conversation (as described in Chapters 3 and 4) which will illuminate this activity, raise awareness and enable the learners to transcend their former lesser-learning selves.

The MA(R)4S (3) (Learning Coach) serves the function of raising the awareness of the Learning Coach about how he or she is conducting the Learning Conversation and judging how well it is going. The coach encourages the learner to introduce the contents of the MA(R)4S (2) (learning interface) into the conversation, partly as a check on the learning process, partly to encourage the learner to so drive the MA(R)4S (2) (learning interface) that it continually improves the quality, sensitivity and accuracy of their obser- vations of their own processes. But most importantly, the content of the MA(R)4S (2) serves as a key input via the learner into the Learning Conversation.

The Learning Conversation between learner and Learning Coach monitored and modelled by the MA(R)4S (3) (Learning Conversation) constitutes the third of our Systems 7.

System 4   Creating Opportunities for Learning

Node 4, the Tasks Supervisor, offers another facility within System 7. We shall elaborate on how Opportunities for Learning are effectively created in some detail, since this is the first occasion on which we have introduced this issue in the book. People who serve in this capacity must have a thorough and in-depth understanding of the learning domain and they must be continually prepared to learn what it is they do not yet know; but more crucially they need to question their own and other people's assumptions about what can or cannot be done in the domain. They also need to be prepared to discover what might be available if they look hard enough and ask the right questions. It is the MA(R)4S (4) (learning opportunities) monitoring and modelling of this activity which enables the Task Supervisor to bootstrap themselves into a more and more productive role.

What the Task Supervisor does is to manipulate the learning domain so that it is offering especially suitable learning opportunities to every learner. This manipulation may initially consist in no more than preparing a special reading list, obtaining a particular training video or getting permission for someone to spend time in a particular department so that they can see what happens to their 'paperwork'. But eventually more will be asked of them. One key role of the Task Supervisor is to see that 'reality has not been altered' when someone is testing their understanding of how things are. Teachers and trainers often tamper with reality, simplifying it so that the trainers' explanation of the textbook answer is simply and clearly shown to work. Helpful friends of a learner may try similar cushioning. Learning from experience needs good, hard, valid experience to learn from.

At first a new Task Supervisor cannot conceive of what might be done beyond the trivial to enhance the Learning Opportunities of Learners operating in the Domain. But as the Task Supervisors converse with Learning Coaches and begin to hear about exactly what it is that the learners are attempting, it soon becomes very clear that most organisations have not been prepared to have much real, hard, work-relevant learning going on in the Learning domain. This is often true, even in education. The Task Supervisor has to work to change this attitude. Project work or short courses where Learning Opportunities are specially created can often open teachers' eyes as to how much can be learned in quite a short time by people who are encouraged to be self-organised and create special Learning Opportunities.

As they become more familiar with the idea of S-O-L, Task Supervisors often experience a surprising shift in perspective. Everything becomes potentially a resource for learning. The Task Supervisors then see their job as a series of problems to be solved. How do I help them get themselves into that position? Can I swap certain duties round? Can I arrange for her to work alongside Mr Soso who is particularly good at that? Can we get an expert down from head office so that they can really grill him about the new revisions procedure? The possibilities become endless and a new selectivity has to be instilled into learners if they are to make effective use of these much expanded resources. The Learners use these Opportunities to ask really penetrating questions of experienced people in the domain. We have found that questions about why something couldn't be done differently are answered by 'We tried that and it did not work'. The further question 'Why did it not work?' may be greeted with silence or annoyance. The Self-Organised Learner is not put off by this. Tactfully, at the appropriate time, and with the right people, they will reformulate their questions more carefully and try again. Often they eventually discover the real weakness in the idea and learn accordingly, but just occasionally relatively naïve learners, in their search for meaning, have insights and ideas that are helpful to the organisation. The same ideas may have been generated many times before but in the absence of a Task Supervisor they have disappeared without trace. This is related to the success of quality circles and certain Japanese methods of management.

In their continual search for ways of helping the organisation become more amenable to learning, the Task Supervisor is in a unique position to act as a conduit for new ideas into the organisation, placing each where it is most relevant and making sure that each is acknowledged and that its career can be traced back to its originator. This can happen equally if not more so in an educational setting. The pupils or students can be exploring all the time, keeping the staff informed and up to date so that the Learning Domain is continually enriched. It becomes a well-ordered set of valuable and relevant resources, including contacts into the community. Eventually the community may come to recognise this gold-mine of resources in its midst and the process becomes two-way. This is potentially even more true for colleges, polytechnics and universities. Such insights could solve many of the problems of financing education.

The Task Supervisor's conversation with the domain, stimulated by the monitoring and modelling of MA(R)4S (4) (learning opportunities), constitutes the third of our Systems 7.

Manipulating the Learning Domain to create special Learning Opportunities

The four nodes, *Learning Domain, Task Supervisor, learner* and *Learning Coach*, come together to produce and amplify the Learning Conversation. The Systems 7 configuration gives an extended form and content to the ideas and methods introduced in Chapters 3 and 4. We should keep in the back of our mind the idea that nodes 2, 3 and 4 could, and to a certain extent should, be nodes of modelling within each Self-Organised Learner, but for the moment let us continue to explore Systems 7 as a description of how an organisation can create a network of conversations which will enable each learner to become progressively more self-organised and more effective. What we have come to call 'defining the learning horizons' is the framework within which the conversation between the Learning Coach and the Task Supervisor takes place. Since this is of practical importance for education, training and learning 'on the job', let us consider it in more detail.

Node 4 revisited the Task Supervisor: industrial, commercial and governmental   We are now firing on four of the five nodes of Systems 7. This allows us to begin to explore where the seven systems are located. System 2 is located around the MA(R)4S (2) (learning interface) which monitors the Learner's interaction with the Learning Domain and raises the learner's awareness of his or her own processes. System 3 is focused around the MA(R)4S (3) (Learning Conversation). This monitors the Learning Conversation and raises the Learning Coach's and the learner's awareness of how the conversation is developing so that the Learning Coach can optimise the impact of the conversation and the learner can, in their own terms, monitor the quality of the learning achieved. These systems enable nodes 1, 2 and 3 to produce Self-Organised Learning. In Node 4 the Task Supervisor arranges special learning opportunities in the learning domain. In the industrial/ commercial world this domain is largely where the learner works.

Arranging Learning Opportunities in the work area can seem a little unusual. In the armed forces training exercises are arranged using as much of the paraphernalia of war as is compatible with peace-time regulations. A fighting ship can be placed in training mode when it can do everything but finally fire its weapons in anger. The Task Supervisor can arrange for a red force and a blue force to simulate war conditions; but without a fuller and more sensitive understanding of what would constitute a good, challenging Learning Opportunity the Task Supervisor sets up just one more training exercise. What is missing is the Learning Coach familiar with the learning purposes of the learners and able to converse in depth about how conditions in the domain might assist or obstruct the learning. This is not to say that the effective Task Supervisor makes things easy for the Learner. Far from it; what he or she does is to use their understanding of the domain and the conversation with the Learning Coach to produce a really good, in-depth opportunity for learning. This could be very different from just another apparently successful training exercise.

Industry and commerce are less familiar with the idea of putting a real, live work area into training mode, although we have one Post Office MLO which has a 'learning shift'. This is a live operational shift specially manned to offer people (S-O-L) an opportunity to try out ideas and skills on the job in ways that provide real, live, hard feedback to the learner whilst not putting the work of the MLO at risk. This idea of a special Learning Opportunity lies in direct contrast to the idea of a training area or school in which the physical, social, technical and time constraints of the reality of work are deliberately excluded.

The emphasis here is to learn from experience on the job. Less extreme examples of some of the ways in which the Task Supervisor can help the Learning Coach to help the Learner are:

1 re-arranging work schedules so that the learner is on a certain duty at a certain time so that he gains experience which he is lacking;
2 timing or placing certain batches of work so that a group of learners have an opportunity to play through their learning strategy;
3 arranging for two people to overlap on their work schedules so that one can act as observer of the other's mode of working;
4 making certain resources available;
5 arranging for a specialist from some other part of the company to be available as a learning resource; and so on.

A good Task Supervisor who is really in touch with the Learning Coach can transform the learning potential of an organisation. This can go wrong in two ways: first, if he does not know the domain sufficiently well to see how it can be manipulated; second, because he believes that he already knows what people really need and therefore does not converse with the Learning Coach. What we are describing is a mutually supportive set of mental models of what might be done.

The Learner is attempting to develop, elaborate and refine their task models so that they become more effective. They aim to increase their understanding of the domain and the job, tasks and relationships within it. The Learning Coach has a model of the Learning Conversation which is tested, elaborated and refined day by day in the real world of Learning Conversations. The coach can use his or her understanding of learning to converse with learners in ways that enable them to organise their own learning better, learn more effectively and increase their appetite and capacity for learning. The coach uses an understanding of each individual learner and their purposes to negotiate with the Task

Supervisor to create more and better opportunities for learning without disrupting the primary work objectives of the organisation. The Task Supervisor has a model of the domain, not only its staffing and resources but also its objectives and real constraints and freedoms. They test out the limits from time to time in order to validate, elaborate and refine their model. They use their understanding to converse with the Learning Conversationalist to continually discover and invent Opportunities for Learning.

The Learner believes, and his or her experience validates their belief, that if they seriously try to learn they will improve their understanding, skill, competence and creativity in ways that enable them to enjoy their work more and do it more effectively. Their experience in the work domain validates this. The Learning Coach believes that the organisation wants him or her to help others to become better Self-Organised Learners and that their increasing competence will feed back into the success of the organisation. The Task Supervisor believes that if everybody is learning, the organisation will thrive and some of these learners will contribute to 'improving' the Domain in terms of how work gets done. These suggestions will become a permanent feature of the progressively improving domain.

Over a period of time the people involved, including the learners, can rotate these roles, gaining greater insight into the organisation as an intelligent S-O-L environment.

Node 4 revisited the Task Supervisor in education   In many educational institutions, it is difficult to identify the four nodes of Systems 7 which we have so far discussed. This is because they are either not there, or the roles are distributed across people in a totally muddled and incoherent way. Why is this? It is either because Systems 7 cannot usefully be applied to education or it is because much of education is in a mess.

A first major difficulty is that, unlike industry, commerce and government, education does not have a primary production process in which the Self-Organised Learner can be given a job and be enabled to learn more and more about it from direct, 'on the job' experience. The Self-Organised Learner is given a job in educational institutions, which is to learn from the teaching. But as this is the primary task, most institutions assume that the students come fully equipped to learn and they just go ahead and teach. They assume that if you teach, then people learn.

It is very difficult in most educational institutions to identify any activity which matches with what we have called Learning Conversations. The personal tutorial is the nearest, but nine times out of ten the tutorial conversation bears very little relationship to a Learning Conversation. It is either social or personal chit-chat, social work aimed at getting the student back to work, or it is closely focused in the topic domain talking exclusively about subject matter. Occasionally there are short courses in fast reading, note-taking or exam technique, but these are themselves instructional skills training in study techniques.

The absence of the Learning Conversation would not be missed if all the new workers in the educational domain had already moved well along the path to Self-Organised Learning, but this is unfortunately not the case.

When we look for Node 4 we find the Task Supervisor there in some guise or another; almost always as teacher or lecturer. However, again the situation is not as it might seem. Whilst the Task Supervisor is often highly skilled and informed about the learning domain, he or she is usually not in conversation with a Learning Coach and does not see any need for it. The domain is manipulated and arranged for teaching purposes, not for learning purposes.

The science laboratory, the language laboratory, teaching companies, project work, work placements in sandwich courses and school practice for trainee teachers are all built into different curricula to offer opportunities for learning in a real or work-like situation; but the skills of the Task Supervisor are not often well developed, nor is a Learning Coach very often available.

Even less often are the 'learning opportunities' and 'learning horizons setting' conversations functioning. Having made this generally pessimistic but well-researched comment, there are obviously many honourable exceptions to this general situation; but these exceptions are usually due to the personal initiatives of intuitively good teachers – teachers who have (inadvertently) developed a tacit understanding of some of the issues we are here making explicit. Unfortunately the managers and senior administrators of most educational institutions do not share our 'meaning as modelling'. They are therefore perceptually blind to these initiatives and therefore cannot recognise, encourage or reward them, so they wither away.

System 5 The Horizons of Learning

Our exploration of how Node 4 could in reality be played out in the world of education, industry and commerce has led us into System 5. The Learning Coach and the Task Supervisor together define the horizons of learning which will meet the aspirations of the learner and the Learning Manager. If the resources or opportunities are not available then the Task Supervisor tries to negotiate or create them. If he or she fails, then they discusses this with the Learning Coach, who negotiates with the Learner to formulate more feasible long-term learning contracts which are compatible with the objectives set by the Learning Manager. If the learner 'knows' what they want to learn but cannot conceive of how this can be done, the Learning Coach negotiates possibilities with the Task Supervisor, and by taking these back to the Learner gradually negotiates a realistic series of shorter-term learning contracts which combine (hierarchically) towards achieving the longer-term objective. These are endorsed through the Learning Manager. If the Learner does not know what they should be learning, then the Learning Coach helps them clarify their needs and formulate their purposes until a feasible long-term Learning Horizon can be envisaged. Part of the Learning Opportunity will be the provision of evidence about how the Domain (that is, the college, the company, the team and so on) views and/or measures the Learner's tasks performances.

It is part of every Opportunity for Learning that it generates various forms of evidence about performance. In some jobs and parts of education this appears, on the surface, to be quite well defined. The professional tennis circuit has a computer rating of players; some schools use examination performance; some sales people use money value of orders earned; but in many situations such seemingly clear and 'objective' measures of job performance are not available. Even where they would appear to be available – for example in league soccer, in educational project work or where a group bonus scheme operates – individual members of 'the team' may experience difficulty in translating the 'job performance' measures of the team back into a reliable commentary on their own contribution. Such seemingly 'objective' measures may be useful indicators of performance, but they are only indicators. Performance is always much more complex and multi-dimensional. Task Supervisors can use their understanding of the domain to elicit a variety of such indicators from it. Much of what is available comes in the form of the subjective judgements of experts. One of the skills of the Task Supervisor is to help task experts improve the quality, relevance, reliability and validity of the judgements they are able to make about other people's job performance.

It is part of the Task Supervisor's job to identify or provoke the learning domain into generating an abundance of evidence which may be used effectively as feedback-for-learning. It is part of the Learning Coach's job to generate the 'referent' dialogue to help the learner decide just what evidence from the learning domain he needs and can use as part of his feedback-for-learning. It is at the 'horizons of learning' that this becomes clear. In practice both in education and training these horizons are often left vague or not even negotiated at all. The fifth system in System 7 is the conversation between Learning Coach and Task Supervisor with the MA(R)4S (setting Horizons to Learning) monitoring and modelling it. Thus System 5 is continually improving the potential quality of learning and the Learning Opportunities that can be negotiated.

System 6 The management of learning

In our action research studies we have gradually identified a need and evolved the role or function of a Learning Manager – Node 5 – who orchestrates all the learning activities. Here again it is an understanding of the conversational approach which enables the Learning Manager to recruit the power of his or her learners' self-organisation to the objectives of the learning enterprise. A more directive approach to the coordination of learning activities can result in the skills for self-organisation being blunted and deflected away from the interests of the enterprise. In the opposite direction, too, a *laissez-faire* approach to the management of learning leaves people uncertain of what objectives they are trying to achieve and why. This can leave each Self-Organised Learner directing their own learning activities without too much understanding of how what they are doing relates to the learning activities of their colleagues. It is this dilemma that has, amongst many other more positive pressures, led us to identify the need for a Learning Manager.

In System 6 the Learning Manager is directly in conversation with each activity in

Systems 1, 2, 3, 4 and 5. Each of these systems is best thought of as a complex, ongoing conversation in its own right. Each is sustained by its own MA(R)4S function. If any one of these five conversations founders, then to that extent the organisation will fail to make effective use of its system of Learning Conversations.

The role of the Learning Manager revealed

Let us summarise the working of these five systems. The MA(R)4S (1) (Learning Domain) is in effect the heart of the learning domain, and to the extent that this includes the work domain it is the heart of the enterprise. It represents the understanding that the organisation has achieved of its own activities and its own capacity for change. It will include all those accounting, work-progressing, methods-reviewing, quality-auditing, process-monitoring activities by which the organisation knows what it is and what it is doing. More than this, in modelling the activity of the enterprise, MA(R)4S is continually testing and exploring to improve the quality, scope and detail of its understanding of all the ramifications of its own activities. It is because they are working in a constructively questioning way that the Self-Organised Learners often provoke this MA(R)4S (1) (Learning Domain) into more lucid activity. Evidence of this will be more openness, understanding and willingness to converse effectively about the activities of the enterprise. In many ways perhaps the process of the MA(R)4S (1) (learning domain) is best understood through the quality of the 'models of the organisation' that are held (and operated) in the heads of everybody concerned with it. Large differences in these understandings of the nature of the enterprise can lead to considerable difficulties in working together, but such differences are very common. System 1 allows this awareness within the Learning Domain to communicate with the Learning Manager.

By monitoring this monitoring of all five conversations the MA(R)4S (6) (management of the five systems) ensures that the Learning Manager is informed as to the nature, level, quality and growth of learning going on in the organisation. It is a conversation, a process of building understanding by using the monitoring process to model the learning being achieved. This understanding can be tested, revised, checked again and improved until it usefully represents what it purports to portray. Each MA(R)4S is monitoring some coherent process within the complete Systems 7. They are monitoring it to achieve operational awareness and control. We have seen earlier that the MA(R)4S (2) (learning interface) is monitoring 'learning activities' to maintain their quality and to enrich and develop them. System 2 consists in the conversation between MA(R)4S (2) (learning interface) and the Learning Manager.

Thus System 1 and System 2 together inform the Learning Manager of how the primary activity of the enterprise is proceeding and what is the state of all the learning that drives it. Neither of these systems is unusual. Every organisation has some conversation going on within System 1 and System 2. Indeed, it would fail utterly if it did not. What is unusual is to think about these activities in this way. The current fashion is to converse within System

2 about human resources. The difficulties arise from the type of models (or imagery) that this evokes. The personnel man may be seen as a type of storekeeper, making sure that the organisation has the right quantity of each of the correctly trained and experienced trade of people from high flyers to copper bottom knockers.

System 3 is the heart of our system of Learning Conversations. The MA(R)4S (3) (Learning Conversation) monitors the quality and extent of all the Learning Conversations going on in the organisation. Again, it does much more than merely record when and how it happens. It models the whole pattern of Learning Conversations, giving them an operational meaning that enables the Learning Manager and the Learning Coach to agree about how to drive them in an increasingly effective way.

System 4 is the conversation between the MA(R)4S (4) (Learning Opportunities) and the Learning Manager. We have seen earlier how the Task Supervisor can amplify the quality and effectiveness of each Learning Conversation by illuminating both the nature and the use learners can make of the learning resources in the domain. The Task Supervisor is the focus of much questioning and innovative activity. This, properly channelled back into System 1, can have a highly beneficial effect on the primary work activities of the enterprise. This is one of the ways in which the organisation may learn. Similarly the System 4 conversation models the Learning Domain as one vast resource for learning. As the Learning Manager begins to experience what System 4 can achieve, the whole interpretation of the 'learning policy of the enterprise' may become very much enhanced. With the support of the Learning Coach and Task Supervisor, he or she is able to agree much more ambitious long-term learning horizons with the budding Self-Organised Learners.

The MA(R)4S (5) system (setting the Horizons of Learning) monitors this ongoing conversation between the Learning Coach and the Task Supervisor. This is the vehicle by which the coach is continually testing and expanding the Task Supervisor's understanding of the needs of the learners and the demands they would like to be able to make of the Learning Domain. In reverse, it is the vehicle whence the Task Supervisor helps the Learning Coach see the increasing possibilities which should inform each Learning Conversation he has with a Learner. By modelling these Horizons for Learning, the MA(R)4S (5) (setting Learning Horizons) offers the Learning Manager a line of understanding (System 5) into the aspirations for learning held within the enterprise. Again this can inform his or her whole implementation of the learning policy.

The MA(R)4S (6) (management of the five systems) is monitoring and modelling how the Learning Manager coordinates his or her conversations with Systems 1, 2, 3, 4 and 5 to implement the learning policy of the enterprise. This is the sixth of our Systems 7.

System 6 has the capacity to represent and compare the models driving each of the five systems. It can also monitor the coordination of each type of conversation to ensure that the system is functioning effectively in its own terms. However, 'effectively' means different things within each situation and even in the same situation at different times. In real, 'natural habitat' situations, unsynchronised and conflicting purposes are often distributed around the system. What System 6 does when it functions effectively is to

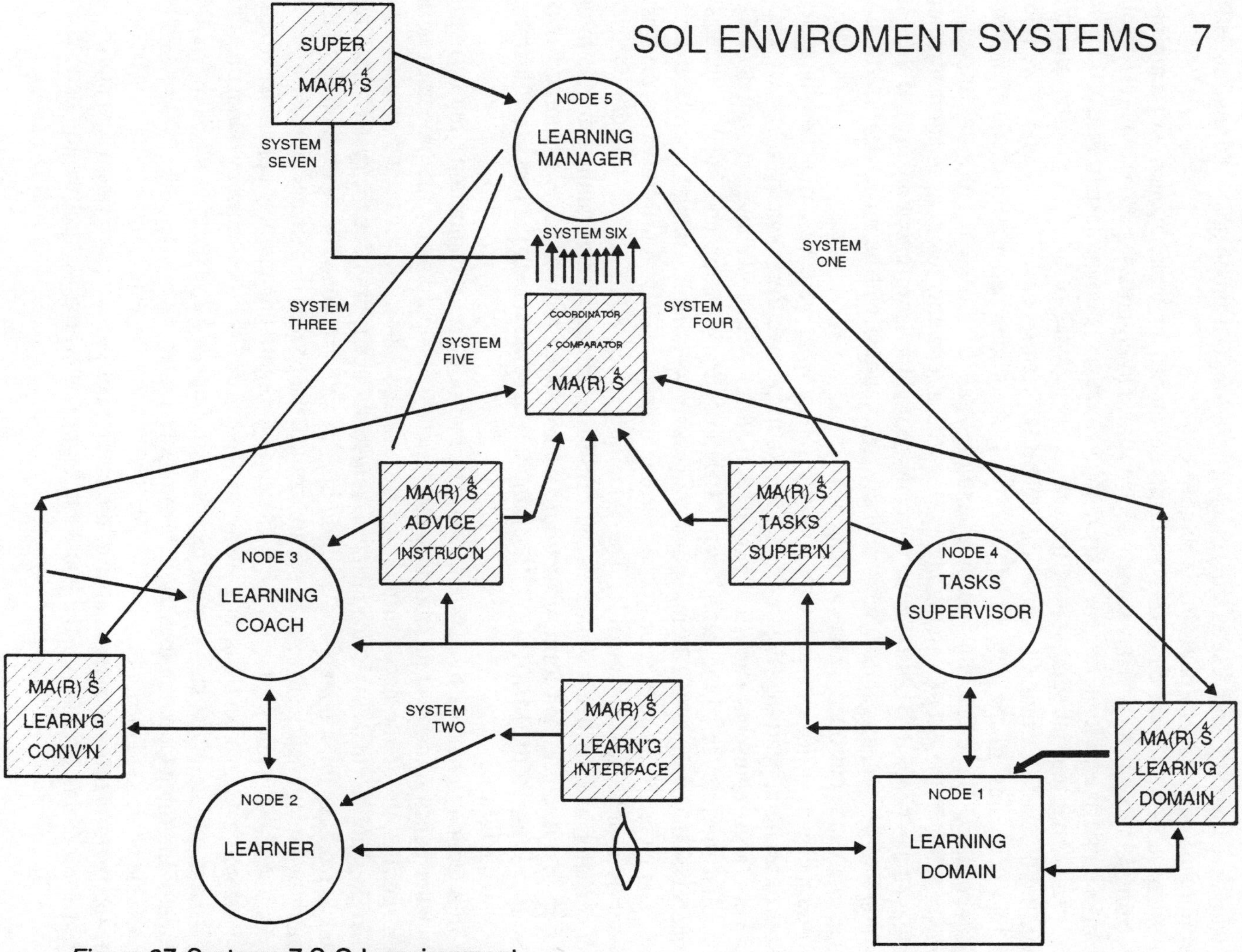

SOL ENVIROMENT SYSTEMS 7

Figure 27 Systems 7 S-O-L environment

negotiate conversationally the intention of the system and then guide, select, diagnose, direct and synchronise the various 'meaning as modelling' operations to achieve the emerging intentionality. Different intentionalities require a different pattern of MA(R)4S settings to drive the conversations. They need to coordinate the different system models, gradually expanding and testing out understanding until a productive, sharing, but still evolving network of understanding is achieved.

We have in a different context (Postscript) developed a simple taxonomy of learning–teaching relationships. This has already been outlined in Figure 24 (p. 204) in Part II. This spans a range of activities from the 'expert demonstration', through 'expert instruction', to the 'traditional tutorial situation' to the two S-O-L modes of the task-focused and the learning-focused Learning Conversation. In Part II (Retrospective Commentary), we refer to this taxonomy in the context of specifying the wider parameters of the Learning Conversation. These teaching–learning activities call for different types and mixes of conversation in the S-O-L environment. How these teaching–learning relationships are achieved can be used to illustrate the meaning behind the term 'intentionality'. If there is no intentionality management, what actually gets learned will be much degraded (as it usually is) and controlled by happenstance.

Another way of looking at intentionality is to use what we have designated the seven faces of teaching–learning (Figure 25, p. 202, Retrospective Commentary to Part II). Each of these faces represents a unique configuration of the Systems 7 conversational network. The first three relate to the *task-focused* Learning Conversation and involve the Task Supervisor in setting up the Domain and conversing with the Learning Coach so that the user can be enabled to set appropriate learning objectives. The fourth involves the Task Supervisor in an assessment role. The remaining three relate to the *learning-focused* conversation and involve a shared awareness of the 'intentionality' guiding the Learning Coach into the level and form of Learning Conversation required. The Learning Coach also makes use of the MA(R)4S (2) (learning interface) to reflect the process of learning back to the user.

In selecting to put the five systems into any one of these configurations, the Learning Manager needs some overall model of the structure and purpose of the processes he is configuring. He or she needs to monitor each conversation to collate and compare the emerging models (meanings) and progressively to define the direction the system is taking. This is fed back for comment and reaction in each conversation. The consequences of the emerging intentionality are used to set and control the pattern of conversations.

On the one hand he or she has the S-O-Learners negotiating learning contracts through the Learning Coach and learning away in 'free form' in the Learning Domain. The S-O-Learners are aided and abetted by the Task Supervisor, who tries to maximise the range of Learning Opportunities available to each learner.

On the other hand the Learning Manager has the Task Supervisor clarifying how he sees the job performance of each member of the enterprise. This allows System 1 to clarify its need for learning (that is, for the learner to learn that which will get the job done more productively, with more quality and with greater cost-effectiveness). This is often wrongly seen by trainers as identifying the training needs of the organisation.

The Learning Manager then has to coordinate the conversation with Systems 1 to 5 to negotiate a series of *task-focused* learning–training horizons with each member of the organisation and to mediate and coordinate the mix of S-O-Learning that goes on in free form and of instruction that is necessary to help the S-O-Learners make the best and most economical use of the expert resources available to them. He or she has to negotiate a *learning-focused* learning contract with each member of the enterprise. This is defined in terms of helping them to increase their capacity for learning. He or she also has to see to it that the Learning Coach works with the learner to implement the contract and must then coordinate the *task-focused* and *learning-focused* contracts with each learner and co-ordinate these to see that each S-O-Learner makes the best use of their Learning Opportunities and the enterprise makes the best use of its Self-Organised Learners.

Much of this discussion will apply with equal, if not more, force to educational and training enterprises. Many are locked into over-learned, well-established and traditionally tolerated robot-like ways of going about their jobs. However, until recently training, with its more immediate needs to provide visible results, was much more innovative and adventurous in its approaches and in its willingness to try new methods than the equivalent sections of education. This has obvious advantages, but it does mean that training seems more likely to be influenced by the latest flavour of the month in method and technology, picking them up, playing with them and putting them down again without developing any long-term stable system of systematic, well-validated development. On the other hand any development may be better than making no attempt to develop one's approach and teaching methods at all.

The difference between the public or private enterprise and the educational enterprise is that in education the prime purpose of all the people and activities in the Learning Domain *is learning*. There are many different interpretations as to what this might mean. One view might be that schools, colleges and universities are the custodians of public knowledge in our society and that children, pupils and students of all ages and levels of achievement have a right and a responsibility to act as S-O-Learners in digesting, evaluating, using and passing on this knowledge (General Introduction). An alternate version of this is to see knowledge as a means of social coordination; as something which is systematically dished out to other-organised learners. Another view is that educational institutions should not only be custodians of knowledge, but that they should also accept the responsibility for creating, developing, sifting, testing and evaluating knowledge to keep it up to date, ahead of our times, predicting possible futures and generating the debates about philosophical and moral issues that keep a society alert and alive. The pupils and students are seen as temporary members of this enterprise.

Yet another view is to see each educational enterprise as having a constituency which it serves. Some are local, some national, some international. Some have a general constituency; others are very specialist or selective in deciding who they will set out to attract or to whom they will offer membership. Those that see themselves in this way may decide that they are not only custodians and generators of public knowledge but they also have a responsibility to see that knowledge is put to good use in their constituency. This provides a good test bed for evaluating the validity of different systems or paradigms of knowledge as these play themselves out in the community or in society over prolonged periods of time.

This preamble is offered simply to provoke the reader into realising that the nature, range, scope and time structure of the Learning Domain of an educational enterprise is not something that should too easily be taken for granted. It is also true that despite what they might say, very few educational enterprises have a coherent, sustained and systematically developing 'learning policy'. Very few have a Learning Policy Committee in the sense that this term is used in Systems 7.

The intentionality of Systems 7: creating the learning policy

Now we have all five nodes of Systems 7 firing and six of the seven systems functioning, but we have not yet fully seen how *intentionality* becomes built into the learning system. How does the educational, commercial, industrial or public enterprise develop a learning policy which can shape, guide and coordinate the direction of all its learning activities? How is this coordinated with its operational (work or educational) policy?

As the learning power within an enterprise develops it becomes possible to make plans for how this power could and should be used and further developed. The Learning Coach, the Task Supervisor and Learning Manager together with representatives of the learners and the Learning Domain can get together to form a *Learning Policy Committee*. The learners and the Learning Domain have special status since they each have 'product' expectations. In education the learners may be directly or indirectly financing the system. They have expectations about increasing their learning capacity and increasing their learning (as new or further developed skills, knowledge and attitudes; that is, as new or developed personal modelling). The Learning Domain has purposes of its own. In a working enterprise it will almost certainly be financing the learning system. It expects the learners, as members of the enterprise, to be able to contribute more and more effectively to achieving its objectives. It may also expect the learning system to add to the enterprise's ability to cope with change; that is, it may expect the learning system to enable the enterprise as enterprise to learn how to learn: Chapter 6 develops this theme. The other three 'members' of the policy-creating committee have 'process' expectations of the learning system. The Learning Coach expects to have the time and resources to enter either directly or vicariously into core Learning Conversations with each Learner. The Task Supervisor expects to have the resources and authority to create imaginative Learning Opportunities in the Learning Domain, and the Learning Manager expects to be able to meet their expectations and to have the resources to be able to negotiate, either directly or vicariously, productive and viable Learning Horizons with each Learner. The Learning Manager is also in the unique position of having monitored and modelled the functioning of the learning system overall. Here the Learning Manager plays out two distinct but related roles. He or she recruits the intentionalities emerging *intrinsically* from within the operations of Systems 7 to coordinate each of the conversations. The *extrinsic* intentionalities – that is, policies of the organisation with which he or she is employed, and which in a top executive director function he or she has helped to formulate – are channelled into Systems 7 to interrelate task policies into learning policies.

First, the members of the policy committee need to share their modelling of the learning system to understand how it is developing and what it is or is not capable of achieving. Having shared a developing understanding of its capabilities, the committee can then work out how the legitimate expectation of the learners and the legitimate expectations of the enterprise can be collated and creatively combined into a coherent learning policy. This should provide the Learning Manager with clear guidelines and adequate criteria to be able to negotiate the Learning Horizons and for coordinating Systems 1–5 to optimise their achievement with high learning productivity and high learning quality, cost-effectively. The 'learning director' is recruited as a resource for the management of the *learning policy*. In Chapter 6 we introduce our conversational technology for 'feedback for learning' in groups. This is an additional important resource that the Learning Manager can use for effectively managing the operational link between organisational and learning policy. The MA(R)4S (7) (creating learning policy) monitors and models this activity. This defines the seventh system.

The Systems 7 aproach can amplify the quality of learning activities. Identifying various malfunctioning or missing features in coordinating Systems 7 may illuminate various problems that arise in current educational institutions and the training functions in private and public enterprises. It may also suggest how getting each of the systems functioning and then effectively coordinating them could transform the quality of learning in such enterprises with which the reader is concerned.

Systems 7 as a community of selves

In the Prospective Commentary we discussed how the learner in a one-to-one situation, individual learners in a group situation, and the group as a learning entity situation, converse with their Learning Domain, supported by the Learning Coach, Task Supervisor, Learning Manager and the executive committee.

Earlier in this chapter we introduced the notion that Systems 7 can be almost wholly addressed within one person as a learning entity. In this sense it can represent a 'community of selves', where all the functions go on in one head. The individual and his or her chosen learning domain becomes the Self-Organised Learning environment. Such a person has not only internalised the Learning Conversation, but also the roles of the Learing Coach, Task Supervisor and Learning Manager. *Systems 7 offers the person a content-independent system through which to become their own conversational support system.* Throughout this chapter we have concentrated on how Systems 7 can represent a whole organisation, where the learner is many people and where there are departments concerned with separating and running the various functions. This has been necessary to show how a whole enterprise (even a very large one) can take on board the promotion of S-O-L. Let us end this chapter with another realistic proposition. Systems 7 can be controlled not only by humans but also by a computer, in which case 'support generators' take on all the functions of their human equivalents. As the 'human' Learner converses with the Learning Domain addressed by the machine, all systems are machine modelled (put through the MA(R)4S process) within a unique Systems 7 configuration. In the Functional Taxonomy of Reflective Tools we outline the specifications for this as the Intelligent Learning System: S-O-L (ILS – S-O-L).

Chapter six

Conversational evaluation and purposive change: the enterprise as a Self-Organised Learning environment

In this chapter we shall consider the practical implications of Systems 7 for the implementation of S-O-L in small and large groups. 'Conversational evaluation' is introduced as a scheme for guiding the process of organisational change. This runs in real time, producing the feedback required to control those parameters of performance that the individual and the organisation values. All the MA(R)4S activities of Systems 7 generate 'knowledge of results' which combine to form a *system of conversational* evaluation. This not only informs each node about its own performance but also informs the organisation so that it can steer its learning policy to achieve its operating objectives.

Anarchy? Self-Organised Learners seek valid feedback

People without direct experience of Learning Conversations sometimes express misgivings that the cultivation of too many Self-Organised Learners within an organisation may be disruptive. They somehow assume that, on becoming self-organised, previously loyal, or at least unquestioning, members of the organisation will suddenly begin to act irresponsibly, pursuing their own unbridled purposes. They equate self-organisation with what they call anarchy. The opposite is actually the case. Learning Conversations are a form of self-discipline which acknowledges that personal fulfilment can often be achieved through working imaginatively and productively with one's colleagues. When Self-Organised Learners find that despite persistent efforts they cannot negotiate a rewarding role within their organisation they will usually feel competent and confident enough to seek an alternative, more satisfying position elsewhere.

In our experience the problems that arise from promoting Self-Organised Learning are different. They are the 'problems' of having alert, loyal, competent, questioning staff concerned with doing an increasingly good job and concerned to have those around them doing likewise. The Self-Organised Learner seeks valid meaning in work. This involves working productively to achieve quality results by cost-effective means. People concerned to work well put pressure on less competent or more complacent colleagues, but what results is not anarchy. It is a systematic drive for controlled change in valued directions. This is achieved by having self-reliant people working cooperatively together to achieve shared negotiated purposes without compromising their independent spirit. Perhaps this is, in its best and original sense, close to anarchy; but it is neither revolutionary nor is it lawless and chaotic.

To move a 'system of Learning Conversations' from an exclusive preoccupation with personally valued learning towards organisationally valued objectives does not, initially, require any effort at all. People are naturally interested in helping the organisation for whom they work to achieve the objectives it sets itself. Amazingly, they see this as being what they have contracted to do. Only after prolonged effort, if learners begin to feel some doubt as to whether what they are being asked to do is being properly appreciated and, anyway, whether they are being asked to do the right things to achieve the objectives, does some disenchantment with the current management or the organisation ensue.

The way in which each person in the chain of command performs depends on how they think and feel about their job. It depends upon how they model their job, the meaning they attribute to it. The 'effectiveness' of each worker, supervisor and manager depends upon how their model 'works'; in handling equipment, in supervising their subordinates, in understanding the needs of their colleagues, and in responding to the requirements of their customers or the other people to whom they answer. Their effectiveness can be evaluated from each of these perspectives both subjectively and more objectively, formally and informally.

Each employee can only perform his or her job according to their own understanding of what is properly required of them. S-O-L projects have shown that many learners have by default been allowed to stabilise on rather inadequate definitions of their job and how it relates to those around them. This is also true for schoolchildren and students, who often have rather peculiar ideas of what 'learning', 'being at school' or 'being a student' is all about.

Each Self-Organised Learner will negotiate learning purposes which seem to them likely to improve their own performance in the terms in which they think and feel it should be valued. This puts the onus on others – such as, teachers, trainers, subordinates, senior colleagues and/or management – to ensure that specific, informal feedback about performance is provided; that it is consistent, within itself and within the stated aims. The terms in which it is offered and its timing operationally defines the job they want done. It should provide an operational context within which viable models of the job can develop.

Each person's effectiveness depends upon how their activities are informed by their appreciation of the objectives of the enterprise or how these can be interpreted from management activities. They translate this appreciation into effective action. They infer the management's intentions from their own day-to-day experience of the demands the organisation makes of them and the feedback they receive about how it values what they do. How they think and feel about their job determines their freedom to respond to the demands of their specific duties and to learn constructively from the feedback they get about their performance. Their 'meaning as modelling' of their job determines how they are able to deal with it, and with change. This understanding of their job is formed in their day-to-day doing of it. Sporadic 'one-off' team briefings or management pep-talks will be interpreted in terms of how well they fit or do not fit in with this operational model.

In the education system, it requires considerable work and some insight for a learner to achieve an understanding of the exact nature, meaning and status of the total pattern of assignments, projects, *ad hoc* tests and formal examinations. Since those vary from one institution to another and within the same instition at different times and for different purposes, it may take a fair amount of MA(R)4S (4) (learning opportunities) reflection in Systems 3, 4 and 5 to provoke the necessary feedback within a conversational framework. The feedback for learning should provide an adequate and viable model within which the learner may judge their performance, both for the purpose of conspicuous achievement and, more subtly, to discover just how well they are thought to be doing within the personal criteria held by valued others in the educational institution. The second purpose is perhaps only achieved conversationally outside the formal teaching situations.

Let us again emphasise that the difficulty with being a Self-Organised Learner in an organisation is the need to establish to your own satisfaction, in your own terms, just how well you are doing. This is not always as easy as it might appear. We have encouraged and enabled people to become Self-Organised Learners in a wide variety of different work organisations. As they become self-organised, our learners always attempt to discover just what it is that the organisation, usually in the guise of their immediate boss, expects of them and just how their success is being judged or measured. This is not something that we build into our programmes in the early stages; rather the contrary. *Experience has shown us that unless or until something radical is done to generate valid and reliable feedback-for-learning, people are best off not relying on being able to obtain it.*

The Learning Practitioner needs to be concerned with this, being committed to helping people increase their capacity for learning. However, in our experience, the more seriously the learner asks to be told how well he or she is doing, the more likely it is that the comments and evidence offered will fall apart in their hands. This happens because job performance appraisal is not often treated as a conversational process, so the MA(R)4S (2) (learning interface) never gets extended outside the learner's head. Very few people feel that they are engaged in a serious, valid and sustained conversation about what they are achieving or what they are learning.

A learner may experience mismatch between a job as explicitly specified and how it is implicitly defined in the procedures that influence the doing of it. The degree of this match or mismatch will determine how they personally understand the job. It also influences their willingness and ability to commit themselves to it. For example, a university lecturer may find that her job is contractually defined as a mix of teaching, administration and research. She may find that the procedures, timetabling and immediate demand structure emphasise the administration and routines of teaching and examining at the expense of research and the quality of teaching. In the longer term, the dedicated researcher and conscientious teacher may find that what is valued for promotional purposes is conspicuous achievement – that is, the number of papers published, and so on. This mismatch is embodied in the bitter academic joke about the Roman centurion: told that Jesus is the greatest teacher the world has ever seen, he then asks why he is being crucified; the answer: 'Not enough publications'. Most jobs differ formally and actually in terms of their short-term pay-offs, long-term pay-offs and organisational objectives.

There is much to be gained by taking a long, hard look at what the shape and the effectiveness of your own organisation would be if everybody did their job:

1 in the way most likely to lead to early promotion; or
2 in the way they really believe it should be done; or
3 in the way that would lead to most approval from (a) their subordinates, (b) their colleagues, or (c) their immediate boss; or
4 in the way it is defined in their job description; or
5 by responding merely to the short-term demands made upon them.

Our Learning Conversation activity has been concerned with helping each learner we have worked with to understand their own job in terms which are personal, but also negotiated with all relevant colleagues. Such understanding is constructed in honest, hard-hitting exchanges of actual first-hand experience gained on the job. It cannot be fabricated out of second-hand experience. People's 'meaning as modelling' of jobs often do not coordinate well one with another. An enhanced personal understanding of each job results from systematic, S-O-L-inspired negotiation about how each job relates to the others around it. This expresses itself in forms that appear to others as greatly increased motivation. We have been very pleasantly surprised by the overwhelming commitment to 'the enterprise' released by S-O-L. This contrasts with the resistance to change that can result when new methods are introduced using 'briefing' which does not allow a collaborative review of the function and content of each job, nor how the proposed change will actually affect it.

In terms of Systems 7 we are talking about the MA(R)4S activities (namely, the conversing about modelling activities that continually raise awareness and improve understanding). If the learner does not feel that the feedback for learning generated by the system is actually a valid commentary on their job performance they have great difficulty in judging whether their learning is making them 'better' at their job. *Intermittent, inconsistent, unreliable and/or invalid information offers misleading and confusing feedback. Such 'control' information makes it difficult to learn to become more effective; particularly in terms which 'the enterprise' will value.*

One often validated observation is that ill-informed judgements and pseudo-'measurements' of people's performance may have led to many under-learners being over-promoted and many self-organised achievers becoming alienated and therefore under-promoted. As the system of Learning Conversations develops, there is increasing pressure for feedback about performance to become more specific, accurate and valid. The provision of such feedback is an essential component of the management of learning.

Both in educational and other enterprises this is more often than not the situation as it is experienced by the learner. The people who know most about how the learner is performing are never asked for an assessment. Used within an enterprise that is committed to learning, the development of systems that recruit peer judgement or even the judgements of those being taught, supervised or managed by the learner can transform the quality of the feedback for learning.

Feedback for learning comes in many forms, but it is useful to identify a simplified two-by-two categorisation. Feedback can be offered *informally* or as part of a recognised *formal* system (such as bonus schemes, counselling, financial accounts, quality audit figures, annual appraisal). Whether conveyed formally or informally, feedback about performance may be offered in the form of *subjective judgements* (for instance, annual appraisal exercises) or in the form of more *seemingly objective measures* (like measures of productivity, quality of service and cost effectiveness, customer satisfaction, even national examination results, and so on). Subjective judgements can be the result of careful systematic critical assessment; or they may be very idiosyncratic and haphazard. Objective numerical measures of performance can be accurate, reliable and very informative; but they can be very confusing if the data are incomplete, arbitrarily selective, misplaced or unreliable. Objective measures can also be wholly misleading if the indices of performance do not separately and together validly represent what they purport to measure.

Feedback for learning: subjective judgement and objective measurement as complementary sources of evidence

So far we have argued that each of the members of any enterprise need to be able to inform themselves about how well they are doing their job. Everybody tries to do this. Minimally it allows them to stay within the acceptable performance requirements, but such information allows the individual Self-Organised Learner a continuing opportunity to understand better and to do what is required of them. In an enterprise manned by S-O-Learners, they can begin to converse one with another about the nature of their jobs and how they can do them better. This will inevitably upgrade their corporate view of what these jobs might be, for them better to achieve their objectives and even to set greater objectives.

Each 'job' has its own 'natural', if minimal, feedback network built in. This is provided by customers, suppliers and colleagues in industry, and by parents, Local Education Authorities, local community, and so on for schools. Those on whom the consequences of the job impinge will minimally provide some level of complaints when things go wrong. They may even offer compliments when things go exceptionally well. Such a network of 'lasting consequences' operates sluggishly and often intermittently. This may lull the complacent into periods of unjustified self-satisfaction interspersed with crises when criticism breaks through.

However, enterprises do not rely totally on the contingency pattern of this 'natural system' to define their activities. They attempt to build some system of 'quickened commentary'; that is, early warnings of when things may be beginning to go wrong and/or early congratulations when things look as if they may be going particularly well. The nature of this 'quickened commentary' will depend upon the 'meaning as modelling' of the 'enterprise'. The explanatory model, the system of causes and consequences that are attributed to the situation will determine and shape what people see as early warnings or reasons for congratulation. Learners testing out these models and, conversing with one another, will often find themselves operating at the constructive and even creative levels in the search for meaning, they will be refining and sometimes re-defining the nature of their jobs. Their greater understanding will allow them to generate better feedback-for-learning information and use this to improve their understanding, and so on. This is the optimistic view; in practice individual learners in an enterprise often experience difficulties in obtaining such feedback for learning. The more outspoken ask for some performance evaluation on a regular basis.

Subjective assessment of job performance: the Feedback-for-Learning package

When learners ask for feedback for learning, some discover that the person nominally in charge of them has little knowledge of how they are doing. Other staff are reluctant, not inclined, or unable to comment on performance even though teaching or supervising the learner face-to-face. 'Counselling' someone is often seen as equivalent to 'tearing him off a strip'. Some Self-Organised Learners even go to the lengths of systematically evaluating their own performance either by using the formal appraisal procedure used by the organisation or as a self-assessment exercise creating their own. This is then presented to the teacher or manager in charge for comment.

Even when the 'appraisal' procedures appear to be working, the underlying reality may be that appraisal forms are treated as paperwork to be fed into the system to keep management happy. The appraisee may get little chance to appreciate fully the assessment of their performance and no opportunity to develop a plan for self-development. Some- times the appraisal means little or nothing to the learner. This may be because a centrally designed appraisal form contains criteria or rating scales that have little operational meaning to the assessor on the spot.

In such circumstances members of an enterprise may express considerable discontent with how people get promoted or put on to a probationary list. Both those who have been passed over and those who have been recognised may feel it was for the wrong reasons. They cannot identify much consistency of judgement in the decision-making. Often the grapevine reports quite bitter rows in promotion boards and staff meetings. This is because there are no really shared criteria, and long-term judgements are made on the basis of isolated, high-profile incidents.

In our action research projects in education and industry, these disquiets about the quality of judgements made of performance have led us into intense discussion with teachers, administrators, supervisors and managers about exactly what criteria they personally would use. We shall briefly describe one commercial situation, and readers whose interests are in the field of education might find it useful to treat this as an allegory and review its relevance to the school, polytechnic or university. Initially we gradually identified a set of fifteen criteria which seemed to represent the major dimensions of personal judgements made by four operational chiefs about the people working for them. From these 'chiefs' criteria' we then developed a Mark I Feedback-for-Learning package designed to produce systematic and reliable judgements of the performance of each employee by those colleagues and immediate superiors who have had an opportunity to see them perform their duties. Suffice it here to note the universal satisfaction shown by all concerned, including union representatives, with subjective assessments which are based on locally relevant criteria and are elicited using systematic procedures for obtaining reliable comparative judgements across the whole range of learners and assessors.

The chiefs' criteria provoked considerable discussion among the assessors, who felt that these were incomplete. We therefore trawled for criteria from a wider franchise of colleagues, supervisors and managers. These were collated, systematized, elaborated and endorsed by more than thirty people in small group discussions. The Mark II Feedback-for-Learning package was thus developed. The twenty-one criteria were grouped into seven major categories; job performance, organisational, communication, man-management, personal and learning skills, as well as outcomes achieved. This was used systematically to obtain reliable subjective evaluations from all those in a position to be able to make a judgement. *It is, however, very important to note that the process of publicly negotiating relevant criteria from all the interested parties to establish a locally accepted and relevant package is probably as important as the particular set of criteria finally decided upon.*

The procedure

The first stage of this procedure is to provide each assessor with a package of materials. In addition to a detailed set of instructions about how it should be used, the package contains:

1 a set of cards each showing the name of one of the learners whose job performance is to be judged;
2 cards labelled 1 to 7 to be laid out on a table top to define the positions on a seven-point scale;
3 a series of 'criteria-defining strips', one for each criterion, to be used in judging the learners' job performance; and
4 a record sheet on which the assessor records his or her judgements.

The first step involves each assessor in selecting those learners 'known well enough on the job to make such judgements'. This is achieved by a comparative card-sorting and scaling technique. The main exercise involves making comparative judgements about all the learners on each criterion in turn. This is achieved by using a similar card-sorting procedure. The completed record sheets from all assessors are analysed on the micro-computer in four different ways, each of which has a place in providing feedback for learning:

(a) *The SPACE-FOCUSed display of the judgements made by one assessor*: This orders the learners according to the cumulative values of their ratings. It also re-orders the criteria putting like with like. This analysis enables the individual assessor to reflect upon how he or she uses the criteria and on how these judgements sort the learners into groups or clusters of similar performers.

(b) *The SPACE-FOCUSed display of the judgements made by all the assessors about any one learner*: This orders the assessors according to the cumulative values of their ratings of this learner. It also re-orders the criteria putting like with like. It introduces a 'worst view', 'best view' and 'average view' for each criterion.

Learners find this analysis particularly useful since it shows them the group view of how they are judged to be doing their job. It also shows *who* judges them in what way on each criterion. This has proved particularly useful in subsequent Learning Conversations when the learner can use this pattern of judgements to establish referents against which they can improve and elaborate their own assessments of their job performance. This allows them to set relevant PLCs.

(c) *The group view of all the learners relative to one another*: This collects all the average ratings from each of the learner's type-2 analysis (item b above) and offers them in one SPACE-FOCUSed display.

This form of the results is particularly useful to the Learning Manager as a summary of job performance. Over a series it can clearly be seen who is judged to be improving and on what criteria.

(d) Finally, on any one criterion, *all the assessors' ratings of all the learners can be SPACE-FOCUSed and displayed*: This can serve as the basis for a hard and precise reflection among the assessors about *how* and *why* they differ in their ratings. This not only reveals assessors who are generally hard, and those who are generally lenient; it also shows which assessors hold certain learners in especially high or low regard. Learning Conversations among the assessors about how they view job per-formance can improve the quality of the informal feedback-for-learning commentary offered to each learner in day-to-day interaction with the assessors.

Figure 28 illustrates the form of the results provided in (b) above.

There is considerable observational and anecdotal evidence that assessors are offering more and better day-to-day feedback quite outside the operation of this procedure. This has been produced informally through the demands of the Self-Organised Learners coupled with the increased awareness by the assessors created by the systematic use of a tool properly designed to meet their local requirements. Thus we were able to transform the subjective judgement aspects of a seemingly arbitrary 'reporting up and kicking down' management information system into one that is acknowledged to be effective,

Figure 28 Feedback for learning: the SPACE-FOCUSed display of the assessor's judgements – Example A

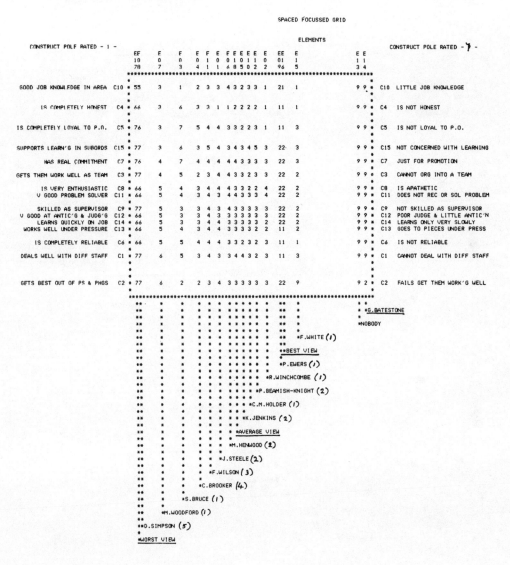

SPACED FOCUSSED GRID

Figure 28 Example B

SPACED FOCUSSED GRID

Figure 28 Example C

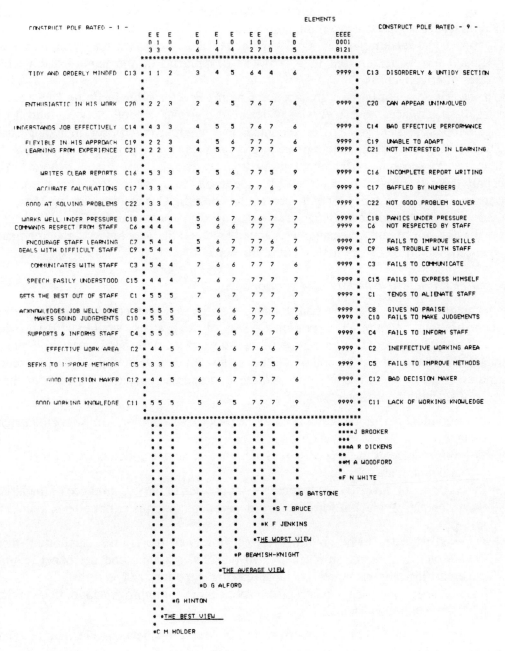

constructive and felt fair for real-time control. The other half of this system provides and uses objective measures of job effectiveness in a similar way. Unfortunately the prevailing tendency to view the chain of command predominately as a 'reporting upwards system' had produced budgetary and production control mechanisms ill-adapted to managing performance and encouraging learning. Regular use of the Feedback-for-learning package highlighted this issue and led to a complete reappraisal of the numerical objective measures of effectiveness.

The clearly apparent fairness and openness of this Feedback-for-Learning Package and the results it produces have met with widespread approval among its users, and it has attracted the attention of some national companies and public enterprises, including Local Education Authorities. The whole procedure only takes an assessor about an hour and a half to record judgements for about thirty to forty people (say, fifteen criteria). The specially tailored software package analyses the results from twenty to thirty assessors in about three hours. It is easily used directly by the Learning Coach and Learning Manager. Experience with this package to date shows it to be a very powerful and flexible resource for managing self-organised change. It is already well on the way towards meeting many of the needs identified earlier in this part of the book.

The search for objective measures of performance

In this action research study we had assumed that the management control information generated in implementing the operational policy of the business would swiftly provide data from which we could cull a pattern of measures of learner effectiveness in terms of productivity, quality of service and cost effectiveness. In fact we optimistically proceeded on the assumption that we could generate these measures separately for each of three aspects of a person's job, namely:

1 the individual performances of each of the people working for them (or being taught by them);
2 the performance of these people working together as one coherent team (or subject-matter course); and
3 the contribution made by the learner's work domain to the performance of the larger work domain of which it forms a part (department, enterprise, or college, year, and so on);
4 we even expected to be able to ascertain how well the learner 'supported' their domain and the people in it (their own personal planning and personnel, course materials, learning resources, personal tutoring' functions and so forth);
5 and how they innovated and accepted responsibility for improvement of the working methods within their domain.

In a number of our studies this way of describing the components of a learner's job has much helped the coach and the learners themselves in their evaluation of their performance and their diagnosis of their learning needs.

POST OFFICE   ROYAL MAIL LETTERS BUSINESS
TRIAL M.L.O   (Machine Letter Office)

PRODUCTIVITY
CHANGE OVER 18 MONTHS

RAISED
BY   **24%**

QUALITY OF **S**ERVICE
CHANGES OVER 13 MONTHS

MAX
100%

RAISED   FROM   TO
1ST. CL.   97% - 99%
2ND. CL.   93% - 98%

COSTS
CHANGE OVER 12 MONTHS

REDUCED
BY   **19%**

Figure 29 Results in one trial office

However, our early attempts to obtain such objective measures of the effectiveness of any individual learner failed in this case. The data just were not available. Nor was there, until much later on, appreciation of the management and control needs for collecting such data and making them available. It has taken two years to encourage the provision of a pattern of objective measures capable of backing and supplementing the results from the subjective Feedback-for-Learning Package.

The design of such objective measures of performance for feedback for learning is a specialist job and varies from business to business in terms of the need to obtain information and indices, which relate unambiguously to the domain of the learner and which hold the major dimensions of the performance in dynamic equilibrium one to another; as well as in terms which truly interpret the objectives of the enterprise; into domain-specific measures; and which can be recombined into measures which reflect the performance of the larger domains of which it is a part, whilst clearly indicating the nature of the contribution that the smaller domain is making to the larger.

Figure 29 shows how one trial office successfully increased their productivity, quality of service and cost-effectiveness over an 18-month period.

The monitoring of learning: the S-O-L spreadsheets and the Personal Learning Biography

After the Feedback-for-Learning Package has been used at regular bi-monthly intervals over a year, the Learning Manager and the Learning Coach can begin to reflect on the amount of 'progress' that was being made by the learners in organisational terms. Progress can be related to the frequency and quality of the Learning Conversations. The Learning Manager can ask for evidence of this relationship because he needs to know whether it would be cost-effective to invest more money in S-O-L activities.

This request presents the Learning Coach with an ethical problem, since the content of individual Learning Conversations should remain confidential. Much of his success depends on the trust that the learners feel they could place in him. To overcome the problem, a category system was developed for the 'type' and 'content' of Learning Conversations, which could be used to provide the Learning Manager with useful general information whilst preserving necessary confidentiality.

The Learning Manager and the Learning Coach began to collate changes in the feedback-for-learning job performance assessment against the types of Learning Conversations that the learners were involved in. This quickly revealed the impact of the Learning Conversations on job performance. Since they found this collating of information so useful, an S-O-L computer spreadsheet was prepared for each learner. This showed the feedback-for-learning assessments criterion by criterion, the sequence and timing of the Learning Conversations and any other S-O-L and training events. They began to add objective numerical measurements of job performance as and when these became available and were judged reliable and relevant enough to warrant attention.

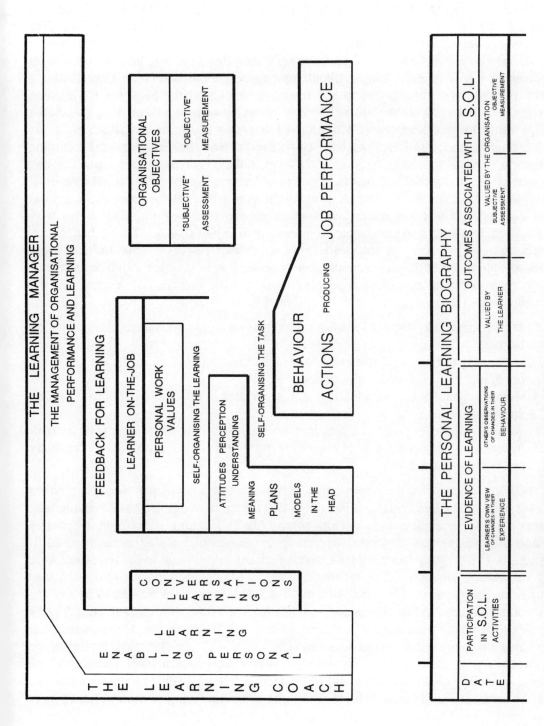

Figure 30 The model behind the Personal Learning Biography

These S-O-L spreadsheets formed the basis for the Learning Managers' review of the learning potential of the organisation. It also provided the Learning Coach and the Task Supervisor with additional systematic information on which to negotiate an extension of the learning horizons (Chapter 5). The Learning Coach also found it to be a sound basis for offering feedback to each learner about how successful or otherwise their Learning Conversations were turning out to be. It also systematised the feedback-for-learning assessments so that the learner had a clear view about how the organisation's view of their job performance was progressing. This allowed them to set more realistic PLCs.

Eventually, the S-O-L spreadsheet can develop into the full Personal Learning Biography method for recording progress. However, there is no point in insisting that this happen before the 'models of the management of learning' in the heads of all concerned can make sense of this more complex information. Figure 30 explains how this system has been developed, how it now works, and how it might evolve in the future. This uses a diary of Learning Events as a sequential basis against which to plot changes. These changes are, firstly, experiential (namely, changes in how individuals perceive, think and feel about work, people and events) and, secondly, behavioural (that is, changes in job performance and ways of behaving at work with people and influencing events). This experiential and behavioural evidence of learning can be evaluated in terms of:

1   self-organisation (whether the evidence reveals changes which were intended by the learner);
2   personal but unintended (different from what the learner intended before the event but in retrospect valued by him or her);
3   work-orientated (changes which are directly related to the objectives of the working enterprise); and
4   valued by the enterprise (changes that are seen by others in the enterprise as contributing towards achieving its objectives more productively, more cost-effectively and with more quality).

The Personal Learning Biography embodies our attempt to develop a '3-by-2' approach (that is, to deal in experiential and behavioural evidence of learning (the '2') and to take note of short-term, medium-term and longer-term (the '3') 'results' of learning. The model behind this biographical method of recording the results of learning is summarised in Figure 30. The Personal Learning Biographical data should be read in the following way. The first column contains a diary record of all the S-O-L activities in which that particular learner has participated. It is anticipated that the S-O-L activities lead first to changes in perception, attitudes and/or understanding in the learner's own view of their work. This is the first (that is, the 'experiential') evidence of learning. The Learning Conversation, the PLC and the other tools in the Learning Coaches' 'kit', are designed to encourage awareness and reflection and lead on to positive personal experimentation. These activities almost inevitably change the 'models' in the learner's head. If the learner does change, only he or she can really know what they are now thinking, feeling about and seeing their work situation. Only the learner has direct access to his or her own experience and consciousness (Prologue).

However, the conversational process usually yields significant indicators of such internal changes. These conversational indicators are probably the most subtle behavioural evidence available to an observer. Other more obvious evidence exists in changes in the way the learner does his or her job and/or interacts with colleagues. Thus others can observe (and machines including simulators can record) changes in the learner's behaviour.

Together the 'the learner's own view' and 'others' observations' corroborate or invalidate the hypothesis that the S-O-L activity has produced learning.

It is theoretically possible that the outcomes of this 'learning' (that is, discernible changes in experience and/or behaviour) might not be valued by either the learner himself or the organisation. However as the learning becomes more and more self-organised the outcomes associated with S-O-L become almost by definition more valued by the learner himself. Whether these outcomes are also valued by the organisation will depend on whether the learner's purposes align with the objectives of the enterprise. Earlier, we described how 'subjectively assessed' and 'objectively measured' indicators can be recruited to provide feedback for learning which could inform and guide the learner towards the organisation's objectives. It also explains how and why these are often missing. In collaboration with the Learning Coach, the Task Supervisor and the Learning Manager, we have worked with the learners and other managers in the organisation to construct such feedback-for-learning processes. *The primary use of performance evaluative data is to act as feedback for learning so that the learner can improve his or her performance in ways that better enable the enterprise to achieve its objectives.*

Self-controlled change in an enterprise and controlled evaluation

The Personal Learning Biography is a tool with which the Learning Manager can co-ordinate the learning of individuals in an enterprise and as a reflective tool with which the individual can represent and put their learning activities through the MA(R)4S process in order to develop an explanatory model of how he or she learns. This explanation is then used to bootstrap the learner's capacity for learning, yielding more evidence against which the model can be further improved. Coupled to the idea of the group-as-a-whole-as-learner is the 'Group Learning Biography'. This offers us a powerful tool for enabling a group (or an enterprise) to move into self-controlled change.

The ways in which the learners, Learning Managers and the organisation took to the spreadsheet and the Personal Learning Biography led us to see it as the core of a conversational method for evaluating the success or otherwise of S-O-L.

Conventional evaluation procedures used by organisations, including questionnaires, *ad hoc* interviews and various organisational performance measures nearly always show significant improvements when S-O-L is introduced, but there are also many other factors at work so that it is impossible to relate 'results' to S-O-L activities. There are also many different perspectives from which S-O-L could be viewed and evaluated. The expectations and values belonging to these perspectives develop and change as S-O-L becomes established. Altogether, our experiences led us to search for better indications of S-O-L effects than those revealed by conventional methods of evaluation.

1   We recognised that S-O-L might be very fruitful for the learner and yet appear to be almost a disaster for the organisation of which they were a member. This was clearly indicated in one technical college with whom we have worked. A series of fairly successful Learning Conversations led the students to clarify their purposes for the first time. About 60 per cent developed strategies for achieving their purposes which involved leaving the technical college to pursue other activities. Despite the fact that the 40 per cent who decided to stay became much more motivated and successful, the staff never saw the value of S-O-L in quite the same terms as we did! Other perspectives on the learning situation also have a legitimate interest in its outcomes, but these may be evaluated differently.

2   We have also recognised that there are short-term, medium-term and longer-term, more enduring, outcomes of S-O-L. Any evaluation has to consider these and how they relate to one another. For example, if a supervisor learns how to handle a difficult operator, does this lead to him finding it easier to supervise the other people in his section? If so, does this reflect in the productivity and quality figures of his section in the next six months or year? Similarly, if a student learns how to read more effectively, does this show up in the quality of her essays? Does this improvement influence the way the student tackles other learning opportunities such as lectures or seminars? How does any or all of this show up as changes in marks in assignments and in the end-of-year exams?

3   We have long recognised the difference between the learner's experience as evidence of learning and other people's judgement or measures of their behaviour.

4   We have so often seen a learner's expectations change during a series of Learning Conversations that we no longer believe that the criteria by which a project should be evaluated can ever be set before it starts. In fact, we believe these criteria to be in a process of continual development and change as experience accumulates and awareness of 'results' begins to influence values and expectations.

5   Taking account of (1) to (4) above, we have gradually evolved the view that the primary objective of evaluation is best expressed in terms of *'the process'* rather than *'the products'*. We believe that the main findings of an S-O-L project are in terms of how well people understand their own processes of learning and how well a group or organisation understands the processes by which it achieves change. These understandings are more important and useful to their future than any specific, product-like achievement in the here and now.

With these five points in mind we saw that the S-O-L spreadsheet and the Personal

Learning Biography held the germ of a method by which we could develop a systematic approach for conversational evaluation.

Conversational evaluation and evaluation of change

The Personal Learning Biography lends itself to conversational evaluation. Those of a working group can be used as a tool for developing and guiding a system in change.

The group begins to understand that there is experiential and conversational evidence of learning and that there is behavioural or performance evidence of learning. They also begin to accept that different psychological and social perspectives have different access to this evidence and have different value systems from within which to infer what learning is taking place. Recognising this leads members of the group to be much more scrupulous in making their evidence available. It also enables them to discuss and negotiate value systems with superiors. This experience within the group alerts them to the need for identifying all those who have an interest in the changes which will result from the learning. Having identified the interested parties, they are recruited into the evaluation conversation. They can form a 'learning policy setting group' to contribute to the intentionality of the 'group in change'.

Alongside this 'perspectives' activity, the Personal Learning Biographies of individuals and of the 'group-as-learner' offer the data out of which each learner, including the 'group-as-a-whole', can begin to build an 'explanatory model' of how the change is happening: how the learning is taking place, how changes in personal meaning lead to changes in performance and how these changes contribute to the change achieved by the group as learner. As the 'model' of the group-as-learner is made explicit, the group achieves awareness of its learning processes. This awareness of process can be used to achieve greater control of the learning. The group as a whole becomes more self-organised.

By clearly representing the time sequence of S-O-L activities, experiential and behavioural changes, and the evaluation of these changes from all relevant perspectives, the Personal Learning Biography offers a language in which to model the process of directed change. As individuals and the group-as-learner achieve greater awareness, the model offers the terms in which greater self-organisation and therefore greater intentionality can be achieved. Thus, the change is not just evaluated from some out-dated point of view. It becomes actively self-regulating, prudently revising its objectives in the light of experience and simultaneously increasing its capacity for self-regulated change by increasing its understanding of the nature of its own learning processes.

Cascading S-O-L: an action plan

Once S-O-L has been introduced into an organisation and a Learning Coach (or Coaches) and Learning Manager (or Managers) have been appointed, strategic decisions will have to be made to manage its growth. The results of conversational evaluation can be fed upwards to the Learning Policy Committee. This enables them to direct future S-O-L activities. There are various ways in which S-O-L can be extended into the operating networks of the organisation. One proven strategy is to introduce an S-O-L cascading mechanism, supported by a learning network.

The action plan for an effective cascade depends on a well-functioning S-O-L base. This may be in one location or distributed through the organisation. The cascade then involves:

1 convening a series of S-O-L workshops for Learning Coaches and a series of seminars for Learning Managers;

2 the formation by these Learning Practitioners of a 'learning network', which allows an exchange of experience and a development of S-O-L skills;

3 the recruitment of experienced and competent Learning Practitioners and Task Supervisors as 'S-O-L installers' in new locations;

4 the familiarisation of all S-O-L installers with the S-O-L implementation model, Feedback-for-Learning Package. S-O-L spreadsheet, Personal Learning Biography and conversational evaluation technologies; and

5 liaison with CSHL S-O-L consultants and advisers on specific S-O-L projects to be implemented in various offices or regions, and on the use of CSHL computer-based back-up facilities.

Retrospective commentary: The implications of Systems 7 for industrial and commercial training and education

Reflexivity of Systems 7: the implications for the Self-Organised Learning entity – individual, pair, team, group or enterprise

The main implications of S-O-L, Learning Conversations and the pattern of conversations represented by Systems 7 are as follows:

1 For the achievement of the fundamental objectives of training, learning must be accepted as an integral part of the main enterprise and as an activity that is continually associated with every department and member of it.

2 Some coherent group of people in the organisation should be responsible for facilitating learning. This is a totally different set of activities from the traditional function of training. It is totally different from seeing 'learning-to-learn' or 'study skills' as some sort of remedial function grafted on to training.

3 If the training department is to be given responsibility for facilitating learning, they can only achieve S-O-L throughout the organisation if they acquire a new philosophy and a new range of skills. They will have to reorganise themselves completely so as to offer a distributed service of both Learning Coaches and learning Task Supervisors. They will also have to accept that the management of learning must remain the responsibility of the operational line management. If the responsibility for managing learning is hived off into personnel or training, then it will fairly rapidly cease to be seen as a central function in the management of all controlled change in the enterprise. It will revert to its role of being just an afterthought, a way of handling technical expertise and the 'people problems' and motivational issues that arise.

4 Once the philosophy has changed and two or three years of S-O-L and Learning Conversations have been built into the shared experience of the members of the enterprise, then the day-to-day activity of the Learning Coach and the creation of Learning Opportunities can and should be gradually handed over to the operational management and supervision. The MA(R)4S (Learning Conversations) and MA(R)4S (learning opportunities) monitoring and modelling activity should remain the responsibility of those responsible for facilitating learning. If this is the training

department, so be it; if it is not, then some alternative, clear assignment of authority and responsibility needs to be set up.

5   The management of learning can now be seen to have two totally interrelated themes. The first is that of managing the content of the learning. This is the function of MA(R)4S (setting the learning horizons). These Learning Horizons are coordinated into the aims and objectives of the enterprise through the Learning Policy Committee (Chapter 5).

The secondary implications are that of how Systems 7 functions – which is the result of how the Learning Manager conducts and coordinates the conversations with Systems 1–5. This is a result of the nature of the shared monitoring and modelling of the system. The quality of the Learning Manager's activities depends on an awareness and sensitive monitoring of Systems 6 and 7. This needs resources and services to achieve anything worthwhile (Figure 31).

Chapters 5 and 6 exhibit how the conversations with Systems 1–5 can be coordinated in various ways to meet the requirements of various types of learning–training contract. Each Self-Organised Learning entity should:

— create a Learning Policy;
— Manage its own learning;
— define the Horizons of its Learning Contracts;
— make and create Learning Opportunities;
— conduct its own core Learning Conversations;
— monitor the Learner in process; and
— define, enlarge and enrich their Learning Domain.

How do learners discover whether they are performing better? In one sense the domain tells them; as they do their job the domain reacts to how they perform. In a more profound sense they evaluate their own performance; but to do this they may need evidence from the domain. The learning domain may or may not be in conversation with itself. For example, a book cannot be aware of itself and it cannot tell the reader how it is being read, but a college library, given the appropriate facilities, provides some sort of commentary to the students on their book-using habits. As we have seen in Chapters 3 and 4, the Brunel Reading Recorder (or software) can record how books are read. The MA(R)4S (1) activity, concerned with monitoring and modelling the learning domain, creates this state of awareness. If the learning domain cannot, of its nature, generate such a MA(R)4S conversation with itself, then it may become necessary for the Learning Practitioner to provide such a function, at least temporarily, until the learners have discovered how to do this for themselves. Where the domain has a capacity for monitoring and modelling its own activities then these may provide the learner with independent evidence about how he or she is performing his or her tasks. It is up to the learner to judge the quality, reliability and validity of this evidence. It is up to the Learning Practitioner to decide if and how to enter into conversation with the domain about improving the quality of the evidence it makes available. *This is often crucial in determining whether the Self-Organised Learner can learn to do that which will contribute to the objectives of the enterprise.*

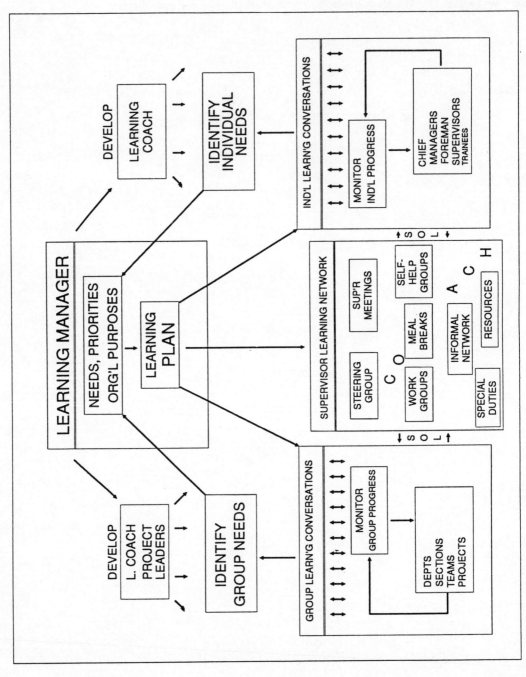

Figure 31 The job of the Learning Manager

A Functional Taxonomy of Reflective Tools

What is a reflective learning tool? How does it amplify the power of the Learning Conversation?

Introduction: Increasing the power of the Learning Conversation – a resource for the Learner and the Learning Practitioner

The embodiments of the conversational technology: a reminder about S-O-L

Let us start by re-stating, but in a different form, what we mean by levels of awareness in the learning process, (Prospective Commentary to Part II). People at work or home, on the sports-field or in any habitat of life fall into at least *three modes of functioning*. They may operate in a *habituated* mode, and in this state not only do their meaning systems rigidify, but their anticipations and actions also assume that they remain in an environment that offers no challenge. This leads to a static *ultra-stability*. In this mode people act as robots; they are task-bound, exhibiting neither awareness nor understanding of what they do (Stage 1 of Figure 11 on p. 96). People who operate almost exclusively as robots are distinguished by their inability to cope with crisis, to adapt to new situations, and who in difficult times become the victims of society, at work, on the shop floor, and in the board room, at school, on our streets, in our homes and in our mental institutions. These are the real disabled, who have become imprisoned in their impoverished and habituated operations in life. In an earlier life one of the authors operated almost exclusively in this way.

People may seek to *operate optimally* – their internal processes work within a negative feedback system of constructive self-validation. Such people can evaluate their own constructions of experience from at least three different sources (Chapter 3, Referent Dialogue, p. 105): the outside world of individual people, the outside world as a community of meaning and standards, and the inside world in which their own organism acts as the test-bed of fitness. Their personal evaluative 'criterion set' functions to influence their adaptive personality and expanding learning style. These are the people who learn from experience and have a capacity to adapt to new situations, practices and technologies. They demonstrate some understanding of what they do and in our terms operate at Stage-2 level of awareness (Figure 11, p. 83). Such people are more flexible and versatile and in Rogers' terms are more 'fully functioning'. Both the authors have sought to create conditions which allow themselves and others to operate this way.

People may, on occasion, *operate creatively* – their 'process of doing' may link back on to their constructive processes to produce a positive feedback of open-ended inventiveness. This relates to the Godel concept introduced in Chapter 2 and to the provisionality phase of any Learning Event as described in Chapters 3 and 4. Their creative conversations with themselves may indicate a Stage-3 level of awareness (Figure 11, p. 96). The maverick who functions this way most of the time is in a sense also a victim, since rarely does he commit himself to one single alternative sufficiently to follow this through into action. One of the authors, on occasions, functions in this way!

'Ultra-stability', 'optimal operating' and 'creativity' define three very different modes of personal functioning. We are all a mix of these three ways of functioning, and how we converse with life determines that unique mix which characterises each of us. The disabled robots exhibit *frozen conversations* as they limp through life. Moments of awareness emerge only under circumstances of extreme dissonance and, locked in their pain and suffering, their understandings remain impoverished. The optimal operators *converse constructively* as their actions and understandings link with more positive feelings of satisfaction, confidence and control. The inventors can sustain lengthy periods of provisionality and exploration as they leap and dance, emanating endless possible alternatives for action.

People who are able to operate flexibly within each of these three modes according to their needs, purposes and resources demonstrate a quality of understanding and level of conscious control which is truly representative of Stage-3 awareness. These are the enlightened ones, the fully functioning beings, the 'natural' Self-Organised Learners. They know when it is effective to act like a robot, when to allow their thinking processes to roam freely; when it is useful constructively to commit themselves to act competently in specific situations, and when to break away to a non-evaluative, highly active period, generating the infuriating range of alternatives which forms the basis for creativity. Reflective tools used within the Learning Conversation enhance its capacity for enabling learners to gain better control of these three modes of functioning, freeing them from their robot in their sustained quest for personal skill, competence and creativity.

The conversational technology, modelling and MA(R)4S

In essence, the Learning Conversation supports greater awareness, review and development as a person functions in his world. To achieve this, personal experience and behaviour as one coherent process must be consciously observed. Awareness and control of this process requires the use of specific tools. Without them, people are unable to distance themselves from their own processes sufficiently to be able to observe themselves. The CSHL repertory grid technology, structures of meaning and flow diagram techniques, THESAURUS and CHART procedures and various forms of behavioural records with associated talk-back procedures represent some of these tools, *but they can only augment the process of researching learning when used conversationally*. Each reflective tool serves specifically to model particular aspects of experience or behaviour. In Chapter 2 we described the nature of the 'meaning as modelling' facility within which each tool plays a significant and integral part. In Chapters 3 and 4 we introduced MA(R)4S as the heuristic for engagement in the process dialogue which supports awareness, the develop- ment of a language to reflect upon learning, and the construction of significant, relevant and viable models.

Modelling and MA(R)4S

If we perceive the outside world by modelling it within us and checking the evidence to guide, validate and develop this construction, then 'working models' of reality can be run more quickly than in real time, thus producing meanings ahead of the evidence for them. Modelling seems to be a way of representing the creative process of meaning construction stimulated by replications of experience. Meaning is changed in such conversational encounters, but meaning is never fully knowable since part of the inner conversation always remains unrevealed. All we can do is represent our meanings (in appropriate forms), and by conversing with these representations the inner meaning is transmuted. We have found it useful to represent this process as shown in Figure 32. MA(R)4S stands for seven stages in the conversational cycle (Chapter 3, p. 131).

It is in the nature of every Learning Event that the learner cannot know what it is that he wants to know until he knows it. This is the function of MA(R)4S. It enables a systematic, directed search for successively better-defined outcomes to be made often from an ill-defined or even totally confused or apathetic starting-point. We have found that applying the MA(R)4S process to the tools within the Learning Conversation provides a conversational technology for constructively bootstrapping the process of Self-Organised Learning. *As a general principle each tool to be described provides a record, and within the MA(R)4S facility, each functions to support the personal modelling of either the behavioural or experiential aspect of the process of learning.*

Experience and behaviour as psychological categories for classifying the tools: towards the Functional Taxonomy

The tools can be categorised by reference to the two psychological methods employed for enhancing awareness of processes of learning; that is, from the perspective of personal experience or/and from the perspective of actions or behaviours (General Introduction). We can then further differentiate them within the functional framework offered by our model of Self-Organised Learning (Figure 5, Chapter 1, p. 62).

Tools that enhance awareness of the construction of personal experience by eliciting representations of personal meaning support reflection upon the anticipatory mechanism which drives behaviour. Tools that record behaviour directly support the reconstruction of experience which generates feedback about the quality of performance. Together, these two types of tool generate evidences which enhance awareness of the meaning-constructing, anticipatory, purposive mechanisms which condition the ultra-stability, optimal operating and creativity modes of functioning already described. They represent the

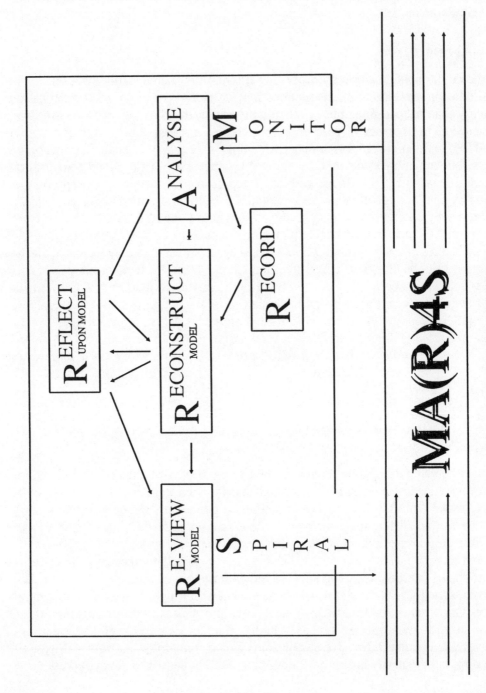

Figure 32 MA(R)4S heuristic

primary categories of our Functional Taxonomy.

It is impossible to do justice to the specific procedures and range of usage for these two types of tool within this book. In the case of the repertory grid, in *Self-Organised Learning* we have written a complete compendium about how we have elaborated this tool and conversationaly recruited it into the Learning Conversation. The tools have been described extensively in various CSHL technical papers and research reports (Postscript). Here, our purpose is to outline the essential attributes of each tool, the procedures for using them, and to suggest how each can be used in specific situations. These tools have either been specifically devised and developed by the authors, or existing techniques have been cannibalised and modified to meet the requirements of the conversational approach. Either way, the specifications guiding their development are summarised as follows:

1 some observational record or representation of meaning which allows *talk-back* to reconstruct the learning experience sequentially;
2 a capacity for applying the MA(R)4S process to a Learning Event in order to identify the 'meaning as modelling' activity which is driving it;
3 the Purpose Strategy Outcome Review (PSOR) heuristic embodied in the PLC for clarifying the organisation and directionality of each Learning Event;
4 a facility to move up and down the hierarchical organisation of any task or topic so that this can be reviewed as a coherent system;
5 a facility for the development of a language in which understanding can be used to enhance levels of skill, and tacit skills can be made explicit and analysed to improve understanding. Thus, behaviour and experience can be articulated in sufficient detail and with such a degree of precision that a new level of awareness is achieved;
6 a capacity to shift the Learning Conversation from the task-focused to the learning-focused level of awareness;
7 a capability for the testing out of alternatives and a system of evaluation which indicates the merits of each and which makes explicit the possible directions in which more adequate alternatives may be sought;
8 a capability to amplify at least one of the three modes or levels of the Learning Conversation – namely, life, tutorial, and learning to learn;
9 a capacity to facilitate an effective exchange of 'meaning as modelling' between two or more developing Self-Organised Learners; and
10 a procedure for gradually dispensing with the tool as an enhanced perception and evolving language for S-O-L is developed.

This Functional Taxonomy is offered as a resource for the Learning Practitioner to manage Learning Conversations effectively in a wide variety of situations. It is only through practice in specific contexts that he or she can become a skilled facilitator of S-O-L.

To continue one of our themes in Part II, *reading* is used as a vehicle for illustrating how specific tools can be used in a Learning Conversation. Since the tools described are *content-independent*, any task, topic or learning skill could have been similarly illustrated.

As in Part II, additional examples are gradually introduced in order to emphasise their generality. We conclude by outlining our most recent development of a computer-based Intelligent Learning System which can be seen as one major tool for promoting Self-Organised Learning (S-O-L – ILS).

Tools for increasing awareness of learning processes: representing personal meaning for reflecting on experience

Here we introduce five classes of tool for representing personal meaning. We aim to show the advantages and disadvantages of each class and to describe the conditions which optimise their usage within a Learning Conversation.

Tools derived from the repertory grid

In our book *Self-Organised Learning* we report a compendium of techniques for using the repertory grid in a Learning Conversation. This grid-based reflective learning technology enables individuals, pairs, groups and organisations to represent their personal meanings on given topics, tasks, people, events and situations in optimal forms for reflection, review and development. FOCUS, TRIGRID and INTERACTIVE TRIGRID optimise the analysis of grid data for feedback. PEGASUS-ICARUS elicits a grid conversationally on the microcomputer and together with the FOCUS suite offers a machine resource for the representation of personal meaning. CHANGE grid offers a tool for comparison over time so that the directions and quality of learning can be personally evaluated. PAIRS and EXCHANGE enables two individuals to explore the nature of their understanding and to identify areas of agreement and disagreement. SOCIOGRID and THESAURUS similarly allow a group to explore their understanding. This integrated technology for representing meaning is a resource for the learner, Learning Coach, Task Supervisor and Learning Manager to use within the Systems 7 S-O-L Environment (Chapter 5). Readers are referred to our book for detailed descriptions of the methods involved.

For purposes of reminding those readers who are familiar with these techniques and to introduce those who have not as yet come across them, Figure 33 represents a combined FOCUSed grid of the authors' construing of psychological tools. The structure reveals their understanding of these tools in terms of practical applications for our work. It was elicited several years ago by means of Laurie's FOCUS algorithm. For simplicity we have not illustrated the hierarchical tree cluster diagrams. The SPACEd layout indicates the distribution of the main clusters of *elements* (the tools) and *constructs*.. Much of what we have since come to value is missing. Reflecting upon this, what else could we have included which would have been more representative of our values as developing conversational scientists? Repertory grid, personal scientist, reflexivity, structures of meaning, behaviour records and talk-back, challenging the robot, Systems 7, ILS-CHAT, and the Learning Conversation are few of the tools we could have included as elements. The original grids were elicited on PEGASUS, and PAIRS was subsequently used to merge the two grids which was FOCUSed as shown. This exercise helped us to consider what was missing from our constructs and what gaps there were among our elements. During our joint REFLECT activity we found that some of the elements we could have added represented more than one item and we therefore ended up with, for example, repertory grid A, B, C, D and E. Each of these reveals the constructs which are more representative of our views of what psychology is and could be used for as a domain for enabling human learning in all walks of life. For reasons of space and clarity we have not included these grids. Their purpose was served by our reflections on our developing theory of S-O-L, which is offered in this book.

In Chapter 4 we referred to the CHANGE grid procedure, which Gwen used in her life-level conversation to reflect on her growing repertoire of needs and purposes for reading. As a result, she was able to explicitly model her own 'purpose taxonomy' (the Functional Taxonomy of Tools) and use this experience to experiment with new reading tactics and strategies. Thus the grid technology combined with records of reading behaviour, the flow diagram and structures of meaning techniques described in detail in this chapter, formed a powerful battery of tools for developing her reading competence.

Here, it may be useful to summarise some of the positive attributes of this grid technology and also to indicate some of its disadvantages, since these lead us to develop our 'beyond the grid' tools, to represent personal meanings for reflection upon experience more comprehensively.

Advantages of the grid technology

1 The elicitation process is explicit and systematic and is completely in the learner's own terms.
2 Meaning is embodied and displayed within a relatively simple two-dimensional format.
3 A structure emerges, particularly when the grid is FOCUSed (elements and constructs clustered so that they are displayed in a new relationship), which shows that a person's meanings may be much simpler than one might initially believe.
4 The structure of meaning so displayed enables the individual, often for the first time, to become aware of the tacit knowing which influences her constructions of experience.
5 The structure is so systematic that the individual can easily begin to explore, review and develop control of the construing process.

However, by its very nature the repertory grid is limited in terms of its sensitivity, its failure to exhibit the relationships between items of meaning and by its low predictive powers.

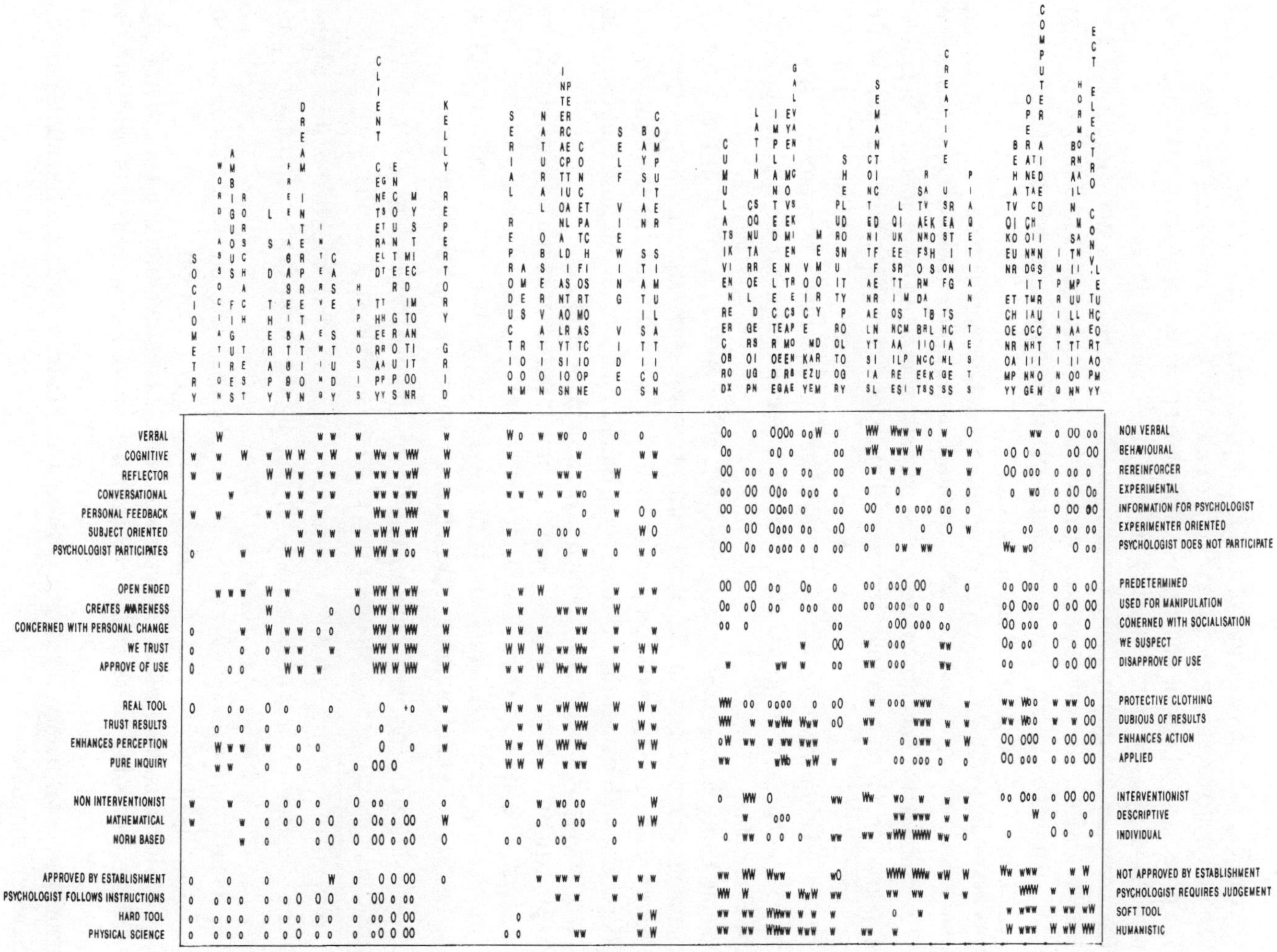

Figure 33 The FOCUSed grid: the authors' construing of psychological tools (1972)

Disadvantages of the grid technology

1   It does not display the natural hierarchy of meaning within a given range of discourse (even in a FOCUSed grid as shown in Figure 1, the hierarchical tree diagrams only serve to indicate the closeness of relationship between elicited items).

2   The grid matrix restricts the pattern of meaning to a two-dimensional format.

3   The process by which the description of meaning is arrived at tends to be reductionist, with the analysis of parts gradually built up into a holistic pattern.

4   The compare-and-contrast bipolar differentiation of elements into similarities and dissimilarities in the ways a person perceives and conceives the inner and outer world may push meaning into convergence very early on in the conversational elicitation, so that much of the potential richness is lost.

5   The grid fails to display the types of relationships between items of meaning; rather, it expresses the characteristics of these items. A construct expresses one dimension of meaning only. This limitation can be partially overcome by means of a 'relationship grid' in which constructs represent dimensions of relationships, but this would be a special case. Even so, it is only when a construct refers to two specific elements that the relationship, such as 'cause and effect' or 'a contains b' represents any real meaning. Only very remote abstractions about relationships can be applied across all the elements.

6   Intentionality is not expressed in the grid, although it is implicit in the range of elements selected and in the repertoire of personal constructs. Every aspect of meaning has a purposive component to it which influences the directionality of construing within an n-dimensional, non-Euclidean space. Exhibiting purpose is an important aspect of mirroring, which is lacking in the grid.

7   As an expression of meaning at one given time it fails to take the sequential process of construing into account. The anticipatory and predictive aspects of the Self-Organised Learner constantly inventing models of his own reality and using these models in the light of ongoing experience, are not made explicit in the grid.

Greater precision and sensitivity requires that the invention of beyond the grid techniques for representing meaning must include some or all of the following criteria:

1   The items of meaning should be 'naturally occurring' and exhibited within a hierarchical system of meaning, capable of tapping the multi-faceted forms of representing and experiencing personal meaning.

2   The relationships between items should be explicitly displayed and these should also be 'naturally occurring' and not constrained by logical thought.

3   The device must be capable of expressing thought and feeling as a pattern in time. Models embodying cause and effect, probabilistic or fuzzy relationships, syntactic structures, embedded structures as in computer programs, general systems as in general systems theory, hierarchic networks or inference machines can all be used to represent meaning.

4 The device must be capable of enabling the individual to become more aware of the intentionality influencing thoughts, feelings and action.
5 The device must support the exploration of meaning in all possible forms, from verbal to non-verbal.

The structures of meaning, flow diagram and personal learning task analysis techniques were invented with these criteria in mind. Non-verbal forms of representation are also referred to.

Structures of Meaning

To compensate for the limitations of the repertory grid technology, the *structure of meaning techniques* invite a richer and more open exploration of a topic, event or situation. The number of items of meaning that can be represented within a given range of convenience can be extended well beyond the 8 to 25 which are the pragmatic limitations of the grid; that is, up to 60 to 100 items or more. The items are not restricted to placings on bipolar constructs nor are they restricted by scaling procedures. The tight differentiation of meaning in the grid is relaxed within a non-formal open relationship. Whatever the range and class of item elicited these can be successively sorted to uncover the enduring relationships between them. A two-dimensional – or, on the computer, a multi-dimensional – pattern of items expressing these relationships can be constructed. Levels of structure emerge as items, clusters, and clusters of clusters. Much of the literature on networks, hierarchies, heterarchies and methods of pruning networks into particular structures has proved useful in enabling us to expand our procedures. Different forms of structures are useful for different purposes, domains and situations.

The general structures of meaning procedure

The procedure offers flexibility in:

1 the elicitation of items of meaning;
2 the sorting of their relationships;
3 the display of a final pattern.

Items of meaning can represent any aspect of a topic, problem or event. None of the restrictions of type, range or number that apply to elements need be considered. This provides a much freer elicitation procedure and ensures a much richer exemplification of the topic. Many different methods can be applied to facilitate this elicitation. Brainstorming techniques, and content-free techniques for enabling different types of associations, including qualifications, refinements, chronological, logical, temporal, analogy, opposite and similar, metaphor, inference, lateral, bizarre, emotive, visual, analytical, casual, intuitive, or pure free association and so forth, are recruited to release suppressed or tacit feelings and ideas. The aim at this stage is to minimise internal monitoring and the tightly evaluative processes which often inhibit the potentially creative meaning-generating process.

At any stage of the elicitation, items can be sorted, using iterative procedures, into clusters of items which are noted, and then the items are returned to the population before selecting a new cluster. Gradually a pattern emerges and stabilises. During this procedure many other items are elicited and these are added to the developing structure of meaning. This stage is analagous to the bipolar scaling procedure but is much freer, less formal, and more intuitive. An alternative, more formal procedure is to compare each item with every other item attributing a similarity score to each dyad. It is also sometimes useful to classify the nature of the relationship between items and to link this to the order mechanisms which influence memory and the retrieval of meaning.

As the number of items expands and they begin to pattern into a structure, less relevant items can be deleted and new ones added as they come to mind. At this stage, the topic or problem is continuously monitored, reconsidered and evaluated. Gradually, a more evaluative, content-free procedure is introduced which encourages the stabilisation of a pattern of meaning which embodies greater relevance to 'purpose' and the topic. By shifting the focus of attention to a more general or more detailed level, a hierarchically organised structure begins to emerge.

A final stage in the structure of meaning procedure involves selection of an optimal mode of display to hold and exhibit the system of personal meaning. Networks, hierarchies, heterarchies, entailment structures, cluster diagrams, and Venn diagrams are some examples. Many techniques used in other fields have potential use here; mathematical forms such as Q-analysis, graph theory, data structures, and developments in computer graphics are some examples, but other cultures have arrived at other techniques for displaying meaning. The tantric model of 'all thought and time' represents one such display. Again, Joycean prose, bardic stances, haiku poems or sonnets and Zen calligraphy, sculpture and architecture are only a few selections of forms for representing personal meaning. The problem with these culture-bound displays is that because of familiarity and highly developed associations with publicly accepted meaning, learners are often incapable of transcending this to construct a meta-awareness of the process involved in constructing personal meaning within these forms. This is why unfamiliar forms such as the repertory grid and structures of meaning are well suited as aids within the Learning Conversation. But obviously unfamiliarity is only one prerequisite. In this section we have tried to highlight some of the others. Within the Learning Conversation, such displays become tools for the articulation of experience and for reflection upon personal meaning. The essential procedure is summarised in Figure 34.

The structures of meaning procedure has been developed into a suite of interactive computer programs which can display two- or three-dimensional representations of personal meanings or even more. An n-dimensional display is represented in three-dimensional projections. By offering dynamic displays, the computer can be recruited to explore the intentionality and anticipatory aspects of meaning, thus offering a vehicle for

Figure 34 The Structure of Meaning heuristic

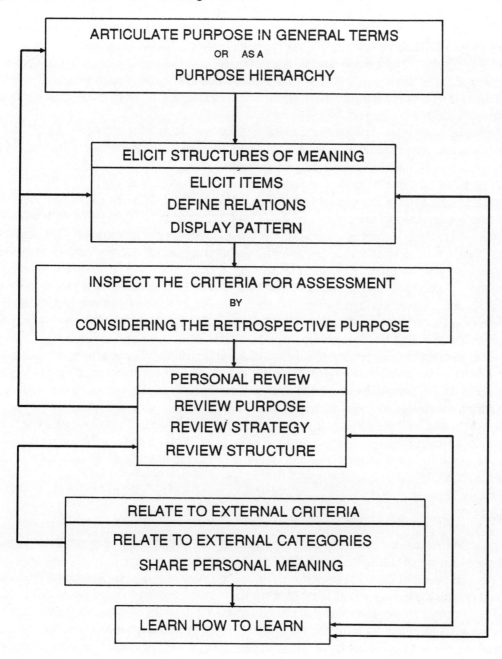

exploring alternate futures. In another culture the Shri-Yantra has been used for similar ends (Chapter 1).

Given this wide variety of alternate methods for eliciting and representing meaning, the Self-Organised Learner can select appropriate representational structures for exhibiting specific aspects of personal meaning. The Self-Organised Learner is free to recruit not only those specialist tools described in this section but also more 'culture-bound' devices (Chapter 1) or more traditional psychological techniques ('Tools from education and training', p. 326).

Once the means for representing meaning is recognised as a reflective tool, all forms of representation can be used as aids for achieving awareness. Indeed, readers will recognise that each was invented to serve this very purpose.

The procedure can be extended for two-person exchange, and Figure 35 illustrates in diagrammatic form a structure of meaning resulting from such an exchange. Learning takes place not only in the context of one's own personal process but also with reference to the processes of others (Chapter 3). Exchange involves procedures for either entering completely into another's world, achieving a compromise, or a more truly joint creative encounter. Additionally, pairs of learners are enabled to choose appropriate outside referents (individuals, multi-media resources, and people as a community) for developing their shared personal understanding. By remaining firmly within their own inner referents, learners are in a better position to relate these precisely within the wider perspective of significant others, public knowledge, and the mind-pools of various cultures.

The compendium of procedures for representing structures of meaning are almost as vast as those for the repertory grid. Here, we can only offer sufficient guidelines for some of these to be practically explored and for the reader to set out on their own tool-constructing voyage. By varying the type of item in the structure, by introducing different categories and by highlighting different types of relationships, the general procedure can be tailored to the specific contribution it is making in the Learning Conversation. The structures of meaning suite of programs and the full range of procedures are demonstrated within the CSHL S-O-L workshops.

Meaning nets for reviewing reading outcomes

Figure 36 illustrates a structure of meaning in the form of a 'meaning net' as originally elicited, and the meaning net revised after talk-back.

As can be seen, Lisa's revised meaning net shows a number of additional items and clusters which she had added after looking back at the text in the course of her review. What this suggested to Lisa was that she had missed quite a lot of what was in the passage. Her original meaning net reflected her understanding of the passage all right, but when she came to review it by comparing it with the passage and with her stated purpose, she found that it was deficient. The outcome was not completely satisfactory. Thinking over the possible reasons for this, she felt fairly happy about the way she had formulated her

Figure 35 Two-person exchange

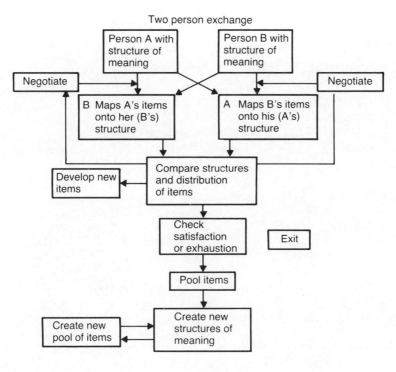

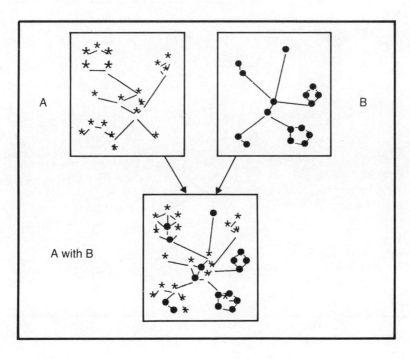

Figure 36 Lisa's meaning net

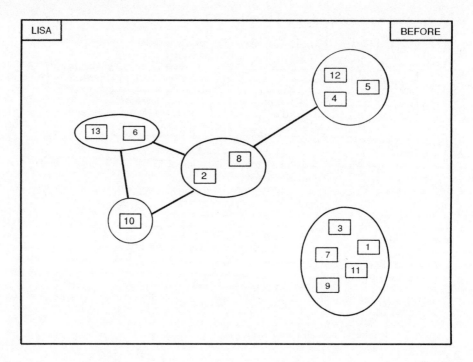

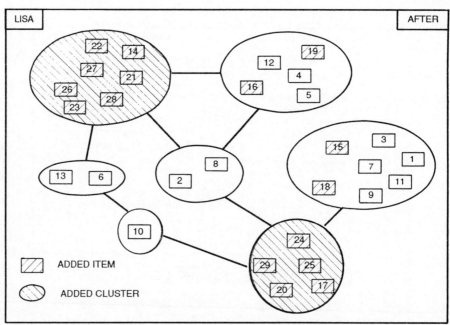

reading purpose but much less happy about her reading strategy, which she felt had been too slapdash. She had employed one quick 'smooth' read followed by a fairly uncontrolled 'item' read. She decided that her purpose, which was of a fairly high order in terms of comprehension demanded (it was 'evaluative'), would have been better served if she had employed a 'search' read and a more rigorous 'item' read.

To explain how the Learning Conversation was conducted, it may be helpful to offer a structure for the flow of questions.

Reflecting on the items:

- How many of the ideas elicited in your net can actually be traced back to the text?
- How many came out of your own experience whilst you were reading the text?
- What does this reveal about your comprehension?
- How selective were you? Did you miss the important things?
- If unselective, did you succeed in achieving an accurate verbatim report of the text?
- Did you modify the text by
    paraphrase
    reorganisation
    inference?
- How evaluative were you?

More specifically on strategy, were you:

- too obsessed with detail?
- too selective?
- too evaluative or not evaluative enough?
- too inferential or not inferential enough?
- over- or under-elaborate in your tactics and overall strategy?

When you were eliciting your meaning net:

- In what order were the items recalled?
- What does this tell you about the way in which you reconstructed the outcome of your reading?

More generally on the outcome:

- What is your current understanding of the passage?
- How does this differ from that expressed in your meaning net?
- Add, delete or rearrange items and clusters to show your present understanding.
- Was your meaning net more or less adequate?

Now, more systematically, review the reading process, taking into account the information provided by the meaning net.

- Review purpose. (Was it specific enough, were there sub-purposes you should have formulated?)

- Review strategy. (Were the tactics the right ones?)
- Review outcome. (What are the criteria?)

As with reading, the outcomes of listening can be represented and reflected upon in the form of structures of meaning. In listening, strings of words invariably follow one another in a linear sequence of presentation, but the personal meaning attributed to them is multi-dimensional. In some of the development activities of our academic staff, the lecturer is often surprised at the 'personal knowing' exhibited by students! They in turn are often surprised at the lecturer's structure of meaning. This type of event often triggers off intense discussions about their appreciation of the subject matter and the lecturer's presentation of it! A Learning Coach often needs to be engaged in very lengthly support dialogues with both students and staff. When effectively managed, this type of encounter can be the vehicle for focusing on the referent dialogue. Learning partners can exchange their structures of meaning in small and increasingly larger groups and as another referent they can compare their understanding with the (expert) lecturer. They are enabled to share their structures of meaning using the three forms of exchange – the give-over/take-over, the compromise and the creative encounter already described.

This structures of meaning procedure has been applied successfully in many other contexts. For instance, managers have been able to use it to reflect on their 'personally significant learning events'. Students use it to explore their learning outcomes as a result of reading, listening, and participating in seminars. One illustration of this is Lisa's reading outcome. Teachers have used it to prepare their lectures and rather than hand out the conventional notes they have used it to communicate more meaningfully with their students. Project groups have used it to record their understanding of the outcomes of meetings and to check out one another's understandings of these events. Scientists have used it to explore the frontiers of their understanding. We shall briefly describe one example.

Structures of Meaning and the creative process

Applying the reflective learning technology in the form of the structures of meaning procedure to enhance the creative process has successfully enabled certain experts to explore the frontiers of knowledge in the domain of their speciality. A senior training adviser in the Civil Service, briefed to design a new national open system of learning; a training manager responsible for radically restructuring industrial training programmes within an international company; a research director of a pharmaceutical company selecting high-risk drug design projects; and a chemistry professor eminent in the field of catalysis and surface chemistry have each been assisted to explore the scope of their topic, to identify the nature of the problem, to generate alternative solutions and to plan a subsequent course of action in systematic yet, for each, refreshingly open and creative ways. Brain-storming on the edge of their knowledge and experience and reflecting upon the structured representations of their own understanding in each case enabled them to make personally significant forward moves.

Professor X, in exploring the dimensions of the problem involved in communicating with colleagues about issues of surface chemistry, was confronted with the inadequacy of conventional methods for representing sophisticated chemical processes. The complexity of the dynamics of change could not be satisfactorily captured within existing forms. Descriptive items were first elicited relating to this topic. Various forms of representative systems were identified and associated with the epistomological advance of chemistry. Each representation became elaborated, modified, but eventually inadequate as questions about the subject could no longer be fully formulated, nor possible answers fully represented out of the existing symbolic components. New systems were evolved to represent more adequately the expanding domain of chemical explanation. Categories of representations were identified from verbal, symbolic, structural, transitional states, time-sequenced, phase-patterned to reality models (for example, hooks on the surface of molecules). Explanations about their respective attributes as effective forms of representation and communication emerged. Attributes such as 'kinetics', 'speed', 'valency', 'types of bonds', 'specificity', 'energy dimensions' and 'physical transformations' were clarified. It became clear that the history of chemistry could be traced in the development or extensions of appropriate categories of symbolic representations of the subject matter. Items spanning different aspects of the topic were gradually elicited and the elicitation process was reflected on as it shifted in intention and direction. The elicitor guided the 'creative learner' to reflect upon areas of doubt, provisionality, certainty, specificity, functionality and applicability; logical, evaluative and inferential construings; different aspects and levels of organisation of the topic; a consideration of alternative representations as well as grey, submerged and less differentiated areas. The conversational encounter enables psychologist and client to take better control of the meta-process involved in this creative problem-solving encounter. Pre-emptive, constellatory and core issues were recognised, and gradually the client got to grips with those aspects of the problem which had hitherto eluded his conscious scrutiny. Items relating to strategies for achieving more satisfactory representations were then elicited and reflected upon as well as items dealing with criteria for effectiveness as valued by himself, colleagues and chemistry as a whole.

Insights into the relationship between representations and 'objective reality' became a topic for discussion. In this context relativistic and functional aspects of representations were explored and evaluated. As the topic was elaborated and reflected upon, additional explanations and further inferences emerged. Was chemistry as a domain of knowledge and experience a language within its own right? Was this language essentially verbal or best expressed in more formal terms? What were the syntactic and semantic rules for formal representational structures? How do these relate to the periodic table? Was there a private language in chemistry in the same sense as the 'personal signatures' of artists and composers to musical scores?

The negotiation of needs and purposes released clusters of items relating to 'private' representations invented whilst struggling with specific problems of catalysis. Comparisons were made between these and conventional representations. A private language used as aids to the imagination, and aids to communication when searching for points of growth at the edge of what was known in this important area of industrial chemistry became the focus of review and contemplation. Grey, non-expressible areas were identified and when pushed or cajoled to reflect on these, one session led to an impasse where demands of teaching and managing the department set other priorities for personal effort. In another session a process of search and reflection at a deeper level was set in motion. Was it laziness, over-anxiety, or insecurity about one's own creative ability which led to a blocking off of some of the real issues? When asked directly, 'How did the fuzzy grey areas affect his own research?' the answer was that he 'tended to slip sideways' to other 'important but more handlable problems' and 'there were plenty of these to keep one busy'. One grey area led eventually to a discussion about new technologies; computer graphic displays capable of representing multi-causal and three-dimensional dynamic structural processes were appraised as 'possibly leading to ideal solutions', 'fantasies remote from reality' and 'trendy but not necessarily useful'. In counterpoint, more familiar and simpler two-dimensional representations were valued as 'aids to communication' on courses and conferences when 'you did not have your expensive high-tech computer with you'. This led to an agreement that interpretation was a personal process, since what may appear simple to an expert could be as meaningless as a Chinese hexagram to an A-level student untutored in inorganic catalysis or I Ching. An understanding of chemistry depended on analogy, metaphor, visual imagery and anecdotes as much as any other domain of knowledge or language with its agreed boundaries. Some of the core meta-issues which emerged for further reflection included the following:

1 When can a representational system be no longer expended to accommodate advances in knowledge?
2 What are the indicators for determining the inadequacy of a conventional system?
3 When does a representational system become redundant?
4 Should alternative forms be sought from within the old? For instance, the representation of bond angles within two-dimensional structures.
5 How is it best to invent forms which capture dynamic processes and energy distribution?
6 Is the idea of holding alternative forms of partial representation simultaneously the precursor of a new, more total system?
7 To what extent do forms of representation constrain one's ideas?
8 To what extent should one compromise for the purposes of communication?
9 Can the process of representation itself be articulated more fully so that the essence of representational systems can be identified?
10 Is it possible to discover the essential components for the design of functionally useful representations in surface chemistry?

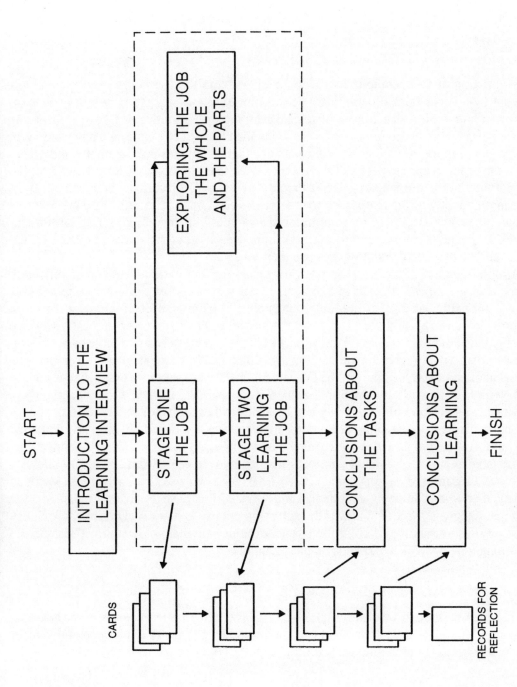

Figure 37 The learning interview heuristic

11 Could such core components become the beginnings of the growth of alternative forms for creating more useful representations?

This process of reflection set in motion an ongoing process of creativity.

Structures of Meaning: The learning interview

One variation of the technique has been developed into the *learning interview schedule* (Figure 37). This elicits a hierarchical description of a task or job and how it is done, as well as a hierarchical description of related learning opportunities and how the learning was achieved. This procedure is often used to launch a series of Learning Conversations in on-the-job learning situations as a means for diagnosing personal strengths and weaknesses in order to initiate personally relevant PLCs. Used in this way, it becomes a tool to be recruited in the life conversation (Chapter 4). This is a technique which can easily be passed on directly to the learner, so that he or she can continue to reflect on their task or job and their learning of it, in a progressive awareness-raising conversation with themselves. Learning partners can also use it to support each other's awareness-raising reflections on how they learn and how they see their job.

A modified form of the learning interview technique facilitates more specific reflection upon particular aspects of a job and how this is learned, or upon a particular range of skills covering a particular duty or area of responsibility. The structures of meaning shown in Figures 38a and 38b and are examples of how one senior supervisor in the Post Office involved in planning represented this aspect of his job to try to become more aware of and improve his own implicit problem-solving algorithm, and how another supervisor involved in managing all the duties during the busy evening shift in a letter sorting office used it to review the way he spent his time on the floor. Both said they learned a lot about the ways they tackled their jobs, although they had been doing these jobs for several years.

The structures of meaning technique has also been modified to form the Personal Thesaurus procedure as a tool for learning a new language. In Figure 18 we illustrate how a new language of air intercept control is learned by trainee officers. Figure 19 shows a Personal Thesaurus of a language for S-O-L. It has been used extensively in Mexican universities where students of science and engineering have to learn English, in the National Language Unit of Wales with adults who choose to learn Welsh, and in Toulouse to help French-speaking air controllers to learn to use English in their job. The example 'Learning to learn Welsh' expands on this technique.

The Personal Thesaurus for learning Welsh

Eliza, a mature student, was learning Welsh in an intensive one-term course at the National Language Unit of Wales. Welsh had become important for her as a junior school teacher in a Welsh-speaking area. She was familiar with the 'occasional Welsh word' though she

Items

55 items elicited and clustered

Items 1—26 describe sequence of 1st cycle of activity

Gather information and when necessary issue commands
40 mins

Do a selective circle around the floor.
Usually quite quick
15 mins

Check staff PEDs

Selective observations of my circle.
More overall check.
Concentrate on PHGs and PEDs

Check bags

Key control points

Primary PHTs
Secondary
Code desks fully manned
Secondary letters
Primary letters SCM and ALF
Staffing of meters
Facing table
Letter sorting
Meter tipping and trays
Primary and secondary packets
Letter sorting
Code desk

Personal model

Checking period

During checking period PEDs will inform about staffing situation sick, overtime, etc.

Check and control implementation of my plan

Now check delivery section.
Mainly walk around

Back to floor.
Check plan — Tea break.
Overall check

Expect collections to start rolling in and start process again

Meal relief arrives.
One hour break

Back on job. This is when my job really begins

Quick cycle but much observation and much control

Continuously monitoring situation

Explanation

Build up plan for shift and begin to control

Selectivity depends on PEDs and situation

Staff report to me if there are problems

At least 10 bags from loading bay

Work out overtime staff requirements.
10 round trips at best.
Much more often at worst

Figure 38a **Structure of Meaning representing managing a shift**

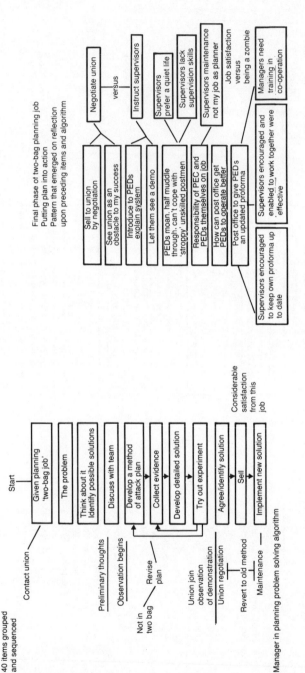

Figure 38b Structure of Meaning representing planning

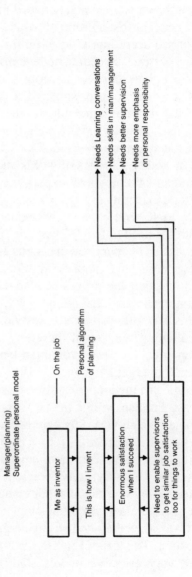

Figure 38b continued

had never spoken Welsh. Eliza was one of a group of twenty adults, each with rather different needs and purposes for learning Welsh.

A feasibility study was launched in which five CSHL reflective learning procedures were introduced as part of their course.

The personal thesaurus technique is briefly described here. This is designed to make explicit the ways in which personal meaning is constructed in a new language. It is based on the concept that a group of ideas or 'items of meaning' become related and personally categorised according to specific functions of language. The range and clusters of items reveal a personal thesaurus or developing system of personal meaning in the new language. Figure 39 gives an example from Eliza's thesaurus. For her, as well as for her peers and tutors, it was quite surprising to discover the structure of her own meanings in Welsh. This bore very little relationship to the daily conversation drills, grammar drills, printed materials, and audio tapes which formed the main part of her language learning resources.

Yet the structure revealed significant insights into the ways in which she constructed ideas in Welsh. Clusters of words and phrases were described as 'nice-sounding words', 'reminders of enjoyable experiences', idiosyncratic visual associations, memories of childhood experiences, 'deep bonds with father', 'commands to do with the children in her class', 'to do with home', 'private language used with her Welsh-speaking husband', 'to do with the need to feel Welsh' and 'pride in being Welsh', and so on.

Eliza used her personal thesaurus as an aid to expand her vocabulary, for effective recall of new terms and phrases, for locating important functions in the language and for reflecting upon the process of language construction itself. This deeply influenced her growing realisation that not only was she embarking on learning a new language, but also that this was influencing her lifestyle, personality and her image of herself.

In eliciting a personal thesaurus from each member of the group, the tutor and the learners together were evolving a language for communicating about their learning processes. The target language, Welsh, was seen to be separate from the process language of learning. This meta-conversation was conducted in the mother language of the learner (in this case English) whilst the target language was being learned. In negotiating the meta-language, Welsh was only referred to to illustrate, emphasise or concretise the learning process itself. At first the group and the tutors found it very difficult to talk about their own learning processes. The meta-language in which to describe these processes was very rudimentary. Initially, considerable resistance was engendered as their partially developed learning skills were made explicit and challenged. This was doubly disastrous since most of them were teachers. Interestingly, the greatest impact was on the course tutors, who went on to adapt their courses to integrate some of the learning-to-learn techniques into the curriculum. The use of English for the meta-language, and Welsh for the target language, proved very effective in this study. As familiarity with Welsh increased, group discussions about learning processes were subsequently carried out in Welsh.

Figure 39 Learning to learn Welsh – a Personal Thesaurus

				Ways I feel, think and use Welsh				
Mainly to do with hobbies and leisure							*Mainly to do with work and family*	
Nice sounding words	Singing	Location where I live	TV/radio jokes and news	Staff room greetings conversation	Praise and activities	Memories of childhood	People in my life	
Diflasi	Mewn'tune'	Canol y	'Pobl y Cwm'	Faint o'r	Da boch chi	Da lawn	Gwr	
Bendigedig	Tenorai	ddinas	'Maehi'	Gloch	Nos da	Bendigedig	Gwraeg	
Anobeithiol	Bass	Swyddfa Post	ynddeg	Ga i	Bore da	Cariad	Cefnder	
Dihuno	Cantre-	Eglwys	'or gloch'-	Cwpaned o de	Prynhawn da	Nos da	Dyn	
Clychau	Gwaelod	De-	TV news	siarad	Os Gwelwch	Blodyn	Bachgen	
Arbennig	O dan y mor	Morganwg	Drama a	a.m.TV	fod yn dda	fach	Merch	
Pysgodyn	a'i donnau	Croeso-	actions	Programme	Sut ydych	Ardderchog	mamgu	
Bendra	Bwmba	Cymru	'seddwch ar	Pwy sydd ar	chi?	Bruallu	dadcu	
Mwnogl	'O Iesu Mawr'	Maes Parcio	y gadair'	'duty'	Dewchi		dyn du	
Peidiwch	Y Marchog	Ty ffarm	Days of	siarad am y	mewn-		merch bert	
a poeni	Hywela	Diwedd	the week –	'plant'	esgysodwchifi		athraw	
Drosy Dibyn	Blodwen	Allan	Dydd,	teachers'	Amser cinio		pergethwr	
Newyddion	Oesgafireto	Pob-Cerbyd	Sul, etc	athrawon	amser te		meddyg	
Defnyddio	Sospan Fach	'Undeb'-on		Family –	-brecwast		glowr	
Hiraeth	Ble ydych chi	Students		teulu		*Pride in*	pysgotwr	
Marw		Building-on-		happenings	un waeth yr	*being Welsh*		
Eira		swper		– 'gartref'	wythnos			
		Insurance		athraw		chwarae pel		
	Enjoyable	Building,		yn mynd	mae'n ddrwg	droed	*Private to do*	
	experiences	Siop dillad		heno?	gen i		*with father*	
	Actions	yr ysgol		ydydd-		y ddraig goch	Mochyn bach	
	through			'Heddyw' –			dysgu penillion	
	songs –			TV Programme		cerdd-oriaeth		
	'Ian a lawr'			Fy hen Ysgol		Dydd Gwyl		
	yn y maes			Clywed llais			Blodau melyn	
	yn yr	*Visual*		chwarae pel		Dewi sant		
	eisteddfodd	*association*		Droed			torri'r gwydr	
	yn y capel	Gwallt		chwerthynam			gwyliau a	
	Ar lan y mor	Ceffyl		bethau bach			mwyn hau	
		yfed cwrw						
		tê dydd Sul		*Commands to*				
		Cwm Penant		*do with children*				
		Dant y llew		*in class*				
				Agor y drws				
				eistedd yn syth				
				Sefyll				
				gwrando				
				edrych				
				paid				

The flow diagram technique

Any meaning which is transmitted in linear form, such as a piece of writing, a lecture, a conversation, can usefully be analysed and represented in a structural form to display the spatial and temporal or chronological sequence. The complete sequence is broken up into smaller 'items of meaning' each of which has some integrity as a separable item within the whole. These items can be categorised and the relationships made more explicit. The original sequencing, the categorisation and relationships between items are displayed in the form of a flow diagram. In this book we use this technique as a means of displaying the organisation of the parts and the chapters (Figure 4). In Chapter 3 we illustrated how the flow diagram and the read record can be used in a Learning Conversation.

The technique has been used very successfully both as an 'expert' guide to a given resource (Figure 40) (for example, lecture, paper, book) or as a tool that learners can use to represent their own understanding of the resource whilst preserving the original temporal sequence. The sharing of a common system of representation makes comparisons between a group sharing the same resources relatively simple and unambiguous.

The display of multi-dimensional relationships between units of meaning in a sequence has certain advantages over the repertory grid and vertical structures of meaning techniques. The vertical axis displays the sequence of items. Arrows specify the relations between them. Levels of description of meaning can be displayed in successive flow diagrams. The elicitation of items is more holist than the grid and more structured than structures of meaning, since each unit of meaning has to be considered in relation to its sub-units and also in the context of the supra-ordinate units before it can be categorised within the descriptions of the flow diagram. Its major disadvantage is that the categories for classifying the items of meaning must necessarily be arrived at early on in the elicitation process in contrast to cluster descriptions or supra-constructs which are open to exploration throughout.

By considering the positive and negative attributes of each meaning representation tool it becomes possible to design and develop additional devices, the specific characteristics of which serve some particular functions. Once the learner perceives the value of these systematic devices *as tools for representing personal meaning* and for using in the MA(R)4S process, in her or his quest for enhanced personal competence, then each culturally bound representational device referred to in Chapter 1 becomes a legitimate tool within a Learning Conversation.

The flow diagram procedure

The basic procedure can be summarised as follows:

- the resource is examined as a whole to get an overview of it (this could be, for instance, a tape of a lecture or a chapter of a book);

- the resource is chunked into smaller units of meaning (in a text, groups of words, sentences, groups of sentences or paragraphs can represent these units);
- each unit is considered carefully in order to categorise it into one of the following four categories: *main theme, qualifiers (derivatives), elaborations (specifics), links (signposts and side comments)*;
- a number is assigned to each unit, preserving the sequence, and it is placed in one of the columns representing the four categories;
- this is done for each unit successively;
- a provisional exploration is essential before the final form is arrived at;
- arrows are introduced to show how each unit relates to the others;
- the units are checked for consistency so that the 'main theme' column creates a meaningful and coherent sequence.

When the learner is familiar with using flow diagrams, it becomes useful for him or her to differentiate *types of relationships*. A coding system on the arrows can make this explicit. The choice of categories and relationships depends on the nature of the resource and on the purposes of the learner. For instance, a team of scientists developed *evidence, theory, review of theory, evaluation, implications* as an appropriate category system for their own reports, and a group of literary critics used *imagery, patterns, plot, situation, characters* for an assessment of the style and quality of prose.

This multi-dimensional flow structure, when charted at different levels of organisation, can reveal how the total meaning derives from the internal relationship of the units at any one level and also from its context, that is, the ways in which it connects to other parts of the resource. Together, the internal structure and the context give to a particular sequence of units of meaning a coherent meaning. To the extent that there is a shared purpose, a shared category system and a shared agreement about size of meaning units, a group can arrive at an agreed structured representation of a given resource. In Chapter 3 we illustrated how a group of students use the technique for exploring the process of comprehending a text.

Personal Learning Task Analysis (PLTA)

In its simplest form, this allows learners to represent their purposive, strategic, causal model of a given task, hierarchically. Each node of description in the hierarchy contains elements of *what* is done, *how* it is done, *why* it is done, *how well*, *where* it is done and *what next*. This hierarchical structure allows the whole task and each of its component parts to be represented in relationship.

The PLTA procedure

By laddering upwards from a given node, the superordinate node can be identified and described. This is achieved by locating the purposive element and asking why you do that

Figure 40 **A flow diagram of S-O-L environments for skill, competence and creativity**

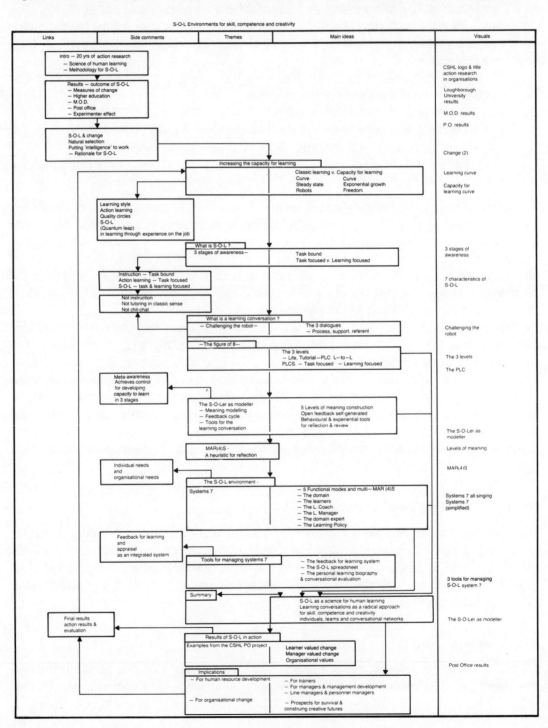

and then asking what must be done to achieve this new superordinate purpose. 'How' reveals the strategy and 'how well' the criteria for review. For the superordinate node 'where' identifies its location and 'what next' locates equivalent nodes at the same level in the hierarchy. By laddering downwards from any given node the subordinate nodes can be identified. This is achieved by locating the strategic element and asking what must be done to achieve that. 'How', 'how well', 'why', 'where' and 'what next' identifies the causal descriptions for this subordinate mode. 'What next' identifies similar nodes at this lower level. Thus, an upwards–downwards and rolling elicitation procedure focusing on the performance of the task derives a comprehensive hierarchical personal description of the task. Figure 40 illustrates in diagrammatic form a Personal Learning Task Analysis representation.

This reflective tool has been used by trainee factory foremen for developing their view of the job, by trainee chefs developing their skills in making omelettes, by managers for re-assessing their roles when new demands are made on them, by experts of a complex task for identifying the key features for simulation by a computer, and by students on work placements.

Unlike the repertory grid, structures of meaning and the flow diagram technique, the PLTA embodies a causal description of a task and can be directly linked with records of task performance for self-validation. Operationally linked in this way, when, for example, learning on a simulator, behaviour and experience are represented together as a coherent process which can be explicitly validated. Thus, by building the PLTA into a simulator, it is possible to represent more fully the ongoing time structure of the personal experience and relate this to the actual consequences of behaviour. We have in our action research projects successfully used records of performance combined with the PLTA as part of a conversational technology for developing learning competence.

Non-verbal forms of representation

In Chapters 1 and 2 we emphasised that the totality of meaning is embodied in the muscle sense, in visual, tactile and auditory forms as well as the almost infinite forms of symbolism that woman- and mankind have invented. As part of the repertoire of meaning representation devices it is important therefore to recruit tools that can exhibit meaning in all its possible forms. In our S-O-L book we showed how the repertory grid can be adapted for the non-verbal expression of constructs. Arts students used this procedure for exploring and developing their criteria for creating sculptures. Tea-tasters and whisky blenders used it for their subjective calibration of quality; but beyond the grid, structures of meaning and flow diagram there are many possibilities.

Psycho-drama and Noh drama are interpretive forms for group Learning Conversations, and mime in all its variant forms can be included here. Music, sign language, as for the deaf and dumb, or used during social intercourse, are some of the extensive resources that can be drawn upon. Pictorial sketches ranging from the more concrete to more abstract

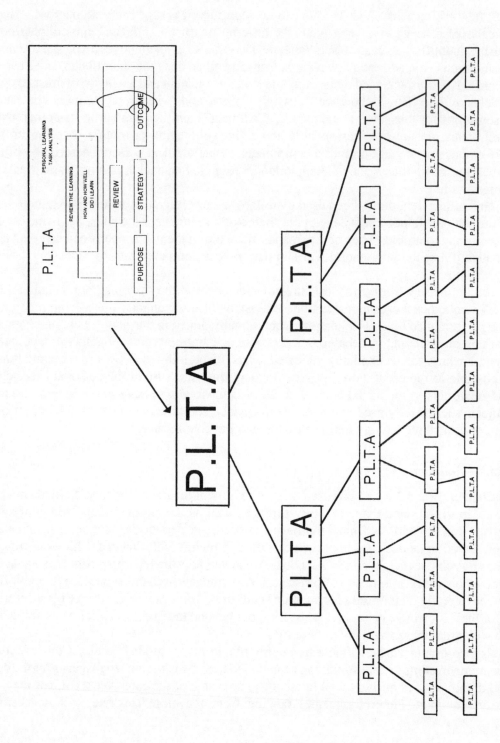

Figure 41 Personal Learning Task Analysis representation

symbolisms become a resource for reflection and review. One of the authors is currently exploring how certain aspects of Jung's primordial symbols can be recruited as a resource for the Self-Organised Learner. Self-hypnosis offers yet another powerful reflective tool for raising awareness of the richness and wholeness of the personal meanings created during learning. In E – Tools from education and training we indicated how techniques within psychology offer a wealth of truly human technologies which can become resources for expanding the power of the Learning Conversation.

Biological tools such as blood-pressure monitors, heart-rate detectors and electrical skin resistor monitors offer well-tested biofeedback devices which can function as aids for modelling our physiological and sensory non-verbal meanings. These devices display the processes of inner behaviours and we have used biofeedback tools together with various combinations of other reflective tools to heighten consciousness of the performance of complex tasks and skills, which are dealt with in the next chapter. These have been particularly useful when challenging perceptual robots (Chapter 3). In implementing the support dialogue of the Learning Conversation these devices are a way of getting to grips with those physiological states associated with anxiety, hostility and stress.

In this section we have indicated how the tools described can be variously recruited for reflecting on personal experience. These meaning representation tools form one of the two main branches of our Functional Taxonomy. The form of each tool is designed to facilitate the construction of appropriate structures for reflection at key points in the Learning Conversation. The other branch of our taxonomy describes the tools for recording behaviour. In the next section we introduce a wide range of behavioural tools accompanied by specific talk-back examples in some instances. We build on the examples referred to in this section and in Chapters 3 and 4 (Part II).

Tools for increasing awareness of learning processes: reconstructing experience by talk-back through records of behaviour

As tool-makers for the conversational development of learning our extensive search for methods of recording behaviour in various learning situations has led us to invent many behavioural techniques. We have explored different types of observational records, their analysis and capability for reliably and validly reconstructing experience. Our first endeavours resulted in the Reading Recorder, Listening Recorder and Manual Skill Recorder in their various hardware and software forms. Since these early initiatives, we have recruited video, audio, and a wide range of computer technologies. The following sections introduce five classes of behavioural tools and their more recent advancements. We shall begin by elaborating the reading example introduced in Chapters 3 and 4 in order to explain in greater detail the techniques involved.

Records of behaviour: reconstructing reading-to-learn

When people read they are seldom aware of how they are reading, nor are they aware of the cognitive and affective processes which underlie their behaviour. The Reading Recorder was developed as a device for making the behavioural processes of reading explicit. Developments in our techniques for recording reading include a robust mechanical machine, various paper-and-pencil methods and computer-driven software. These are explained in detail in various published papers and in our book *Reading-to-Learn* (Methuen).

The read record shows *how time was spent in reading a text*; it shows changes in pace, hesitation, skipping, backtracking and note-making. A simplified form of a read record is shown in Figure 41. The vertical axis of the graph shows the position in the text. The horizontal axis shows progression in time. This record shows the reading of a 400-line article in twenty minutes. We can see that the lines were not read at an even rate of 400/20 (twenty lines per minute). The first 100 lines were read in five minutes (that is, at an average of twenty lines per minute), but the reader spend five minutes not reading at all. In fact, he was thinking for three minutes and made some notes, though this, of course, does not appear on the graph. From the tenth minute to the fifteenth he read more slowly from line 100 to line 150. Then he speeded up and read from lines 150 to 250 in two minutes.

At line 250 he stopped and turned quickly back to line 150. He stayed on line 150 for a minute. (Actually, he wasn't reading at this point, he was making notes.) He then read very quickly and without stopping at all from line 15 to line 400 in two minutes (that is, at a rate of 250/2 = 125 lines per minute).

A reading record like this immediately makes one wonder:

1 What was in the first 100 lines that made the reader pause and think after reading them?
2 He read lines 100 to 150 rather slowly. Why? What was it in these lines that was difficult to read?
3 Why did he go back from line 250 to line 150?
4 Why was it then so easy to read through from line 150 to the end?

If we explain that the first 100 lines were a simple introduction; the next fifty lines examined in detail the author's intentions; line 250 referred to an idea first dealt with in line 150; and the last 150 lines repeated the author's intentions more elaborately, then we can begin to infer quite a lot from the reader's behaviour.

For a read record to become meaningful in a Learning Conversation it has to be put through the MA(R)4S process with sensitivity and care. In Chapters 3 and 4 we illustrated this as we described how the process, support and referent dialogues were conversationally recruited to enhance the quality of reading-to-learn. The verbal ability for talk-back is not the same as a perceptual ability to recognise significant events in the process of reading from the recording emitted by the machine. The learner must attempt to *relive the experience and account for his or her behaviour.* The record and the original text is used to elicit a personal explanation of the reading process. Talk-back also involves a later phase of evaluation which requires detailed justification for the behaviour at a micro-level in terms of purpose, text structure, strategy and outcomes.

When the flow diagram of the text is combined with the reading recorder a more powerful representation of the personal causal processes of reading is possible. In Chapter 3 we have illustrated this. When the full power of the conversational technology is brought to bear, using the *repertory grid* and *purpose hierarchies* to explore needs and purposes, the *flow diagram* to systematically describe the structure and organisation of the text, the *read record* to represent behaviour and *structures of meaning* to represent reading outcomes, a fully fledged and coherent awareness of the whole process of reading-to-learn is achieved. This is described fully in *Reading-to-Learn* (Methuen). The CSHL Reading-to-Learn software suite enables this level of awareness to be developed for any text that the learner may choose to read (Postscript).

A writing recorder offers similar facilities for talk-back through records of personal writing, and a listening recorder uses a modified form of the conventional tape recorder for talk-back through records of listening. Thus we have developed a number of mechanical devices for obtaining records of learning behaviour to use for talk-back. We have also simplified the technology by developing paper-and-pencil observational procedures for

Figure 42 A simple read record

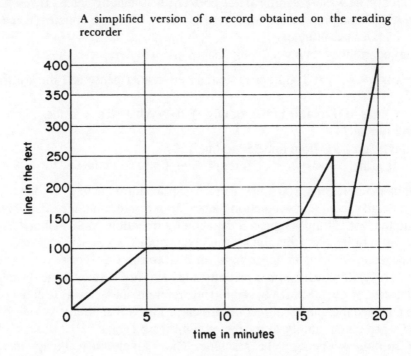

A simplified version of a record obtained on the reading recorder

use when the mechanical devices are not available. We have also developed conversational software for those who use the facilities of the micro-computer.

Talk-back using records of reading has been used to support the development of reading-to-learn skills within a large number of educational, training and commercial centres. Teachers have used this tool with 6- to 8-year-olds to help them overcome their almost total lack of awareness of their reading processes. Their almost robot-like intern-alisation of the 'reading out loud' syndrome (that is, sub-vocalisation) which constrains speed and comprehension, has been successfully challenged. Purposiveness in reading and an awareness of processing texts differently for different purposes represent new skills which they were able to develop successfully. Our transcript of Susie and Nick in Chapter 3 illustrates this. Again, scientists in industry have used it to enhance their search skills and, combined with the flow diagram technique, they have been able to improve their report writing skills. Managers have used it to improve the quality of their speed reading and their summarising and evaluation skills. Whilst the reading recorder and the software offer technical precision for recording the time/structure of reading in detail, the simpler paper-and-pencil procedures have sufficient power for those who do not have this techno-logy. This technique is explained in the simple example that follows.

Branwen is using the 'hand-tracking technique' shown in Figure 42. Her reading purpose was 'to evaluate the findings of a report that reading standards have declined in recent years in Britain'. She is in fact a teacher in a junior school. Before she began the exercise she had been engaged in a life conversation about her needs as a teacher, her purposes for improving her skills in reading and her particular purposes for reading the text that she herself had chosen.

She kept a pencil in her hand, and as she read she traced in the margin of the page her progression through the text. She attempted to monitor her reading. She tried to be aware of the relationship between her hand movements in tracking her own reading and the movements of her eyes as she perused the text. Figure 43 shows an extract of her read record and her own explanation, elicited during talk-back, of what was going on in her head as she read the text.

Having familiarised herself with the method by using the technique several times on different texts, Branwen was able to improve her monitoring of how she processed a text for different purposes. Each time she was continuously surprised at the richness of her own explanations, which only emerged during talk-back of her read records. A fuller flavour of the process of such reflective MA(R)4S conversations was offered in Chapter 3. Here we generalise on the structure of such talk-back.

- What does my record tell me?
- I read the text twice. On the first occasion I wanted to get a good preview, so that next time round I could select important bits. On the second read I zoned in on these bits, and searched between paragraphs for . . . .
- I paused on lines so-and-so because:
     I couldn't understand the phrase/word/term.
     I found it interesting.
     It was important for my purpose.
     I disagreed with the author.
     I made notes.
     I was daydreaming.
     I was linking it to what went before, etc.
- I skipped forward on lines so-and-so because:
     I could tell it wasn't relevant.
     I knew about it already.
     I was challenged by the author, etc.
- I made notes on lines so-and-so because:
     I wanted to recall this exactly.
     I wanted to check it later.
     I thought I could use these for reconsidering my outcome.
     It's a habit I've got – I always make notes.
- My notes were:
     Very detailed.

Figure 43 The hand-tracking technique

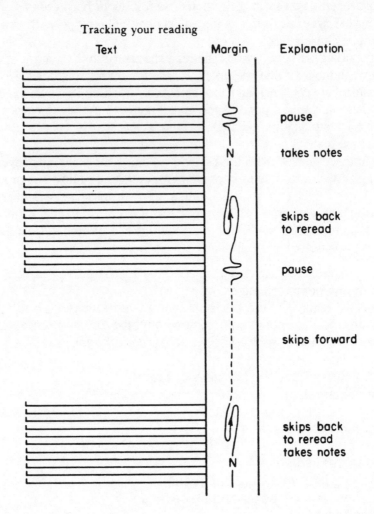

Tracking your reading

Very brief.
Actually maps.
Actually lists.
— In my second read, I searched back and forward:
  between sentences in paragraph so-and-so because I . . .
  between paragraphs so-and-so and so-and-so because I . . .
  between phrases in sentence so-and-so because I . . .
— At the end I find it helpful to make notes about how I read.

- When I have finished, I stand back from the details and ask myself some questions about the read as a whole:
    How long did I take?
    Did I read it more than once?
    Was the way I read it different when I read it again?
    How was it different?
    Did I read smoothly?
    Did I skip forward or track back?
    Did I pause in the right places?
    Did I make notes in the right places?
- Then, of course, the hard question . . . if I had to read it again, what changes would I make in the way I read it?

Records of a manual task and talk-back

A manual skills sensor and recorder was developed to monitor the movements made by a person carrying out a manual skill. This is achieved by having a series of 'sensors' which signal the breakpoints between the elements of a task. The sensors are photo-electric, touch-sensitive, proximity-sensitive with various types of specific-purpose devices including micro-switches and capacity and resistant gauges. These are placed strategically on the machine or workplace at which the skill is performed, and they signal the learner's movements to the central recorder. This records the time taken for each element of each cycle of the task. This device offers a choice between different types of feedback for learning.

During a practice run the learner might start by choosing to see his or her cycle times on the task. As they proceed they may become interested in one particular part of the task; namely, one or more elements in a cycle. The learner can choose to obtain a printed record. As learners become more skilled they can choose the time taken to complete a selected number of cycles. Thus, they can practise stamina training. Finally, the pen recorder can be adjusted to plot histograms of the relative times taken for each element of the task during successive cycles. This allows the learner to concentrate on increasing his or her productivity.

Developmental learning studies have used this manual skills sensor recorder in the assembly of television printed circuit boards, on Capstan lathes and a variety of machine and assembly mass-production tasks.

By using a mix of feedback it is possible to talk-back through the records so that the learner is enabled to *build up a model of the manual skill on the job*, and thus acquire production speeds in about a quarter of the normal training time. As with the reading recorder, this is an effective talk-back tool for promoting Self-Organised Learning. Since it is used as a conversational tool, the device allows learners to dispense with it once they

Figure 44 Branwen's read record with talk-back

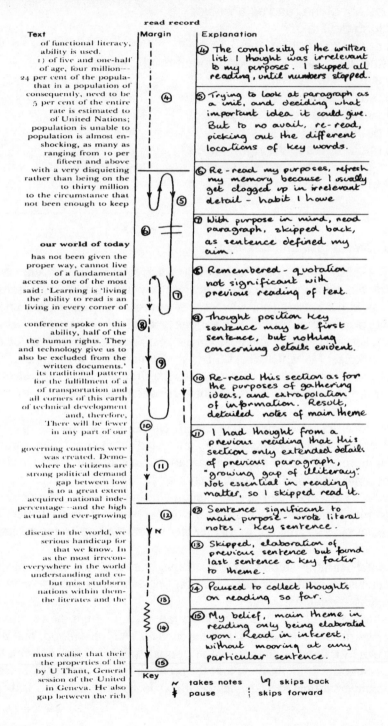

are able to observe and monitor themselves learning a manual skill. Many of the recording devices described have now been integrated into a manual skill software suite.

Observational records and talk-back

So far we have explained how a reading recorder, writing recorder and analagously a pen recorder linked to a cassette player can be used to monitor reading, note-making and listening skills. Manual skills in industrial production training have been monitored using the flexible time and quality recording aid. In this section, we show how *observational techniques* can be used to monitor individual and group learning.

There are many situations and events in which records can be obtained for talk-back about learning using comparatively simple direct observational monitoring and charting techniques. For instance, any pair in a one-to-one exchange situation, and any group in which its members are concerned with the quality of their learning, in the group situation, can use modifications of the original Bayles technique as a reflective device. We have used this with management teams in business settings, air traffic controllers to evaluate the quality of their debriefs after a practice sortie, university staff to reflect upon the nature of their teaching, language students to reflect on their strategies for learning a language, with young chefs to reflect on their skills in making omelettes or with ourselves to reflect on the quality of our Learning Conversations with our clients.

There are two modes in which such records can be obtained: either by direct observation of the live, all-singing, all-dancing situation or indirectly by observations, using video or tape recordings. Either way the records are used carefully to reconstruct the complex process of interaction in a group learning situation.

Each pair or group, according to its needs and purposes, *invents its own category system* for observation and then reconstructs together the meanings of each event without recourse to the usual potted normative systems of analysis offered by micro-teaching and social skills training. Recent developments, including the computer control of the video for rapidly defining and categorising items and for a structured access to this behavioural resource, have offered a superb reflective learning tool. The selective access video recorder is further described in the next section.

Here we shall explain briefly how group observation categories have been used with a team of managers in a business environment and with ourselves as conversational researchers. We shall also outline different types of observational methods we have used for charting tasks in a workplace, for charting the pattern of a student's activities over time, and for keeping a detailed time record of young chefs using film loops as they learned to make omelettes. All of these were used for group talk-back.

Observations of learning by discussion

One form of the modified Bayles technique for recording discussion consists of a chart in which the vertical columns represent each participant and each row represents a fixed period of time; for example, 30 seconds. We use a simple letter code based on a problem-solving algorithm.

The categories used are as follows:
P identifying and defining the problem,
A analysing the situation,
I additional information,
S tentative solutions,
T testing a possible solution, and
N negotiating an agreed solution.

The conversation is charted in these terms.

This was used with a team of managers who were meeting daily in a business setting. They felt that they were not performing as a good problem-solving group.

During the early talk-back reconstructions, the team were astounded to discover that their conversation meandered up and down and round and round through what they saw as the logical development of the problem-solving algorithm, but later they gradually appreciated that problem-solving is a systematic and cyclic activity and that testing possible solutions can lead one back to a better formulation of the problem.

After a number of such talk-back sessions, individual managers identified what they saw as their own personal lack of skills. For example:

M1 saw her problem as talking too much and not really contributing;
M2 felt she was always missing opportunities and saying the wrong things at the wrong time;
M3 was worried that he never opened his mouth;
M4 was always negatively censoring everything he heard;
M5 was trying to listen to it all and soak it up as gospel;
The chairman felt he was always allowing the discussion to get out of hand.

Having arrived at this self-diagnosis through talk-back, the participants moved on to a more advanced method with talk-back. Combining their observational chart with a tape recording of the discussion, each reconstructed *what was going on in his or her head when they were not talking*. They then produced six parallel 'inner conversations' in the form of personal notes. As the group exchanged hidden conversations, they realised just how much of the group resource was going to waste. Further practice in subsequent meetings gave them insight into the kind of contribution each could make and how the chairman could manage the group better.

Charting a task in a workplace: the diagnostic flow process chart and talk-back

This technique is used for detailed observation of how materials move from one operation to another within a production area. A symbol system is used for charting progress. This is shown in Figure 44. The learner tracks the product's progress through the area to produce the flow process chart. He then uses this in a talk-back session to identify the points at which evidence of incipient problems may appear, such as waste of materials, lack of productivity or a drop in quality. Having identified as many sources of information as possible, he then reflects on the remedial action to be taken. He adds these perception and control loops to the chart as shown.

This tool enables a supervisor to build an appropriate model of an area and reflect upon how she or he uses this to control the area effectively and to appreciate the supervisory process. Using this technique a group can quickly identify differences between their models and explore their agreements and disagreements.

We have used this technique in many different industrial situations including a rental laundry, a letter sorting office in the Post Office, and with a well-known chocolate manufacturer.

The CHARTing technique: recording a pattern of activities over time

This is a generally applicable technique for recording the pattern of activities in which an individual takes part over a period of time. For example, students can use it to reflect on the activities implicit in their courses of study. They start by identifying a range of topics in a particular course. They then develop a category system to cover all their activities concerned with these topics. These might include lectures, seminars, tutorials, practicals, tests, chats with peers, private study, use of the library and so on. They then use these as categories on the vertical axis. The horizontal axis represents time (hours in a day/days in a week).

As activities concerned with the range of topics occur, they are entered in the chart indicating the exact nature of the subject matter; for example, the osmosis experiment carried out, the various theories about diffusion and osmosis reviewed, the various physiological effects on the tissues of plants and animals, and so forth. Talk-back through one week's chart enables the student to identify how their activities relate to one another, revealing the pattern of learning opportunities, thus *diagnosing how differentiated their study strategies are*. A series of observation and talk-backs enables them to become increasingly aware of their developing effectiveness in tackling the job of being a student.

This CHARTing technique can be applied to *any* operational task demanding a range of activities over a period of time and is equally useful as a conversational tool in commerce, for research, teaching or production management. It is available as a software package.

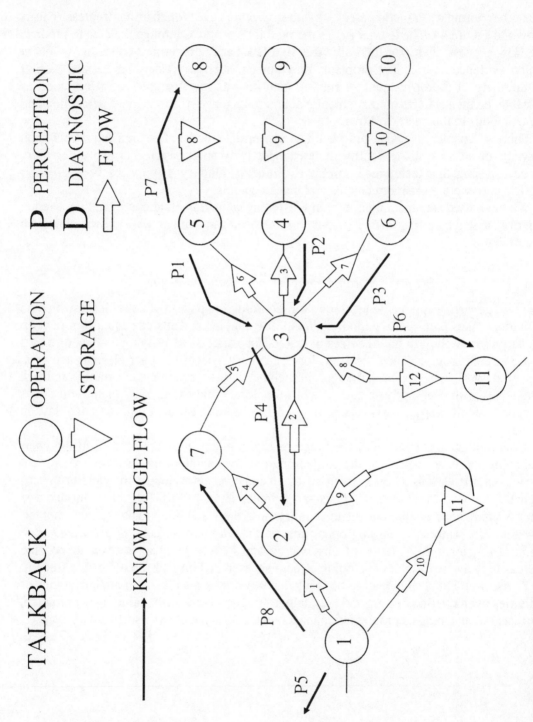

Figure 45 The flow process chart

Recording the use of training materials

Trainee chefs learning to make omelettes

In an action research project in the early 1970s for the Hotel and Catering Industry Training Board we produced a hierarchically organised set of forty-eight super-8 cassetted film loops of how to make an omelette. These ranged from a loop showing the whole process from beginning to end, down to a detailed slow-motion loop of how to beat the mixture with a fork. There were also loops showing faults and quality omelettes. In a controlled experiment, learners, after a short initial briefing, were provided with the materials (eggs and so forth), the utensils (including a frying pan), the equipment (a gas stove, for instance) and an individual cassette-loading film projector. They were asked to use these facilities as an opportunity for learning how to make high-quality omelettes. The only other provision was a panel of experts who would judge the quality of each omelette made, using seven dimensions of quality, each expressed as a five-point scale.

The observational technique consisted in keeping a detailed record of how each learner spent his or her time. We developed a detailed coding scheme which allowed the observer to note which loops were viewed when and for how long, how the learner distributed time over the various preparation, cooking and omelette-serving activities, how many eggs were used, how many omelettes were made and the quality of each omelette as judged by the panel.

Talk-back through this behavioural record quickly revealed the degree of self-organisation in learning. Some were able to reconstruct the learning activity as a coherent attempt to use those film loops which were particularly relevant to the specific learning they wished to try out in the practice cooking: then to use the panel's evaluation of the product of their cooking both as a means of assessing their success so far, and as evidence about what exactly they should learn next. Others had much less-developed strategies, using a very hit-or-miss non-strategy, almost pulling out the loops at random.

Reflection upon their reconstructed 'strategy of learning' led the less Self-Organised Learners first to recognise their state of disorganisation and then to begin to build a more coherent strategy. The insights obtained were reported to have fed over into other areas of their learning.

Putting a detailed 'monitoring of use' shell around an expert system, in this case addressing omelette-making skills, provides the learner with the talk-back opportunity to reconstruct their progressive modelling of professional knowledge in the system.

Observational records for conversational scientists reflecting on their own experiment

The 'conversational experiment' is a method which the authors have developed to deal with the issues that arise when one sets out systematically to investigate the process of Self-Organised Learning. We see the conversational experiment as a hierarchically organised system of events, each of which has its own time span and each of which can be viewed as an experiment which has aims of its own contributing to the higher-order, longer-term aims of the experiment of which it is a part. The fact that learning is taking place by both learner who intends to become self-organised and by the experimenters who intend to develop a theory of Self-Organised Learning shows that records of progress can have a *double function*. This example serves to illustrate how we used categories of observation of our own experiment (that is, involving ourselves with our subject) to help us theorise about Self-Organised Learning. The example used a machine driven Bayles-type interaction recorder which we developed ourselves.

Our early research activities with the reading recorder, manual skills recorder and FOCUSed repertory grids provided initial opportunities for the construction of tentative forms of observational categories. These were used as paper-and-pencil procedures both during sessions and subsequently in the analysis of video recordings of the same events. The development of these systematic observational procedures is a necessary stage for the implementation of the conversational method, since this provides another tool for use with our learners and also for use to research our theory. The conversational experiment can only be managed effectively if we can monitor and reflect on it.

The example shows how some of our criteria for a Learning Conversation are used as categories for feedback to ourselves when conducting an experiment with learners using the ILS-CHAT software, a simulator, and supported by a Learning Tutor (Postscript). To indicate the value of using such observational techniques for ourselves, we list some conclusions we drew from conducting this conversational experiment with seven learners over a period of six weeks.

Management of the Learning Conversations was concerned with such interventions as:

- task debrief and learning debrief activities;
- diagnosis of strengths and weaknesses in playing the game and in learning to play the game;
- setting learning goals and constructing plans for mini-games;
- personal support during processes of experimentation in both task and learning skills;
- clarification and encouragement during elicitation of Personal Learning Contracts;
- aspects of the affective states of the learner which contribute to learning;
- regulation of movement between open-provisional and decisive and more convergent phases in the learner-player activities;
- constructions of creative alternatives during play or during contract elicitation;
- awareness and growth of predictive skills as an example in pattern recognition in detecting the enemy's intentions and in missile control;
- channelling the level of the Learning Conversation:
    process reflection in learning the task (tutorial level of the Learning Conversation);
    process reflection on challenging the partially developed strategic skills
    (learning-to-learn level of the Learning Conversation);

　　　process reflection on relevance within a wider context (life-level of Learning
　　　Conversation);
- part-task negotiation and relating these to mini-games;
- guiding sequences of specific learning contracts;
- progressive clarification of machine-elicited contract structures;
- negotiating and reflecting on personal learning styles;
- negotiating learner needs into purposes;
- guiding learner reflection during play;
- overall guidance in engagements with the software;
- non-verbal gestures during learner support;
- content-based conversations to do with the experiences of the game and of personal
  learning history as extensions of the learner's own referents;
- overall guidance on the use of the software;
- empathising with the learner's own strivings for improvements;
- buffering the learner's stress, often initiated whilst he challenges his incompetence;
- entering into the learner's understandings of and difficulties with a task;
- appreciative attention to the learner's 'here and now' responses;
- being appreciated by the learner in acting as observer of the learner as he or she
  continues to learn, thus providing a human participant during the learning process.

Video records and talk-back

There are many situations in which task performance and learning activity can be captured
on to video tape: for example, in sport, in the classroom, on training courses and in
dialogues such as personal tutoring, or bank manager–client, psychotherapy, doctor–
patient interviews or negotiations between architect and client or union representatives and
employers. The example closest to home is 'learner–Learning Conversationalist'. Given a
little time to familiarise themselves with the initially unnerving experience of being
recorded and then 'seeing ourselves as others see us', most participants quickly settle down
to accept the video record as a powerful reflective learning aid, but there is a crucial
difference between using it as an instructional device and as a tool for awareness-raising.

　　Teachers and trainers are inclined to use video recorders for critical debriefing. This can
be pre-emptive, cutting off participants from understanding their own behaviour, or
performance, in their own terms. It is, therefore, very useful to use the MA(R)4S heuristic
to talk the learner back through his or her record, letting him stop and re-play, skip back or
forwards, until he has fully reconstructed the experience (namely, the modelling which
drove the original behaviour). Once the experience has been reconstructed and awareness
achieved he can be encouraged to explore his modelling more deeply by producing a more
explanatory talk-through. This will require him to reflect on the terms (criteria) in which
he would evaluate his own performance. It is only when a participant has achieved this
state of self-organised awareness that he is in a position creatively to make use of 'peer' or

'expert' criticism, without either being taken over by it or prematurely rejecting it (Chapter 3).

Once the learner has achieved this primary process of self-organised awareness there are many selective observational category systems available for helping him or her sharpen his perception of certain aspects of his performance or behaviour which experts have found to be important. Social skills training and micro-teaching offer fairly well-known examples, but work study (for example, two-handed operator process charts), dance (choreographic notations or Laban movement analysis), interview training, TA (transactional analysis), or the professional analysis of golf strokes could be cited.

We have found that whilst these systems are initially very useful in offering the participant an alternative way of viewing their own activity and so focusing their perceptual processes, they can soon become counter-productive. Having an expert point of view thrust upon them can often inhibit the development of the participant's own, more personally relevant perceptual sensitivity. It can be experienced as rather gimmicky. Eventually, the participant should be offered two alternative sets of observational categories for interpreting the same recording. This provokes them (frees them) to construct their own category system. Groups that we have worked with have found it deeply rewarding to search for an observational category system best-suited to their own particular set of purposes. The expert systems are then seen as resources which may contribute to this process. This self-organisation of the observational process leads to a revealing upsurge in the relevance and immediacy of the talk-back process.

The use of video disks

The recent advent of WORM (Write Once, Read Many times) video disks offers possibilities for a much more flexible and effective approach to the talk-back through video records of one's own performance. The WORM technology driven by a micro-computer enables the user to partition the recording into self-defined 'events'. Once defined, these events can be accessed without delay, so they can be called, compared and contrasted, classified and reorganised at will. This increases the power of the talk-back process and offers a MA(R)4S monitoring and modelling facility which completely transforms this awareness- raising activity. This process can, for example, be used to create experiential events that can be used in a repertory grid. The computer-aided PEGASUS type of conversation can be based on elements of behaviour or performance (Postscript). There are almost infinite possibilities for developing this very immediate type of computer-driven talk-back activity.

Computer-logged records of complex tasks and talk-back

So far we have tried to show how paper-and-pencil observational techniques, mechanical devices, video and audio recorders, and relatively simple software systems such as the CSHL Reading-to-Learn and ILS-CHAT suite can provide resources for recording behaviour and how, by using records for talk-back, a learner can better articulate and control his or her performance on a wide variety of tasks. In these last examples we show how high-fidelity simulators can be transformed from practice devices mainly involving 'playing the whole thing through again' to negotiating learning constructively.

Our main illustration is taken from one of our Ministry of Defence projects; the second and third are forward-projected commercial examples in which we are currently involved. In one system a complex expert knowledge system is being developed as a resource for developing highly skilled performance on a complex task. The other is concerned with simulating a working area for improved efficiency, productivity and quality of service.

In each case computer-based facilities such as logged time/structure records, replay facilities and methods for enhancing feedback of performance and the CSHL PEGASUS and structures of meaning expert knowledge elicitation systems are used to enhance MA(R)4S facilities. Additionally, CSHL-ILS software, including PEGASUS, CHAT and CHART are used as additional learning aids within the Learning Conversation as a whole for promoting Self-Organised Learning. In the appendix to Chapter 3 we presented some selected transcripts to demonstrate how computer-logged records are used in a Learning Conversation. Here we set these in the context of the skills to be learned, describe the procedure involved, and indicate the range of possible applications.

Replay talk-backs of a war game: patterns in the sea

The game simulates a war between two opposing forces. The aim is to locate with sonar and destroy by firing the opponent's force of submarines. It is played in a series of discrete actions either between two players or between one player and the computer. The game demands an appreciation of tactical moves in complex patterns and in a capacity for prediction and risk-taking. It is an exercise in command and control.

At the end of the game the player can replay in fast or slow time and call upon a number of additional learning aids for enhancement of feedback for learning.

John's protocol, which follows, was produced during a first replay.

Action 1
Initial position; get to Best Tracking Position (BTP)

Action 2
Different games are not the same. This could be because of the defensive position of subs.

Action 3
How do I best get into BTP?

Action 4
I can't remember my last input of choices, therefore I may waste time putting in the same movements (M) again.

Action 5
I will have to test different strategies for patterning my subs to find every enemy sub.

Action 6
I will use the time limit between actions to the full.

Action 7
Still no detection of any enemy sub.

Action 8
What different strategies could I now be using?

Action 9
Found one! Now relax! Try to work without anxiety. What should I do?

Action 10
Sort out my strategy.
   step one – find subs – roughly
   step two – take action to locate exact position
   step three – destroy enemy subs – how?

Action 11
I must use 'speed' and 'movement' and I must use my missiles most efficiently.

Action 12
Perhaps I should take more chances – experiment in order to learn.

Action 13
Is it better to stop and then fire or to keep moving?

Action 14
I'm getting anxious about running out of time before I can input my commands – I must try to remain calm, confident, relaxed. . . . I must retain a feeling of control. Why am I getting flustered?

Action 15
How do I know when and where the enemy subs are moving?

Action 16
Damn it! The enemy subs are escaping! Sh——!

Action 17
Use other vessels as reserves.

Action 18
There's a problem of enemy subs going past R around position 10.

Action 19
I'm not very good at estimating 5 squares. I don't know, I haven't properly appreciated fullest capabilities of my subs. There are gaps in my firing.

Action 20
Distractions, the missiles are running out.

Action 21
I must accommodate in thinking how to do various different things at once.
    I must destroy detected subs around R.
    I must locate the subs that are passing A and G.

Action 22
Why did I move so quickly?

Action 23
I don't know about distances and positions (directions) of Fire (F). The result is that I destroy my own ships. Which could I have destroyed?

Action 24
I'm listening to the disk drive – I think it gives me hints about enemy moving.

Action 25
I am beginning to judge distances across the screen. It's 25 x 25.

Action 26
Why should I move quickly? I've got 3 minutes to move in, think it out. Breathe deeply to give myself the illusion of control. Events crowd in on me. Movement is really quite slow. There's a lot of time.
    How do I loose these feelings of panic?

Action 27
I'm not testing things out properly so the enemy is slipping by.

Action 28
I was too influenced by what happened last time.

A self-debrief, at the end of the replay, which had involved John in re-living and then explaining the rationale underlying his activities, led him to identify new bits of language about his learning. These are listed below.

   – positional thinking
   – seeing ahead
   – approximate calculating
   – seeing picture in my head

- depicting two more positions in my head
- thinking how positions are related to detecting and firing
- seeing the invisible enemy
- imagining 'the sea' as a 25 x 25 matrix
- preparing ahead of events
- following strands of thought
- panic
- anxiety
- disruption
- focusing attention
- keeping a broad view
- concentrating
- taking all variables into account, e.g. speed, velocity, direction
- changing positions
- capabilities of objects in particular submarines, e.g. passive sonar, missiles, engines; i.e. maximum power
- imagining the enemy
- capabilities of enemy's vessels
- Best Tracking Position
- defence cordon.

The explanations elicited in relation to each action only emerged after careful periods of reflection, and John reported that this gave him a much clearer picture of what was going on and how he was reacting to it. This self-debrief activity on replay immediately after each game became an important component of John's self-directed learning schedule. Talk-back allowed John to identify what he needed to concentrate on for learning. Each of the seven learners' talk-back sessions yielded similarly rich resources of insight into processes of learning. For those readers not accustomed to simulators, it is important to point out that the reconstruction of personal experience by means of computer-driven replays involves as much emotional reaction as analytical thought, and learning to use emotional responses for effective command and control is crucial. The four variations of the replay facility made possible by this computer extended the possibilities of talk-back. Not only can each move be slowed down, giving time for a deeper reflection at a micro-level, but the moves can be speeded up for reflection on the pattern of moves as a whole. Again, replays from different points of view broaden strategic thoughts. Such facilities enable a more thorough reconstruction of the nature of anticipatory skills and the invention of personal methods for acquiring such skills to take place. Progress made by learners supported to use these facilities within a Learning Conversation were spectacular.

The following reported examples of sections from replay talk-backs illustrate the kind of learning taking place.

Example 1

As the replay with the enemy shown begins to unfold the learner begins to comment on the pattern of enemy movement. He had only been thinking in terms of individual enemy ships and how he could detect them.

As he sees the first passive sonar detection occur and watches himself move in another ship to obtain a cross-bearing, he realises that this has opened up a large gap in his defensive screen.

In another sequence he cannot understand why, when the enemy ship is so close, the passive sonar does not detect it. This leads him into a much more careful analysis of how the slow speed of the enemy and his own rapid movement combine to cut down the range of detection. This had wide-reaching ramifications for his subsequent defensive strategy.

At another point he is viewing a part of the battle where he had made a detection and fired missiles from all three of his ships and yet failed to sink the enemy. In the original game this had completely baffled and temporarily demoralised him. He now saw that he had been unconsciously assuming that, because the passive sonar detection line extended four spaces, the enemy ship was therefore at some distance from him. The replay revealed that the missile 3 x 3 squares had overlapped with each other thus reducing what he called the 'kill area'. More significantly, it also revealed that the enemy vessel was in fact almost adjacent to his own ship. This was quite contrary to the assumption that he had made during the game, which was that the enemy had 'got away'; that is, moved out of range. This led him to move off 'in chase' at top speed thus confirming his wrong belief by moving out of detection range (1) of the stationary enemy.

In his next game he demonstrated that he had learned much from this replay and in fact succeeded in sinking the first detected enemy. Unfortunately he later fired close to his own ship and, forgetting that he was moving diagonally towards where the missile would explode, he sunk himself. Thus does learning progress.

This learner rapidly moved towards a much more careful appreciation of the need to judge distances accurately, to understand the exact nature of the missile power, the sonar detection ranges, and how the movement of his own and enemy ships combined with these to produce results which baffled him until he viewed the replay. Much of the effectiveness of this learning can be tracked back to ways in which the Learning Conversations raised his awareness back from winning the game to encourage him to analyse how he was playing the game, and then to begin to reflect upon how he could use the replay facility to develop his game-playing skills.

Example 2

This learner had used the replay facility a number of times. He was beginning to reflect upon how he could detect enemy ships, even pinpoint them, and yet then lose contact with them. He had seen the more obvious mistakes he was making in earlier replay debriefs analogous to those described for the learner in Example 1.

In this reported learning sequence he is beginning to turn his queries more subtly inwards. Having played the game, he carefully tried to reconstruct it from memory, making sufficient notes to remind himself of the exact nature of the reconstruction. He then replayed the game showing only his own vessels – that is, seeing only what he had seen as he played.

This was a very salutary experience as there were a number of occasions on which he had 'remembered' events taking place much more quickly (in fewer actions) than they had actually occupied. There were also related errors in his memory of distances and movement. The Learning Manager guided him into a systematic examination of his 'cognitive model' of the battle process. This led to a series of 'ah-ha' comments and some apparent change in what he thought 'caused' what.

Having improved the precision of his perception and memory of what was going on, he pursued this same learning strategy one step further after the next game. He played the game, refining his memory and understanding of the expectations and decisions that produced his play by replaying the game from his point of view without showing enemy vessels, and then went on to replay a second time with the enemy vessels revealed. Having committed himself to a clear and careful reconstruction of what he had been expecting, thinking, inferring and doing, he was forced to see exactly where his inferred view had parted from the reality of enemy movements. Because he had already thought through the informational and modelling basis of his inferences he became very sensitive to information (from one or more moves before) which had been available to him but which he had not carried forward into his consideration of later events.

His play improved rapidly, in contrast to another learner who misrepresented his own decision process to himself and only selectively perceived events in the replay. Guided conversations with the Learning Manager had begun to reflect this back to him during the last session.

S-O-L, computer-based knowledge elicitation conversations and talk-back through behaviour

Current expert systems are, on the whole, limited by the skill of the knowledge engineer in eliciting the 'reservoir of meaning' from the expert in terms that can be represented as an inferential, rule-based system. This is a rather inexact science. However, interesting advances in the elicitation of knowledge have recently been achieved by using some of the PCP ideas and computer-based repertory grid techniques developed at CSHL during the 1970s (*Self-Organised Learning*, by Laurie F. Thomas and E. Sheila Harri-Augstein, Routledge & Kegan Paul, 1985).

But these techniques are rather restricted by their dependence on George Kelly's idea of a personal construct system which is essentially a hierarchical structure of bipolar constructs. As such, this approach is only scratching the surface of the future possibilities of the ideas and techniques offered in this book.

The LISP computer programming language has the fascinating facility (shared by only a few less-well-known approaches to the constructing of computer software) of being able to generate programs which can treat their own code as data and their data as code. Unfortunately LISP has been used mainly in Artificial Intelligence (AI); that is, it has been used in attempts to simulate human intelligence. This is probably an ultimately abortive activity, as Searle has so eloquently argued. It is better employed in creating *conversational amplifiers of 'human intelligence'*. The LISP language lends itself to the conversational representation of meaning as this term has been developed in this book. It can be used to generate very powerful reflections and reconstructions of meaning which can be recruited into the Learning Conversation.

We have, therefore, been playing with the possibilities of re-presenting meaning not as a static display (for instance, our paper-and-pencil techniques), not even as inferential rule-based 'knowledge' systems, but as heterarchial networks of the rote, descriptive explanatory, constructive and creative heuristics postulated in our discussion of meaning as modelling in Chapters 1 and 2. The code-manipulating powers of LISP enable us to represent some of the inner conversational meaning construction activities. These representations enable us to converse with our conversational construction of meaning, thus acting as meaning amplifiers.

For example, this conversationally elicited representation of meaning (that is, modelling of reality) can be run against situation scenarios to produce re-presentations of behaviour. Through conversational exchange the learner can be encouraged to compare and contrast these anticipated behaviours with records of actual behaviour faced with 'the same' scenario. This amplified 'talk-back' through behaviour' enables the learner to reconstruct experience much more fully and veridically than is normally the case. This reconstruction of experience is the basis of the bootstrapping Learning Conversation with the representation of meaning (modelling of reality) with which we started this paragraph.

Alternatively, we can use the PLTA techniques outlined in Chapter 3. Here we start with the record of behaviour, and conversationally decompose and represent it to generate a more fully explanatory reconstruction of the experience. This can serve as a conversational resource out of which the Self-Organised Learner can generate and represent constructive and possibly creative reconstructions of his or her meaning (as a modelling of reality).

Thus, we have *the twin possibilities of feeding highly sophisticated representations of meaning and very detailed records of behaviour into the same computer-aided Learning Conversation*. This offers a facility in which computer-aided awareness-raising is amplified from both the experiential and the behavioural sides of our conversational heuristic. This approach recognises the 'intelligent' technology as a power amplifier of human learning and therefore as a means for enhancing the quality of human living.

We would make a plea for more resources to be fed into the development of such a conversational science for educational and training purposes.

A Royal Mail Machine Letter Office simulator – a forward projected example

Developments in computer programming have made it relatively easy to develop the specifications for what we have called the MLO (Machine Letter Office) construction kit. This is intended as a software package which offers each District Post Office in the country the possibility of configuring a simulator which purports to replicate most of the relevant features of their own MLO; it offers an extendible building kit of MLO components, coding desks, automatic sorting machines (ASMs), pre-sorters, manual sorting frames packet frames, trays and so on.

It can represent the manning of this equipment with postmen, supervisors, chiefs and the MLO manager. It can also simulate all the traffic streams (letters, packets and large flats) through this manned system. This descriptive system can be separately defined by each user. *These perspectives on reality can be compared and contrasted so as to highlight similarities and differences in the modelling of the MLO by its constituent members.*

This descriptive system of components, manning and traffic can then have operating characteristics assigned from any perspective. For example, people can be assigned characteristics of performance and quality of service. The traffic streams can be charac-teristics of volume, timing and movement. As these operating characteristics are run through the descriptive systems, insight is gained into the modelling of the MLO as seen from many different perspectives within it.

Linking this modelling facility to sources of real-time data (that is, records of staff movement and traffic flow) allows the simulator to model 'reality'. By feeding this working model of the MLO with real-time information about the perceived state of affairs, it becomes in effect a sorting office *which can record events.*

It can therefore be used as a *powerful learning aid to all concerned.* It can provide any one coding desk operator or manual sorter with a cumulative record of their performance. This can be used for talk-back and for S-O-L. Similarly, any supervisor can replay the sequence of events in his or her control area through a shift in fast time. They can use this to reconstruct the experience of supervising the area. Given that it has been fed the appropriate real-time manning and traffic information, the simulator can show them the performance of each of the people working for them, the hour-by-hour performance of their area as a whole, and the ways in which the activity in the area contributed (or did not contribute) to the larger scene. These performances can be expressed in terms of pro-ductivity measures, measures of quality of service and its contribution to the cost-effectiveness of the whole operation (MA(R)4S (1), Chapter 5; objective measures, Chapter 6).

Besides talking the supervisor through his or her version of events it can show how modelling of the activities maps on to these as seen from other perspectives. This could provide a considerable opportunity for learning by each individual, by work teams, and by the enterprise as a whole.

This simulator is planned to be surrounded by an 'intelligent' Self-Organised Learning shell; namely, on the theory and practice of Learning Conversations and the configurations of Systems 7 (ILS – S-O-L, p.333). The shell consists of a series of conversational learning aids to the activities of the learner, the Learning Coach, the Task Supervisor and the Learning Manager (Chapter 5). This is outlined in diagrammatic form on p. 217.

So far we have shown that records of behaviour when used for talk-back in the Learning Conversation are primarily useful in raising awareness of experience and that representations of experience are primarily used to raise awareness of the anticipatory mechanism which drives behaviour. Let us now build on this in our quest for a more fully functioning Taxonomy of Conversational Tools.

C

Experience and behaviour expanded into purpose and review: an elaboration of the Functional Taxonomy

The reconstruction of experience by *representing personal meaning* in the systematic form of the repertory grid, structures of meaning, flow diagram and Personal Learning Task Analysis (PLTA) procedures described in A – Representing personal meaning and by *talk-back through the various records of behaviour* described in B – Reconstructing experience by talk-back is the *fundamental activity which fuels the Learning Conversation*. The three essential dialogues – *process reflection, support and referents for self-evaluation* (Chapter 3) – depend on this. MA(R)4S offers a heuristic for using these tools for modelling the personal processes of learning. Once this has been initiated, the language of Self-Organised Learning (that is, the terminology and the theory) acquires its relevance for each participating individual and continued self-exploration, supported by the Learning Practitioner in the early phase, leads to the 'figure-of-eight' configuration of the three levels of the Learning Conversation; life, tutorial and learning to learn (Chapter 4).

Awareness of this meaning-constructing, anticipatory action-orientated and feedback process, which we have described as 'meaning as modelling' (Chapter 2), can be further enhanced by the recruitment of additional tools which make explicit the *purposive* and *review* aspects of the learning process. Thus, it becomes possible to map our developing Taxonomy of Conversational Tools on to our model of the Self-Organised Learner as conversational scientist described in Chapter 1 (Figure 5).

People are often only partially aware of how their needs become translated into specific purposes which in turn become operationalised into strategies. *To the extent that they are unaware, their purposive mechanisms remain undeveloped.* In education and training, purposes are restricted to those embodied within the professionally recognised system and are set outside the learner. Unless sensitively negotiated, these become arid tasks or ritual assignments, to be performed like a robot according to standards which are also determined extraneously. 'Purpose tools' facilitate an articulation of the person's implicit intentions which in turn drive his or her own processes. 'Self-review' tools provide the means for the development of self-generated criteria for evaluating the growth of personal competence. 'Purpose tools' expand the power of the process dialogue and 'review tools' elaborate the power of the referent dialogue in the Learning Conversation.

The Personal Purpose Taxonomy (PPT)

A diary of learning events combined with the PEGASUS repertory grid elicitation procedures or structures of meaning procedures in which the 'elements' of 'items' are 'personal reasons for doing or learning' yields clusters of constructs or higher-order nodes of meaning which can be formulated in terms of a purpose taxonomy. The learner can be guided into recognising his or her current repertoire of purposes and into identifying a greater range of alternatives. These can be operationalised within the Personal Learning Contract (PLC) (Chapter 4) and gradually evolved into the personally significant repertoire of purposes.

It is in the nature of learning that one cannot know what one is learning until one has learned it. Extraneous purposes may not be understood or agreed with. A tentative but progressive negotiation of purpose and the adjustment of corresponding strategies to meet the gradually clarifying purposes is an essential component of flexibility and competence in any skill. Fixed strategies entail predetermined and unnegotiable purpose. Thus, the PPT and the PLC together facilitate an ever-expanding and differentiated awareness of purpose. In *Chapters 3 and 4* we referred to Gwen's grids on purposes, as one example of a PPT. The detailed procedures for eliciting a PPT and actual illustrations are presented elsewhere (Postscript).

The process of need negotiation (life conversation – Chapter 4), and the encouragement of the growth of a personal and growing taxonomy of learning purposes compatible with those needs, require self-exploration over many cycles of PLCs. In managing Learning Conversations we have discovered that many of the emotional blocks to learning which students experience – in, for example, maths, classic literature, or science – are better operationally defined as a malfunctioning mechanism for identifying and articulating purposes in operational terms (personal myths, General Introduction). This leads to emotional hang-ups which may endure through life unless grappled within the Learning Conversation.

The Purpose Hierarchy and the Purpose/Resource grid

As purpose-awareness develops and as learning is operationalised it becomes important to integrate the longer-term goals with the medium- and short-term purposes. A progressive refinement of purposes is part of the process of learning, and to the extent that this can be monitored into awareness, the process is the richer, and better regulated into effective tactics and strategies. The here-and-now purposes which initiate immediate actions can then be elaborated in a Purpose/Resource grid.

In initiating learning within a PLC it is useful to order purposes into levels of generality to form a hierarchy. This provides a useful guide to organise one's learning. As actions are taken within the PLC and learning purposes clarified, this hierarchy can be elaborated. At the review stage of the PLC this hierarchy can be used as a referent against which to evaluate the outcomes. Exhibiting purpose in this form – that is, in a tree structure – is also a valuable tool for the tutor/assessor better to appreciate and comment on the learner's own functioning of a given task. This feedback commentary from an external source is correspondingly enriched.

As the learner progresses through the PLC the Purpose Hierarchy can be used to identify appropriate resources. The most general level guides the learner to consider and locate the type of resource, books, tapes, articles, computer files; the learner level guides him or her into the detailed processing of each resource. Thus implementing a Purpose Hierarchy and Purpose/Resource grid during the action phase of learning serves to heighten awareness and improve control of the process.

Once a Purpose/Resource grid has been constructed it becomes possible to consider exactly what skills are required to process a particular resource for a given purpose. The cells in the grid can be used to relate resource to purpose by specifying the kind of mental operation required to achieve an appropriate outcome. This cannot be specified in advance since only learners, as they explore the resource, will be able to integrate their own unique past experience, knowledge and values to the articulated purposes and the structure and content of the resource itself. A resource which may prove boring or too challenging to one may prove exciting and highly relevant to another.

In education and training, resources are often prescribed, and criteria for assessment often do not include the learner's own. This is partly what we mean by other-organised learning, referred to in the General Introduction. In refining the processing skills demanded by the Purpose/Resource matrix, many learners encounter difficulties. This leads to the learning-to-learn conversation, where existing skills get challenged and alternative skills become identified and explored. We can here quote numerous instances where learners begin with a factual/rote approach to a chosen resource and gradually, through cycles of experimentation, the explanatory, causal, constructive and creative conversational skills are developed (see Types of meaning, Ch. 1, p. 65 These different skills imply different tactics and strategies and these alternative possibilities need to be explored to develop a wider repertoire of personally significant learning strategies.

Tools for identifying review criteria

We have constantly reaffirmed throughout this book that the criteria for evaluating personal competence must remain primarily with the learner. In Chapter 3 and earlier in this chapter we pointed out the three principal sources for identifying evaluative criteria. It may be useful to summarise these here:

1　outside the learner, significant others;
2　outside the learner, a community of meaning, groups, cultures;
3　inside the learner, internally derived from past experience.

First, the EXCHANGE grid procedure and sharing of structures of meaning are ways in which learners can systematically expand their personal system of referents. These can be practiced in peer-group networks, or as novice–expert exchanges when such opportunities arise.

Second, as a member of any organisation – for example, home, school, factory, commercial enterprise, or in athletics – an individual is exposed to an evaluative commentary both formal and informal. A Self-Organised Learner needs to develop skill in interpreting such comments from 'significant others' within the organisation or community, be they parents, teachers, bosses, friends, colleagues or subordinates. Such comments need to be interpreted by S-O-Learners in terms of *their own performance* and also in terms of some understanding of *the other's evaluative meanings* – that is, internal model of understanding. Additionally an organisation may generate various performance judgements (such as job appraisal or written exams). Often these take the form of uncalibrated, subjective views, either expressed in terms of ratings on an agreed set of scales (e.g. from 1–7 or grades (e.g. A, B, C, D, E). The CSHL Feedback-for-Learning software package (Chapter 6) describes how such a system can be elicited, conversationally calibrated and used as a referent for personal learning.

Third, the Personal Purpose Taxonomy, Purpose Hierarchy and Purpose/Resource matrix are means by which they can refine and constructively build their own repertoire of evaluative criteria: their 'personal criteria set'.

Given the exchange procedures and the internally generated criteria based upon their own purposes, learners are more able to consult the expert, or public sources, as these may be relevant. It is here that various taxonomies of learning derived from psychology and education may be useful resources. We have guided learners to Bloom's Taxonomy of Educational Objectives, in both cognitive and affective domains, and a Purpose Taxonomy developed by one of the authors (*Reading-to-Learn*, Methuen), as well as to Guildford's three-dimensional model of cognitive processing. Readers may be aware of numerous others.

It is in establishing personal referent criteria for evaluating personal competence that quality emerges fully into focus. What are the criteria for judging quality when all else has been taken into account? It is here that originality makes its highest demand. It is here that the quality of the Learning Conversation itself turns back on itself to facilitate a personal quantum leap of the self-assessment of personal processes. Quality in the Pirsig sense must be an integral part of the conversational meaning system within which each of us operates. For it is the quality of this criterion-generating review stage of the Learning Conversation that carries the potential for fully fledged Self-Organised Learning and self-fulfilment in its deepest sense, and comes closest to Rogers' creative encounter, Maslow's self-actualisation, Zen and nirvana.

D

Charting progress as a Self-Organised Learner

The Personal Learning Biography (Chapter 6) has been developed as a tool for charting progress of a Self-Organised Learner. This is not just a method for recording results; neither is it only a method for tracing out the chain of cause and effect between the major activities; that is, cycles of PLCs making up the *tutorial conversation* and the figure-of-eight sorties into the *life* and *learning-to-learn* conversations. If self-organised change is to be sustained, the *Personal Learning Biography must function as a feedback tool for self-evaluation of long-term progress*. This drives the direction and controls the quality of Self-Organised Learning. Thus, as a tool for recording the results, seeking out personal principles of causal change, and MA(R)4S-ing progress over time, the biography becomes an integral tool with the conversational technology.

The Personal Learning Biography

Table 7 illustrates the Learning Biographies of a 'chief' and a supervisor in the letter sorting office of a Head Post Office (The Systems 7 – S-O-L environment (Chapters 5 and 6)). As part of the Learning Biography we have developed an elaborate coding system for recording individual Learning Conversations; the quality and power of the PLCs, the relationships between the 'before' and 'after' phases of each PLC, the learning logic shown by the sequential development of a series of PLCs, and the growing vocabulary of words and phrases associated with the developing language of Self-Organised Learning.

The Personal Learning Biography is the penultimate tool in the repertoire of tools making up the conversational technology, and as such it remains for some considerable time under the control and guidance of the Learning Coach and Learning Manager. Even when PLCs and the whole battery of tools for reconstructing personal experience and behaviour described in these two chapters have been mastered by learners themselves, the Personal Learning Biography may remain the responsibility of these external support agents. Perfectly viable S-O-L environments may persist in this mode indefinitely. It depends on the size of the system, the complexity of the tasks and the competencies and purposes of all those concerned. In most of our action research projects this is the level which has been finally achieved. However, just occasionally, the insightful and dedicated change agents have evolved the Personal Learning Biography as part of the battery of tools directly under learners' control. *In achieving this, Systems 7 itself becomes internalised by the learner.*

We have tried to bring these tools together into a conversational technology. *The symbolic relationship between theory and practice introduced in the General Introduction finds expression in this Functional Taxonomy of Tools.*

In developing a Self-Organised Learning capacity, the external Learning Conversation becomes internalised so that learners can sustain this, unsupported by the Learning Coach. Further progress along this trajectory depends on internalising all the functions embodied in the S-O-L Systems 7. This community of S-O-L functions are then all sustained inside one person, who becomes his or her own Learning Manager. Ultimately, the conversational technology becomes obsolescent as internal control of learning is fully achieved. *This technology is unique in that embodied within it is the means of its own demise. All that remains is the conversation itself, sharpened by the experience of using the tools.* It is this capacity to sustain conversation with oneself and others about learning in *the absence of tools*, which imparts an enduring characteristic to it. The Learning Conversation, its language, form and functions, becomes the ultimate tool for maintaining 'on the job' and through life an ever-spiralling capacity for Self-Organised Learning.

Table 7 Charting progress as an S-O-Learner: a Personal Learning Biography

Personal Learning Biography: a chief

Date	Participation in S-O-L activities	Evidence of learning		Outcomes valued by the learner	Outcomes associated with S-O-L.	
		Learner's own view: changes in attitude and understanding	Others' observations: changes in the learner's behaviour		Outcomes valued by the post office	
					'Subjectively' assessed	'Objectively' measured
March – April	S-O-L meetings with LOM(LM) and 20 other chiefs re S-O-L policy organisation and resources	Very gradual shift from seeing staff dev. as task-centred and training resources to learning-centred with resources for learning 'on the job'	More positive actions to support S-O-L activities as these affected his area		Still a hard-nosed directive chief	
May	S-O-L and staff appraisal elicitation of chiefs criteria for dev. of S-O-L feedback/appraisal package. Results of 1st round of computer analysis of PEB and PEC responses fed back	Gradual development of understanding of function of learning in staff dev. More sympathetic to S-O-L approach. Learning from experience on the job less to do with time, i.e. no. of years, and more to do with learning skills and dev. of task expertise	Less confrontatory in promotion meetings. More useful comments re staff competence	New insights gained into other chiefs and PECs views on acting men	More sensitive approach to staff valued by PECs (Annual counselling and daily briefs)	
June	S-O-L support in annual counselling/ appraisal sessions: confidential	Considerably enhanced confidence in conducting annual appraisal interviews, especially 'tricky ones'	More frequent follow-up dialogues with PECs concerned – better rapport with individual PECs re job competence and 'personal problems'	Better daily working relationship with my men		
July	Attended Basingstoke encounter weekend and participated in Learning Conversation role play exercise	Increased confidence in S-O-L approach for myself	Much more sensitive to others' needs and purposes	Sees 'change' as something relevant to me – a mind-blowing experience	PECs begin to see him in a new light	
September	Attended national LM seminar at Rugby CSHL	Began to appreciate national significance of managing staff learning	More supportive of S-O-L activities at Reading – especially in relation to Acting PEDs .Used results of feedback for learning / appraisal package for decision making re promotion of acting men	Sees S-O-L within an ever increasing perspective	PEDs and PECs value 'personal' changes in chiefs' approach to them – a transformation. Offers more feedback and advice to CSHL team re operations. Makes more use of the learning coach system	
	Involved in on-going S-O-L meetings with M.Osbourne – S-O-L 318 *Duties* and LOCS project. (with G. Batstone, D. Smith and CSHL team)	Greater understanding of a theory of control as feedback for individuals' performance	Used S-O-L project as a resource for review of 318 *Duties* in his area and created his own special duty project recruiting a newly promoted acting man to complement this	Begins to recognise a chief's function as a learning manager	Control proformas in OLO in process of revision	Some increase in Productivity and Quality of Service in his area – the most difficult area in the office
	Visited Tonbridge with PED on special project to inspect their software					
October December	Supported S-O-L substantive PED workshops	More confidence in tasks as chief. More skill in managing control data	Made sure his men were available for S-O-L workshops. More discussions with MLO manager re S-O-L .Called his men to thank them for the way they responded during Christmas period. Goes on developing new ways of dealing with staff on operations on his floor		New control forms developed for his area. MLO manager recognises and values improvement in his management skills. Three named PECs comments – before S-O-L he was loud in instructions on the floor and a bit of a bully. After S-O-L – more adult. More thinking , more dedicated, more confident, more appreciative of his staff	

Table 7 continued

Personal Learning Biography: a difficult case

Date	Participation in S-O-L activities	Evidence of learning		Outcomes associated with S-O-L		
		Learner's own view: changes in attitude and understanding	Others' observations: changes in the learner's behaviour	Outcomes valued by the learner	Outcomes valued by the post office	
					'Subjectively' assessed	'Objectively' measured
15.1.86						Put on the acting list
3.2.86	S-O-L acting PED workshop (WK-SP.A.D.)	I feel embarrassed and cannot learn this way. I have always hated school and training	Non-co-operative and anti-S-O-L. Made no contribution	I told them	All the signs are that he will not make it (potential failure)	
10.2.86	First learning contract and follow-up LC \ ILCFCO	I suppose I may be able to learn from the PEC and other PEDs	Appears lackadaisical and slightly resentful	I am doing alright	723 weekly assessment shows 'C's'	
17.2.86	Routine follow-up ILCFCO	No comment from my PEC	He does the job		723 shows 'C' s	
3.3.86	Routine follow-up ILCFCO	Job in yard is like being a traffic warden	Shows no enthusiasm	I am a good supervisor	723 shows 'C' s	
10.3.86	Task focused learning contract ILCFCO Missing data	Still no comment from PEC. Must be OK. I am getting 'C's on 723	No response		723 shows 'C's Coach reflects on inadequacy of 723 comment in identifying problem	
12.5.86	Group discussion with other APEC from his WKSP/ GLCOCO	Maybe I should be doing something differently. But I cannot understand what it might be	No interest A bit better	Funny. The other Acting PEDs seem to be getting more out of the job than I am I knew I was doing well	723 after group discussion shows 2 'B' ratings	
19.6.86	CSHL feedback for learning pack is available. Coach takes him through his results in detail	My God! S-O-L strikes again. These evaluation ratings do not align with my 723 results. They must be wrong	Shows no interest – just gets by	I know I am as good as PED "X". Why has he been rated so highly – and promoted?	The CSHL feedback for learning results show him to be rated 16th out of 20 Acting PEDs	
21.7.86	Senior coaches and supervisors attend Basingstoke weekend. Coaches play out this difficult Acting PEDs attitude in role-playing Learning Conversation. Two senior PECs who have known him well as PHG work out strategy for conducting series of serious and searching Learning Conversations with this man	I shall appeal			Coach's comment: that is much nearer his mark than his 723 gradings	
24.7.86	PEC conducts Learning Conversation with him	I had not realised just how I have been behaving, I must work out why I am so resentful	He appears galvanised. Seems to be much more involved	My boss and my postmen treat me differently	An all round improvement. A new man. 723 shows straight 'B's	
6.10.86	Many PL Contracts completed on the job				Coach and senior supervisors believe that without S-O-L this APED would have eventually been removed from acting list. 2nd CSHL feedback for learning results show him 16th out of 25 operational PEDs	
3.1.87	2nd CSHL feedback for learning pack results S-O-L-S PROJ-9	This new way is challenging and enjoyable	He gets to grips with his problems on the job	I'm not yet a good supervisor but I am going to make it	Coach's comment: he is going to need more coaching and support to do really well	Promoted to substantive PED

E

Tools from education and training

Once the essential characteristics of a conversational tool have been personally understood through practice, a wide range of techniques currently used in education, training and management can be recruited in to the Learning Conversation. Within a physical science paradigm, these remain tools for the teacher, trainer and traditional researcher, but within 'conversational science' they become tools for the Learner, Learning Practitioner and action researcher.

These tools can be recruited to challenge personal robots and create awareness at various points within the S-O-L feedback cycle (Chapter 1, Figure 5 and Chapter 2, Figure 8, on pp. 62 and 72). For instance, 'role playing' activates behavioural awareness, enabling learners to review their models of people in specific social situations. Experimenting with alternative behaviours will have consequences for how one thinks and feels. Experimenting with perceptual skills, as in an 'Encounter group', offers a protected situation for enriching sensitivity to the internal models of others, and so to externalise in a social context the imprisoned inner aspects of a learner's awareness of others. Again, various 'observational techniques' such as flow charts used in work study, Bayles' Interaction Analysis and other techniques used in social skills training, as well as video playback in micro-teaching enhance perceptual awareness. This in turn feeds back to change thoughts, feelings and actions. Similarly, tachistoscopic exposure to subliminal stimuli and Ames Room challenges perceptual inputs and can be used for exploring how alternate models relate to alternate perceptions. 'Transactional Analysis' (TA) offers a developmental model for experimentation with different ways of modelling personal worlds. This in turn will alter perceptions and actions. 'Lateral thinking' can change aspects of modelling, enabling the learner to break free from a monolithic perceptual feedback and action set. 'The Inner Game' allows the learner to play out in varitime alternate models in the head, and allows him or her to experience more richly sensation and feelings linked with action. 'Behavioural Modification' techniques can be recruited to raise awareness directly at the feedback stage of the cycle by selecting and emphasising self-rewarding consequences of specific actions. Precision Teaching builds on this approach.

Any of the psychometric tests used in education (Personality, IQ, Reading Age and so on can be recruited for a *conversational diagnosis* and used as a person-centred referent for challenging current skills and competences. Other educational tools such as 'the essay', 'poem', 'biographical account', 'film', 'simulator', 'physical model', 'map', or diagrammatic specifications such as an architectural plan, logic chart or electrical circuit, if used in isolation, may not produce change, but within an awareness-raising Learning Conversation each can function for promoting Self-Organised Learning.

Conclusions: S-O-L and the enhancement of the quality of learning

A comprehensive, though not exhaustive, survey of the reflective learning tools within a functional model of Self-Organised Learning has been attempted. *Representations of personal meaning* (experience) and *records of behaviour* are used to enable 'personal modelling' of experience. *MA(R)4S* is the modelling heuristic which guides this activity. Modelling experience enhances awareness of personal learning processes of the functioning being. The *Tutorial Conversation* with its PLC operates the three dialogues of the Learning Conversation (process, referent and support) so that a personal model of action in the world is constructed. Each or all of the 'experience and behaviour' tools can be recruited to augment its power. The current state of the art underlying personal functioning becomes challenged, alternative modes of functioning are explored and growth is achieved.

Within a figure-of-eight configuration the Learning Conversation may be diverted into the *learning-to-learn conversation* if the conversation at the *tutorial level* seizes up because of lack of specific skills. The robot-like processing of perceptual/motor skills at the micro-level is challenged and alternatives are explored so that new levels of competence are achieved. Process, referent and support dialogues operate at the *learning-to-learn level* of the conversation to raise awareness and to challenge robot-like micro-skills. Each or all of the experience/behaviour tools can be recruited at this level. The conversation is re-diverted to the *tutorial level* when successful learning-to-learn encounters are achieved.

Failure to involve the person wholly in becoming fully functioning due to lack of motivation diverts the conversation to the *'life level'*. This challenges relevance, needs and personal goals, and enhances awareness of directionality in life. Alternative needs and values are explored, facilitated by the experience tools described in the Functional Taxonomy. New insights achieved here enable the figure-of-eight to loop back to the *tutorial* Learning Conversation. Effective Learning Conversations make possible the development of fully functioning beings engaged in creative encounters with their world.

Thus, the experience and behaviour MA(R)4S conversational technology is recruited to augment the power of the Learning Conversation. The primary tool is the Learning Conversation with its embedded form and function, and as this becomes internalised (that is, models of the Learning Conversation itself are acquired) the lower level technology becomes redundant. Internalisation of the Learning Conversation promotes Self-Organised Learning. The Systems 7 S-O-L environment provides the systems technology of the teaching–learning modes which can also be internalised to produce the mega-ecology of a 'community of selves'; of learner, Learning Coach, Task Supervisor/instructor and Learning Manager, all inside one person. When the Systems 7 S-O-L environment is extended beyond the individual to teams and enterprises, another aspect of the technology, the feedback-for-learning, the S-O-L spreadsheet, and the conversational evaluation techniques (Chapter 6) are required to *challenge the group or institutional 'robots' and to explore alternatives which can lead to more creative enterprises.*

We have briefly traced out the overall function of the conversational technology and how this is integral to the theory and practice of Learning Conversations as described in Chapters 3 and 4 and the Systems 7 S-O-L environment described in Chapters 5 and 6. Our Functional Taxonomy of Reflective Tools embodies all of this. Table 8 summarises this taxonomy in a form which attempts to create a *syntony* between East and West. Table 9 illustrates how the conversational tools work to achieve Self-Organised Learning.

In the 'General Introduction' we defined S-O-L in its simplest and most abstract form, as

the conversational construction, reconstruction and exchange
of
personally significant, relevant and viable meanings
with awareness and controlled purposiveness.

These two tables and this definition represent our attempt to abstract the fundamentals of the theory and practice of S-O-L. *They are the heart of this book.* The flow diagram of this book on p. 42 is another form of representing the meaning in it. Now that we have presented our model of S-O-L in these alternative forms, we have been able to indulge in using our con- versational technology for our own communicative purposes. In the spirit of S-O-L, readers are asked to reflect upon these alternative versions of the meaning of our book to enhance their own understandings of it. Self-Organised Learners are able to achieve 'Syntony' (Jung) in their creative inner Learning Conversation provoked by having alter- native versions of the same system of meaning.

We have one last purpose to achieve. Let us briefly outline our functional specification for a content-independent Intelligent Learning System (Table 10, ILS – S-O-L). *This can be attached as a shell around any domain that can be addressed by a computer.* Whilst the conversational technology is embodied in the S-O-L software, the system still relies on some back-up from a human Learning Manager. *Thus, in the person/machine interaction the learner, the software and the human support become engaged in a triadic conversation.* This specification may be useful to those who are concerned with the development of computer-aided learning systems, but we introduce this here primarily as a resource for those practitioners interested in launching a fully human S-O-L environment. The precision of a systems approach has a pay-off for the more conventional

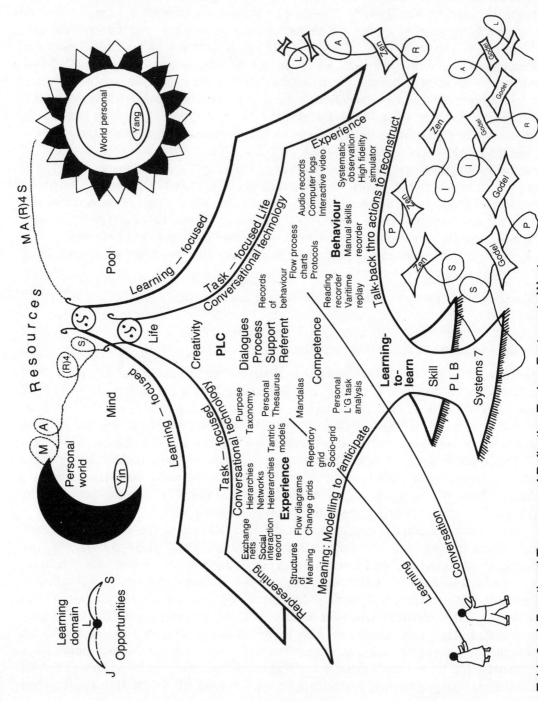

Table 8 A Functional Taxonomy of Reflective Tools – East meets West

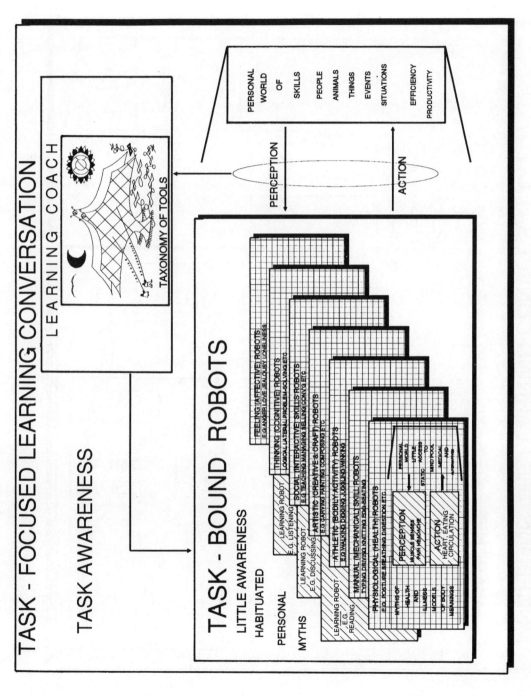

Table 9 Self-Organised Learning in action – theory and practice as one

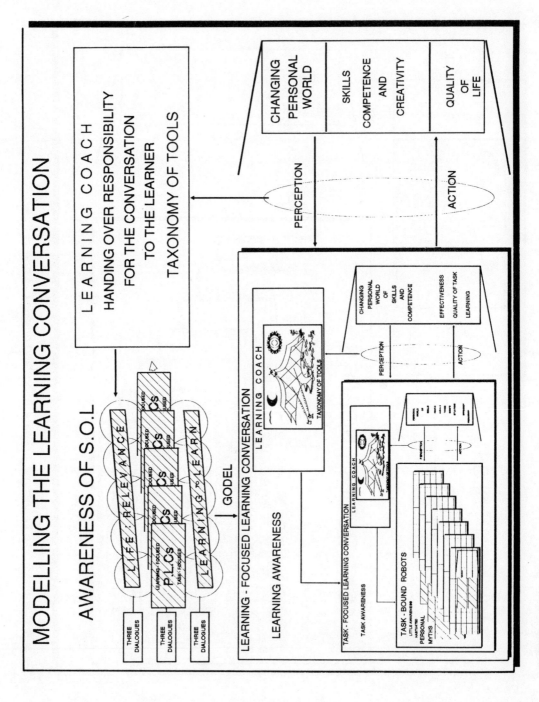

MODELLING THE LEARNING CONVERSATION

Table 9 continued

MODELLING THE THEORY AND PRACTICE OF S.O.L

TOTAL AWARENESS

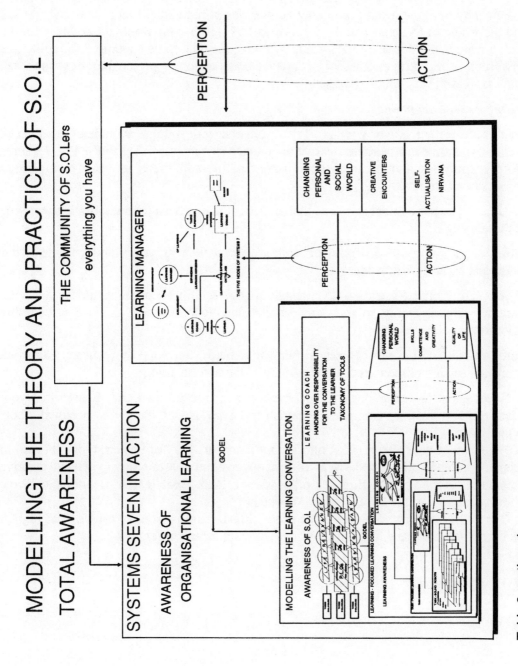

Table 9 continued

training–learning environment, since the conversational heuristics are essentially the same, whether they are played out through the machine or through a totally human interface. In the General Implications we indulge in our vision of the prospects for how S-O-L in its man/machine and in its person-to-person interface can transform our world.

Few may have the resources to play out a series of individual Learning Conversations and the whole of Systems 7 in the form of an ILS – S-O-L environment as addressed by such a computer-aided learning system. We have the luck to be supported for doing just this. But it is of central importance to appreciate that anyone – person, pair or group – can start, as we did, very simply (Origins).

To begin at the beginning!

Recruit one learner, maybe yourself. Try to converse with yourself about learning. Recruit one or two paper-and-pencil reflective techniques as conversational tools. Try out some more techniques and, should they prove useful, add these to your portfolio of conversational tools.

Make sure you use a relevant mix of both experiential *and* behavioural tools. Throw some of these away.

Work with a group of learners, work with a team, work with your family, friends, your mates and colleagues at work.

If you can, recruit Systems 7 to manage change within an organisation as a whole. Continue experimenting so that you can develop your expertise as an S-O-Learning Practitioner.

Enrol on our S-O-L short courses. Be our diplomates. Be our postgraduates. Construct your own version of the Centre for the Study of Human Learning!

Never allow the technology to become the means to its own end. Ensure that your Learning Conversations continue to flourish and grow. Never allow your personal robots to take over.

Take care of your Faculty X (Colin Wilson). Use the Way of Eastern thought (Tao) to deepen your approach. Use the Way of the conversational technology to achieve creative encounters. Achieve rare glimpses of Maslow's Peak Experiences or Nirvana. 'Rage against the dying of the light' (Dylan Thomas).

Our S-O-L journey continues to be professionally and personally tough, challenging, exciting, life-giving and hilarious. So be it with you, dear learner!

Good Luck.

Sheila & Laurie

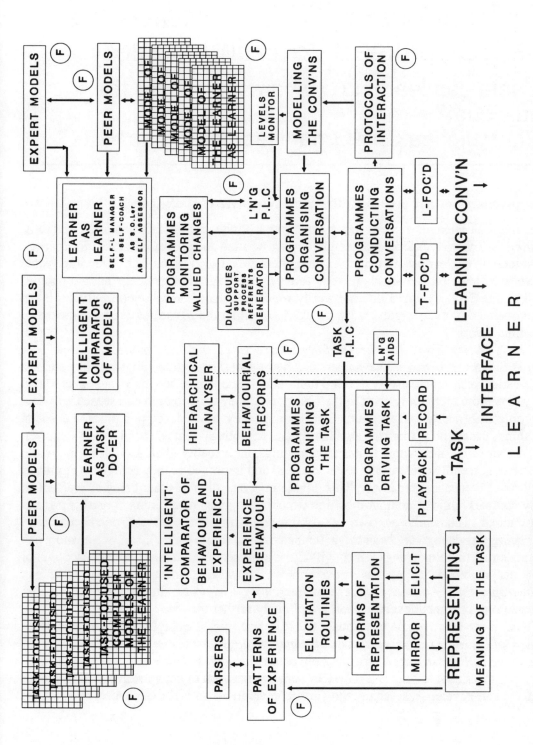

Table 10 The ILS–S-O-L learning shell

General Implications: Towards the Self-Organised Learning Society

Where can learning conversations take the individual?
What might a Self-Organised society achieve?

The prospects for our evolution: the mind takes over from the genes

One major problem of modern society and for each individual within it is often said to be *coping with change*. Science and technology are running ahead of ethics. Pollution, genetic engineering, nuclear power, acid rain, computers are all seen as things that are impossible or very difficult to understand and therefore very difficult to adopt in the natural habitats of life. The Self-Organised Learner warily welcomes change as an opportunity but is not overwhelmed or over-impressed by the claims of either the advocates or the detractors of any innovation.

The Self-Organised Learner is fully aware since they are modelling their own model-building processes. They understand how events acquire meaning; and they are able to question, test and creatively develop their models and thus refine these meanings so that they may more effectively achieve their purposes. They know that in one sense their view of 'objective reality' is a pattern of meanings they have developed from the social meanings passed on to them through family and schooling – that is, socialisation – and yet, in another sense, they know that these meanings, their reality, their models of the world have been carefully constructed, tested, revised and improved as they achieve ever greater skill, competence and creativity. This double understanding of there being a 'real' infinitely complex, infinite domain in which we exist as nodes of meaning construction; and that each of us constructs our own view of this reality from the purposive perspective *is an incredibly freedom-giving knowledge*. It means that the more we really know, the more can we construct those meanings which will allow us to achieve whatever we choose; but not only can we know but we can know how we know. *This means that each of us can bootstrap ourselves into any and every direction we wish to go.* Some may not go as fast and as far as others but everyone can go infinitely further than we now envisage.

This is not only true of individuals but it is also true of organisations and society. *A system of Learning Conversations and the methodology for the conversational evaluation of change outlined in Part III free us from being the victims of change.* We can model the change process not as one causal system but as a 'network of conversations'. This means that we can develop, test, share and further develop an agreed explanation of what the changes are and how they are being driven. This explanatory understanding offers the possibility of creatively controlling the change rather than being a victim who at best can merely cope. It also offers the possibility for the mind to free itself from the shackles of the genes, not by ignoring our biochemical and archetypal symbolic past, but by conversing with them (Chapter 2). To the extent that the individual Self-Organised Learner can evolve towards greater freedom, a fully participative corporate network of S-O-Learners (teams, departments and organisations) can similarly evolve. *The mind-pool of an enterprise, society, and a given culture can free itself from the 'gene pool' and static past by conversing with it.*

Possible futures with Self-Organised Learning

Myths that spawn the instabilities of our time

The technological, educational and social changes of the last hundred years have produced an age in which we no longer believe in the traditional myths by which earlier generations lived (General Introduction). Their interlocking personal myths enabled our forefathers unknowingly to maintain a stable, if unequal and often unhappy and unhealthy society. Previously unimagined universal compulsory education up to the age of sixteen, votes for everybody over eighteen, micro-computers, cheap foreign travel and the images which the press and television bring into our homes now mould our expectations. We demand, however unclearly, more from life than our grandparents achieved. Yet perhaps we also envy their certainties. Our expectations exist alongside, and contribute to, the stresses and strains of living in the late twentieth century.

Our material progress leads us to feel that we should be free to work, play and relate to others with more enjoyment and fulfilment than we actually experience. *But most of us do not know what such living would entail.* The few of us who think we do know what we truly want do, at the gut level, believe that we can achieve it for ourselves. The majority ride mindlessly on the family, school, and local job-opportunity escalator into a life they find, at best, vaguely unsatisfactory and, at worst, intolerable. Smoking, alcohol and other, less legal, drugs are just some of the means of escape and of achieving a pseudo-satisfaction.

Our schools and the organisations in which we work are built on corporate myths which assume us to be the other-organised receivers of consequences not of our making. Our implicit models of such situations are built up unknowingly to contain such assumptions as threats of redundancy, job changes and re-training, environment changes, houses priced out of our reach, new technology in the home and at work and so on, but at the explicit conscious level we are encouraged to believe ourselves to be autonomous. In charge of our own destiny, we are exhorted to accept responsibility for what happens to us. It is the incompatibility of these implicit and explicit myths which produces most of our stress. Education or training or the lack of them, money and religion or the lack of them, even politics in its many forms can all plausibly be blamed for this state of affairs.

We, the authors, believe that it is both more helpful and more hopeful for each of us to accept the responsibility for learning to converse with ourselves. We can then resolve the mismatches between the models implicit in our patterns of behaviour and the myths by which we consciously attempt to live. We can conversationally explore how to understand ourselves better, define our needs more clearly, and learn to achieve them more effectively. Once we are consciously making our own choices we can each negotiate our own compromise with ourselves; about what we will accept and what we will work to change – both within ourselves and and in the world out there. This applies to the apparently trivial but all-pervading activities of everyday relationships at least as much as to the longer-term issues of how and why we live our lives. In a phrase it would be more personally effective to create those conditions within which we could each 'become more self-organised'– self-organised, that is, in our achievement of understanding, in doing what we want to do; and in learning to be and do both more effectively.

It is our contention that *networks of Learning Conversations* generated within many of the formal and informal groupings in our society could enable us quietly but irreversibly to reconstruct ourselves into more fully functioning people, and transform our environment into a better place to be. Minimally such networks would make life more interesting and personally exciting.

Here we will firstly explore the philosophy behind S-O-L a little more deeply. We will explain how we think this can generate the personal myths by which our generation can create a stable but more happy and healthy society. Later we will use our action research experience to imagine how these myths might play themselves out in different areas of contemporary life.

S-O-L: a unifying and constructive myth

Many people first met the ideas of S-O-L and the Learning Conversation during a period of crisis. This is because the majority of people and most organisations only become interested in radical new ideas when they are in some kind of trouble. For example, individuals may be in conflict with the law or with their friends and family; they may have failed an examination that is important to them; or they may feel themselves to be in danger of losing their job or their partner in life. Organisationally the parents, pupils, staff, headmaster, governors, local government and central government may not all completely agree about the role a school should play in its local community and/or society at large. Nor will they reasonably agree about how this should be achieved. A social services department may find itself suddenly and unhappily in the public eye. An industrial or commercial enterprise may find itself facing strong new competition and feel that it rapidly has to increase its productivity, its quality (of service) and its cost effectiveness. People under pressure tend to see the Learning Conversation as a means for dealing with some newly perceived deficiency. It may be seen as a method for helping the less able to keep up in school, college or university, or as a technology for enabling the less successful (be they worker, supervisor, manager, director or owner) to learn how to do their jobs more effectively. From within a crisis this seems a reasonable point of view. Given that we can identify an effective tool for challenging their relevant robots and supporting them through the anxious process of re-constructive change, then the Learning Conversation is indeed an effective way of assisting people and organisations through periods of externally induced change. But such remedial functions are not central to the philosophy which has grown up with and informed our work.

Crises may reveal the need for more effective performance, but it is not always clear to the uninitiated that the best and most enduring way to achieve this is to help people to increase their capacity for learning. It is often only after a traditional training approach has been tried and failed that the Learning Conversation is considered as a more radical alternative. Traditional training treats people as other-organised, as the receivers of established public knowledge. Despite the apparent freedom of many training techniques, if in the end there is one right answer, if there is one pre-determined, organisationally approved, ultimately unnegotiable position which everybody is expected to accept and believe in, then the training process is essentially manipulative. Being manipulated – that is, unknowingly organised by others – encourages people to look to others for answers. This can work temporarily if the answers to one's immediate problems are those on offer; but in a rapidly changing society, more and more often the answers still have to be discovered; or if they are out there somewhere, then nobody has yet got round to searching them out and presenting them to us on a plate. This is why traditional training often fails to produce the expected results, and it is why S-O-L, which really does leave the learners to establish their own personally relevant and viable meanings (answers), has a much greater potential for truly helping people in crisis. *Paradoxically, S-O-L achieves this not by resolving their crisis for them, but by aiding and supporting their search for their own ways of resolving it.* Sometimes the S-O-Learner will arrive at what is superficially the same answer as the trainer was offering; but now it is set in a context of having explored the nature of the problem, having set criteria for evaluating alternative solutions and having really selected it as that best suited to his or her needs. This increases a hundredfold the probability that a S-O-Learner will more fully understand his situation, will be prepared to tailor the answer to suit his requirements and to change and adapt it as the situation develops.

Many outside observers of S-O-L do not understand this. If the trainer's solution is used in the end, then they think that 'surely it would have been quicker just to tell the (stupid) supervisors, students, members of parliament the right answer rather than have them fluffing about looking for it'. Even if the solution was unknown before the S-O-Learner discovered it, such observers will often be left thinking in retrospect, now the answer is known, that if only the trainer had done his or her homework properly we could have saved ourselves a lot of trouble. People taking part in Learning Conversations do not suffer from these misperceptions. They know that the really valuable changes have taken place in them; and that however effective their task solutions have proved to be, their real gain is in their increased capacity for coping with new changes in the future. Unfortunately, the visibly efficient managers or administrators who simplistically believe that 'if it can't be explained on one side of an A4 sheet then you haven't thought it through properly' often blind themselves to this. They are so busy being visibly efficient that they have not yet time to take part in Learning Conversations. They cannot see that their superficial efficiency is inevitably preserving the crisis-laden status quo since the easily understandable is that which fits in with the models already in their head, and it is these models that are preventing them from dealing with the crisis. Their 'efficiency robot' needs challenging. Such people can be amazingly grateful once they have reconstructed their robots into models for achieving longer-term effectiveness.

Having experienced the Learning Conversation from the inside, the S-O-Learner no longer sees it as a means for recovering from the brink of disaster. It is seen as a gateway to a personally more rewarding and socially effective existence. It is accepted as a means for enriching the personal quality of life, from infant school or earlier, through a potentially infinite set of alternative lives to a fulfilled and active retirement. It is better seen as a way of living rather than as a life-line to the disabled learner.

It is this ability to engage creatively with change and the increased confidence in oneself and others that this engenders that makes S-O-L the myth most likely to succeed. A group of people who share this belief in one another become a stable yet flexible and adaptive team.

The personal philosophy that informs the Learning Conversation

Self-Organised Learning is 'content-independent', so it is misleading to offer examples unless these are sufficiently various and superficially contradictory to encourage the reader to search out the coherent message that runs through them. We have been concerned to present examples that help the reader achieve this and to explain the processes which enable S-O-L as a conversation which challenges existing behaviours, understandings and beliefs and supports learners through periods of reconstructive change.

In the Prospective Commentary to Part I we have suggested that conversing about one's learning requires a language, and that the quality of this language for conversing about learning will contribute to but not determine the power of the conversation. In Chapters 1 and 2 we have seen that a language is more than just a vocabulary of new words. We can have non-verbal languages with which to communicate visually, by touch or through other modes of representation. The words or other primary units of the language do not carry meaning in themselves. They only acquire meaning as they are used to represent experience, and experience has structure and coherence only inasmuch as the models in our head enable us to construct and attribute meaning to events. Language in its many forms is the vehicle and the tool through which we construct and embark on conversational voyages. *This book has been an attempt to converse with you, the reader, in constructing a language with which to explore the nature of learning and how it and you can become more self-organised. We have suggested that the successful end to a Learning Conversation is that it has no end, since effective Self-Organised Learners have learned to converse with themselves and continue so to do.* Here our purpose is to explore the forms, paths or trajectories that such long-term conversations might take.

There is no one simple way of describing this since by definition creative conversation is unpredictable and each will be different. But as our experience of such conversations accumulates it is possible to see some repeating patterns of events. By examining these and reconstructing the processes that shaped them we are able to identify at least the skeleton of an anatomy of Learning Conversations. The first recurring event we identified disturbed and surprised us at first, but we have now come to accept that it is a natural sequel to the initial impact of these ideas and practices. Quite a number of our clients have reported that after first being exposed to the ideas and some practice sessions they could not stop 'conversing with themselves'. Some were quite worried to find that they were actually talking to themselves. Others found a conversation running on out of control in their head.

One fifty-five year old reported in detail being fascinated and a little frightened by all the things he recalled, thought and felt, over a more or less continuous period of three days. His meaning construction processes had been prodded into action and he found the inner conversation working overtime. It was only after he had begun very obliquely to hint of this to others that they revealed a similar hyper-activity of their internal modelling processes. We then found ourselves recalling similar experiences. It would appear that this phenomenon is most likely to happen to those of us who had lost the habit of internal conversation and who find the ideas and experience spreading out from the immediate topic of the Learning Conversation into other areas and times in their life. It is a little like suffering from a fever. *The result is that we discover that we are accessing a lot of resources within us with which we had lost touch.* Children taking part in Learning Conversations do not seem to experience such trauma, partly because they don't have such a back-log to sort out; and partly because they already 'naturally' have much imaginative activity going on. *This hyper-activity is usually followed by a period of more solid reflection in which the process is gradually organised and brought back under conscious control. This self-organisation of one's own thoughts and feelings is a key step in recognising just how much of one's own inner process has been running like a robot.*

This hyper-activity of the modelling process does not happen initially to the majority of clients. Many choose to get down more quickly into practical, task-oriented, learning contracts. These enable them to rapidly show some results. Many people find this to be a safer feeling and a more controlled way of dipping one's feet (or head) into the S-O-L water. However, reflectivity is an essential ingredient in any effective ongoing Learning Conversation. If some exceptional tapping of one's past experience, one's internal resources is not achieved initially, there are probably good reasons why this is so. There are many opportunities for this increased awareness, this power to tap your own resources, to happen in the course of a sequence of Learning Conversations. For some, this happens piecemeal, so gradually that it is only much later that they realise just how much they have changed.

The course of any Learning Conversation will be determined not only by the needs of the learners and the learning opportunities they create for themselves. It depends also on the skill of the Learning Practitioners and the emphasis they give to the different dialogues and levels in the conversation, and to their skill in introducing and using the appropriate tools at the relevant points in the delicate process of enabling a learner significantly and successively to increase their capacity for various types and modes of learning.

A conversation that consists in an endless sequence of successful learning contracts may be all that the client desires, but seen in the long term it is merely enabling the client to organise their existing skills into achieving their most obvious and salient task/topic learning needs. However much of a significant advance this may appear to the client at the time, it is only really scratching at the surface of the potential results that might be achieved.

The task-focused learning activity

As we have seen in Part II, the heart of the Learning Conversation is the Personal Learning Contract (PLC). Within the *task-focused* activity this contract may easily be achieved. The learner can define a task or topic and learning purpose, can work out a feasible strategy of achieving this purpose, can clearly recognise the outcome of the contract and have well defined the criteria by which they will judge the quality of what they have learned. The contract works. All the practitioner has to do to sustain this level of activity is to check that learners are able to formulate such contracts for themselves without the aid of a supportive conversation. One extremely simple form that might be taken by this long-term Learning Conversation is merely to monitor their situation for whenever it would be useful to learn something new, and to formulate and carry out PLCs to achieve these objectives. This is the least the Learning Conversation can do. It enables one systematically to organise one's current learning capacity and bring it to bear on the jobs in hand; but for most clients, there is more to it than that.

If the 'task' or 'topic' is already well known and the problem consists in raising one's understanding and performance to new levels, then the process will almost certainly involve challenging the existing task robots. This will involve a process dialogue. The conversational problem or skill is how to raise the client's awareness of their current understanding or performance. This can be done merely by getting the learner verbally to reflect upon and reconstruct the process, but more often than not significant improvement will require more than mere verbal reflection. The tools for recording behaviour are recruited in to record the current robot-like behaviour in terms that add meaning, pattern and precision to the learner's reflection. Such a record can then be used to help the learner systematically and veridically reconstruct what he was perceiving, thinking and feeling at each stage of the process. Given an imaginative and practical choice of tool this can be a very powerful aid to helping the learner really bump up his or her performance. If sufficient support is provided to help the learner through the reconstructive period, and if the learner can see clearly what an improvement in performance would entail, then the occasional task-focused conversation with behavioural recording tool back-up can be all that a learner feels he or she will ever need. Again, some clients will feel very rewarded that they have achieved such insight and will not wish to go further.

However, this is to undervalue the support and referent dialogues. Many a learner's major problem consists not in the learning itself, nor is it exactly in knowing what it is that they want to learn. No; the problem consists in knowing what understanding or performing better would be like. For example, a supervisor may know that he should be supervising 'better' but he cannot conceive of what exactly this would entail. Similarly a maths student may know that she needs to work out her proofs better, but she cannot for the life of her imagine what 'working them out better' would look or feel like. This is where the referent dialogue comes in. This dialogue pursues the issue of where the learner should look for exemplars of what a better understanding or a better performance would be like. We have discussed this issue earlier. For example, a really good athlete, writer or actress would each be able to describe in some detail events or periods in their career during which their view of what 'their task was all about' went through a period of change. If they had the powers of process observation and the support necessary to achieve it, this 'new view of my craft' will have set the standards by which they improved their performance. To understand the significance of the referent dialogue is to have put one's foot on the first rung of increasing one's capacity for learning. It is at this level of understanding of the Learning Conversation that we find many of the very good 'performers', be they in the arts, in the performance of arts, in sport, in the instructional sides of education, or in the operational activities of any industrial or commercial enterprise. This is the state in which many Self-Organised Learners stabilise. The Learning Conversation in their head allows them to achieve their ambitions in their craft, profession, hobby or career, and this suffices.

However, as we have seen, it is only really the tip of the Learning Conversation iceberg. There are still levels in the *task-focused* conversation and the whole of the *learning-focused* conversation yet to come.

In Part II we suggested that it is useful to see the Learning Conversation as a kind of figure of eight. The waist of the eight is the learning contract conversation. If it fails, the conversation dips into the lower loop of the conversation into the *learning-to-learn* level. If the contract is successfully completed but what is achieved is not as valuable as was expected then the Learning Conversation goes up into the upper loop of the figure of eight, into the *relevance or life* conversational level.

Let us deal with the upper loop first. What the practitioner is trying to do is to get the learner to stand back and see his current learning contract within a wider perspective and over a longer time-span of a series of contracts. Within this wider perspective the learner is encouraged really to explore his or her reasons for learning, inner needs and outward looking ambitions, and to examine the constraints and opportunities in the situation facing them. Having used whatever tools are best suited to facilitating this process of inner and situational exploration, the learner is then asked to work out a longer-term plan within which each individual learning contract would acquire its relevance.

A series of failed contracts in the context of the learner really wanting to learn what he is attempting is an indication that the learner has a learning problem. This may be resolved using the PLTA analysis by showing the learner that he is putting too much into one contract. If the learner is able to formulate a longer-term learning plan which breaks down the learning job into a series of feasible contracts, then the learner's problem is solved and he or she can resume their task-focused Learning Conversation. If their problem is not a learning task organisation one, then they need to move into the learning-focused conversation.

However, before proceeding into this area, let us reflect on where our long-term learner-driven Learning Conversation might be going if she or he were able to sustain the full task-focused conversation with relevance discussions thrown in. These can be very powerful for the person who has a clear view of where they want to go and has the basic learning skills to allow them to achieve their objective. Many great performers probably fall into this category, but if they are not able to generalise and transfer their understanding of how to learn into other areas or phases of their life, then they may well become rather lop-sided people.

The learning-focused activity

Most people experience serious difficulties in understanding the difference between the *task-focused* reflective activity and the *learning-focused* reflective activity. This depends on a full understanding of the explanation we offer in the Prospective Commentary to Part II. 'But we have been talking about learning all along,' they will claim. 'In fact I have never spent so much time thinking about learning in my whole life.' (The coach ducks the discussion about what happened whilst they were at school, and proceeds.) 'Yes, we have been talking about how you could set about learning to be a better (supervisor, chemist, olympic rower and so on) but we have not talked about how well, how fast, and with what quality and economy you are learning.' After some time sorting this out, the Learning Coach begins to discuss whether the strategies they have been using in their PLCs were really the best for that particular learning task. Then they are off. They can begin the learning-focused Learning Conversations. They can begin to use their task-focused activity as a vehicle for investigating the quality of their learning as opposed to keeping their nose pressed too close to their concerns about the quality of their task performance and understanding.

As this conversation progresses they can begin to reflect on the range and power of their learning skills and how they recruit these into their *task-focused* PLCs. They can begin to formulate *learning-focused* PLCs which use the *task-focused* PLCs as a resource or strategy for investigating the quality of their learning. The first impact that awareness of the quality of our learning can have is that we can begin consciously to take control of our learning activities. We can access our learning skills and improve our ability to recruit our full learning capacity into each task-focused reflective activity that is undertaken. Organising one's existing learning skills and developing them more effectively can be seen by observers as a considerable increase in a capacity for learning. It may even be seen in this way by learners themselves.

However, this is to blind oneself to the much greater potential that lies waiting to be constructed by systematically working at improving learning skills. *Now we are working on the skills by which we learn*; for example, reading as a learning skill, listening as a learning skill, discussion as a learning skill, remembering as a learning skill, thinking or problem-solving as a learning skill. As one begins to work at it, the potential unfolds. The difficulty often lies in getting the learner to see the difference between exercising the skill generally and exercising it specifically so that one learns effectively. For example, there is a vast difference between being 'good in discussions' and 'being able to use discussion as a means for systematically learning something'. Once this difference has been appreciated then the 'learning to learn' really takes off. Learners begin to appreciate that 'learning how to learn' and 'increasing my capacity for learning' will pay off for evermore in everything they do. *This takes us back to the ideas of the models in our head being the plans that configure the feedback systems by which we achieve coherence and directionality*. We can begin to see that the relevance or life conversation within a learning-focused Learning Conversation takes on a special significance.

As we begin to explore just how we can represent our understanding and how different forms and types of understanding contain the dynamics of different directionalities, we can begin to reconstruct the phenomena which led Freud to invent the unconscious. This was and is no more than a language for describing those directionalities in our psychosomatic processes which we have either not yet recognised or, if we have recognised a directionality, we have not yet learned to converse with the models in our head that produce it sufficiently well to bring it within range of our self-organising skills. Thus therapy becomes an extension of the Learning Conversation concerned specifically with those of his or her own activities which are unacceptable to the learner, to their family or to the wider groupings (including the community and society) within which they attempt to live. Be this as it may, much of the activity of psychotherapy, marriage guidance, and various counselling services may be more usefully construed as special Learning Conversations.

This raises an important issue. Any given Learning Conversation is conducted within a social setting which carries an implied contract between the learner and the practitioner. The school, the college, the company or even just the relationship between two individuals implies boundaries and constraints about what is acceptable content for negotiation. These constraints should be kept in mind and should be explicitly negotiated within the Learning Conversation.

The theory is the method: the language with which we can negotiate what learning might become

So far we have used the language established in Parts I to III to summarise and consolidate our presentation of the 'models in our heads'. *These models are the deep structures informing this language.* It is our contention that this language would be mere jargon unless informed by these models, and the models would be merely 'interesting but not very practical ideas' if our language in the fullest sense of the word were not an effective operational tool kit for putting these ideas to work. Thus, for us, each of the 'behavioural' and 'experiential' tools outlined in the Functional Taxonomy is an extension of the language. The deep structure is more than the container and generator of the language. It is the modelling that drives our skills, competence and creativity in conducting Learning Conversations and exploiting these ideas.

As you achieve personal insight, the language will develop. The degree of personal understanding about your own learning processes that you achieve will largely determine the quality of the Learning Conversation that you can sustain with others, but it is equally true that once you can get a Learning Conversation launched, the experience of conducting the conversation will feed meaning into the ideas which we have here tried to portray, darkly, through the media of words. The 'theory *is* the method' and the true processes of the Learning Conversation and of being an S-O-Learner are the real contents of the theory. The model in the head, the language of learning and the process of the Learning Conversation are symbiotically interrelated. As you come to understand this personally you may find that your capacity for processing, for learning on the job from your experience, grows.

A network of Learning Conversations within the Systems 7 paradigm

Now that we have explored, at least in outline, the nature of the Learning Conversation, and now that we have developed some understanding of how we construct meaning by conversing within ourselves and with the referents of our meanings, we are in a position to revisit the idea of a 'learning network' introduced in Part III.

The basic idea is that learners should be encouraged to talk to one another about learning. Once this practice has become more or less established they should get advice about how to improve the quality and effectiveness of these conversations. This chapter, up to this point, and in more detail, the whole book, is intended as a guide towards how this might be done. Gradually some shared understanding and expertise will grow up among the people participating in the network but at this stage each Learning Conversation is a separate enterprise. Gradually, as people begin to share some understanding of what is going on, they also begin to realise that some of the conversations are concerned with the learning of very similar topics and/or tasks. The people in such similar Learning Conversations begin to work together and pool their resources in pursuing their common aims.

*Also there gradually emerges an agreement that nobody should be a Learning Prac-
titioner unless they are or have taken part in Learning Conversations as a learner.*

Depending upon the distribution of age, expertise and experience in the group, some
groups develop a consciously egalitarian structure in which everybody has to be prepared
to serve as learner and Learning Practitioner in turn. As the structure of the Systems 7
organisation emerges, if it does, these egalitarian groups try to share out and rotate all the
roles so that everybody gets experience of everything. In other groups, seniority, expertise
or just plain power or pushiness determines who serves in what capacities. As the networks
develop people begin to realise that there is a lot more to creating effective learning
opportunities than at first appeared.

The learners with their Learning Coaches keep in close contact with domain experts so
that they can really find out what learning resources are available and so that the domain
expert so well understands what they are trying to do that he or she will begin to make
suggestions about possible strategies and resources that no one had actually thought about
before. Eventually the network grows up and it begins to realise that a lot of their
negotiations among one another might be viewed as rather an amateur attempt to manage
the learning, and eventually they will recognise the need for some form of learning
management. Sometimes the job is delegated by the group to one of its members or is
hijacked by one of the members on the basis of 'it's my ball you're playing with, so I'm
going to be the Learning Manager'.

As these specialist roles evolve there is a danger that the conversational activities
become routine, so various forms of the MA(R)4S awareness-raising, conversation-
improving, reflective-processing facility evolves. This serves as a form of quality control
and quality improvement activity on the Learning Conversation.

Psychology as 'conversational tool-making'

Twelve years ago we, the authors, wrote a paper with this title, but it was never published.
The ideas and experience which had led us to reformulate the job of the psychologist in this
way were not then fully formulated. Figure 33 in the Functional Taxonomy shows some of
our thoughts at this time. Our problem was that the more we worked with other psychologists and the more the ideas of S-O-L grew, the more worried we became about the role
psychology seemed to be playing in society. On the one hand we were becoming more and
more disenchanted with the types of psychology which worked within a physical science
paradigm for developing psychological knowledge. The type of psychologist who built
theories about people without consulting them in depth about the adequacy of this theory
we came to see as a 'dangerous blunderer'. This was true even when he or she was working
'harmlessly' in a laboratory, because their ideas, books and journal articles were escaping
and influencing generations of educationists, managers, trainers and other recipients of the
latest psychological tests, packages and fashionable ideas. But he or she became ten times
more dangerous when let loose directly on those in need. The film *The Clockwork Orange*,

part of which was filmed in our own university, Brunel, made this point more eloquently than our writing.

But psychology contains its own most able critics, and the humanistic psychologists developed their ideas of 'personal science' in which the client was responsible for learning to understand his or her own problems. The psychologist merely provided the conditions which best enabled the client to get in touch more fully with his own processes, thus becoming better able to diagnose his own problems and formulate solutions to them. This was the base from which we ourselves worked. But we found this 'soft' psychology too amorphous and undifferentiated for our purposes, so we started to develop 'hard tools' for 'soft psychologists' to use. But again the reflexive nature of what we were doing swung full circle and we saw that the tools we were developing were of more use to practitioners. What role was there, then, for the psychologist?

We began to see that psychologists were best seen as tool-makers. At the ground level, psychologists could create the tools that their clients could use to solve their 'psychological problems'. These tools should be conversational since it is only by conversing with themselves and others that people can become more psychologically alive, skilled, competent and creative. The *Self-Organised Learning* book was one product of this way of looking at how psychologists work. The CSHL Reflective Learning Software was another. It is hoped that the Learning Conversations techniques, tools, philosophy and language are another step in re-defining the work appropriate to those who study the nature of man, woman and child.

Management as the enabling of learning

Finally, our action research projects have brought us in close touch with 'managers' in industry, commerce and education. When managers can be encouraged by means of Learning Conversations to reconstrue the nature of their job, then exciting things begin to happen to them and to those who work for them. They discover that managing, organising and doing are cooperative, reflective and fulfilling activities. Managing starts from developing one's own capacity to learn on-the-job, and from enabling others to learn and to take responsibility for the quality of their own learning. Given this, the task-based activities follow on. Managing an S-O-L environment as a 'learning culture' in any organisation has repercussions far beyond current practices. The quality of individual, team and organisational achievements depends on a radical shift in emphasis towards Self-Organised Learning.

Our research suggests that conversational tools can become the tools that psychologists hand over to teachers, trainers and managers to develop S-O-L among those working and studying with them. Perhaps these should form part of the core curriculum within management and teacher-training programmes, so that trainee managers and teachers are offered the experience to learn about S-O-L, learn to conduct Learning Conversations, and learn to manage using these skills.

In the spirit of the alternate Ways of conversing about learning:

Nature knows all
Man knows not
Follow the Way and seek to learn
Be happy in the striving.

A haiku poem

Examples of possible futures with Self-Organised Learning

The personal myths about learning (General Introduction), our approach to learning as 'modelling meaning' (the Functional Taxonomy), the theory and practice of Learning Conversations (Part II), the creation of an S-O-L Systems 7 environment (Part III), and the conversational technology (Part IV) may all fall into place as we put flesh on our S-O-L alternative futures. This flesh may be white, black, red, blue, or the myriads of hues in between and beyond. Let us stroll around the rainbow habitats of life, into the year 2010, and portray the ecology of learning for that time. The multi-hued cameos which follow are designed to challenge your own, our valued readers', personal myths about the future of learning.

The Fordcam-Brumit (1) College of Learning: the future in education

All the members of Fordcam-Brumit College are students of Human Learning but each is also expert/learner in one or more topic areas. There is an intricate network of Learning Conversations in each of which there are three roles: the learners, the Learning Practitioners and the reflective observers. A large multi-media database is completely cross-referenced to enable members rapidly to identify others with whom they might most productively converse. Members may be active or passive. Active members have contracted into the 'learning network' for a fixed period and in one of three levels/ degrees of commitment. Each level (full-time, short intensive and part-time) requires the member to serve severally in all three roles in different Learning Conversations.

Members of Fordcam-Brumit College became very serious and considerable contributors to their chosen topic areas. Quite often a topic/task group such as a parallel processing computer development group, a dance ensemble, a sports team or a Buddhist knowledge group makes a considerable impact on their peers in the topic area; but the constitution of Fordcam-Brumit ensures that when the involvement of a person or group with the topic takes precedent over their involvement with personal learning then they are placed in 'translation' (popularly known as living limbo). 'Translation' is the membership condition which emphasises the 'cloning off' or 'entrepreneuralisation' of a task-focused activity into an independent enterprise. The support (the expert commercial, legal and academic management advice) that Fordcam-Brumit offers during this period of translation has now become very sophisticated. It is highly lucrative to Fordcam-Brumit and ensures that almost all 'Fordcam-Brumit translations' are very successful in their various endeavours as independent enterprises.

Fordcam-Brumit College offers services to its catchment communities in each of the topic areas known to its members. Its catchment communities vary from local to national to international, depending upon the conversational links developed by its members. Members also form into task-focused groups of their own design to pursue industrial, commercial and social-service enterprises. Each college service group and each enterprise partakes of the Learning Conversation network. Many members of the college are also members of professional institutes and academic societies for which most of them have qualified by public examinations, although some have been invited and elected by acclaim. Fordcam-Brumit has a high reputation in its communities both through the services it offers, which are of high quality, efficient, advanced, down to earth and highly innovative, and through the enterprises it is continually cloning off into society. These include a mime group with an international reputation, a dairy, a canal barge transport company, a company offering workshops in perceptual motor training to many special groups including paraplegics, sports coaches and chemistry lab technicians. An electronics group are marketing a successful air bicycle which is power-assisted by a potent mini heat pump, a massage-in-your-own-home network and plumbing without leaks.

Its passive members serve both as a potential resource to the active ones and as a complex liaison network into its communities and are free to move into an active phase when they can and wish to negotiate a contract to do so.

This is the first page of its constitution.

Fordcam-Brumit College: an S-O-L future in education

Some observations about teaching and learning from an S-O-L perspective indicate interesting forms into which educational enterprises may evolve.

1 *You never really learn a subject . . .*
   (a) because the more you know, the more you realise how much you don't know,
   (b) until you try to teach it,
   (c) until you try to use your understanding to solve significant problems in 'real life situations',
   (d) until you try to set examination questions which truly test a learner's understanding, explore with at least two other experts how you have marked the answers, and then
   (e) feed back the marks and your assessment criteria conversationally to the learner (S-O-L) in their peer groups and under open public scrutiny.
2 *The belief that good teachers are born, not made* only continues to be held because skill in conducting Learning Conversations is not offered as part of teacher training.

3 *If lessons and lectures were exposed to a true market economy (in which the consumers were Self-Organised Learners) many subject matter middle men would rapidly be forced out of business.*

4 *The real job of a teacher is . . .*
   (a) to help children and students develop robust learning skills,
   (b) to encourage learning and show the delights, joy and satisfaction to be obtained from it,
   (c) to help them to manage the learning of their students,
   (d) to reveal the excitement, power, logic, mystery, imagination and fascination of the subjects in which they are 'expert',
   (e) to help learners identify the true resources, i.e. books, people, learning opportunities, laboratories, workshops and community resources, etc. where well-tested, living, first-hand knowledge is to be found, and to be able easily and properly to identify the criteria by which the rubbish is made apparent.

5 *There is a seeming paradox between the ability of S-O-Learners to use good quality didactic 'authoritarian' teaching because they remain free within it,* and the inability of the other-organised learner to use the wealth of learning opportunity around them when it has not been specially garnered and carefully presented for step-by-step consumption.

6 *One major function of an educational enterprise is to keep examples of first-generation understanding before its students.* It can only do this by offering services to its catchment community and by generating and developing new knowledge in ways and by processes that are visible to all learners.

7 *An educational enterprise should be the keeper, developer, critic and refiner of its constituents' conscience.*
   The primary function of Fordcam-Brumit College is to enable its members to increase their capacity for learning. It does this by creating an ever more effective network of Learning Conversations among its members. Fordcam-Brumit is an open, self-governing, self-financing institution and has temporary, part-time and full-time members who can opt in and out of the active and passive modes of membership.

The Battersea Ballistics Soccer Team: S-O-L future in sport (leisure)

Roy Rover likes to reminisce about how, after spending some years on the continent, first as a player and then as coach and assistant manager, he was asked to come back to England to manage the Ballistics. They had just dropped disastrously from the First Division to the Third Division in two years. If pressed he will reluctantly tell you how, early on in his career, he dropped out of Fordcam-Brumit because at the age of 22 his Learning Conversations were rapidly bootstrapping him towards the position of top goal-scorer in the league. He became more and more reluctant to take part in the football-task group conversation where he felt worried about 'revealing my secrets' to possible competitors.

Also he had a deep-seated belief that 'now that I was getting there, talking about it might undermine my natural playing ability'. Then he will recall the terrible year he had with the United team when he was 27. 'I thought I was past it.' He paid his forfeit and went back to Fordcam-Brumit. He conversed and played his way through a conversion into a mid-field player. In this position he got more England caps than he had won as a number 9. 'What I learned about learning in sport at Fordcam-Brumit has stood me in very good stead here at Ballistics.'

What I did first when I arrived was to spend three or four hours with each player giving them a Learning Interview (the Functional Taxonomy of Tools). I got them to describe the whole job/life of being a professional footballer. I got it all down on cards and got them organising and adding to the cards until they felt that what was there was a good first stab at describing their 'perceptions, thoughts, feelings and activities' in a reasonably coherent way. Having numbered and cross-referenced the cards so that they could reconstruct the pattern, I told them to go away and think about how they had learned each of the skills and competences involved in their description; I also told them that this Learning Conversation was confidential.

Two weeks later I got the squad together and explained what I had been doing and how we were now going to proceed. I told them that we were going to have a one-week S-O-L workshop in which they would conduct Learning Conversations with each other and pool their findings so that they could begin to outline a series of detailed descriptions of what playing football was all about and how they thought and believed the real skills were learned. Keeping in mind the problems I had with talking about it, I suggested that video tape might be useful as an additional means of representing their meaning. The boys really got down to it, and most of them remember that week as a watershed experience.

Anyway, when they got back they each began to work on their game. I deliberately kept out of the 'task'-focused activities. I concentrated on organising their conversations. They worked in threes and all came together twice a week with notes and video to report progress and pass on what they were learning. But they also did a lot of informal chatting. We kept on with the twice-weekly practice games. I was on call to advise on how they might improve the quality of the Learning Conversations. We also had two seminars a week on the theory and practice of Learning Conversations. I remember a series of these sessions where people were being 'talked back' through video records of their 'playing behaviour'. We gradually learned not to comment on other people's play until they had completely debriefed themselves. We also learned to debrief ourselves 'descriptively' before we did any evaluation. The sessions during which we developed our own video record protocol analysis categories taught me more about football than I ever thought there was to know. Anyway, one way or another we began to do a lot better in the league.

I had got the players working in self-help groups but I also offered individual

Learning Conversations to those who requested them. I could go on for hours about the problems and ideas those players had. Then they formed a 'back-to-basics' group who worked incredibly hard at improving their ball skills. 'Micro-analysis' techniques and the 'run-as-his-shadow' game worked wonders. The boys were very generous in trying to share their tricks of the trade. That's when we began to zoom. I was truly bucked when they asked me to start a 'master class', although I must admit that really began to pay dividends when we invited back some of the 'golden oldies' to contribute.

But, and I always keep this till the end, what I really think did the trick for us was when we developed our game of 'alternative versions'. We would watch the video of Saturday's game and decide on the 'key 15 minutes'. Sometimes this was when things were really going well for us, but, as we came to value what we could learn from these sessions, more and more often we would pick the tough bit. I don't mean dirty play, I mean when we had lost our grip and things were really getting out of control.

Anyway, we would pick the '15 minutes' and make 16 copies of it. Then each of the players, the reserves, the coach and myself would take our copy off to our own video recorder. The players' job was to dub the tape with a complete reconstruction of what was going on in their head as they played that bit of the game. That was all. Nothing about what they could see on the video that they hadn't noticed at the time. Just a completely honest reconstruction of the 'inner game' that they were playing during that 15-minute period. The rest of us reconstructed our viewing of that 15 minutes as we had experienced it watching live on Saturday.

We had two hours to reconstruct the 15 minutes and dub the tape. Then Ted, our electronics wizard, would add the comments on to the fifteen audio channels on our computer-controlled random-access video-disk machine. Listen to the jargon, that's how you get on in this game. Anyway, then you settle down and gradually familiarise yourself with everybody's experience of that same bit of the game. It's amazing the different views, feelings, plans, horizons.

'It's completly changed our ideas of what football is all about.'

'Did you know the boys have actually got together in the squad and come to me with an idea of how they can rotate membership of the team so that we can have a go at the Championship, the Cup and the European thing next year?'

'Also, we have really got the youth teams going. Some of the squad have developed a system of Learning Conversations and "little master classes" among those lads.'

'The rest of the squad thought it was more important to get these ideas going among all the groups that use our "sport and leisure" facilities. Our Fordcam-Brumit work placement task group is over the moon.'

'Oh, and Fordcam-Brumit has asked us to do a one-day workshop for their members.'

The Allpeer Secondary School Experiment: feedback for learning – the future in schools

Timothy Fairbody was appointed Headmaster of Allpeer some seven years ago. Later, he was faced with the need to introduce a system of teacher job-performance appraisal. He was faced with a moral dilemma. He believed that teachers, like everybody else, best learn to do their job properly when they are getting good-quality commentary back about how others evaluate what they are doing. He was also convinced that teachers often do not get such feedback and can gradually let their standards slide and their performance become sloppy, variable and sometimes hardly acceptable. He also realised that his teachers all seemed to have different ideas about what 'good' education was and what a local government-funded secondary school was supposed to achieve. He saw a spectrum of values which might be represented by 'teaching as a subversive activity' on the one hand to 'the black papers on education' on the other, and from Summerhill to Arnold's Rugby. Timothy was studying for an Open University degree. He went to a summer school where one of the Fordcam-Brumit professors was running a seminar on 'If we become Self-Organised Learners, where do our standards come from?'. He got into a quite violent argument with some of the other students that evening and ended up negotiating a three-month contract at Fordcam-Brumit to examine 'standards and appraisal' with three of the others. These others all disagreed with him and with one another. In particular, Timothy was convinced that 'we will not learn anything if nobody is going to teach us', and said, 'I bet there's really a lot of surreptitious teaching going on! You'll see.' Those three months part time changed his life.

One of his experiences at Fordcam-Brumit consisted in having someone do a repertory grid on his significant learning experiences. This was FOCUSed and he was talked back through his own perception, thoughts and feelings about 'learning – what is it really and how does it happen to you?'. Fellow students in his task group also became interested in the repertory grid technique and together they worked their way through Thomas and Harri-Augstein's *Bible on Self-Organised Learning*. This was originally called *Self-Organised Learning with the Repertory Grid* until their publisher talked them out of such a long title. Anyway, Timothy's task group organised a trip to CSHL at Brunel University where they attended a workshop on the CSHL 'Feedback for Learning' system and micro-computer software package. To cut a long story short, Timothy took it and his new ideas about teacher appraisal back with him to Allpeer.

First of all Timothy got his staff together and told them that he had no intention of imposing an appraisal system on them and that he intended to work with them to evolve a scheme of peer appraisal. He would be an equal member, appraising and appraised with the rest of them. This was not believed and was not received very well. It was seen as a management 'con' by some of the staff and as wishy-washy rubbish by others. Timothy agreed with everybody.

He then suggested that each member of staff should draw up a list of six dimensions on which they felt that their job performance could and should be properly appraised. Timothy had prepared his own six criteria in advance and had produced a sheet listing these and offering a space against each for recording a rating on a seven-point scale. He gave one of these sheets to each member of staff and asked them to rate him (Timothy) on each of his six criteria. As they completed their sheets he filled in their ratings on his summary sheet. This he FOCUSed and showed to the group on an overhead projector. He used it to provoke discussions. Firstly he used the variation among the ratings offered on the first criterion to get the staff to clarify exactly what he had in mind when he postulated the seven-point scale.

1	2	3	4	5	6	7
Gets the best out of his staff						Tends to alienate or discourage his staff

The ensuing discussion was heated and very illuminating in terms of what his staff thought he had been doing to help, encourage, badger, browbeat or discipline them into performing better. In the end they decided that they should re-rate him in the light of the discussion, firstly in terms of how much he had influenced each one of them separately and then, having each given their reasons with examples for the rating, they should each give him a general rating in terms of how much he had helped staff as a whole. This new set of ratings was much more consistent and the reasons for what differences in judgement remained were clearly understood by everybody. In fact, someone commented that the ratings tell you more about us, the raters, than they do about Timothy. They then went through the same type of negotiation to substantiate their ratings of Timothy on each of his other five criteria.

Timothy now took their ratings seriously and put them through the CSHL computer package. He then picked out what he felt was indicated as his greatest weakness as a headmaster. He asked them to help him formulate a Personal Learning Contract which would help him learn to perform better in this area. Timothy then checked that they all understood what was wanted from them in terms of the six criteria which they felt would best express the standards by which they would want their own job performance evaluated. He also asked them for a short explanatory paragraph on each criterion which would help the other staff understand what was intended.

Within three days they had all given Timothy their sheets. These he photocopied and gave all to every member of staff to complete. He asked them to hand back each sheet to the staff member being rated so that they could each privately collate their colleagues' views of them. He suggested that each member of staff arrange a discussion with his or her peer group to explore the implications of their views and formulate a Personal Learning Contract to deal with what they saw as the major criticism. He also suggested that they each choose a Learning Coach with whom they could carry on their Learning Conversation. After much debate and some painful negotiations they came to accept, and indeed to look forward to, these 'Learning Conversations'.

However, Timothy was not finished yet. Staff were encouraged to develop and refine their six personal criteria for evaluating excellence as a teacher within an evolving network of Learning Conversations and after a year of this activity Timothy arranged another one-day workshop with his staff. This time they were all given a set of cards each representing one criterion used by all the staff. They were all very familiar with these 6 x n criteria since they had all been rating everybody on his or her own criteria monthly over the year. Timothy asked them each to spend thirty minutes grouping and re-grouping the cards until they felt that like was with like. When they had done this he got them to work in threes, comparing their groupings and combining these into an agreed hierarchical category system of criteria. He then got all four groups of three to pool their ideas and come up with an agreed, re-worded set of between ten and fifteen criteria that still included everybody's main ideas and values. When this had been agreed he gave each member of staff a set of cards describing these twelve new criteria. He asked each of the teachers to sort them out into rank order from 'most relevant to me in understanding my performance and what I might do to improve myself as a teacher' to 'least relevant to me in these terms'. Timothy had sheets made up for each staff member showing the same set of agreed criteria but each one listing the criteria in that teacher's own order of perceived relevance. Each teacher rated everybody, including himself, on all twelve criteria once a month and each teacher interpreted these peer evaluations from within their own set of values. The Learning Conversations continued.

All this happened three years ago and now Allpeer has extended this system of peer review to the pupils. The children run their own peer appraisal scheme topic by topic, subject by subject and have set up a network of Learning Conversations among themselves. Teachers are finding it hard work to keep up with what are to them the frighteningly high standards that the children are setting and consistently achieving among themselves.

You would not believe the public examination results that Allpeer is now achieving.

The Moulting Fennicaps Village Hall Goings-On: the future of human relationships in a community

Once upon a time, two psychologists who were members of Fordcam-Brumit were talking about the idea of Learning Conversations and what they could achieve. They had experience in clinical work, in psychotherapy, in co-counselling and in marriage guidance. Whilst they were concerned and informed about what these activities tried to offer people they were not convinced that any of them were really as effective as they might be. They could see that, in general, opportunity to converse was probably the life-line that was needed by many people in society. They could see that Nightline and other such activities served a crucial service for individuals in extremity who no longer had any other resource for supportive and regenerative conversation; not in the family, nor at work, nor in the local community. They could see that, say, marriage counselling provided a very useful service for couples who lacked the skills and resources to talk to each other fully and properly before things got too bad between them. They could see that it also provided a lot of factual information about the legal position of wives and husbands and the kinds of resources and services which were available to them. But they also knew of research which had shown that what one marriage counsellor saw as the purpose of counselling was not necessarily similar to what another took their purpose to be.

As they talked they began to think that perhaps what society needed was a network of Learning Conversations threading through families, friends, leisure societies, Darby and Joan clubs, football fan clubs, and so on. So they decided to pursue a task project dedicated to the organic growth of just such a network in one small town.

They would rent the Village Hall for one night a week and offer a free facility for villagers to 'come and learn to talk productively to each other'. They spent some time designing a nice poster to put outside and then set up shop each Friday. The first week nobody came but the next week two very shy teenagers turned up. Joan and Darby, our two psychologists, just chatted to them at first and it gradually emerged that Peter, the thirteen-year-old lad, had a talking problem. No one could hear what he said. 'Well, you don't seem to have any problem with us,' said Joan. 'Oh well, this is different. We are all sitting round this table and you seem interested in what I have to say.' 'You should see him at school,' said Shirley, his friend. The two psychologists spent two hours very informally chatting to the two teenagers, systematically conducting an initial learning interview. They explored what they thought their lives were about, what they thought their skills were and how they thought they had learned what they knew and what they could perform.

The next week Peter and Shirley came back and another man turned up, so Darby looked after the new man and Joan worked with the two teenagers. The new man seemed very uncertain as to why he was there, but as he said 'I had nothing else to do so I just dropped in', Darby conducted a very relaxed learning interview with him and tried to get him to identify what he saw as his learning needs. 'I would like to learn how to get on with people better.' So Darby began to try to negotiate this rather diffuse and generalised need into something more manageable which might form the basis for a Learning Conversation. Meanwhile, Joan had got the two teenagers trying to negotiate learning contracts with each other. Peter ended up deciding that he would 'like to hear what I sound like when I am speaking so that I can see what people are complaining about'. Shirley drew up a very careful contract about how she would 'learn to look after Pickles, my cat, rather better than I do'.

The next week all three came back, although Peter was accompanied by his parents who came to see just what was going on down in the Village Hall on Fridays. Four other youngsters also looked in about half an hour later. They were in a very giggly state and had stood outside the door for some time, occasionally pushing one another forward but rapidly backing out again. Darby and Joan took no notice of them until they eventually came forward in a very polite way and introduced themselves as Tom, Dick, Harry and Penelope. Joan offered them tea or coffee and asked them to sit down for a bit until she was free to talk to them. She then asked Peter and Shirley if they would mind if Tom and company joined them.

After five weeks the numbers had grown to about a dozen, and Darby and Joan were getting people to work in pairs, conducting very elementary Learning Conversations with each other. Then they offered to spend the next Saturday running a workshop which would explain some of the ideas behind this activity and offer an opportunity for people to try out some of the techniques. Eight of the Friday people came, bringing six newcomers with them.

The Conventional Construction Company: a future of S-O-L in work

CCC was started by two brothers, Ben and Bill Blossom, the sons of a potter who ended up selling flowers at Shepherd's Bush. They are life members of Fordcam-Brumit College of Learning where CCC is always referred to as the Constructive Conversation Company. Ben and Bill were part of a small enterprise task group at Fordcam-Brumit making dog kennels and garden sheds. They then moved into making garages and fully fitted portable buildings. As CCC weaned its way out of Fordcam-Brumit's domain it grew into a close-knit partnership of surprisingly successful independent firms. In their fifties, Ben and Bill have converted their holding company into a charitable trust which, besides being the sole investor in each of its own companies, launched a series of non-profit-making enterprises, some in collaboration with Fordcam-Brumit and some with its commercial offspring. Some of CCC's companies have developed their woodworking know-how into furniture-making; but its most successful enterprise was the one which developed a system for constructing full-scale industrial and commercial buildings. This was immensely successful not only because it lived up to its motto 'quick, quiet, clean and tidy construction' but also because its high-quality, cost-effective, conventional-looking buildings could be redesigned internally to meet the changing needs of the client. Clients were amazed at the speed with which floors, walls, doors, stairways and even lifts could be dismantled and rebuilt into a new 'permanent' layout that looked as if it had always been an integral part of the building.

Each CCC enterprise has its own constitution and is run as an apparently complex partnership in which seniority and personal income depends on the rolling average of a three monthly index of 'total contribution to the firm', which is computed from measures of 'job performance', 'length of service', 'position in the firm' and 'experience'. The basic criterion of 'felt fair' has enabled each CCC enterprise to use the CSHL repertory grid technology to clarify the 'models in the head' about rewards for work. Each has negotiated its own shared model and converted this into robust and stable indices which are accepted as an equitable basis for sharing out the financial rewards of their own company's success and for partaking in the overall profitability of the group. There is also a generous pension scheme which has a sliding scale of early retirement schemes and a matching, but higher, scale of requested retirement schemes.

Everybody in CCC has a well-defined job in the operational hierarchy or in the support and advisory services such as the finance, quality audit and manufacturing equipment departments. There is a well-monitored system of occasional job-swapping which is organised so that everybody not only fully appreciates and understands the jobs that impinge on their own, but is also encouraged to acquire the skills, experience and openly evaluated reputation which informs the staff learning, staff development and promotion procedures. The CSHL Feedback for Learning system, originally developed as a research tool and applied in the British Post Office, was the basis from which these procedures developed. In addition, everybody from tea boy to managing directress has to spend at least 5 per cent of their time (that is, roughly one day per month) observing somebody else doing their job. This system has grown up over many years as a result of suggestions made through a scheme developed by ChatSHLe.

This suggestions scheme gradually evolved as 'newcomers to jobs' who were Self-Organised Learners kept being frustrated by having their suggestions received with the comment, 'Oh, yes, we tried something like that years ago and it didn't work out.' The scheme now has its own Sugboard in the canteen which shows each suggestion that has been made and how far it has progressed (with dates and who is responsible) through its formulation, initial evaluation, feasibility trialing, public scrutiny meeting, and installation phases. There is also an accessible hypertext database which holds full details, specifications and history of all suggestions, past and present, with their costings and continuing cost-effectiveness audit. As one suggestion builds on previous ones this is accumulated into the audit. This scheme has spawned the CCC Inventors Club, some of whose members make significant additional income from developing ideas for the suggestions scheme. This club also offers a 'formulation and presentation' service to other employees/partners in CCC who have suggestions they wish to put forward. It also provides legal advice on licensing to those who are in collaboration with CCC and provides all types of intellectual property to outside firms and agencies.

As might be expected coming out of Fordcam-Brumit, the original members of CCC were deeply involved in using its network of Learning Conversations as a basis for all kinds of learning, from experience, on the job. This activity carried over into CCC, where a supervisor or manager who did not have an effective ongoing Learning Conversation with each of those working for him or her would rapidly come under scrutiny within their own job performance feedback for learning. This almost never happens, since there is always a demand for good quality feedback for learning by those answering to them. The ChatSHLe system evolved from a learning audit that Ben and Bill asked CSHL to carry out in the CCC. Sheila and Laurie's 'chatshow' combined with the abbreviations 'CSHL' and 'le' for learning gave this idea its name; the term 'SOLdered' came about when some new entrants to the welding department (who were (as all new entrants do) attending Fordcam-Brumit) were being discussed by the established members of that department. It has come to mean 'bright, keen, questioning and awkwardly persistent'. The ChatSHLe scheme is run by the CCC staff association to provide an independent learning service to any staff or members of their families who wish to make use of it.

The Improved Health Through Silent Conversation Movement: the future in health

Fordcam-Brumit members, over the years, have been widely and variously interested in how people can learn to live with more positive health. They have played with yoga, with various forms of alternative medicine, and with various methods of providing biofeedback about how the body is functioning. There has always been the feeling that 'if you can psycho-somatise yourself ill' you should be able to 'psyche yourself well again'. About five years ago one task group got interested in the Alexander technique and read *The Use of Self*. They were impressed, but very scathing about Alexander's ideas of about how to teach people to control their posture and body processes. Anyway, the group decided to do an in-depth study of how, how much and how finely you can learn to control your own body processes. It became quite a thing at Fordcam-Brumit. People did not just watch themselves in mirrors. They wired up with tele-sensing recording devices and began talking themselves back through their breathing, heart rate, the distribution of blood flow through the body. They used all the yoga, tai-chi, Zen, and other techniques to begin really to discover how their thoughts influenced their body processes and how various forms of exercise influenced their perceptions, thoughts and feelings. They developed Thomas's PEGASUS/DEMON/ICARUS original interactive grid elicitation computer program until they could actually monitor how their construing was changing with their physiology. One of the drug companies got hold of that to use as a sensitive measure of their new drug's influence on the brain.

Anyway, some of them began to work with athletes, and they got quite involved with the Battersea Ballistics at one time. As they got the athletes not just recording their physiology, but also silently playing the inner game, this group realised that the related muscle systems were actually working at a covert level, so they developed the body simulator. This used a whole network of sensors on the athlete's body to pick up the physiological correlates of the 'inner game'.

They spent a long time pursuing the myth that 'the same game' played out as 'the same physiological processes' in everybody. The real breakthrough came when they realised that all that stuff about models and different modes of sensory representation in the Harri-Augstein and Thomas book (Chapters 1 and 2) probably means what it says. Each person represents his or her internal meanings differently and therefore we must each develop our own personally scientific understanding of how it is for us. That's where the Body Simulator came in.

You could video yourself 'running, jumping and standing still' and then reconstruct the 'inner game' whilst watching the video wired up to the physiology recorder. You can then gradually instruct the body simulator to perform your movements on the screen as you have the silent conversation (inner game) in your head. Gradually you can train your version of the simulator to play your game under the influence of its sensing of your physiological processes. It's very simple once you have done it.

However it is incredibly powerful, because it gives you a way of short-cutting through the verbal language barrier. You can learn to converse directly with your body processes without having to translate things into inadequate word pictures and back again. Of course, once you have the process going in outline, you can zoom in on different body systems: breathing, blood circulation, digestion, the lymph stuff, etc. – it's incredible what these new micro-computers can do.

Once the Body Simulator was available the thing took off. All sorts of groups began to use it to learn what they were doing to their bodies and to learn how to change abuse into effective healthy use. Stutterers, asthmatics, and others all tried it.

Of course we now realise that the Body Simulator wasn't necessary. It's fairly easy, with those new silent conversation techniques, to listen to your own processes with all the sensors of your own nervous system connecting your body to your brain. You can then build your own Body Simulator as a model in your head. You get more and more sensitive as you practise. The trick is to explore and vary the model until you are really able to perceive what is going on in your own body. People have developed all sorts of non-verbal talk-back techniques and you would not believe the discoveries we are making about what influences what. You can see what Pranic power is about, and why acupuncture points produce the effects they do.

Now people are beginning to ask why the NHS doesn't take it on board and offer Body S-O-L courses and, by handing people the means of accepting responsibility for their own health, enable them to remain healthy. People estimate that 75 per cent of illness is self-induced – totally unconsciously, of course – but once the processes can be raised into non-verbal consciousness we can take control again.

Anyway, the Health through Silent Conversation Movement and Fordcam-Brumit seems to have caused quite a stir among the people concerned about the cost of the NHS.

The Fordcam-Brumit (2) College of Hi-Tech Learning: the future of S-O-L in educational technology

Some twenty years ago now, in the 1990s, Fordcam-Brumit College faced its greatest crisis. A group of its full-time members formed a strong task group on the topic 'Why can't computers conduct Learning Conversations?'. At first the rest of the college looked on this group with friendly, if slightly scornful, tolerance, confidently expecting that it would turn out to be just another of those misdirected task group enthusiasms. It was generally believed that rigorous Learning Conversations would soon show these people the fundamental defects in their ideas. Unfortunately or fortunately, depending upon your point of view, such conversations had the opposite result. The task group unearthed a complete set of the CSHL ILS – S-O-L software packages from the university archives. These reflective learning systems blew their minds, or rather opened their eyes to the possibilities of 'computer-aided conversations with yourself and with others'.

The task group re-vamped and improved all these primitive programs and then laid on a five-day ILS – S-O-L workshop for all members of the college. As a result, a proposal was put to senate that 'This college develop and then equip its computer network with a software system capable of sustaining a Learning Conversation with each member of the college'. Many members saw this as a threat which would, in the name of progress, tear the human heart out of the whole Fordcam-Brumit enterprise. The senate meeting ended in deadlock but members of the college were far too skilled in the art of effective and civilised conversation not to be able to solve their dilemma. Gradually the solution evolved. They would clone off the college so that there would be two parallel faculties: the Faculty of (Humanistic) Learning and the Faculty of (Hi-Tech) Learning. The necessary constitutional and financial changes were negotiated and agreed. Each 'college' went off successfully in its own direction.

However, very soon members began wanting to swap back and forth between the two faculties. First a trickle and then a flood of joint task projects grew up and gradually the hard-core and soft-core members of both faculties began to see that they were still wedded to a common set of aspirations and shared both a theory and a method for achieving these. The Humanistic group began to realise that the computer facilities were really quite useful, taking the tedium out of some of the more repetitive parts of routine Learning Conversations. The Hi-Tech group realised that, clever as their software was, it could not do everything. There were many new tricks and skills that the Humanistic group were developing which were not (as yet) built into the computer software. Numerous true incidents were elaborated into stories of how senior members of the Humanistic group had key learning experiences when they tried to use the computer system in order to ridicule it, and the humanists had their stories about how the top systems analyst spent days in conversation with his computer only to have his problem resolved over lunch in casual conversation with the Dean of the Humanistic Faculty.

Eventually, the issue was resolved when a joint faculty project group came across the report of an experiment carried out by CSHL for the Ministry of Defence in the early 1980s, 'S-O-L and Computer Aided Learning: Simulators which Invite Users into Learning Conversations', and then by digging around came across a subsequent project proposal that CSHL had put to the MoD in 1985, but which had not been pursued: 'Implementation of a Learning Shell around a Complex Simulator'. But they then found out from one of their members who happened to come across an extinct machine in the engineering stores at the headquarters of a commercial organisation that in 1991 they had installed a working prototype of the CSHL – ILS – S-O-L system in two of their main offices. That was before top management got worried by the welter of suggestions from supervisors about how to revamp most of the man management systems as well as their control measures on which productivity, cost effectiveness and quality of service were based.

The inside story goes like this. Educational technology grew up shaped by the ideas of its time. Instruction and other-organised learning was the prevailing philosophy. Almost inevitably the all-singing, all-dancing commercial versions of software embodying these ideas is usually five, ten, twenty years behind the original research work (for example, UNIX, hypertext and so on). *Most of what was called computer-aided learning in the 1970s and 1980s was actually computer-aided instruction.* Teachers usually feel that the best way to help someone who is having difficulty learning something is to simplify it, popularise it or explain it to him better. So, too, the educational software used its graphics and its interactive facilities to present subject matter in the clearest possible form and to check understanding step by step, leapfrogging when understanding was good, back-tracking, repeating and elaborating when understanding was poor. *But understanding was almost always checked against what the teacher, expert or software writer knew to be the right answer.* Terms like 'individual learning', 'personalised learning' or even 'auto-nomous learning' were hijacked and abused to mean no more than that each user could make their own path through the *teacher-specified materials*, at their own pace and in their own time, *to the teacher-specified answers*. Individual instruction is not personal Self-Organised Learning. The organisation of the material remains with the teacher, albeit cloned into the machine. In its more sophisticated forms, this educational technology became an expert system in which the facts, the logic, production rules and inference systems of the 'expert' were incorporated into the computer program so that they could be consulted, questioned and interrogated by the user. Clever! Yes, but the result was still instruction from which the user was expected to learn. This they could only do by allowing themselves to be other-organised.

Another facility produced by the educational technologist also copied the instructional practices of the teacher. Generations of students have sat through tutorials which consisted of you working at subject questions in maths or science and having the teacher check them (or finding the answers in the back of the book) and go over the ones that were causing difficulties. The computer is very good and patient in generating 'examples' which fit a series of constraints, checking the answers or even the steps in the working out, re-working those that prove difficult, and setting more of the same until you have mastered it. Yet another facility which was later introduced was educational games, but pupils soon got bored with games that were dressed up to disguise the message that teacher knows best.

Self-organisation was encouraged differently by the educational technology of the eighties. The computer can offer the self-organised user many back-up facilities. The word processor, the spreadsheet, the database, CAD (computer-aided design) and desktop publishing can all be fantastically helpful to people with ideas of their own. Similarly, the programming environments of third- and fourth-generation languages can vastly amplify the software workers' ability to produce new systems. There are many educational pro-grams that offer a user similar back-up resources in more specialist areas. Perhaps the best-known example of this type of learning resource in educational technology is LOGO.

Whilst these back-up resources for the self-organised user might be claimed to make practising new skills and experimenting with new ideas easier and more productive they do not, in the words of the original Fordcam-Brumit task group, 'conduct a Learning Conversation with you'. The task group set out to use the facilities of the day to develop and if necessary transform the CSHL conversational technology of the late eighties. Both faculties agreed to test out the prototypes which were symbiotically related to the ideas in this book. They subjected them to rigorous 'on-the-job' testing in order to generate feedback to help the task group refine the Fordcam-Brumit ILS – S-O-L specifications.

The S-O-L vision: Bootstrapping ourselves securely and compassionately into the future

The politics of S-O-L

In 2030 the Elders of Fordcam-Brumit College commissioned some of their members to do a repertory grid study of a representative sample of the members of each political party in Great Britain. They used the computer software of the day to identify rapidly the *core constructs* of each participant. There is no space here to explain how they got the politicians to co-operate except to deny the two contradictory rumours: one about somebody being killed in the rush, and the other that there was a distinct cooling-off of interest when it was announced that individual contributions were to be treated as strictly confidential.

The Elders were politically motivated in commissioning this study. They felt that politics (namely, Western democracy, Russian neo-communism, South American dictatorship, South African nationalism, Chinese communism, African statesmanship, and all the variations on these that existed in the countries of the world) was as yet a very immature and undeveloped discipline and that people had yet to find a way of living effectively together. In particular they felt that for a country as old, experienced and by reputation as civilised as Britain to be governed on a rigidly party basis was farcical.

The results of the repertory grid study were interesting. *It was found that in no political party did its members share any core constructs.* Quite to the contrary; they discovered that in each party (except the very extreme fringe ones) a whole range of different core constructs were represented. More, they found that there was a greater variation in perceptions, thoughts and feelings within each party than there was between parties. Many senior party members ridiculed this finding, but the Royal Statistical Society, when called in as arbiters, showed that, given the size of each party, the distribution of constructs within and between them compared to the distribution of the total population, left only one chance in 10 trillion that this find could have emerged by chance.

There was a greater distribution of perceptions, thoughts, and feelings about the main issues of the day within each party than there was across all parties as a whole. It was stated positions, political robots, personal ambition, public service and the power of the whips that kept the parties together and pitted one against the other. This came as a greater surprise to the politicians than it did to the intelligent layman who had long since been of the opinion that if only we all got together and worked things out we could make the world a much better place to live in.

Having established its basic premises, the Elders of Fordcam-Brumit began to raise the issue of how the people of 'the community', the region, the county, the metropolis, the country or the world could better live, work and play together. The issue began to be discussed in many of the conversational networks that had developed among the wide variety of groups who had found S-O-L (and/or all its developments and derivatives) a useful way of life.

Gradually a consensus emerged. If 'everybody' could be encouraged to move some way towards becoming more self-organised and a more Self-Organised Learner, then there would be much less need for the other-organising functions of many of the existing social systems. Greater awareness of one's own condition led to the possibility of a wide range of social contracts being drawn up. There was a powerful working party on the criteria needed to judge the equitability of a contract.

All legal operations were made free so that everybody was actually equal before the law. Education was redefined as opportunities for learning. The resources available for helping each person develop their capacity for learning from the cradle to the grave were increased tremendously but separated from the institutions responsible for helping people develop skills and knowledge. These in turn were kept separate from those institutions responsible for passing on and developing the values and culture of each and every grouping of people from Church of England to the Communist Party, from chemists to witches, from the Green Party to the Friends of *Homo Sapiens* and from the Mothers' Union to the Ship-workers' Union.

In search of an S-O-L golden age: a technological odyssey

Following on from Wittgenstein, Pirsig, Searle, Warnock and Bach, the Elders of Fordcam-Brumit College struggled in their pursuit of quality. Neither the subjectivity of the idealists nor the objective view of truth of the classical thinkers which pointed the way to scientific materialism inspired them. One of them said: '*Quality is prior.*' The Elders all agreed that for them this is achieved through a meta-reflective awareness of the conversational process in which both subject and object becomes an interrelated system.

Alongside researchers of Artificial Intelligence (AI), now called Inferential Intelligence (II), they speculated on the nature of the underlying principles for intelligent machines. One challenging question for them was 'Is it possible for a non-biological machine to address S-O-L competence and so achieve quality?' They agreed with Searle that it is difficult to imagine that the rules for an intelligent machine could be predictably specified, and that in any case this would be a most cumbersome approach. They were in tune with his argument that they should seriously question the obvious 'pattern recognition' alternative considered by Minsky and others, in which specific connective patterns are wired in to the hardware/software. The inherent adaptability and reflectivity of conscious thought contradicts this alternative approach and was therefore, for them, untenable. They also knew they had to go beyond the 'Chinese room' syndrome in which the manipulator simply behaves 'as if' it is intelligent. For them, quality must play through the environment of a real mind and body (that is, a biological body) which behaves unpredictably and which demonstrates not only a capacity for understanding, but also a capacity for awareness, for learning, and for constructing uniquely personal experiences.

They recognised that those who assumed a 'pattern recognition' approach would have seen 'human capacities' as products of a specific biochemistry. As biological machines we 'just do it'. Followers of Socrates' suicidal attempt to convince himself that 'abstract knowing' does exist might go along with this philosophy. Followers of Platonic thought might insist that 'rules' do exist but these are innate since ideas and generalities are innate. They agreed that Chomsky had fallen into this trap in his explanations for the *generation of human language*. Was there yet another alternative?

The Elder's *reflections on the human/machine prospect* lead them to continue their search. They recognised that just because *we* do it and that the capacity to achieve quality is embedded in us, *we can not readily observe it*. Therefore we find it difficult to draw up a generalisable rule system for it. They saw the way forward: to see the rule system itself as part of a *biological conversational process*. They went on to propose that:

1 *Conversational entities*: If unpredictability and freedom to explore and invent alternatives in our quest for quality are real (and we all *know* that they are), then the 'intelligent' entity must be conversational. We have a capacity to learn and achieve quality because we are organisms capable of the construction of conversational meaning. An awareness of *how we converse* is the real measure of our freedom. It is conversation with its power of reflectivity which allows us to stand outside ourselves and express inside ourselves *both at the same time*. Neither Socrates, Plato, Descartes nor Godel has got it quite right. We construct the rules as we converse with life. We also reconstruct them and change our worlds. *Conversation is prior*.

2 *Constructing our S-O-L replicates*: If we can build our own non-biological replicates, then we may have the capacity to match God at Its game. To prevent these representations of our constructions becoming merely the 'effects' – that is, the psychological specifics – the machine replicates must demonstrate a capacity to model their own constructions and so achieve freedom and quality. It must also be capable of challenging their own 'machine myths' and to bootstrap its activities purposefully and adaptively within an open system of change.

Throughout the history of mankind few humans have broken free of the specific meanings they intuitively construct to achieve freedom and quality. These are the recognised geniuses or mavericks of our cultures; the so-called 'gifted ones' or 'enlightened ones'. The S-O-L adventure has shown that many more can achieve this awareness, generality, control, freedom and creativity and so attain quality. Quality lies in the power of creative conversations with ourselves and our world.

3 *Constructing machine mega-stars*: What if we can build our own S-O-L

non-biological replicates? Can we then beat God at Its game? Nature, life and the source of all living matter, including ourselves, is becoming the God-head! If the power of the conversation *is* God, then *God is freedom*.

But one of the Elders said, 'Why go so far in our philosophical pilgrimage when there is so much else we must do to save ourselves and reconstruct our destinies? What if we are locked within our biological boundaries as Koestler insistently and pessimistically proposed? And what about the realism of our everyday life in an increasingly alien world?'

4 *Constructing a compassionate world*: The meta-reflective awareness and mega-skills required to generate an S-O-L species of machine capable not only of surviving the rigours of natural and man-made selection, but also of making a quantum leap into a new type of evolutionary trajectory, demands insights and skills and a research effort of star-war proportions.

Who is to make this investment and for what purpose? This is only justified if the S-O-L machines become our simulated laboratory for standing outside ourselves, Godel-like, in order to understand our potential selves so that we can learn to self-organise ourselves into a compassionate future. The S-O-L Way may help us all to achieve this more human goal.

Intellectually, the Fordcam-Brumit Elders have still some way to go to combine the science of West and East constructively to achieve a new science, a new syntony for Human Learning. This remains their ultimate quest.

Given where we are and attempting to look backwards into antiquity and forwards towards new destinies.

5 In Lao-Tzu's words:
In the pursuit of learning one knows more every day;
In the pursuit of the Way one does less every day.
One does less and less until one does nothing at all
And when one does nothing at all there is nothing that is undone.

Learning Conversation and the philosophy of science: S-O-L as a paradigm of human inquiry

In the archives of Fordcam-Brumit the Elders unearthed several unpublished CSHL papers. They found one of them particularly interesting!

We find that the paradigm of inquiry is based upon what are for us five self-evident truths.

Five Axioms for Conversational Science

Axiom 1   That the elements of inquiry are conversational beings engaged in conversational endeavours. Human beings are one example of such elements.

Axiom 2   Conversation is a process in which meaning is negotiated. Thoughts, feelings and perceptions about the negotiation of meaning cannot be negotiated within the explanatory systems of traditional (human) science. We need new ways of conceiving how one thing influences another.

Axiom 3   The methods of Conversational Science express the knowing of it; and the knowing of Conversational Science is informed by its methods: method and knowledge co-exist in a symbiotic relationship.

Axiom 4   Conversational Science offers fresh insights into other forms of scientific inquiry. This is because the knowing and the methods of conversational science can enable other sciences (and paradigms) to re-negotiate their meanings with themselves and with one another.

Axiom 5   Conversational Science offers people the means for self-organising their own change; self-organised change is the most meaningful definition of freedom.

Commentary on Axiom 1: On the nature of conversational beings engaged in conversational endeavours

Each converser has a unique perspective. All meaning is therefore relative, dependant upon the perspective of its generator; but, since generators of meaning can converse, all meaning is potentially related. Relative but related meanings are the subject matter (the material) of conversation. Other sciences, e.g. physics, suggest that issues of relativity are illuminated when a proper referent is identified within the subject matter. Examples of this are 'the speed of light', 'action at a distance', 'God', 'life', the 'table of elements' and entropy. These have all served as proper referents for clarifying the meaning domains of various conversational endeavours. *In studying human activities* (including other scientific activties) we would suggest that a *proper referent is the conversational being*. At different times, in different places and in differing circumstances human beings can become conversational but at other times, in other places and in other circumstances they may better be seen as a (cordant or discordant) community of conversational beings or occasionally as constituents within a more comprehensive conversational being (such as a team, a family, two people in love, Maslow's creative encounter or a nation under threat). This proper referent for the study of human experience and behaviour we have designated 'the conversational being' (C-being).

C-beings embody two co-existent parallel conversations: one directed inwards, composed among its own meaning-generating constituents: and one directed outwards towards its own conversational community. Thus *each conversational being is a conversation and can take part in conversations with others*.

A C-being in action is a conversational endeavour. One person may become a number of C-beings, each engaged in its own conversational endeavour; and a number of people nature or with technology (Pirsig with his motorcycle) becoming a constituent in a C-being larger than oneself. This is the nature of art. Another example is the way Brecht sees audiences in the theatre.

Each conversational endeavour produces its own *Domain of Meaning* (e.g. any school in science or movement in art). The domain of meaning of an endeavour defines, refines and confines the quality of understanding that the C-being can achieve. In other words, it influences and is influenced by the quality of modelling, the reflection upon others' meaning (Konrad Lorenz: 'Behind the Mirror').

When C-beings begin to model their own processes they achieve awareness. This is the seed of self-organisation. It endows the C-being with Godel-like open-system properties.

Commentary on Axiom 2: Conversation is a process within which meaning is negotiated

We have suggested that personal learning may be viewed as the construction of significant, relevant and viable meaning. Meaning acquires these characteristics if it is continually regenerated in the heat of ongoing experience. We call such personal meaning 'first generation knowing' since it changes in each regenerative cycle.

The paradox of conversation is that although it would appear to involve the exchange of meaning, this is hardly possible if meaning is continually being regenerated. This paradox indicates the trap into which strands of human inquiry have fallen, e.g. computer-based 'expert' systems, much education and training and indeed almost all of AI (Artificial Intelligence). They regard information, pre-digested meaning or nth generation meaning as the coinage of conversation. This is to view pre-digested dogmatic meaning as the coinage of teaching, of learning and of therapy; it is not.

This paradox is resolved when we recognise that meaning cannot be transmitted or received; it can only be represented. Representations of meaning can be interpreted through the spontaneous generating of new first generation meaning.

Two C-beings each representing their first generation meaning and interpreting the representations of the other are the minimal conditions for conversation, as we define this term. As these processes synchronise and begin to operate iteratively with feedback the conversation comes alive and a new C-being is born.

Commentary on Axiom 3: The methods express the knowing and the knowing informs the methods

The essence of S-O-L is its conversational method. It is systematic but not ritualised. It is content-independent but always requires specific meaning to be generated. It is reflective upon actual first-hand experience and it is person-sensitive whilst remaining pragmatic.

This conversational method is intrinsic to the conversational paradigm and the quality with which it operates is core. Tools are recruited into this conversational method as and when they may enhance its quality. Used non-conversationally, the same tools will impede, dismember or even kill the C-being. This has been true, for example, of a lot of repertory grid usage.

Like all human experience, the conversational method has a tendency to lose its integrity over time. When this happens it withers away and dies unless refreshed by reflection upon the processes by which meaning is generated and negotiated.

MA(R)4S is a model enhancing tool which we invented to be used conversationally. It can be used to enhance a C-being's awareness of the nature of their own conversational processes. It is therefore a means by which the method can refresh the method. Indeed, the method can bootstrap the method into new realms of experience. Thus, the method is the conversational knowing in action, and the conversational knowing is generated for multiple representations of the experience of the method.

Commentary on Axiom 4: Conversational Science offers fresh insights into other forms of human inquiry

It seems to us that most forms of human inquiry coincidentally or accidentally achieve mystification. This is because the real experience of the endeavour, its intrinsic process, is not that in which its findings are reported, nor its 'apparent methods' described. Hence the need for scientists to write non-scientific biographical accounts of how things really happened (e.g. J. Watson and F. Crick, *The Double Helix*) and hence, also, the artists' reluctance to examine their 'creative' processes for fear of dismembering them.

This comes about because the explanatory concepts of traditional science do not serve to express or represent the processes of conversation. We have found it necessary to progressively discard most of these explanatory devices and to develop new languages, such as the language about learning that we have used in this book to converse about conversation. We believe that we are forging the means whereby significant, relevant and viable meanings can be generated about the processes of conversation.

As these new languages emerge they reveal a new paradigm of human inquiry. What sustains us in this endeavour is having discovered that many other areas of human inquiry are illuminated by the conversational paradigm. It embraces other paradigms, each of which can then be seen at first to conceal, but later to reveal fresh facets of the conversational method. As each endeavour is further demystified it illuminates the conversational process.

Commentary on Axiom 5: Conversational Science, Self-Organised Change and Freedom

As people converse about their own processes they achieve awareness.

As they begin to experiment with these processes they move towards self-organisation.

As they reflect on the nature of these experiments they become more aware of the processes by which change happens.

As they begin to experiment with their ways of experimenting they become more able to organise change.

Self-Organised Change is needed if we are to avoid the consequences of our non-conversationally driven technological and scientific endeavours.

The Domain of Meaning which is being generated by the various and varied attempts to reflect upon more conversational methods and paradigms, is the arena within which C-beings can pursue truly human-scaled endeavours.

Where the C-beings are fragments of a person we are confronting questions of personal freedom, i.e. the goals of therapy and education.

Where the C-beings are people endeavouring to work together we are confronting the issues of organisation and social freedom.

Where the C-beings are humanity, we are confronting the issues of universal freedom and a healthy world.

Postscript: the Centre for the Study of Human Learning S-O-L environment and information technology

To support those teachers, trainers and managers who may be at various stages of S-O-L implementation, strive to carry out their S-O-L initiatives, the CSHL continues to offer its reflective learning technology and its published materials as a resource. We are also setting up a Fordcam-Brumit Open Learning Opportunity Scheme for those who wish to qualify as accredited CSHL S-O-L Learning Practitioners. Those interested in promoting S-O-L from all walks of life and all levels of industrial or educational res- ponsibility are invited to take part.

About the Centre for the Study of Human Learning

Postgraduate studies

The CSHL offers its own postgraduate research programme for the award Master of Philosophy and Doctor of Philosopy in Human Learning. The postgraduate programme is based on 'on-the-job' action research projects, thus combining an academic and job-orientated sandwich approach. Postgraduates are accepted from education and industry, government and commerce, for part-time study. Overseas students are also accepted on an external postgraduate basis. Further details are available on application to Brunel University for its Postgraduate Prospectus.

The Certificate and Diploma in S-O-L for Learning Practitioners

As part of its academic activities, the CSHL is currently seeking to accredit its S-O-L courses so that Certificates and Diplomas in Self-Organised Learning can be awarded. The Institute of Training and Development intends to recognise the S-O-L Certificate, Diploma and higher degree by research as professional qualifications for Membership of the Institute.

Courses, consultancies and contracts

The CSHL negotiates in-house short courses and consultancies based on S-O-L techniques and methods, and accepts action research contracts within industry, commerce and government for the introduction of the S-O-L methodology and technology into training departments or directly into on-the-job learning within organisations. Such initiatives are applicable from the shop floor through to various levels of supervision and management, including top executives. To develop S-O-L at any given level, the CSHL requires that at least one superordinate and one subordinate node becomes involved, so that S-O-L seeds itself effectively.

Over a twenty-year period the CSHL has procured contracts with the Social Science Research Council, the Department of Education and Science, Nuffield Foundation and the Ministry of Defence as well as with organisations such as ICI, Kelloggs, Marks and Spencer, Clarks Shoes, the Post Office and a number of smaller industrial companies, and directly with schools, colleges, polytechnics and universities.

CSHL publications

The CSHL produces its own publications; a Publications Booklet is available directly from the CSHL which lists technical working papers, reports, and contributions made to journals and books, as well as theses submitted for postgraduate award.

CSHL Reflective Learning software

Through contract research and personal research, the CSHL has developed its own Reflective Learning Technology, made up of suites of micro-computer programs and packages designed to support different aspects of S-O-L. These include:

1 An *Integrated Repertory Grid-based conversational suite of programs* for eliciting grids (PEGASUS/ICARUS), analysing grids for individual feedback (FOCUS/TRIGRID), measuring personal change over time (CHANGE grid), as well as for systematic differentiation of levels of perception and construing (PERCEIVE and EVALUATE) and for paired exchange of specific experiences (EXCHANGE) and group sociometric feedback (SOCIOGRID and SOCIONET).

2 *A learning-to-learn suite of programs* for elicitation, action and review of Personal Learning Contracts. The learner is free to work on any given topic and task (for example, from writing essays on any manual tasks to almost any aspect of man-management skill). The programs are menu-driven, and hard-copy printouts of learner responses are provided at various stages of the conversational man–machine interaction. This software has been used effectively by researchers, students, and managers as part of their S-O-L activities within various educational and industrial organisations. It has also been used as part of an S-O-L 'Intelligent' Learning

Software System (S-O-L – ILS) for use with a variety of simulators demanding skilled performance on complex tasks.

3 *A reading-to-learn suite of programs* record actual reading behaviour and use talk-back procedures for raising awareness of purpose, strategy, outcome and review criteria in reading-to-learn. The original and unique flow diagram technique for mapping out the structure and organisation of self-selected texts is available as part of this software and a bank of actual flow diagrams of selected texts is also available. Using word-processor facilities the user is free to incorporate his or her own text resources.

4 *S-O-L spreadsheet procedures* for recording and monitoring learning progress:
   Personal Learning Contracts – daily or weekly
   Self-initiated and staff-initiated appraisals based on regular weekly or equivalent
      short-term intervals
   Office-based appraisals based on quarterly or annual assessments.

5 *An Appraisal and Feedback for Learning computer-based package* for the elicitation of assessment criteria, from a specific group of managers, teachers or consultants, incorporating analysis procedures for diagnosing individual learning profiles (strengths and weaknesses), and for initiating Personal Learning Contracts.

Further details are available directly from the CSHL.

A Self-Organised Learning environment and information technology

Much of the software on offer in education and training falls into the area of the task-focused conversation. Most of it also has a very restrictive and authoritarian Task Supervisor built in. Just occasionally the function of the learner can configure the domain for different purposes. Very little of the available software offers any of the functions of the Learning Coach. None seems aware of the need for the management of learning nor the coordination of intentionality. This seems to us to be a significant opportunity that is being missed.

Throughout this book we have referred, where relevant, to various forms and versions of the CSHL Reflective Learning Technology which form part of an Intelligent Learning System (ILS).

Some of this is in the form of paper-and-pencil techniques which can be recruited into the S-O-L environment to act as amplifiers of some component of one of the MA(R)4S processes (Chapter 5). Individual FOCUSed grids, structures of meaning and CHART serve to represent meaning in different forms so that it may be reflected upon. Other techniques such as PEGASUS, CHANGE, interactive PAIRS, SOCIOGRIDS and EXCHANGE & CONVERSE serve more directly as enhancers of the process of conversation. Many of these techniques are now available as CSHL software packages. The micro-computer and the power of information technology can be recruited into the enhancements of various component conversations in the S-O-L environment.

For some time we have been concerned with building a software-driven S-O-L environment around specific domains. So far we have made three attempts at this. The first was in a Ministry of Defence project which was concerned with developing an Intelligent Learning Support System for Naval Command and Control (Thomas and Harri-Augstein, 1986). The second consists of the CSHL Reading-to-Learn techniques which are all addressed within a suite of conversational software.

ILS Reading-to-Learn

The Reading-to-Learn software has been designed as an aid for learners to work independently to develop further the effective use of reading as a learning skill and to use texts which they encounter in their normal studies as a more effective resource for self-organised study. The software replaces the Learning Coach and to some extent the Learning Manager and enables learners to develop their skills in the following ways:

1 to identify a wide variety of needs and purposes in order to plan specified
   strategies;   P
2 to select from a wide variety of strategies in order to achieve specified
   purposes;   S
3 to assess the quality of reading outcomes within the context of specified
   purposes;   O
4 to review systematically the whole process (purpose-strategy-outcome) in
   personal terms.   R

The software is divided into two major groups of programs. The Reading-to-Learn programs are located on the Pupils Reading Activities Disk – PRAD. The Organisation of Resources programs are located on the Teacher's Resource Organisation Disk – TROD. TROD allows teachers to examine text resources provided by the CSHL on a Text Resource Engineering Disk – CSHL-TREND – and to prepare, copy, file and organise their own text resources on their own Teacher's TREND Disk. PRAD enables pupils to become more aware of their own reading processes and to examine, reflect upon, review and develop their reading-to-learn skills. The central activity of the system uses MA(R)4S based on a behavioural record of reading the text. This enables learners to model their reading-to-learn process and so to review and develop their skills. A Personal Record Organising Disk – PROD – allows them to keep a record of the results of their reading-to-learn activities, so that they can progressively review their progress. The CSHL-TREND Disk offers twenty-seven texts for use with PRAD. These are grouped into eleven major categories which offer teachers and pupils a flexible and wide-ranging resource.

Our third endeavour is a domain-independent learning-to-learn Personal Learning Contract software system.

ILS Chat-to-Learn

The system comprises a suite of programs which explain themselves to the learner, offers them choices of activity, and leads them through the elicitation procedures of model building; that is, MA(R)4S. The learner can choose to be addressed as a 'Novice', when they will receive full explanatory annotations to the procedures, or as an 'Expert', when the explanations are withheld. The learner is free to traverse the elicitation and associated procedures in almost any order he or she chooses, although some routes are suggested as more sensible than others. The dialogue conducted via the VDU and the keyboard is augmented by hard-copy printouts of the learner's models which may be accompanied by non-evaluative comments which draw the learner's attention to omissions in the model or suggestions for the learner to reflect on. The software system cannot comment on the meaning of any of the contents of the learner models because it has, as yet, no language-understanding mechanism. However, a human Learning Coach, where available, can take on this function.

There are essentially three activities available to the learner, corresponding to the three modellers: PSOR contracts, Intensive Conversation, and Reflect-al A. *The system provides no constraints on the contents of the learner's contracts.*

The PSOR modeller leads the learner through the elicitation of his or her contract, always prompting the learner to formulate the contract with the utmost care and to revise its contents, repeatedly if necessary. This emphasis reflects the importance attached to the process of contract-making as one which itself induces change to the learner. The learner is asked to define the contract *topic*, its *purpose*, *strategy*, *outcome* and *outcome criteria*, and to specify the *resources* they will need or draw upon to execute their contract. An expansion of the contract follows, although here as elsewhere the learner can opt out of the suggested sequence. The learner is asked to specify both a superordinate context and a set of subordinate elements for each of the components of their contract, so that they are constructing a *three-level hierarchy*. Again they have the opportunity to revise their contract. When they are at least provisionally satisfied, they can attempt to execute it. The suggested sequel is the contract review procedure, in which the learner reconstructs all the components of this contract and their resource list in the light of their experience. A comparison of before- and after-task versions of a contract is provided as a hard-copy print-out (ORACLE) and the learner is invited to reflect on the differences and to plan future activities.

Each of the three modelling activities conducted in the current version of the system is self-contained and can operate in the absence of a human Learning Coach, although such a person can play a useful part in steering the learner between activities: Figure 46 outlines the current version. The three modellers can be supplemented by a pencil-and-paper version of the Debrief, which is most effectively used after task execution and before contract review. The pencil-and-paper version of a procedure can be seen as an inter-mediate stage in the implementation of a procedure which initially exists only in the head

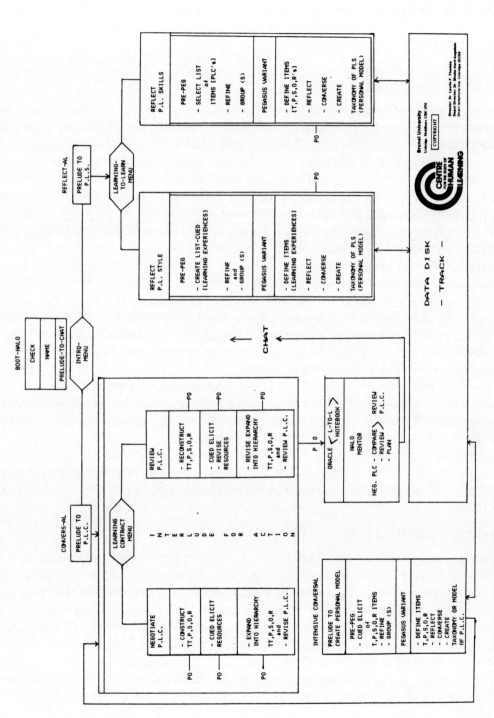

Figure 46 ILS Chat-to-Learn

of the skilled Learning Coach. This process of externalising and articulating the skills of the Learning Coach is the first step towards a machine implementation, and is served by a research strategy based on empirical study.

The CSHL research strategy

Starting from the assumption that in the early stages a human being is more likely to be able to offer a facility than a machine, we find that with experience we begin to be able to describe the models that drive us sufficiently clearly to write computer programs to do all or part of the job for us. In theory this saves time and effort in not having repeatedly to offer the same human services and enables us to offer a distant learning software resource. In practice the computer programming can become all-absorbing in itself and, until recently, our programs could not (like us) learn from experience. However, the programs do serve a very useful purpose by implementing what we think is our model of an activity and then offering it at a distance, without us. The programs illustrate how well or how badly we understand what we, as researchers, are doing. They act as a dynamic representation of our meaning upon which we can reflect. This is almost always salutory. Either we realise that we have only partially captured what we should have meant, or we realise that much of what we are doing could be done much more simply and economically. Either way, as conversational researchers we learn a lot. Thus, the action research approach is incremental and the results at each stage feed back to increase the range and sharpen the precision of our MA(R)4S modelling facilities.

We have briefly outlined how we have embodied various aspects of the Systems 7 S-O-L environment into software and we also have a whole variety of software aids that can be recruited into the human Learning Conversation to sharpen this and improve its quality. We are now well into our first attempts to fully implement Systems 7 as a concurrently running 'learning shell' around certain specialist domains involving high-fidelity simulations and complex knowledge bases. We are also introducing an S-O-L environment for supporting Learning Conversations throughout one large organisation.

Where do we go from here?

Let us speculate where the implementation of an S-O-L environment might take us.

Our experience in using Systems 7 to engender self-directed change convinces us that the quality and effectiveness of learning in most educational and training situations could be many times greater than it is. In fact we are convinced that an S-O-L environment could quite transform many different areas of endeavour. Self-Organised Learners go on learning in the absence of the Learning Practitioner. In creating their own destinies they will extend the range of convenience of the constructs in our mind-pool.

Bodily health is one other major area in which an S-O-L environment could make an impact. Yoga and the Alexander technique demonstrate what can happen when we learn to reflect on our own body processes. Biofeedback monitoring techniques being used within a supportive Learning Conversation could transform the treatment of heart disease and respiratory problems. As medicine develops more non-intrusive diagnostic techniques, the range could expand.

We would like to think that certain readers will appreciate the power of Systems 7 as a *content-independent environment* for channelling and amplifying creative activities such as psychotherapy, design, quality control, staff appraisal and even the philosophy of science itself.

Index